SOME ASPECTS OF RABBINIC THEOLOGY

Some Aspects of Rabbinic Theology

By
Solomon Schechter
M.A., Litt.D. (Cantab)

WIPF & STOCK · Eugene, Oregon

Wipf and Stock Publishers
199 W 8th Ave, Suite 3
Eugene, OR 97401

Some Aspects of Rabbinic Theology
By Schechter, Solomon
Softcover ISBN-13: 978-1-6667-3346-4
Hardcover ISBN-13: 978-1-6667-2812-5
eBook ISBN-13: 978-1-6667-2813-2
Publication date 8/5/2021
Previously published by The Macmillan Company, 1910

This edition is a scanned facsimile of
the original edition published in 1910.

To

LOUIS MARSHALL, ESQUIRE

JEW AND AMERICAN

PREFACE

THE contents of this book have grown out of a course of lectures delivered at various learned centres, and a series of essays published in the *Jewish Quarterly Review*. These essays began to appear in the year 1894. They attracted some notice, and were utilised by several writers on theological subjects, both with and without due acknowledgment. They are now presented to the public in an expanded form, revised and corrected, and increased by new chapters and other additional matter, amounting to about half of the bulk of this volume.

The first chapter, which is introductory, offers the reader a fair notion of the nature of our subject as conceived by the author, the point of view from which he approaches it, the inherent difficulties in its treatment, and the manner in which he has tried to accomplish his task. Yet a few supplementary remarks seem to be necessary.

This volume represents no philosophic exposition of the body of doctrine of the Synagogue, nor does it offer a description of its system of ethics. Both the philosophy of the Synagogue and its ethics have been treated in various works by competent scholars belonging to different schools of thought. The main aim of such works is, however, as it would seem, interpretation, more often re-interpretation. The object of the following pages is a different one. The task I set myself was to give a presentation of Rabbinic opinion on a number of theological topics as offered by the Rabbinic literature, and forming an integral part of the religious consciousness of the bulk of the nation or "Catholic Israel."

Keeping this end in view, I considered it advisable not to intrude too much interpretation or paraphrase upon the Rabbis. I let them have their own say in their own words, and even their own phraseology, so far as the English idiom allowed. My work consisted in gathering the materials distributed all over the wide domain of Rabbinic literature, classifying, sifting, and arranging them, and also in ascertaining clearly and stating in simple, direct terms the doctrines and theological concepts that they involved, in such a manner as to convey to the student a clear notion of the Rabbinic opinion of the doctrine under discussion. In cases where opinion differed, the varying views were produced, and so were inconsistencies pointed out, stating, however, when there was sufficient authority for doing so, what the prevailing opinion in the Synagogue was. Where such authority was lacking, it was assumed that the Synagogue allowed both opinions to stand, neither opinion containing the whole truth, and being in need of qualifications by the opposite opinion.

On the other hand, I made little use of such matter as may be described as mere legend and fancy, falling within the province of folk-lore and apocalypse rather than belonging to the domain of theology. These represent the chaff, an inevitable growth in the field of religion. Now and then a grain of truth may be detected in it, but as a rule the chaff serves more often to hide the grain of truth from sight. To the practised eye of the student, such passages appear as "theological curiosities," either heedlessly repeated or surreptitiously inserted in the text. The works in which this chaff grew most exuberantly have a strong family likeness with certain Pseudepigrapha, which were a product, not of the Synagogue, but of the various sects hovering on the borderland of Judaism, on which they may have left some mark by a few stray passages finding their way even into the older Rabbinic literature. The Hebrew works, however, which are especially conspicuous for the affinity of their contents or the larger part of their contents with those Pseudepigrapha, are of a later date. They make their appearance under disguise, betraying sufficiently their origin by their bewildering contents as well as by their anachronisms. They were admitted into the Synagogue only under protest, so to speak. The authorities seem to have been baffled, some disowning them, whilst others are overawed by their very strangeness and apologise for their existence,— or, reinterpret them. The writings are thus of little help to the student of Rabbinic opinion, though they may be of service to the worker on the field of the Pseudepigrapha.

As really representative of such opinion, we can only take into account the Talmudic and the recognised Midrashic literature, or the "great Midrashim." But even in these authoritative works we have first to separate all that is stray and peculiar of the nature just indicated, and to eliminate a great deal of polemical matter only uttered under provocation in the heat of controversy, and to subject the whole of it to the test of the religious consciousness of Israel.

This literature covers, as stated elsewhere, many centuries, and was produced in widely differing climes amid varying surroundings and ever-changing conditions, and was interrupted several times by great national catastrophes and by the rise of all sorts of sects and schisms.

This last circumstance — besides being productive of bitter polemics, as just hinted at — could not fail to create new "theological values," as the modern phrase is, leading, for instance, to the emphasis upon the significance of the Law and even the Oral Law and other doctrinal points, which, though questioned by none, were never before stated with such distinctness and in such a challenging manner.

The influence of the historic events may perhaps be best illustrated by the literature bearing upon the belief in the advent of the Messiah. Whatever doubt there may be as to the high antiquity of this doctrine or as to the varying phases it passed through in the early stages of its history, no such uncertainty prevails as to the opinion held by the Rabbis with regard to it. This opinion can easily be ascertained from Rabbinic literature, which permits of no doubt that the belief in the advent of the Messiah in its general and main features was a firmly established doctrine of Rabbinic Judaism. The main outlines are given by Scripture and tradition, but it is history which furnishes the details. These appear sometimes in the form of apocalypses, reflecting the events of their age, whilst the prolonged suffering of Israel, and the brooding of the nation over the wrongs inflicted upon the people of God, have the unfortunate result that fancy and imagination busy themselves more with the anti-Messiah and the punishment awaiting him than with the Messiah and the bliss coming in his wake. To such an extent does this proceed that in some of these apocalypses the universalistic features of the Kingdom are almost obscured, although, in truth, Israel never abandoned them even amidst the worst distress.

Notwithstanding, however, all these excrescences which historic events contributed towards certain beliefs and the necessary mutations and changes of aspects involved in them, it should be noted that Rabbinic literature is, as far as doctrine and dogma are concerned, more distinguished by the consensus of opinion than by its dissensions. On the whole, it may safely be maintained that there is little in the dogmatic teachings of the Palestinian authorities of the first and second centuries to which, for instance, R. Ashi of the fifth and even R. Sherira of the tenth century, both leaders of Rabbinic opinion in Babylon, would have refused their consent, though the emphasis put on the one or the other doctrine may have differed widely as a result of changed conditions and surroundings. On the other hand, a careful study of the Agadic sayings, for instance, of R. Akiba and R. Meir of the second century, will sufficiently prove that there is little or nothing in the dicta of these great teachers which would have prevented them from subscribing to the same general theological beliefs that inspired the homilies contained in the *Seder Elijah* and the *Agadath Bereshith* compiled in the seventh or in the eighth century, if not much later. Indeed, many statements in these books appearing at the first glance as new can often be traced as mere amplifications of teachings occurring in some older collection of the second and third century in a less diffuse form.

It was in view of this fact that I did not consider it necessary to provide the quotations given from the Talmud and the Midrash with the date of their authors, assuming that as long as there is no evidence that they are in contradiction to some older or even contemporary opinion they may be regarded as expressive of the general opinion of the Synagogue. Such a treatment of the subject was, I thought, the more justified as it did not lie within the scope of this work to furnish the student with a history of Rabbinic theology, but rather, as already indicated, to give some comprehensive view of a group of theological subjects as thought out and taught by the Synagogue. It should be remembered that the field lay entirely barren until a comparatively recent date. Indeed, when I began to write on the subject there did not exist a single book or even essay from which I could derive any instruction or which could serve me as a model in the conception and construction of the work. Conditions have since considerably improved, and I have had occasion in the course of this book to gratefully refer to those who have rendered substantial contributions to this subject. With the great lack of preliminary studies and the absence of monographs on subjects of Rabbinic theology, a history of its development would thus be premature. Not only will the whole of the Agadic literature as well as the Targumin have to be carefully studied, but the Halachah also will have to be consulted, for this was very sensitive to all shades and changes in theological opinion, and in many cases reverberates with it. But what is mainly needed are good treatises on individual doctrines and theological terms based on primary sources and giving the necessary attention to detail.

The legitimate successors of the Talmud and the Midrash are the legal codices and the works of edification known as Books of Discipline (*Sifre Mussar*) of the Middle Ages, constituting the Halachah and the Agadah of post-Talmudic Judaism. Not only do they restore to us occasionally passages from ancient Rabbinic collections now lost to us, but they afford us some insight into the workings of Rabbinic opinion after Israel had, through the medium of the Arabic vernacular, been brought into contact with Greek thought, or what professed to be Greek thought, of different schools and had, for the first time perhaps, become really conscious of the obstacles on the path of belief. A few extracts from this literature are sometimes given in the text by way of illustration.

As a treasure-house of "theological sentiment," we may regard the *Piyutim*, or the hymnological literature of the mediæval Synagogue, aptly described sometimes as a continuation or development of the Psalms and the ancient liturgy of the Synagogue. Nowhere, perhaps, are the teachings of the Synagogue in reference to the close relations between God and Israel and the permanency of the Covenant with the Fathers expressed with greater conviction and more depth than in the hymns recited in the Sabbaths between the Passover and the Feast of Weeks. Again, the doctrines as to the meaning of sin in its aspect of rebellion and its terrible consequences, the efficacy of repentance, and the helplessness of man to obtain pardon and reconciliation without assistance from heaven — all these doctrines receive nowhere a more emphatic expression both in strains of the most exalted joy and of the deepest humiliation than in the mediæval Synagogue compositions for the Penitential Days, especially for the Day of Atonement. This will be found to be the case with other doctrines, such as the inspiration of the Scriptures, the significance of the Commandments as a saving factor, which forms the theme of the Synagogue poetry for the Feast of Weeks, or the doctrine of the advent of the Messiah, and the restoration of Israel to the Holy Land, which constitutes the subject of elegies for the Ninth of Ab and the Consolation Sabbaths succeeding it.

It is true that these poetical compositions cannot be considered as representative of universal Rabbinic opinion, in the same measure as the Talmud and the Midrash. To a certain extent they enjoyed only local authority, each country having in addition to the common Prayer Book a liturgical collection of its own. The ritual of the Spanish Jews, for instance, contains but few compositions emanating from the Franco-German School, or even from their earlier models written in Palestine and Babylon. It is distinguished by the simplicity of its diction and its symmetrical form. It is, further, less cumulative of its epithets of the Deity, and is sparing in allusions to the Talmud and Midrash, whilst there is in it but a minimum of Angelology, which forms such a prominent feature in the sacred poetry of other schools, reflecting unmistakably the influence of the Chapters of the Chambers and similar mystical productions.

Such differences, however, vital as they may appear to the metaphysician, affect but slightly the main features of such doctrines as are above referred to and are discussed in the course of these pages. In these the consensus of opinion was maintained even after Aristotle became *the* sage of Jewish literature and the wisdom of the Greeks was discovered to be "bordering on the path of the faith." Nor could it be otherwise. Starting from the same premises, such as the inspiration of the Scriptures, their binding authority upon every Jew, and fully admitting the claim of the Rabbis to be the only legitimate interpreters of these Scriptures, — much as the various schools differed in their definition of inspiration and in their method of eliminating isolated Rabbinic opinion, — and sharing in the same hope of the nation as it found expression in the doctrine of the advent of the Messiah, — much as they differed in the description of his person and the miraculous details accompanying his appearance, — they could not but arrive at the same general conclusions. Practically, they only differed to agree in the end. It was only in this way that it came to pass that Maimonides' résumé of the Creed became soon the object of numberless hymns accepted by the Synagogue at large, and even mystics wrote commentaries to it; whilst there were very few — perhaps none — of the rationalising school who would have had any scruples to read their prayers from the common Prayer Book used in Germany or France. If it was not exactly uniformity, the unity of Israel was well maintained — "union of doctrines, of precepts, of promises."

It is one of the most interesting of religious phenomena to observe the essential unity that the Synagogue maintained, despite all antagonistic influences.

Dispersed among the nations, without a national centre, without a synod to formulate its principles, or any secular power to enforce its decrees, the Synagogue found its home and harmony in the heart of a loyal and consecrated Israel.

There was no school of thought to which it was not exposed, no great philosophic or spiritual influence which did not reach into its life and is not reflected in its development. These foreign-born ideas were all thoroughly assimilated by the Synagogue, and mingled even with its devotion and contemplation. The hymn, "Royal Crown," by R. Solomon b. Gabirol, in the Spanish ritual, and the "Song of Unity," in the German ritual, both recited on the Day of Atonement, are sufficient evidence of this fact, apart from some customs and usages of non-Jewish origin, which were thoroughly converted to Judaism by the Synagogue in the process of time. Having gained an entrance by a process of natural selection and unconscious absorption, the power of Judaism was manifested in its obliteration of all that was strange and objectionable in such accretions, so strong were its digestive powers. But equally, the vitality of the Synagogue was manifested in what it eliminated and rejected as inconsistent with its existence. Whenever any influence, no matter by whom advanced or by whatever power maintained, developed a tendency that was contrary to a strict monotheism, or denied the binding character of the Torah, or aimed to destroy the unity and character and calling of Israel, although it may have gained currency for a time, the Synagogue finally succeeded in eliminating it as noxious to its very existence.

It is this body of Israel in which the unity of the Synagogue was and is still incorporate that I called occasionally as witness in some cases of religious sentiment wholly unknown to the outsider. I may as well state here that it was my knowledge of this Israel which gave the first impulse to these essays. Having been brought up among Jews who did live under the strict discipline of the Law and were almost exclusively nurtured on the spiritual food of the Talmud and Midrashim, and having had occasion thus to observe them for many years, both in their religious joys and in their religious sorrows, I felt quite bewildered at the theological picture drawn of Rabbinic Judaism by so many writers. I could not but doubt their statements and question their conclusions. These doubts were expressed to friends, who were at once affected more or less by my sceptical attitude and urged me to write down my thoughts on the subject, which in the course of time took shape in essays and lectures. The reader will, therefore, pardon if, in addition to the written evidence, I appeal also in a few cases to living testimony.

The foregoing remarks will suffice to prepare the reader for what he has to expect from this book and in what he will be disappointed. I have also prepared him for my point of view, which is further developed in the body of the book. I have only to warn the reader that this volume is by no means exhaustive of Rabbinic opinion on all theological subjects dealt with in Rabbinic literature. This book represents only *some* Aspects of Rabbinic Theology. Some doctrines, such as, for instance, Immortality, Resurrection, were only slightly touched upon; whilst others, as the Eschatology of the Rabbis with regard to the Day of Judgement, Eternal Punishment, and similar topics, hardly found any place in this volume. The guiding motive in the choice of subjects was in general a selection of those large and important principles in which Rabbinic thought and Israel's faith were most clearly represented and which I found were most in need of elucidation, because so often misunderstood and misinterpreted. If God gives me life and strength, I may perhaps one day write more aspects of Rabbinic theology.

As to the nature of the literature with which I had to deal, the reader will find the necessary information about it in the Introductory Chapter. I desire only to add that I did not wish to multiply references in my Notes when the additional references brought no further information with them. Both the Talmud and the Midrashim are now provided on the margin or the foot of the page with ample references to parallel passages, and the student who is anxious to farther pursue the subject can easily turn to the original sources with the aid of the references given in the Notes. I have also purposely avoided in my transliteration of Hebrew words or names all bewildering devices for representing the actual sound of the word, contenting myself with the ordinary Roman alphabet, in spite of its shortcomings.

In conclusion, I wish to thank Dr. Alexander Marx, Professor of History in the Jewish Theological Seminary of America, who prepared the list of Abbreviations for me. I am also indebted to Mr. Joseph B. Abrahams, Clerk of the Seminary office, who was always at my call during the progress of this work. I can further hardly express sufficiently my obligations to my friend Rabbi Charles Isaiah Hoffman, of Newark, N.J., for his painstaking reading of the proofs and for ever so many helpful suggestions, by which this volume has profited. And last, but not least, I have to record my special obligations to my friend, Miss Henrietta Szold, who likewise read the proof, and made many a valuable suggestion. I am particularly grateful to her for the excellent Index she has prepared to this work, which will, I am convinced, be appreciated by every reader of this volume.

S. S.

CONTENTS

CHAPTER		PAGE
I.	INTRODUCTORY	1
II.	GOD AND THE WORLD	21
III.	GOD AND ISRAEL	46
IV.	ELECTION OF ISRAEL	57
V.	THE KINGDOM OF GOD (INVISIBLE)	65
VI.	THE VISIBLE KINGDOM (UNIVERSAL)	80
VII.	THE KINGDOM OF GOD (NATIONAL)	97
VIII.	THE "LAW"	116
IX.	THE LAW AS PERSONIFIED IN THE LITERATURE	127
X.	THE TORAH IN ITS ASPECT OF LAW (MIZWOTH)	138
XI.	THE JOY OF THE LAW	148
XII.	THE ZACHUTH OF THE FATHERS. IMPUTED RIGHTEOUSNESS AND IMPUTED SIN	170
XIII.	THE LAW OF HOLINESS AND THE LAW OF GOODNESS	199
XIV.	SIN AS REBELLION	219
XV.	THE EVIL YEZER: THE SOURCE OF REBELLION	242
XVI.	MAN'S VICTORY BY THE GRACE OF GOD, OVER THE EVIL YEZER CREATED BY GOD	264
XVII.	FORGIVENESS AND RECONCILIATION WITH GOD	293

CHAPTER	PAGE
XVIII. Repentance: Means of Reconciliation	313
Additions and Corrections	345
List of Abbreviations and Books not quoted with Full Title	349
Index	353

SOME ASPECTS OF
RABBINIC THEOLOGY

SOME ASPECTS OF RABBINIC THEOLOGY

I

INTRODUCTORY

My object in choosing the title "Some Aspects of Rabbinic Theology" is to indicate that from the following chapters there must not be expected either finality or completeness. Nor will there be made any attempt in the following pages at that precise and systematic treatment which we are rightly accustomed to claim in other fields of scientific inquiry. I have often marvelled at the certainty and confidence with which Jewish legalism, Jewish transcendentalism, Jewish self-righteousness, are delineated in our theological manuals and histories of religion; but I have never been able to emulate either quality. I have rather found, when approaching the subject a little closer, that the peculiar mode of old Jewish thought, as well as the unsatisfactory state of the documents in which this thought is preserved, "are against the certain," and urge upon the student caution and sobriety. In these introductory paragraphs I shall try to give some notion of the difficulties that lie before us.

To begin with the difficulties attaching to the unsatisfactory state of Rabbinic documents. A prominent theologian has, when referring to the Rabbis, declared that one has only to study the Mishnah to see that it was not moral or spiritual subjects which engrossed their attention, but the characteristic hairsplitting about ceremonial trifles. There is an appearance of truth in this statement. The Mishnah, which was *compiled* about the beginning of the third century of the C.E., consists of sixty-one (or sixty-three) tractates, of which only one, known by the title of "The Chapters of the Fathers," deals with moral and spiritual matters in the narrower sense of these terms. Still this is not the whole truth, for there are also other tractates, occupying about one-third of the whole Mishnah, which deal with the civil law, the procedure of the criminal courts, the regulation of inheritance, laws regarding property, the administration of oaths, marriage, and divorce. All these topics, and many similar ones relating to public justice and the welfare of the community as the Rabbis understood it, are certainly not to be branded as ceremonial trifles; and if the kingdom of God on earth means something more than the mystical languor of the individual, it is difficult to see on what ground they can be excluded from the sphere of religion. But, apart from this consideration — for it seems that theologians are not yet agreed in their answer to the question whether it is this world, with all its wants and complications, which should be the subject for redemption, or the individual soul, with its real and imaginary longings — there runs, parallel with this Mishnah, a vast literature, known under the name of Agadah, scattered over a multitude of Talmudical and Midrashic works, the earliest of which were compiled even before or about the time of the Mishnah, and the latest of which, while going down as far as the tenth or even the eleventh century, still include many ancient elements of Rabbinic thought. In these *compilations* it will be found that the minds of the so-called triflers were engrossed also with such subjects as God, and man's relation to God; as righteousness and sin, and the origin of evil; as suffering and repentance and immortality; as the election of Israel, Messianic aspirations, and with many other cognate subjects lying well within the moral and spiritual sphere, and no less interesting to the theologian than to the philosopher.

It is these Talmudic and Midrashic works, to which I should like to add at once the older Jewish liturgy, which will be one of the main sources of the material for the following chapters. Now I do not want to enter here into bibliographical details, which may be found in any good history of Jewish literature. But it may have been noticed that I spoke of "compilations"; and here a difficulty comes in. For a compilation presupposes the existence of other works, of which the compiler makes use. Thus there must have been some Rabbinic work or works composed long before our Mishnah, and perhaps as early as

30 C.E.[1] This work, or collection, would clearly have provided a better means for a true understanding of the period when Rabbinism was still in an earlier stage of its formation, than our present Mishnah of 200 C.E. Is it not just possible that many a theological feature, characteristic of the earlier Rabbis, found no place in the Mishnah, either because of its special design or through the carelessness or fancy of its compiler, or through some dogmatic consideration unknown to us? Is it not likely that the teaching of the Apostle Paul, the antinomian consequences of which became so manifest during the second century, brought about a growing prejudice against all allegoric explanations of the Scriptures,[2] or that the authorities refused to give them a prominent place in the Mishnah, which was intended by its compiler to become the great depository of the Oral Law? But whatever the cause, the effect is that we are almost entirely deprived of any real contemporary evidence from the most important period in the history of Rabbinic theology. The Psalms of Solomon may, for want of a better title, be characterized as the Psalms of the Pharisees; but to derive from them a Rabbinic theology is simply absurd. They have not

[1] See D. Hoffmann, *Magazin für die Wissenschaft des Judenthums* (Berlin), 8, p 170.

[2] See the ל״ב מדות of R Eleazar b. Jose of Galilee, where we read that the *Mashal* (allegoric interpretation) was only used in the Prophets and in the Hagiographa, "but the words of the Torah and commandments thou must not interpret them as *Mashal*" Cf. Bacher, *Terminologie*, I 122.

left the least trace in Jewish literature, and it is most probable that none of the great authorities we are acquainted with in the Talmud had ever read a single line of them, or even had heard their name. The same is the case with other Apocryphal and Apocalyptic works, for which Rabbinism is often made responsible. However strange it may seem, the fact remains that whilst these writings left a lasting impress on Christianity, they contributed — with the exception, perhaps, of the Book of Ecclesiasticus — little or nothing towards the formation of Rabbinic thought. The Rabbis were either wholly ignorant of their very existence, or stigmatised them as fabulous, or "external" (a milder expression in some cases for heretical), and thus allowed them to exert no permanent influence upon Judaism.

Passing from the Mishnah to the Talmud proper (the Gemara) and to the Midrash, the same fact meets us again. They, too, are only compilations, and from the defects of this, their fundamental quality, we frequently suffer.

There is, for instance, the interesting subject of miracles, which plays such an important part in the history of every religion. Despite the various attempts made by semi-rationalists to minimise their significance, the frequent occurrence of miracles will always remain, both for believers and sceptics, one of the most important tests of the religion in question; to the former as a sign of its superhuman nature, to the latter as a proof of its doubtful origin. The student is accordingly anxious to see whether the miraculous formed an essential element of Rabbinic Judaism. Nor are we quite disappointed when we turn over the pages of the Talmud with this purpose in view. There is hardly any miracle recorded in the Bible for which a parallel might not be found in the Rabbinic literature. The greatest part of the third chapter of the Tractate Taanith, called also the "Chapter of the Saints," is devoted to specimens of supernatural acts performed by various Rabbis. But miracles can only be explained by more miracles, by regular epidemics of miracles. The whole period which saw them must become the psychological phenomenon to be explained, rather than the miracle-workers themselves. But of the Rabbinical miracles we could judge with far greater accuracy if, instead of the few specimens still preserved to us, we were in possession of all those stories and legends which once circulated about the saints of Israel in their respective periods.[1]

Another problem which a fuller knowledge of these ancient times might have helped us to solve is this: With what purpose were these miracles worked, and what were they meant to prove? We are told in 1 Corinthians (1 22), that "the Jews ask for signs as the Greeks seek for wisdom." As a fact, however, in the whole of Rabbinic literature, there is not one single instance on record that a Rabbi was ever asked by his

[1] About the probability that there may have existed other collections of such stories, see Rapoport, *Bikkure Haittim*, 12 78 79.

colleagues to demonstrate the soundness of his doctrine, or the truth of a disputed Halachic case, by performing a miracle. Only once do we hear of a Rabbi who had recourse to miracles for the purpose of showing that his conception of a certain Halachah was the right one. And in this solitary instance the majority declined to accept the miraculous intervention as a demonstration of truth, and decided against the Rabbi who appealed to it.[1] Nor, indeed, were such supernatural gifts claimed for *all* Rabbis. Whilst many learned Rabbis are said to have "been accustomed to wonders," not a single miracle is reported for instance of the great Hillel, or his colleague, Shammai, both of whom exercised such an important influence on Rabbinic Judaism. On the other hand, we find that such men, as, for instance, Choni Hammaagel,[2] whose prayers were much sought after in times of drought, or R. Chaninah b. Dosa, whose prayers were often solicited in cases of illness,[3] left almost no mark on Jewish thought, the former being known only by the wondrous legends circulating about him, the latter being represented in the whole Talmud only by one or two moral sayings.[4] "Signs," then, must have been as little required from the Jewish Rabbi as from the Greek sophist. But if this was the case, we are actually left in darkness about

---

[1] See *Baba Mezia*, 59 b.
[2] *Taanith*, 24 b, cp *Jer. Taanith*, 64 a, 64 b.
[3] See *Berachoth*, 33 a, and *Jer. Berachoth*, 10 b.
[4] *Aboth*, 3 9. See Bacher, *Ag. Tan.* I 288, p. 2.

the importance of miracles and their meaning as a religious factor in those early times. Our chances of clearing up such obscure but important points would naturally be much greater if some fresh documents could be discovered.

As another instance of the damage wrought by the loss of those older documents, I will allude only here to the well-known controversy between the school of Shammai and the school of Hillel regarding the question whether it had not been better for man not to have been created. The controversy is said to have lasted for two years and a half. Its final issue or verdict was that, as we have been created, the best thing for us to do is to be watchful over our conduct.[1] This is all that tradition (or the compiler) chose to give us about this lengthy dispute; but we do not hear a single word as to the causes which led to it, or the reasons advanced by the litigant parties for their various opinions. Were they metaphysical, or empirical, or simply based, as is so often the case, on different conceptions of the passages in the Scripture germane to the dispute?[2] We feel the more cause for regret when we recollect that the members of these schools were the contemporaries of the Apostles; when Jerusalem, as it seems, was boiling over with theology, and its market-places

[1] *Erubin*, 13 *b*.
[2] For other controversies of a theological nature between the same schools, see *Gen. R.*, 12 14, *Rosh Hashanah*, 16 *b*; *Chagigah*, 12 *a*; *P K.* 61 *b*. Cf. Bacher, *Ag. Tan.*, I 14.

and synagogues were preparing metaphysics and theosophies to employ the mind of posterity for thousands of years. What did the Rabbis think of all these aspirations and inspirations, or did they remain quite untouched by the influences of their surroundings? Is it not possible that a complete account of such a controversy as I have just mentioned, which probably formed neither an isolated nor an unprecedented event, would have furnished us with just the information of which now we are so sorely in need?

In the Jewish liturgy we meet with similar difficulties. It is a source which has till now been comparatively neglected. Still, its contents are of the greatest importance for the study of Jewish theology; not only on account of the material it furnishes us, but also for the aid it gives us in our control over the Talmud. For the latter is a work which can never be used without proper discretion. Like many another great book of an encyclopædic character, the Talmud has been aptly described as a work "full of the seeds of all things." But not all things are religion, nor is all religion Judaism. Certain ideas of foreign religions have found their way into this fenceless work, but they have never become an integral part of Jewish thought. Others again represent only the isolated opinions of this or that individual, in flagrant contradiction to the religious consciousness of Catholic Israel; whilst others again, especially those relating to proselytes or the Gentiles, were in many cases only of a transitory character, suggested by the necessities or even the passions of the moment, but were never intended to be taught as doctrine. In like manner the exaltation, by sectarians, of one special doctrine at the cost of essential principles of the faith led at times by way of reaction to an apparent repudiation of the implied heresy; whilst the synagogue, through its interpreters, recognised the true nature of this apparent repudiation and continued to give the objectionable doctrine its proper place and proportion among the accepted teachings of Judaism.[1] Some test or tests as to the real theological value of a Talmudic saying will, therefore, always be necessary in making use of the old Rabbinic literature as a source of theology. The Jewish liturgy, which was from earliest times jealously guarded against

---

[1] See Weiss דו״ד I 287 and Joel's *Blicke*, 2 170, seq. As an illustration we refer here to the well-known objection to the explanation of certain laws (Lev. 22 28 and Deut. 22 6 and 7) on the mere principle of mercy, "for he (who does so) declares the attributes (or the laws dictated by such attributes) of the Holy One, blessed be he, mercy, whilst they are only commands" מפני שעושה של הקבה רחמים ואינן אלא גזירות See *Mishnah Berachoth*, 5 8; *Megillah*, 4 9; *Jer Berachoth*, 9 c and B. T. *Berachoth*, 33 b, text and commentaries. Cf. also Bacher, *Ag. Am.*, 3 728. All these authorities, however, were set aside by the synagogue which continued the tradition of Pseudo-Jonathan to Lev. 22 28 (see Berliner, *Targum*, 2 85) and never hesitated to explain such laws on the principle of mercy. See *Gen. R.*, 75 18; Deut. R., 6 1; *Tan. B.*, 3 48 a. Cf. also *Gen. R.*, 33 8, where with reference to Ps. 145 9 the words occur שדן מדותיו הוא מרחם. As to mediæval authorities for the *paitan* Kalir, see Buber's note to *P. K*, 98 b. Cf. also Nachmanides Commentary to Deut., 22 6 and 7, and the reference there to Maimonides. See also ילקוט יצחק by Isaac Zaler, Warsaw, 1895, 3 59 a and b and 5 45 b and 46 a.

INTRODUCTORY

heresy,[1] and which in its essentials always was under the control of the synagogue at large, may fairly be regarded as such a test. Now there is no reason to doubt that in its broad outlines this liturgy — as far as the Prayer Book is concerned — has its origin in the earliest Tannaitic times, whilst certain portions date from the pre-Christian era, but it is at present so overgrown with additions and interpolations, that the original contents are hardly discernible from the constant accretions of succeeding ages. The Talmud, and even the Mishnah, occasionally quote some ancient liturgical passages, and these might prove useful in helping us to fix their date.[2] But, unfortunately, it was not thought necessary to give these quotations in full. They are only cited by the word with which they begin, so that we are left in uncertainty as to the exact contents of the *whole* prayer, and have only guesses to rely on.

Even more embarrassing than these textual difficulties are those defects which are inherent in the peculiar nature of old Rabbinic thought. A great English writer has remarked "that the true health of a man is to have a soul without being aware of it; to be disposed of by impulses which he does not criticise."

---

[1] See I. Elbogen, *Geschichte des Achtzehngebets*, Breslau, 1903, 34, note 4.

[2] See *Mishnah Tamid*, 5 1. *Pesachim*, 118 *a*. Cf. Landshut הגיון לב to the שמונה עשרה, and Elbogen, as quoted above. See also Schechter's notes to *The Wisdom of Ben Sira* (edited by S Schechter and C. Taylor), to XXXVI 17 *c* (p. 60) and LI 12 *c* (p. 66), and *J. Q R.* 10³, p. 654.

In a similar way the old Rabbis seem to have thought that the true health of a religion is to have a theology without being aware of it; and thus they hardly ever made — nor could they make — any attempt towards working their theology into a formal system, or giving us a full exposition of it. With God as a reality, Revelation as a fact, the Torah as a rule of life, and the hope of Redemption as a most vivid expectation, they felt no need for formulating their dogmas into a creed, which, as was once remarked by a great theologian, is repeated not because we believe, but that we may believe. What they had of theology, they enunciated spasmodically or "by impulses." Sometimes it found its expression in prayer "when their heart cried unto God"; at others in sermons or exhortations, when they wanted to emphasise an endangered principle, or to protest against an intruding heresy. The sick-bed of a friend, or public distress, also offered an opportunity for some theological remark on the question of suffering or penance. But impulses are uncertain, incoherent, and even contradictory, and thus not always trustworthy. The preacher, for instance, would dwell more on the mercy of God, or on the special claims of Israel, when his people were oppressed, persecuted, and in want of consolation; whilst in times of ease and comfort he would accentuate the wrath of God awaiting the sinner, and his severity at the day of judgement. He would magnify faith when men's actions were lacking in inward motive, but he would urge the claim of works when the Law had been declared to be the strength of sin. When the Law was in danger he would appeal to Lev. 27 43, "Those are the commandments which the Lord commanded Moses," and infer that these laws, and no others, were to be observed forever, and that no subsequent prophet might add to them.[1] At another time he would have no objection to introduce new festivals, *e.g.* the Lighting of the Chanukah Candles, and even declare them to be distinct commands of God,[2] so long as they were, as it seemed to him, within the spirit of the Law. He would not scruple to give the ideal man his due, to speak of him as forming the throne of God,[3] or to invest him with pre-mundane existence;[4] but he would watch jealously that he did not become, as it were, a second god, or arrogate to himself a divine worship. I shall have frequent occasion to point out such apparent or actual contradictions.

The Rabbis, moreover, show a carelessness and sluggishness in the application of theological principles which must be most astonishing to certain minds

[1] See *T. K.* 115 *d*.

[2] *Shabbath*, 23 *d*. See also *Jer. Sukkah*, 53 *d*

[3] See *Gen. R.* 47 6.

[4] See *Gen R.* 1 1 about the pre-mundane existence of the *name* of the Messiah. Cf. *ibid.* 2 4, about the soul of the Messiah. *Ibid.* 8 4 mention is made of the souls of the righteous with whom God took counsel when he was going to create the world. See also *PRE.* 3, text and commentary. Cf also Joel, *Blicke*, 2 181 and *S. E* 160, text and notes, and below, p. 70. See also Dr. L. Ginzberg, "*Die Haggada bei den Kirchenvatern*," p. 4, note 1.

which seem to mistake merciless logic for God-given truths. For example, it is said: "He who believes in the faithful shepherd is as if he believes in the word of him whose will has called the world into existence." . . . "Great was the merit of the faith which Israel put in God; for it was by the merit of this faith that the Holy Spirit came over them, and they said *Shirah* to God, as it is said, 'And they believed in the Lord and his servant Moses. Then sang Moses and the children of Israel this song unto the Lord.'"[1] . . . Again, "Our father, Abraham, came into the possession of this world and the world hereafter only by the merit of his faith."[2] Of R. Jose it is recorded that he said: "If thou art desirous to know the reward awaiting the righteous, thou mayest infer it from Adam the First, for whose single transgression he and all his posterity were punished with death; all the more then shall the good action of a man confer bliss upon him, and justify him and his posterity to the end of all generations."[3] Another Rabbi tells us that by the close contact of the serpent with Eve, he left in her a taint which infected all her seed, but from which the Israelites were freed when they stood before Mount Sinai, for there they came into immediate contact with the divine presence.[4]

---

[1] *Mechilta* (ed Friedmann), 33 a. By *Shirah* שירה is meant the Song of Moses (Exod. 15).

[2] *Mechilta, ibid.*

[3] *T. K.* 27 a. Cf Delitzsch, *Hebrew Translation of the Romans* (Leipzig, 1870), p. 82.

[4] *Jebamoth,* 103 b.

To the professional theologian, it is certainly distressing to find that such sayings, which would have made the fortune of any ancient Alexandrian theosophist or modern Hegelian of the right wing, were never properly utilised by the Rabbis, and "theologically fructified," nor ever allowed to be carried to what appears to the scholastic mind as their legitimate consequences. The faithful shepherd and the bliss-conferring righteous were never admitted into the Rabbinic pantheon; the concession made to the patriarch was never extended to his posterity, faith only modifying and vivifying works, but not superseding them, and even the direct contact with the Deity, which the fact of being present at the Revelation of Sinai offered to every Israelite, were conceived of only as the beginning of a new life, with new duties and obligations.

This indifference to logic and insensibility to theological consistency seems to be a vice from which not even the later successors of the Rabbis — the commentators of the Talmud — emancipated themselves entirely. I give one example: We read, in the name of R. Akiba, "Everything is foreseen; freedom of choice is given. And the world is judged by grace, and yet *all is according to the amount of work.*" This is the usual reading. But some of the best Mss. have the words, "And *not* according to the amount of work."[1] The difference

[1] See Dr. Taylor's *Sayings of the Jewish Fathers*, Appendix 152. I add here Ms. Oxford Heb, c. 17. Parma, 802, 975. See *Machzor*

between the two readings being so enormous, we should naturally expect from the commentators some long dissertation about the doctrines of justification by grace or works. But nothing of the sort happens. They fail to realise the import of the difference, and pass it over with a few slight remarks of verbal explanation. Perhaps they were conscious that neither reading ought to be accepted as decisive, each of them being in need of some qualification implied in the other.

It will, therefore, suggest itself that any attempt at an orderly and complete system of Rabbinic theology is an impossible task; for not only are our materials scanty and insufficient for such a purpose, but, when handling those fragments which have come down to us, we must always be careful not to labour them too much, or to "fill them with meaning" which their author could never have intended them to bear, against which all his other teachings and his whole life form one long, emphatic protest, or to spin from the harmless repetition by a Rabbi of a gnostic saying or some Alexandrinic theorem the importance of which he never understood, a regular system of Rabbinic theology. All that these fragments can offer us are some aspects of the theology of the Rabbis, which may again be modified by other aspects, giving us another side of the same sub-

Vitri, pp. 514, 515. Compare also *Die Responsen des R. Meschullam ben Kalonymos*, by Dr. Joel Muller (Berlin, 1893), p. 11, note 19. See below p 306.

ject. What we can obtain resembles rather a complicated arrangement of theological checks and balances than anything which the modern divine would deign to call a consistent "scheme of salvation." Still, I am inclined to think that a religion which has been in "working order" for so many centuries — which contains so little of what we call theology, and the little theology of which possesses so few fixities (whilst even these partake more of the nature of experienced realities than of logically demonstrated dogmas) — that this religion forms so unique and interesting a phenomenon as to deserve a more thorough treatment than it has hitherto received. It is not to be dismissed with a few general phrases, only tending to prove its inferiority.

This brings me to one other introductory point which I wish to suggest by the word *Aspects*. Aspects, as we know, vary with the attitude we take. My attitude is a Jewish one. This does not, I hope, imply either an apology for the Rabbis, or a polemic tendency against their antagonists. Judaism does not give as its *raison d'être* the shortcomings of any of the other great creeds of the civilised world. Judaism, even Rabbinic Judaism, was there before either Christianity or Mohammedanism was called into existence. It need not, therefore, attack them, though it has occasionally been compelled to take protective measures when they have threatened it with destruction. But what I want to indicate and even to emphasise is, that my attitude towards Rabbinic theology is necessarily different from that taken by most commentators on the Pauline Epistles. I speak advisedly of the commentators on Paul; for the Apostle himself I do not profess to understand. Harnack makes somewhere the remark that in the first two centuries of Christianity no man understood Paul except that heathen-Christian Marcion, and he misunderstood him. Layman as I am, it would be presumptuous on my part to say how far succeeding centuries advanced beyond Marcion. But one thing is quite clear even to every student, and this is that a curious alternative is always haunting our exegesis of the Epistles. Either the theology of the Rabbis must be wrong, its conception of God debasing, its leading motives materialistic and coarse, and its teachers lacking in enthusiasm and spirituality, or the Apostle to the Gentiles is quite unintelligible. I need not face this alternative, and may thus be able to arrive at results utterly at variance with those to be found in our theological manuals and introductions to the New Testament.

The question as to how far the theology of the Rabbis could be brought into harmony with the theology of our age is a matter of apologetics, and does not exactly fall within the province of these essays. With a little of the skill so often displayed by the writers of the life and times of ancient heroes, particularly New Testament heroes, it would certainly not be an impossible task to draw such an ideal and noble picture of any of the great Rabbis, such as Hillel, R. Jochanan ben Sakkai, or R. Akiba, as would make us recognise a nineteenth-century altruist in them. Nor would it require much ingenuity to parade, for instance, R. Abuhah as an accomplished geologist, inasmuch as he maintained that before the creation of *our* world God was ever constructing and destroying worlds;[1] or again, to introduce as a perfect Hegelian that anonymous Rabbi who boldly declared that it was Israel's consciousness of God which was "the making of God":[2] or finally, to arrogate for R. Benaha the merit of having been the forerunner of Astruc, because he declared that the Pentateuch was delivered not as a complete work, but in a series of successive scrolls.[3] Indeed, the Rabbinic literature has already been described as a "wonderful mine of religious ideas from which it would be just as easy to draw up a manual for the most orthodox as to extract a vade-mecum for the most sceptical." But I have not the least desire to array the ancient Rabbis in the paraphernalia of modern fashion, and to put before the reader a mere theological masquerade, or to present the Talmud as a rationalistic production which only by some miracle escaped the vigilant eye of the authorities, who failed to recognise it as a heretical work and exclude it from the Synagogue. The "liberty of interpretation," in which so many theologians indulge, and which they even exalt as "Christian freedom," seems to me only another

[1] See *Gen. R.*, 9 2.   [2] See below, p. 24, note 2.
[3] See *Gittin*, 16 *a*.

word for the privilege to blunder, and to deceive oneself and others.

To show, however, that Rabbinic theology is, with the least modicum of interpretation or re-interpretation, equal to the highest aspirations of the religious man of various modes of thought, occasional illustrations have been given from the works of philosophers and mystics, thus proving the latent possibilities of its application by various schools in different ages. As to "modernity," it entirely depends whether there is still room in its programme for such conceptions as God, Revelation, Election, Sin, Retribution, Holiness, and similar theological ideas; or is it at present merely juggling with words to drop them at the first opportunity? If this latter be the case, it will certainly find no ally in Rabbinic theology, or for that matter, in any other theology.

II

GOD AND THE WORLD

AMONG the many strange statements by which the Jewish student is struck, when reading modern divinity works, there is none more puzzling to his mind than the assertion of the transcendentalism of the Rabbinic God, and his remoteness from man. A world of ingenuity is spent to prove that the absence of the mediatorial idea in Rabbinic Theology is a sign not of its acceptance of man's close communion with God, but of its failure to establish the missing link between heaven and earth. Sayings of a fantastic nature, as, for instance, when a Rabbi speaks of God's abode in heaven, with its various partitions;[1] epithets for God, such as Heaven or Supreme, which antique piety accepted for the purpose of avoiding the name of God "being uttered in idleness"; terms expressive of his providence and his sublime holiness, as the Holy One, blessed be he, the King, the Lord of the World,

---

[1] See Weber, *System der Altsynagogalen Palästinenischen Theologie* (Leipzig, 1880), pp. 158, 159 See B. Jacob, "*Im Namen Gottes*," p. 171. It is interesting that in the very passage in *Chagigah*, 5 *b*, where this sharp division between the inner and outer departments is given, it is also stated that in the latter God is mourning over the misfortunes of Israel.

or the Master of all Creation; Hellenistic phrases, which crept into Jewish literature, but which never received, in the mouth of a Rabbi, the significance which they had with an Alexandrine philosopher, or a Father of the Church,—are all brought forward to give evidence of the great distance which the Rabbinic Jew must have felt, and must feel, between himself and his God.

How strange all this to the Jewish student! Does the Jewish Prayer Book contain such passages as — "O our Father, merciful Father, ever compassionate, have mercy upon us. . . . Thou hast chosen us from all peoples and tongues, and hast brought us near unto thy great name forever in faithfulness, to thank thee and proclaim thy Unity in love; blessed art thou, O God, who hast chosen thy people Israel, in love":[1] or are they Christian interpolations from some unknown hand? Is the Jew taught to confess his sins daily in the following words: "Forgive us, our Father, for we have sinned; pardon us, our King, for we have transgressed . . . blessed art thou, our God, who art gracious and dost abundantly forgive":[2] or is this formula borrowed from a non-Jewish liturgy? Has the Jew ever heard his mother at the bedside of a sick relative, directing prayers to God, and appealing to him as "the beloved name, the gracious helper, the merciful Father, and

---

[1] See *Daily Prayer Book*, edited and translated by the late Rev. S. Singer (1890), p. 40; Baer, עבודת ישראל, Rodelheim, 1868, p. 80.
[2] See Singer, p. 46; Baer, p. 90.

the dear God": or was it some Christian neighbour to whom he was listening? Are the millions of worshippers in the synagogue addressing themselves directly to God, the king and creator of the universe, the Father in Heaven; or do they, in their thoughts, substitute for all these terms the Memra or the Logos, or some other abstraction, of which the writer of those prayers was unaware? For, according to what we are told by many theologians, God is too far off, the King of the Universe too cosmopolitan, and the Father in heaven too high for the mind of the Jew, and is thus an impossible object for worship. These are questions which readily suggest themselves when one, for instance, reads Weber's book, *System der Altsynagogalen Palastinensischen Theologie*, which has within the last decades become the chief source of information for the great majority of the writers on this subject. The thesis which Weber sets himself to prove through all his work is evidently that of the predominance of the legalistic element in Jewish theology, which was so overwhelming that it crushed even God under its oppressive burden, or, what is the same thing, removed him out of the world. Hence the strange arrangements of subjects in Weber's work, treating first of nomism (or legalism), then of the character of the oral law, the authority of the Rabbis, etc., and last of all, of the Jewish notion of God. The general impression conveyed by such a representation is that this Jewish God is not the God from whom the Torah has emanated, and on whom its authority rests, but that he is himself a feeble reflex of the law, improved occasionally by some prophetic notions, but jealously watched by the Rabbis lest he should come into too close contact with humanity.

This is very different from the impression which the Jewish student receives from a direct study of the sources. Quite the reverse! The student is overwhelmed by the conviction that the manifestation of God in Israel's history was still as vivid to the mind of the Rabbis and still as present as it was to the writer of Deuteronomy or the author of Psalm 78. "All souls," say the Rabbis, "even those which had still to be created, were present at the Revelation on Mount Sinai." [1] The freshness with which the Biblical stories are retold in the Agadic literature, the vivid way in which they are applied to the oppressed condition of Israel, the future hopes which are based on them, create the impression that to the Rabbis and their followers the Revelation at Sinai and all that it implies was to them not a mere reminiscence or tradition, but that, through their intense faith, they re-witnessed it in their own souls, so that it became to them a personal experience. Indeed, it is this witnessing, or rather re-witnessing, to revelation by which God is God; without it he could not be God.[2] People who

[1] *Exod. R.*, 28 6.
[2] See *P. K*, 102 b, and *Sifre*, 144 a, with allusion to Is. 43 12. Cf. also Hoffmann's *Midrasch Tannaim*, I 72, for more striking instances. The expression כביכול (as if it were possible to say so) is used in *Sifre*.

would doubt his existence and say, "There is no judgement and no judge," belong rather to the generation of the deluge, before God had entered so openly into relations with mankind.[1] To those who have experienced him through so many stages in their history, such doubt was simply impossible.

A God, however, who is mainly reached, not by metaphysical deductions, but, as was the case with the Rabbis, through the personal experience of his revelation and his continuous operations in the world, cannot possibly be removed from it, or be otherwise confined to any particular region. Such a locally limited conception of the deity could, according to the Rabbis, only be entertained by a newly fledged proselyte, who had not as yet emancipated himself from his polytheistic notions. To the Jew, God was at one and the same time above, beyond, and within the world, its soul and its life. "Jethro," say the Rabbis, "still believing that there was some substance in other gods, said, 'I know that the Lord is greater than all the gods' (Exod. 15 11). Naaman came nearer the truth (though still confining God to one part of the universe), for he said,

---

Cf. Bacher, *Terminologie*, I 78, for the etymology and a more precise explanation of this term. It may be remarked that in most cases this term כביכול is used by the Rabbis, when the anthropomorphism which they imply is carried *further* than that implied by the Bible. The instance which I have just cited from the *Pesikta* is a case in point Cf. also the numerous instances given by Kohut in his *Aruch Completum*, s.v. יכל [2].

[1] See *Gen. R.*, 26 6 and *Pseudo-Jonathan*, *Gen.* 4 8.

'Now I know that there is no other God in all the earth, but in Israel' (2 Kings 5 15). Rahab (made even further progress, and) placed God both in heaven and earth, saying, 'For the Lord your God, he is God in heaven above and in earth beneath' (Josh. 2 11); but Moses made him fill all the space of the world (or universe), as it is said, 'The Lord he is God in the heaven above, and upon the earth beneath': there is none else (Deut. 4 39), which means that even the empty space is full of God."[1]

He is indeed to the Rabbis, as may be gathered from the various appellatives for God scattered over the Rabbinic literature, not only the Creator of the world, or "he who spake and the world existed,"[2] but also the Father of the world,[3] the goodness (or the good one) of the world,[4] the light of the world[5] the life of the world,[6] the stay of the world[7] the eye of the world,[8] the only one of the world,[9] the ancient one of the world,[10] the righteous one of the world,[11] the master or the lord of the world,[12] and the space (*makom*)

---

[1] *Deut. R.*, 2 27. cf *Mechilta*, 59 a. Cf. *Tan. B.*, 4 15 a; *M.T.*, 19 8, 22 2, 62 8; cf. Bacher, *Ag. Am.*, I 182.

[2] *Jer Pesachim*, 18 b. Cf. Low, *Gessammelte Schriften*, I 185, note 3.

[3] *Midrash Prov.*, ch. 10.   [4] *P K.*, 161 a.

[5] *Tan. B.*, 4 24 b.   [6] *Tan.*, כי תשא, 24.

[7] *Tan. B.*, 50 b.   [8] *Gen. R.*, 42 2.

[9] *Gen. R.*, 21 5.

[10] *Yalkut* to *Chronicles*, section 1074, but the reading is rather doubtful. Cf. *Ruth R*, 2 1, and commentaries.

[11] *Yoma*, 37 a. Cf. *Yalkut* to *Prov.* § 346.

[12] *Berachoth*, 4 a.

of the world.¹ In another place God is compared by a Rabbi to the soul "filling the whole world, as the soul fills the body,"² a comparison which may probably have suggested to later Jewish writers semi-pantheistic notions; as, for instance, when the author of the Song of the Unity says: "There is nothing but thy existence. Thou art alive, omnipotent, and none is be-

---

¹ *Gen. R.*, 68 9 and *P R* 104 a, and notes Cf. E. Landau's essay *Die dem Raume entnommenen Synonyma für Gott in der Neuhebraischen Literatur* (Zurich, 1888), pp. 30 seq, where the whole literature on the subject is put together: to which Bacher, *Ag Tan.*, I 207, and Jacob, *Im Namen Gottes*, 119 may be added. According to the passage from the *Mechilta*, 52 b, given there by Bacher, מכאן לב״ד, הגדול שהוא קרוי מקום it is the divine court of judgement which is called מקום. Cf. *Mechilta of R Simon*, ed. Hoffmann, 81. See also Lewy, *Ein Wort über die Mechilta des R Simon*, p. 9, note 4. See also *Midrash Temurah*, § 2 I believe, however, that in spite of all these authorities, that the older commentators of the Mechilta, explaining the passage to refer to the court or the Sanhedrin, were in the right, the reading of ב״ה in the *MHG* probably resting on some clerical error. The term is mainly indicative of God's ubiquity in the world and can best be translated by "Omnipresent." Cf. Taylor's *Sayings of the Jewish Fathers*, p 53, note 42, though it is difficult to say with any certainty whether it is Jewish or Hellenistic in its origin On Landau's note 1, p. 40, it may be remarked that the text of Gemara in the *Mishnah Berachoth*, 5 1, has לאביהם שבשמים instead of מקום. Cf Mishnah, *Rosh Hashana*, 4 8, ומשעבדים את לבם לאביהם שבשמים, where Mr. Lowe's ed., p. 62 a, reads ומכוונים instead of ומשעבדים. Bishop Lightfoot's quotation (in his *Commentary to the Colossians*, p 213) from בחיי on the *Pentateuch* (to Exod. 34 20), according to which God is also called בכורו של עולם, the "first-born of the world," is not to be found in the older Rabbinic literature, and seems to be only a later cabalistic term.

² See *Lev. R.*, 4 8.

sides thee. And before the All thou wast the All, and when the All became thou filledst the All." [1]

It is true that there are also other appellatives for God, placing him "above the world," as the heaven,[2] the height of the world,[3] and the high one.[4] Nor is it to be denied that there is a whole circle of legends mostly concentrated round the visions of Ezekiel, which give mystical descriptions of God's heavenly habitations. Here is an instance of the economy of the seventh heaven which is Araboth. It is with reference to Ps. 68 4: "'Sing unto God, sing praises to his name: extol him that rideth upon the Araboth (the heavens).' Araboth is the heaven, in which are righteousness and grace, the treasures of life, the treasures of peace and the treasures of bliss, and the souls of the righteous, and the souls and the spirits which are about to be created, and the dew with which the holy one, blessed be he, is to revive the dead . . . and there are the Ophanim, the Seraphim, and the holy Chayoth and the ministering angels and the throne of glory, and the king, the living God, high and exalted, rests above them, as it is said: 'Extol ye him that rideth upon the Araboth.'" [5] This passage, and a few others

[1] שיר היחוד, 3d day.

[2] See Rab. Dictionaries, sub. שמים. See also Schürer 2 : 539.

[3] *Tan.*, כי תשא, 27.

[4] See *Baba Bathra*, 134 *a*, and Rab Dictionaries sub. גבוה. Cf. also Landau and Löw, about all these expressions.

[5] See *Chagigah*, 12 *b*, 13 *a*; and *P. R.*, 95 *b seq*. Cf. Ginzberg, *Die Haggada bei den Kirchenvatern*, p. 11.

of a similar character, dating perhaps from the first century, are developed later in the eighth and ninth centuries into an extensive mystical literature known under the name of Chapters of the Chambers,[1] which enlarge upon the topography of the heavens with great minuteness, besides giving very detailed descriptions of the various divisions of the ministering angels who dwell there, and their various functions, and producing even some of the hymns which are sung in heaven on particular occasions.

But first we must note that the fact of God's abiding in a heaven ever so high does not prevent him from being at the same time also on earth. "Thou art the Lord our God," runs the text of a prayer, which is still recited every day, "in heaven and *on earth*, and in the highest heavens of heavens";[2] whilst the fact of God's appearing to Moses in the bush is taken as a proof that there is no spot on earth be it ever so lowly which is devoid of the divine presence.[3] When a Rabbi was asked as to the seeming contradiction between Exod. 40 34, according to which the glory of God filled the tabernacle, and 1 Kings 8 27, in which it is said: "Behold, the heaven and heaven of heavens cannot contain thee," he answered, that the matter is to be compared to a cave by the shore of the sea; once the sea became stormy and inundated the land, when the cave filled

---

[1] פרקי היכלות existing in various versions, strongly reminding of the Book of Enoch and similar other Pseudoepigrapha.

[2] See *S. E*, p. 118, and Introduction, p. 80   [3] *P K.*, 2 *b.*

with water, whilst the sea lost nothing of its contents; so the tabernacle became full of the glory of the divine presence, whilst neither heaven nor earth became empty of it.[1]

Secondly, and this is a point which cannot be sufficiently emphasised, that whatever mythologies and theosophies may be derived from the notion of heaven or height, on the one hand, or whatever pantheistic theories may be developed from the conception of the God-fulness of the universe, on the other hand, neither of these opposing tendencies were allowed to influence the theology of the Rabbis in any considerable degree.

Theirs was a personal God, and a personal God will always be accommodated by fancy and imagination with some sort of local habitation. The "Not-Ourselves" will always have to be placed somewhere else. Loftiness and height have always and will always suggest sublimity and exaltation, and thus they could not choose a more suitable habitation for the deity than the heavens, or the heaven of heavens. But theology proper, or religion, is not entirely made up of these elements. It does not suppress them, but with happy inconsistency, it does not choose to abide by their logical consequences.

Thus the very R. Simon b. Lakish, to whom we owe the Rabbinic version of the myth of the seven heavens, in the highest of which, as we have seen, the throne of glory is placed, declared the patriarchs (as models of

[1] *P. K.* 2 *b*; *P. R.*, 19 *a*. Cf. Bacher, *Ag. Tan.*, 2 27.

righteousness) to be the throne (or the chariot) of God; whilst his colleague and older contemporary, R. Jochanan, laid down the axiom, that every place where "thou findest the greatness of God mentioned, there thou findest also his humility"; and he further added illustrations from the Pentateuch, the Prophets, and the Hagiographa. The illustration from the latter is the very verse which partly suggested the legend of the seven heavens, namely the verse, "Extol ye him who rideth upon the Araboth"; being followed by the words, "A father of the fatherless, and a judge of the widows, is God in his holy habitation" (Psalm 78 5). Thus we may maintain safely that with the Rabbis distance does not imply aloofness or any interruption of God's communion with man. Notwithstanding all distance, "God is near in every kind of nearness."[1] For though the distance between heaven and earth is so infinitely great, yet "when a man comes to the synagogue and prays, God listens to him, for the petitioner is like a man who talks into the ear of his friend."[2] The same is the case with repentance, "the power of which is very great." Directly a man has a thought of repentance, it instantly reaches the throne of God.[3]

Something similar may be remarked of the conception of God's Kingship, forming, as we shall see in the sequence, an important feature of the theology of the Rabbis which undoubtedly contributed in some

---

[1] *Jer. Berachoth*, 13 a.   [2] *Jer. Berachoth, ibid.*
[3] *P. R*, 185 a. See also below, p. 335.

measure towards confining God to a *locale*, the elevation of which would not only suggest exaltation, but also convey to our mind a sense of security against all intrusion, so as to keep those below at a respectful distance. Yet this distance does not cause either remoteness and separation. These are only brought about by the evil actions of man. This we gather from such a passage as the following: It is with allusion to Ps. 18 12, "He made darkness his hiding-place, his pavilion round him." "This verse," it is explained, "David only said in the praise of the Holy One, blessed be he, he who is יי, ruling in the height ... and he dwells in three hundred and ninety heavens ... and in each of them there are ministering angels and Seraphim and Ophanim and Cherubim and Galgalim and a Throne of Glory. But thou must not wonder at this thing; for behold, the King of flesh and blood has many habitations, both for the warm and the cold (seasons), much more so the King who lives for eternity, to whom all belongs." But the author of this mystical passage winds up with the words, "When Israel performs the will of the Omnipresent, he dwells in the Araboth (the seventh heaven) and removeth not from his (world) in any way, but in the time of wrath he ascends on high and sits in the upper heavens.[1]

[1] See *D. E.* ch. 2. Cf. Friedmann נספחים 10, note 2, for parallels and the history of this passage The word in brackets is given after an emendation of R Elijah of Wilna A good collection of comparisons

The fact is, that the nearness of God is determined by the conduct of man, and by his realisation of this nearness, that is, by his knowledge of God. "Thus taught the sages, Thy deeds will bring thee near (to God), and thy deeds will remove thee (from God). How so? If a man does ugly things his actions remove him from the divine presence, as it is said, 'Your sins have separated between you and your God' (Isa. 59 2). But if a man has done good deeds, they bring him near to the divine presence. . . . And it is upon man to know that a contrite and humble spirit is better than all the sacrifices (prescribed) in the Torah."[1] It is in conformity with this conception of the nearness of God that we read, "Before Abraham made God known to his creatures, he was only the God of the heaven; but afterwards he became (through Abraham's proselytising activity) also the God of the earth."[2] Hence the patriarchs are, as just quoted, the very throne of God,[3] whilst those, for instance, who speak untruth, are banished from his holy presence.[4] Indeed, "his main dwelling is among those below," and it is only sin and crime which cause God's removal to the upper regions.

between God and the King of flesh and blood, entering into such details as his throne, his palace, his legions, his court, his administering justice, etc., is to be found in *Die Konigsgleichnisse des Midrasch*, by Dr. I. Ziegler (Breslau, 1903). See especially the Hebrew section of this book.

[1] *S. E.*, p. 104. Cf. also the reading in the old editions of תרב״א, ch. 18.

[2] *Gen. R.*, 59 8.   [3] *Gen. R.*, 47 6. See below, p. 84.

[4] *Sanhedrin*, 102 b. *P. K.* 1 a. Cf below, p. 223.

That such appellatives as space, or master of the world, are not meant to imply severance or remoteness, may be seen from the following instances: "Beloved are Israel, for they are called children of Space" (*makom*), as it is said: "Ye are children unto the Lord your God."[1] "He who helps Israel, is as if he would help space" (God).[2] "Israel (on the waters of Marah) was supplicating and praying to their Father in Heaven, as a son who implores his father, and a disciple who beseeches his master, saying unto him: Master of the world, we have sinned against thee, when we murmured on the sea."[3] Even the term *strength*, by which God is sometimes called,[4] occurs in such connections as: "When Israel does the will of God, power is added to strength."[5] In the Babylonian Talmud one of the most frequent appellations of God is "the merciful one," and it is worth noticing, that this term is mostly used in Halachic or casuistic discussions, which proves, by the way, how little in the mind of the Rabbis the Law was connected with hardness and chastisement. To them it was an effluence of God's mercy and goodness.[6]

---

[1] *Aboth*, 3 18. [2] See *Sifre*, 22 *b*.

[3] *Mechilta*, 45 *b*. See *Aruch*, s.v. גדר See below, p. 336.

[4] *Mechilta*, 48 *b*. *Shabbath*, 87 *b*.

[5] See *P. K*, 166 *a* and *b*. Cf. Kohut's *Aruch*, s.v. גאל. See below, p. 239.

[6] See references of Kohut's *Aruch*, s.v. רחם. In *Tractate Pesachim* alone it occurs about forty-one times, but always in Halachic controversies.

Eager, however, as the Rabbis were to establish this communion between God and the world, they were always on their guard not to permit him to be lost in the world, or to be confused with man. Hence the marked tendency, both in the Targumim and in the Agadah, to explain away or to mitigate certain expressions in the Bible, investing the deity with corporeal qualities. The terms *Shechinah* and *Memra* in the former are well known, and have been treated of by various scholars.[1] As to the Agadah, we find the general rule applied to the Bible, that the Scriptures only intended "to make the ear listen to what it can hear"; or as it is elsewhere expressed, "to soothe the ear (so as to make it listen to) what it can hear," which might be taken as implying a tendency towards mitigating corporeal terms.[2] This tendency may also be detected in the interpretation of the Rabbis given in God's answer to Moses' question, "What is His name" (Exod. 3 13). "The Holy One, blessed be he, said to Moses, Thou wantest to know my name? I am called according to my deeds. When I judge the creatures I am named *Elohim*, when I wage war against the wicked I am named *Zebaoth*, when I suspend (the punishment of) the man's sins, I am named

[1] See Schürer, I 147, note 38, about the literature on this point. The term שכינה is very frequent in the *Talmud* and *Midrashim*, see Kohut's *Aruch*, s.v. שכן. Less frequent is דבור. Cf. Landau (as above), pp. 47 *seq* and p. 53; Bacher, *Terminologie* 2 86.

[2] *A. R. N.*, I, c. 2, ל"ב מדות, § 14. See Reifmann, משיב דבר, p. 31; Bacher, *Terminologie*, I 8.

El Shadai, and when I have mercy with my world, I am named by the *tetragrammaton*."[1] The words, "The Lord is a man of war" (Exod. 15 3), are contrasted with (Hos. 11 9) "For I am God, and not man," and explained to mean that it is only for the love of Israel that God appears in such a capacity.[2] In another passage we read that the divine presence never came down, and Moses never went up to heaven, as it is said, "The heavens are the Lord's, and the earth hath he given to the children of men."[3]

This last passage is not only in contradiction with some of the quotations given in the foregoing pages, but is also directly opposed to another Agadic interpretation of this very verse from the Psalms, according to which the line drawn between heaven and earth was removed by the Revelation, when God came down on Mount Sinai (Exod. 19 19), and Moses was commanded to come up unto the Lord (*ibid.* 24 1).[4] This objection of the Rabbis — though only feebly expressed — to take the scriptural language in its literal sense must be attributed to a polemic tendency against rising sectarianism, which, laying too much stress on the corporeal terms in the Bible, did not rest satisfied with humanising the Deity, but even insisted on deifying man. To the former, that is, the humanising of the Deity and

---

[1] See *Exod. R.* 3 6.
[2] *Mechilta*, 38 *b*   See also below, p 44, note 1.
[3] *Sukkah*, 5 *a*.   See Bacher, *Ag. Tan.*, I 185.
[4] *Exod. R.*, 12 8.

endowing him with all the qualities and attributes which tend towards making God accessible to man, the Rabbis could not possibly object. A great number of scriptural passages, when considered in the light of Rabbinic interpretation, represent nothing else but a record of a sort of *Imitatio hominis* on the part of God. He acts as best man at the wedding of Adam and Eve;[1] he mourns over the world like a father over the death of his son when the sins of ten generations make its destruction by the deluge imminent;[2] he visits Abraham on his sick-bed;[3] he condoles with Isaac after the death of Abraham;[4] he "himself in his glory" is occupied in doing the last honours to Moses, who would otherwise have remained unburied, as no man knew his grave;[5] he teaches Torah to Israel, and to this very day he keeps school in heaven for those who died in their infancy;[6] he prays himself, and teaches Israel how to pray;[7] he argues with Abraham the case of Sodom and Gomorrah not only on equal terms, but tells him, If thou thinkest I acted unworthily, teach me and I will do so.[8] Like man he also feels, so to speak, embarrassed in the presence of the conceited and overbearing, and says, I and the proud cannot dwell in the same place.[9] Nay, it would seem that the

---

[1] *Gen. R.*, 8 8 18. Cf. Commentaries and *ibid.* 18 1.
[2] See *Gen. R.*, 27 4.   [3] *Gen. R.*, 8 13.   [4] *Gen. R., ibid.*
[5] See *Gen. R., ibid.*, and *Sota*, 9 *b*.
[6] *Exod. R.*, 28 5, and *Abodah Zarah*, 3 *b*
[7] See *Berachoth*, 7 *a*, and *Rosh Hashanah*, 17 *b*.
[8] See *Tan. B.*, I 46 *a*.   [9] *Sotah*, 5 *b*.

Rabbis felt an actual delight in heaping human qualities upon God whenever opportunity is offered by Scripture. Thus with reference to (Exod. 15 1) "I will sing unto the Lord," the Rabbis say, "I will praise him," that he is terrible, as it is said, "A great God, a mighty and a terrible" (Deut. 10 17). "I will praise him," that he is wealthy, as it is said, "The earth is the Lord's, and the fulness thereof" (Ps. 24 1). "I will praise him," that he is wise, as it is said, "For the Lord giveth wisdom: out of his mouth cometh knowledge and understanding" (Prov. 2 6). "I will praise him," that he is merciful, as it is said, "The Lord, the Lord God, is merciful and gracious" (Exod. 34 6). "I will praise him," that he is a judge, as it is said, "For the judgment is God's" (Deut. 1 17). "I will praise him," that he is faithful, as it is said, "Know therefore that the Lord thy God, he is God, the faithful God" (*ibid.* 7 9).[1]

What the Rabbis strongly objected to was the deification of man. Thus with reference to Exod. 6 and 7 1, God is represented by the Rabbis as having said to Moses, "Though I made thee a god to Pharaoh, thou must not become overbearing (and think thyself God); *I* am the Lord."[2] To Hiram, the Prince of Tyre, who said, "I am God; I sit in the seat of

---

[1] *Mechilta*, 35 a. Cf. *MHG.*, 677 *seq*, about the seventy names of God, and note 12 to col. 681. Cf also Saalfeld, *Das Hohelied Salomons*, p. 137.

[2] *Tan. B.*, 2, 13 a.

God" (Ezek. 28 2), God is supposed by the Rabbis to have answered, "Did Elijah, notwithstanding his reviving the dead, bringing rain, and making the fire to come down from heaven, ever make the claim to be a God?"[1] Both Pharaoh and the Prince of Tyre are, of course, only prototypes of persons deified in the times of the Rabbis, be it Roman emperors or Jewish Messiahs. And it was, as we may imagine, under the pressure of this controversy that the Rabbis availed themselves of any appellatives for God, as well as of any allegorical interpretation, that served as a check against this deification tendency.

It would, however, be a mistake to think that the Rabbis attached to appellatives for God, such as Shechinah, or Word, the same meaning which they have received in Hellenistic schools, or in the theology of the Fathers of the Church. Hallam somewhere quotes the shrewd remark of Montaigne, to the effect that we should try a man who says a wise thing, for we may often find that he does not understand it.

I am not quite certain as to the wisdom of the allegorical method and the various appellatives for God, some of which may perhaps have been of Hellenistic origin. But I am convinced that the Rabbis hardly understood the real significance and the inevitable consequences of their use.

Indeed, it soon must have become clear to the

[1] *Tan*, בראשית, 7. Cf. Jellinek, *Beth Hammidrash*, 5, p. 111 and Introduction.

Rabbis that the allegorising method could be turned into a very dangerous weapon against the very principle which it was meant to defend. Not only was it largely used by the adversaries of the synagogue, as a means for justifying the abolition of the Law, but the terms which were accepted in order to weaken or nullify anthropomorphic expressions were afterwards hypostatised and invested with a semi-independent existence, or personified as the creatures of God. This will explain the fact that, along with the allegorising tendency, there is also a marked tendency in the opposite direction, insisting on the literal sense of the word of the Bible, and even exaggerating the corporeal terms.[1]

---

[1] See Weiss, דו"ד. I 111. Weber (pp. 153 and 179) makes a difference between the Targumim and the later Rabbinism. This theory is based chiefly on the assumption of the great antiquity of the former, which is still doubtful. A good essay on the various heresies which the Rabbis had to face, and which would, as I believe, throw much light on the inconsistencies of the Targumim and of the Rabbis concerning the question of anthropomorphism, is still a desideratum That too much Targum only served to increase the danger, may be seen from the following extract from the *MHG.* (Ms.), to Exod. 24 10,
ויראו את אלהי ישראל ∙ אמ׳ ר׳ אליעזר כל המתרגם פיסוק בצורתו
הרי זה בדאי ∙ וכל המוסיף בו הרי זה מחרף ומגדף כגון שתרגם ויראו
את אלהי ישראל וחזו ית אלהא דישראל הרי זה בדאי ∙ שהקב״ה רואה
ואינו נראה ∙ תרגם וחזו ית יקר שכינת אלהא דישראל הרי זה מחרף
ומגדף שהוא עושה כאן שלשה יקר ושכינה ואל "R. Eliezer said: He who translates a verse (from the Bible) literally is a liar. He who adds to it commits blasphemy. For instance, if he translated (the above-quoted verse), *And they saw the God of Israel*, he spoke an untruth; for the Holy One, blessed be he, sees, but is not seen. But if he translated, *And they saw the glory of the Shechina of the God of Israel*, he commits blasphemy, for he makes *three* (a Trinity), namely,

GOD AND THE WORLD

We have unfortunately no sufficient data enabling us to form a real picture of this great theological struggle. What we perceive is rather confusion and perplexity.

The following fragment from a controversy between a Jew and a certain heretic will perhaps give us some idea of this confusion. We read in Exod. 24 1, "And unto Moses he said, Come up to the Lord." Said the heretic to the Rabbi, "If it was God who called Moses, it ought to be: And unto Moses he said, Come up *to me*." The Rabbi answers that by the word *he* is meant the angel Metatron who commanded Moses to ascend to God, the Rabbi identifying this angel, "whose name is like that of his master," with the angel spoken of in chapter 23 20, 21. What follows now is not quite clear, but we see the heretic claiming quite logically worship for Metatron (and perhaps also the power of forgiving sin), whilst the Rabbi retorts, "Faith in thy hands! We have not accepted him even as a messenger, as it is written, 'If thy presence

Glory, Shechina, and God." See *Das Fragmententargum* by M. Ginsburger, p 43, where this rendering of Exod. 24 is to be found. See also *Kiddushin*, 49 a, and *Tosephta Megillah*, p. 228, and commentaries, and cf. Berliner *Targum*, 2, pp 87 and 173 Our version proves that the objections were of a dogmatic nature. The fact that א״ר is introducing it makes me believe that the passage may have been in the פרקי דר״א (perhaps c. 45). In the older Jewish literature, the Christians are never introduced as Trinitarians. Instructive is also the fact that some Genizah fragments of the Passover Hagada have after the words לא על ידי שליח, the addition אלא הקבה בעצמו, לא על ידי הדבר. Cf. the phrase אנום על פי הדבור. Cf. the Jewish Quarterly Review, vol. x (1897–8), p. 51.

go not (with us), carry us not up hence'" (Exod. 33 16). The heretic thus urges logical consistency and is ready to develop a whole theology from a doubtful interpretation; the Rabbi is less logical, but merely insists upon the fact that Israel refused to give angels divine honours or divine prerogatives.[1]

The fact is that the Rabbis were a simple, naïve people, filled with a childlike scriptural faith, neither wanting nor bearing much analysis and interpretation. "Common sense," is somewhere aptly remarked, "tells us what is meant by the words 'My Lord and my God'; and a religious man upon his knees requires no commentator." More emphatically the same thought is expressed in the quaint answer of a mediæval Rabbi, who, when asked as to the meaning (philosophic or mystic) he was wont to give to his prayers, replied, "I pray with the meaning of this child."[2] Such simple people, however, were unequal to the task of meeting on the battlefield of speculation the champions of the Alexandrine schools. The *aperçu* stigmatising the Rabbis as the "virtuosi" of religion is well known and has in it some appearance of truth. A single letter, or a mere suffix or prefix, or a particle, would suffice for the Rabbis to derive therefrom, if not exactly a new custom or law, at least to give the latter

---

[1] See *Sanhedrin*, 38 *b*, and commentaries (also Edeles). The text is somewhat corrupt. Cf. Rabbinowicz, *Variæ Lectiones a. l.* and the commentary of R. Chananel *a. l.* Cf. Joel, *Blicke*, 1 127; Bacher, *Ag. Am.*, 3 708, and Jacob, *Im Namen Gottes*, p. 41, n. 1.

[2] See *Responsa* of R. Isaac b. Shesheth, § 157.

some foundation in the Scriptures. But the *aperçu* would have more point and be more complete, if we would add that the antagonists of the Rabbis were just as expert "virtuosi" in dogmas and theosophies. What to the Rabbis was a simple adjective, a reverential expression, or a poetical metaphor, turned in the hands of the Hellenists into a new deity, an æon, or a distinct emanation. The Rabbis felt perplexed, and in their consternation and horror went, as we have seen, from one extreme to the other.[1]

The consternation felt by the Rabbis, at the thought of possible consequences, may perhaps be realised by the following passage with allusion to Exod. 19 2: "The Holy One, blessed be he, appeared to them on the (Red) Sea as a mighty warrior (Exod. 15 3) and revealed himself on Mount Sinai as a scribe teaching Torah, and was also visible to them in the days of Daniel, and as Elder teaching Torah (Dan. 7 9) he (therefore) said to them, 'Think not on account of these manifold appearances, there are many deities. I am the Lord thy God. The God of the Sea is the God of the Sinai.' The warning comes from God himself and shows the danger of the situation; indeed, it had become so threatening that even such innocent rhetorical exclamations as 'My God, my God, why hast thou forsaken me?' (Ps. 22 2) were apparently subject

[1] The difference between the Rabbi and the Hellenist in this respect may perhaps be reduced to this: The Rabbi may speak of the *Dibbur* or the *Memra*, but means God; the Hellenist may speak of God, but means the *Dibbur* or the *Memra*.

to misinterpretation, so that it was necessary to emphasise on this occasion, too, the God of the Red Sea is the God of the Revelation." [1]

Even more striking is the following Rabbinic homily on Exod. 3 7, "And the Lord said I have surely seen the affliction of my people": "God said to Moses, 'Thou seest only one sight, but I see two sights. Thou seest them coming to Mt. Sinai and receiving there my Torah; but I see also their making the golden calf. When I shall come to Sinai to give them the Torah, I will come down with my chariot of four *chayoth* (Ezek. 1 5-10), from which they will abstract one (of the four — the ox or the calf), by which they will provoke me.'" [2]

Amidst all these embarrassments, contradictions, confusions, and aberrations, however, the great principle of the Synagogue, that worship is due only to God, remained untouched. Into the liturgy none of the stranger appellations of God were admitted. "When man is in distress," says R. Judah, "he does not first call upon his patron, but seeks admittance to him through the medium of his servant or his agent;

---

[1] See *P. K.*, 109 *b*; *M. T.*, 22 16. אלי בים סוף אלי בסיני. Cf. *P. R.* 100 *b* and 101 *a*, and note 31 to the last page. See also *Tan. B.*, 2 40 *b*. Cf. *Kuzari*, ed. Cassel, 313, note 1.

[2] See *Exod. R.*, 3 2; 42 5, text and references given there in the commentaries. Cf. Ezek. 1 9 and 10; Ps. 106 19 and 20 See also Nachmanides to Exod. 18 1, who gives fuller and better readings of the passage in the Midrash. Cf. Bacher, *Ag. Pal.*, 1 48. About the notion that God came down from Mt. Sinai with the chariot, see *P.K.*, 107 *b*.

but it is different with God. Let no man in misfortune cry either unto Michael or Gabriel, but pray unto me (God), and I will answer him at once, as it is said: 'Whosoever shall call on the name of the Lord shall be delivered'" (Joel 3 5).[1] "Come and see," says another Rabbi, "that in the portions of the Scriptures treating of sacrifices, no other name of God is ever used than the Tetragrammaton. This is done so as not to give room for heretical interpretations,"[2] which might claim divine worship for some other being. When the Rabbis fixed the rule, that no form of benediction is permissible in which the name of God does not occur,[3] they were probably guided by the same principle. At a certain period in history, when the heresy of the new sects was threatening to affect larger classes, the Rabbis even enforced the utterance of the Tetragrammaton in every benediction, lest there should be some misunderstanding to whom prayer is directed.[4]

[1] *Jer. Berachoth*, 13 *a*.
[2] See *Sifre*, 54 *a*. Cf. *T. K.*, 3 *c*. See Bacher, *Ag. Tan.* I 422.
[3] *Berachoth*, 40 *b*.
[4] See *Tosephta Berachoth*, 9, ed. Schwartz, and notes (Graetz, *Geschichte*, 3 458). See also Jacob, *Im Namen Gottes*, p. 174.

III

GOD AND ISRAEL

We saw in the preceding chapter that neither the terms of space nor heaven as applied to God, nor the imaginary descriptions placing his particular abode on high, meant for the Rabbis remoteness from the world. Whatever the faults of the Rabbis were, consistency was not one of them. Neither speculation nor folklore was ever allowed to be converted into rigid dogma. As it was pointed out, when the Rabbis were taught by experience that certain terms meant for superficial proselytes only a reflex of their former deities, they not only abandoned them for a time, but substituted for them even the Tetragrammaton itself; a strong measure, taken in contradiction to ancient custom and tradition, and thus proving how anxious the Rabbis were that nothing should intervene between man and God.

We shall now proceed to show how still more intimate and close was the relation maintained and felt between God and Israel. He is their God, their father, their strength, their shepherd, their hope, their salvation, their safety; they are his people, his children, his first-born son, his treasure, dedicated to his name, which it is sacrilege to profane. In brief, there is not a single endearing epithet in the language, such as brother, sister, bride, mother, lamb, or eye, which is not, according to the Rabbis, applied by the Scriptures to express this intimate relation between God and his people.[1] God is even represented by the Rabbis as saying to Moses, "As much as thou canst exalt this nation (Israel) exalt it, for it is as if thou wert exalting me. Praise it as much as thou canst, glorify it as much as thou canst, for in them I will be glorified, as it is said, 'Thou art my servant, O Israel, in whom I will be glorified'" (Isa. 49 3).[2] "What is his (God's) name? *El* Shaddai, Zebaoth. What is the name of his son? Israel!"[3] Nay, more, though a king of flesh and blood would resent to hear one of his subjects arrogating his title (as Cæsar Augustus), the Holy One, blessed be he, himself confers on Israel the names by which he is himself distinguished, as wise, holy, the chosen ones, and does not even deny them the title of gods, as it is written, "I have said, Ye are gods" (Ps. 82 6).[4]

This intimacy of relationship is reciprocal. "He (God) needs us even as we need him" was a fa-

[1] This feature is so strongly represented in the Rabbinic literature that I must satisfy myself with a few general references. See *T. K.*, 44 *c*; *Mechilta*, 28 *a*, 29 *b*, 41 *b*, 43 *b*, 44 *a*, 57 *a*, 62 *b*; *P. K.*, 1 *a*, 1 *b*, 4 *a*, 4 *b*, 47 *a*, 47 *b*, 50 *a*, 104 *a*, 157 *a*; *Gen. R.*, 81; *Exod. R.*, 15, 20, 27, 33, 52; *Lev. R*, 2. See also *Sifre*, 68 *a*, בני אברהם יצחק ויעקב שנקראו אחים ‎ • • • וכל לשון חבה. The various Midrashim as well as the Targum to the Song of Songs is permeated by the same tendency. Cf. Elbogen, *Religionsanchauungen der Pharisaer*, p 60 *seq*

[2] *Lev. R.*, 2 5.   [3] See *P. R*, 15 *a*. Cf. *P. K.*, 4 *b*.
[4] See *M. T*, 21 2; *Exod. R.*, 8 1.

vourite axiom with certain mystics. In the language of the Rabbis we should express the same sentiment thus, "One God through Israel, and one Israel through God. They are his selected people, and he is their selected portion."[1] "God is the help and the support of all mankind, but still more of Israel." "They recognised in him the King, and he recognised in them the masters of the world. . . . Israel declares (his unity) in the words, 'Hear, O Israel: The Lord our God, the Lord is *one*' (Deut. 6 4); and the holy spirit (or word of God) proclaims their election (in the words), 'And who is like thy people Israel, a nation that is *one* (or alone) in the earth'" (1 Chron. 17 21).[2] "He glorified them when he said, 'Israel is my son, even my first-born,' whilst they sang a song unto him in Egypt."[3] Israel brought him down by their praise (from all the seven heavens to earth, as it is said, "And let them make me a sanctuary, that I may dwell among them") (Exod. 25 9), and he lifted them by his praise above [to the heaven], as it is said, "That the Lord thy God will set thee on high above" (Deut. 28 1).[4] "Blessed be his (God's) name for ever," exclaims a Rabbi, enthusiastically, "who left those above and chose those below to dwell in the Tabernacle because of his love of Israel."[5] Indeed, the Holy One, blessed

[1] *Sifre*, 134 b.

[2] See *Mechilta*, 36 b; *Chagigah*, 3 a, 3 b, and parallels. Cf. Bacher, *Ag. Tan.*, I 285, and Levy, *Talmud. Worterbuch*, s. אמירה, 2, and חטיבה.   [3] *Mechilta*, 35 b.

[4] See *Cant., R.*, 5 16.   [5] *Tan. B.*, 3 8 a. Cf. *Tan. B.*, 2 47 a and b.

be he, says to Israel, you are my flock and I am the shepherd, make a hut for the shepherd that he come and provide for you; you are the vineyard and I am the watcher, make a tent for the watcher that he guards you; you are the children and I am the father, — it is a glory for the father when he is with his children and a glory for the children when they are with their father; make therefore a house for the father that he comes and dwells with his children.[1]

Israel bears in common with the angels such names as gods, holy ones, children (of God). But God loves Israel more than the angels. Israel's prayer being more acceptable to him than the song of the angels, whilst the righteous in Israel are in closer contact with the Deity than the angels, and are consulted by them as to "what God hath wrought." [2]

---

[1] *Exod. R.*, 33 8.

[2] See *Chullin* 91 b. *Yalkut* 1 § 890 (quotation from the *Yelamdenu*). *Yalkut to Prov.*, § 951, and *Shabbath* 8 d. Cf also Friedmann, נספחים, p. 47, to which more passages of a similar nature can be added. It should, however, be remarked that the rationalistic school rather objected to this teaching of the inferiority of angels. Cf. Schmiedel's *Studien über ... Religionsphilosophie*, p. 70 seq , and p. 78 *seq.* Cf. also R Meir ibn Gabbai's עבודת הקדש, the ten first chapters of the section תכלית. In general, the belief in angels was fairly maintained by Rabbinism throughout all its history, although it was only David Bilia (fourteenth century) who raised it to the importance of a dogma. Cf. Schechter, *Studies in Judaism*, p. 203. For opposing tendencies in comparatively early times, see *Exod. R.*, 17 5, ועבר ה' לנגוף את מצרים יא ע"י מלאך וי"א הקב"ה בעצמו. See also מהרח"ו to this passage. Naturally, it was subject in the course of history to all sorts of interpretations, qualifications, and modifications. Cf. Professor

Again, "He who rises up against Israel rises up against God; hence the cause of Israel is the cause of God; their ally is also his."[1] For God suffers with them in their suffering and is with them in their distress.[2] Their subjection implies his subjection,[3] and his presence accompanies them through their various captivities among the Gentiles.[4] Therefore their redemption is his redemption,[5] their joy is his joy,[6] their salvation his salvation,[7] and their light his light.[8]

Their cause is indeed so closely identified with God's cause that on the occasion of the great historical crisis at the Red Sea, God is supposed rather to resent the lengthy prayer of Moses, and says unto him, "Wherefore criest thou to me? (Exod. 14 15). I need no asking for my children, as it is said, 'Wilt thou ask me concerning my children?'" (Isa. 45 11).[9] The recognition of this fatherhood is all that God wants from Israel. "All the wonders and mighty deeds

---

Blau's article *Angelology*. Occasionally, the authorities would have to enter their protest against such excesses as invocations addressed to the angels soliciting their intercession. See *Kerem Chemed*, 9 141 *seq.*, and Zunz, *Synagogale Poesie*, p 148 *seq.*

[1] *Mechilta*, 39 *a*, 39 *b* ; *Sifre*, 29 *b* and parallels

[2] *P. K* , 47 *a*. By Israel is also meant the individual. See *Mechilta*, 17 *a*, 119 *b*, אין לי אלא צרת ציבור צרת יחיד מנין, etc., *S. E.*, p. 89. Cf. *Sabbath*, 12 *b*.

[3] *Mechilta*, 16 *a*.

[4] *Sifre*, 62 *b* ; *P. K.*, 113 *b*. Cf. Bacher, *Ag. Tan.*, I 288, note 2.

[5] *Mechilta*, 16 *a*.   [7] *Lev. R.*, 9 8.

[6] *Ibid.*, 56 *a*.   [8] See *P. K.*, 144 *b*.

[9] See *Mechilta*, 30 *a*. Cf *Num. R* , 21.

which I have done for you," says God unto Israel, "were not performed with the purpose of being rewarded (by you), but that you honour me like children and call me your father."[1] The filial relationship suffers no interference, whether for good or evil, of a third person between Israel and God. Israel loves him and loves his house, no man indeed knowing the love which is between Israel and their Maker. And so does the Holy One, blessed be he, love them. He wants to hear Israel's voice (as expressed in prayer), and is anxious for them to listen unto his voice.[2] According to another explanation (of Exod. 14 15), Moses was given to understand that there was no need for his prayers, the Holy One by his intimate relation to Israel being almost himself in distress.[3]

This paternal relation, according to the great majority of the Rabbis, is unconditional. Israel will be

[1] *Exod. R.*, 32 5.   [2] *M. T.*, 116 1.
[3] *Mechilta*, 29 *b*, in the name of R. חנינה בן חלינסי. Some parallel to this strong confidence in the identity of Israel's cause and God's may be found in various utterances of Luther, as, "Know that God so takes thee to himself, that thy enemies are his enemies"; or, "He who despises me despises God"; or, "God suffers and is despised and persecuted in us." And when anxiously waiting for news from the Diet at Augsburg, "I know," he was overheard saying, or rather praying, "that thou art our father and our God; I am certain, therefore, that thou art about to destroy the persecutors of thy children. If thou doest this not, then our danger is thine too. This business is wholly thine. We come to it under compulsion. Thou, therefore, defend." See the preface of the Bishop of Durham (p. xi) to the volume, *Lombard Street in Lent.* See also Mr. Beard in his *Hibbert Lectures*, p. 87.

chastised for its sins, even more severely than other nations for theirs; but this is only another proof of God's fatherly love. For it was only through suffering that Israel obtained the greatest gifts from heaven,[1] and what is still more important to note is, that it was affliction which "reconciled and attached the son to the father (Israel to God)."[2] "The Israelites are God's children even when full of blemishes," and the words, "A seed of evildoers, children that are corrupt" (Isa. 1 4), are cited as a proof that even corruption cannot entirely destroy the natural relation between father and child.[3] Indeed, when Isaiah received the call, "the Holy One, blessed be he, said unto him, 'Isaiah! my children are troublesome and rebellious. If thou dost take upon thyself to be insulted and beaten by my children thou wilt be sent as my messenger, not otherwise!' Isaiah answered, 'Yes, on this condition. As it is said, "I gave my back to smiters and my cheeks to them that plucked off the hair (Isa. 50 6)," I am not even worthy to carry messages to thy children.'"[4] But Elijah, the Rabbis say, who in his zeal denounced Israel, saying, "I have been very jealous for the Lord God of hosts; because the children of Israel have forsaken thy covenant, thrown down thine altars, and slain thy prophets with the sword" (1 Kings 19 14),

---

[1] See *Berachoth*, 5 a, and *Exod. R.*, 1 1.
[2] *Sifre*, 73 b. Cf. *M. T.*, 96 [3] *Sifre*, 133 a, 133 b.
[4] *Lev. R* , 10 2 and references. Cf. also *Exod. R.*, 7 8, regarding the call of Moses and Aaron.

was dismissed with the answer, "I have no desire in thy prophecy"; and his prophetic office was transferred to the milder Elisha, the son of Shaphat, who was anointed in Elijah's place (19 16). Likewise is the Prophet Hosea rebuked for his refraining from praying for Israel, God saying unto him, They are my beloved ones, the sons of my beloved ones, the sons of Abraham, Isaac, and Jacob. For this is indeed the glory of both patriarchs and prophets, that they are prepared to give themselves (as an atoning sacrifice) for Israel; as, for instance, Moses, who said in case God would not forgive the sin of Israel, "Blot me, I pray thee, out of thy book which thou hast written" (Exod. 23 32). Jeremiah, however, who proved himself just as jealous for the glory of the son (Israel) as for the glory of the father (God), saying as he did, "We have transgressed and have rebelled: thou hast not pardoned" (Lam. 3 42) (thus though confessing Israel's guilt, still reproaching God, so to speak, for his declining to forgive), was rewarded by the continuation of his gift of prophecy, as it is said, "And *he adds* besides unto them many like words" (Jer. 36 32).[1] And, it is on the strength of this view of childship that some of the prophets pleaded with God on behalf of Israel. "Behold," they said to the Holy One, blessed be he, "thou sayest (because of their transgressions) they are not any longer thy children,

[1] See *Mechilta*, 2 a. See also *Pesachim*, 87 a and *S. E. Z.*, p. 187, text and notes.

but they are recognisable by their countenances as it is said, 'All that see them shall acknowledge them that they are the seed, which the Lord has blessed' (Is. 61 9). As it is the way of the Father to be merciful with his children though they sin, so thou wilt have mercy with them (notwithstanding their relapses). This is (the meaning of the verse): 'But now, O Lord, thou art our father. . . . Be not wroth very sore, O Lord, neither remember iniquity forever'" (Isa. 64 8, 9).[1] Indeed, God says, after you (Israel) stood on the mount of Sinai and received the Torah and I wrote of you that I love you; and since I loved you, how could I hate you (considering that I loved you as children)?[2]

The only opponent to the view of the majority regarding the paternal relation is R. Judah, who limits it to the time when Israel acts as children should act.[3] When R. Akiba, in a time of great distress, opened the public service with the formula, "Our father, our king, we have sinned against thee; our father, our king, forgive us," he only expressed the view of the great majority, that Israel may claim their filial privileges even if they have sinned.[4] The formula of the daily confession, "Forgive us, O our Father, for we have sinned," points in the same direction. In fact, the

[1] *Exod R.*, 46 4.
[2] See *Exod. R.*, 32 2. Cf. Commentaries *a. l.*
[3] *Sifre*, 133 *a* and *b* Cf. also 94 *a* and *Kiddushin*, 36 *a*.
[4] *Taanith*, 26 *b*. See Rabbinowitz, *Variae Lectiones, a. l.*, and Baer, p. 119, text and commentary. Cf. Low, *Gesammelte Schriften*, I 181.

GOD AND ISRAEL

term "Father," or "Our Father, who is in heaven," or "My Father, who is in heaven," is one of the most frequent in the Jewish Prayer Book and the subsequent liturgy. The latter seems to have been a favourite expression with the Tanna of the school of Elijah, who very often introduces his comments on the Bible (a mixture of homiletics and prayer) with the words, "My Father in heaven, may thy great name be blessed for all eternity, and mayest thou have delight in thy people Israel."[1] Another consequence of this fatherly relation is that Israel feels a certain ease and delight in the fulfilment of the Law which to slaves is burdensome and perplexing. For "the son who serves his father serves him with joy, saying, 'Even if I do not entirely succeed (in carrying out his commandments), yet, as a loving father, he will not be angry with me'; whilst the Gentile slave is always afraid lest he may commit some fault, and therefore serves God in a condition of anxiety and confusion."[2] Indeed, when Israel feels uneasy because of their having to stand in judge-

[1] See *S. E.*, pp. 51, 53, 83, 89, 100, 110, 115, 121. The formula אבי שבשמים occurs on p. 112 eight times. Cf. Friedmann's Introduction, p. 80.

[2] *Tan.* נח, 19. Israel's relation to God seems only then to assume the aspect of slavery, when the whole nation is determined to apostatise. Then God enforces his mastership over them by the right of possession. This seems to me the meaning of the rather obscure passage in *Exod R.*, 24, 1, ד"א אם אביך למה קנך. Cf *ibid.* 3, § 6, where a distinction is made between the individual and the greater number of Israel, to the former free action being left; this contains undoubtedly a deep historical truth. See also *Sifre*, 112 b.

ment before God, the angels say unto them, "Fear ye not the judgement. . . . Know ye not him? He is your next of kin, he is your brother, but what is more, he is your father."[1]

[1] *M. T.*, 118 10.

IV

ELECTION OF ISRAEL

THE quotations in the preceding chapter will suffice to show the confidence with the Rabbis felt in the especially intimate relations existing between God and Israel. This renders it necessary to make here some reference to the doctrine of Israel's election by God, which in fact is only another term for this special relation between the two. "To love means in fact, to choose or to elect." The doctrine has found no place in Maimonides' Thirteen Articles of the Creed, but still even a cursory perusal of Bible and Talmud leaves no doubt that the notion of the election always maintained in Jewish consciousness the character of at least an unformulated dogma.[1]

The Rabbinic belief in the election of Israel finds, perhaps, its clearest expression in a prayer which begins as follows: "Thou hast chosen us from all peoples; thou hast loved us and taken pleasure in us, and hast exalted us above all tongues; thou hast sanctified us by thy commandments and brought us near unto thy service; O our King, thou hast called us by thy great and holy name." These words, which

[1] See Weiss, דו״ר, 3 801. Cf Kaufmann, *J. Q R.*, 2 442.

still breathe a certain scriptural air, are based, as may be easily seen, on the Biblical passages of Deut. 10 15, 14 2; Ps. 149 2; and Jer. 14 27.[1] There was thus hardly any necessity for the Rabbis to give any reasons for their belief in this doctrine, resting as it does on ample Biblical authority; though, as it would seem, they were not quite unconscious of the difficulties which such a doctrine involves. Thus Moses is represented by them as asking God: "Why out of all the seventy nations of the world dost thou give me instructions only about Israel?" the commandments of the Torah being mostly addressed to the "children of Israel" (*e.g.* Exod. 3 15, 31 30, 33 5, Lev. 24 2);[2] whilst in another place we read, with reference to Deut. 7 7, that God says to Israel, "Not because you are greater than other nations did I choose you, nor because you obey my injunctions more than the nations; for they (the nations) follow my commandments, even though they were not bidden to do it, and also magnify my name more than you, as it is said, 'From the rising of the sun, even unto the going down of the same, my name is great among the Gentiles'" (Mal. 1 11).[3] The answers given to these and similar ques-

[1] See Singer, p. 227, and Baer, p. 247. This is the introductory prayer to the original liturgy for the festivals. In olden times the morning prayer for Sabbaths began with the same prayer. See Zunz, *Die Ritus*, p. 13. The benediction over the sanctification cup on festivals opens with a similar formula.

[2] See *P. K.*, 16 *a seq.* and *Lev. R.*, 2 4.

[3] *Tan.*, עקב, 2. See also *Tan. B.*, 5 9 *a*.

tions are various. According to some Rabbis, Israel's election was, as it would seem, predestined before the creation of the world (just as was the name of the Messiah), and sanctified unto the name of God even before the universe was called into existence.[1] Israel was there before the world was created and is still existing now and will continue to exist in the future (by reason of its attachment to God).[2] "The matter is to be compared to a king who was desiring to build; but when he was digging for the purpose of laying the foundations, he found only swamps and mire. At last he hit on a rock, when he said, 'Here I will build.' So, too, when God was about to create the world, he foresaw the sinful generation of Enosh (when man began to profane the name of the Lord), and the wicked generations of the deluge (which said unto God, 'Depart from us'), and he said, 'How shall I create the world whilst these generations are certain to provoke me (by their crimes and sins)?' But when he perceived that Abraham would one day arise, he said, 'Behold, I have found the *petra* on which to build and base the world.'" The patriarch Abraham is called the rock (Isa. 51 1.2); and so Israel are called the rocks (Num. 33 9).[3] They are an obstinate race and their faith in God is not a shifting one, and, as a later author expresses it, if you leave them no

[1] See *Gen. R*, 1 4 and *S. E.*, p. 160. [2] See *Tan.*, נצ, 12.
[3] *Yelamdenu* quoted by the Yalkut, *Num.*, § 766. Cf *Exod. R.*, 15 17. See also below, p. 173.

alternative but apostasy or crucifixion, they are certain to prefer the latter.[1] "Hence the thought of Israel's creation preceded the creation of the world." According to other Rabbis, Israel's claim to the election is because they declared God as king on the Red Sea, and they said, "The Lord shall reign for ever and ever" (Exod. 15 18). According to others again, it was on account of their having accepted the yoke of his kingdom on Mount Sinai.[2] Why did the Holy One, blessed be he, choose Israel? Because all the other nations declared the Torah unfit and refused to accept it, whilst Israel agreed and chose God and his Torah.[3] Another opinion maintains that it was because of Israel's humbleness and meekness that they were found worthy of becoming the chosen people.[4] This may perhaps be connected with the view expressed that God's reason for the election of Israel was the fact that they are the persecuted ones, all the great Biblical characters such as Abraham, Isaac, Jacob, Moses, David, having been oppressed and especially chosen by God.[5] From another place it would seem that it is the holiness of Israel which made them worthy of the election.[6] It is worth noting, however, that the passage in which the reason of Israel's meekness is advanced concludes with the reminder that God

---

[1] See *Exod. R.*, 42 9. Cf. Nachmanides to *Deut.* 7 7, and see also Friedmann, הציון, p. 12.

[2] See *P. K.*, 16 *b* and 17 *a* and parallels.

[3] *Num. R.*, 14 10.   [4] *Tan. B.*, 5 9 *a*.   [5] See *Lev. R.*, 27 6.

[6] See *Sifre*, 94 *a* (§ 97), but the meaning is not quite clear.

says, "My soul volunteered to love them, though they are not worthy of it," quoting as a proof from the Scriptures the verse, "I will love them freely" (Hos. 14 5).[1] This suggests that even those Rabbis who tried to establish Israel's special claim on their exceptional merits were not altogether unconscious of the insufficiency of the reason of works in this respect, and therefore had also recourse to the love of God, which is not given as a reward, but is offered freely. When an old Roman matron challenged R. Jose (b. Chalafta) with the words, "Whomsoever your God likes he brings near unto him (elects)," the Rabbi answered her that God indeed knows whom to select: in him whom he sees good deeds he chooses him and brings him near unto him.[2] But the great majority of the Rabbis are silent about merits, and attribute the election to a mere act of grace (or love) on the part of God. And he is represented as having answered Moses' question cited above, "I give these instructions about Israel (and not about the nations) because they are beloved unto me more than all other nations; for they are my peculiar treasure, and upon them I did set my love, and them I have chosen."[3] "Praised be the Omnipresent" (*makom*), exclaims the Tanna of the school of Elijah, "blessed be he, who chose Israel from among all the

---

[1] *Tan. B.*, 5 9 a.

[2] See *Midrash Shemuel B.*, 8 2, and *Num. R.*, 3 2, text and commentaries.

[3] *Tan.*, כי תשא, 8.

nations, and made them verily his own, and called them children and servants unto his name . . . and all this because of the love with which he loved them, and the joy with which he rejoiced in them."[1]

It must, however, be noted that this doctrine of election — and it is difficult to see how any revealed religion can dispense with it — was not quite of so exclusive a nature as is commonly imagined. For it is only the privilege of the first-born which the Rabbis claim for Israel, that they are the first in God's kingdom, not the exclusion of other nations. A God "who had faith in the world when he created it,"[2] who mourned over its moral decay, which compelled him to punish it with the deluge, as a father mourns over the death of his son,[3] and who, but for their sins, longed to make his abode among its inhabitants,[4] is not to be supposed to have entirely given up all relations with the great majority of mankind, or to have ceased to take any concern in their well-being. "Though his goodness, loving-kindness, and mercy are with Israel, his right hand is always stretched forward to receive *all* those who come into the world, . . . as it is said, 'Unto me every knee shall bow, every tongue shall swear'" (Isa. 45 23). For this confession from the Gentiles the Holy One is waiting.[5] In fact, it did not

---

[1] See *S. E*, p. 129 and p. 127. Cf. *Tan. B.*, 4 9 a.
[2] *Sifre*, 132 b.
[3] *Gen. R.*, 27 4. Cf. *Sanhedrin*, 108 a. See also above, p. 37.
[4] *P. R.*, 27 b and parallels.
[5] See *Mechilta*, 38 b Cf. *M. T*, 100 1.

ELECTION OF ISRAEL

escape the composers of the Liturgy that the same prophet by whom they established their claim to election called God "the King of the Gentiles" (Jer. 10 7), and on this the Rabbis remark that God said to the prophet, "Thou callest me the King of the Gentiles. Am I not also the King of Israel?"[1] The seeming difference again between "I am the Lord, the God of *all* flesh" (Jer. 32 27), and "the Lord of hosts, *the God of Israel*" (ver. 15), or between the verse "Three times in the year all thy males shall appear before *the Lord God*" (Exod. 23 17) and another passage enjoining the same law, but where God is called "the Lord God, the God *of Israel*" (34 23), is explained by the Rabbis to indicate the double relation of God to the world in general, and to Israel in particular. He is the Lord of all nations, while his name is especially attached to Israel.[2] Of more importance is the interpretation given to Deut. 6 4, "Hear, O Israel," etc.

---

[1] *M. T*, 93 1.

[2] See *Mechilta*, 102 *a*, and *Sifre*, 73 *a*. The text is in a rather corrupt state. I have partly followed here the text of the *MHG*, which on Exod. 34 24 reads . את פני האדון אני על כל באי עולם ׃ יכול
אף אתה כיוצא בהן ת״ל אלהי ישראלו יכול עליך בלבד ת״ל את
פני האדון ה׳ ׃ הא כיצד אלוה אני על כל באי עולם ושמי יחול עליך.
Friedmann's suggestion (in *Mechilta*, *ibid.*, note 156) that the original explanation was in כי תשא (not משפטים) is thus confirmed, though, of course, the *Mechilta* of the compiler of the *MHG*. is not the same as ours. In Deut. 6 4, the same Ms. has כיוצא כו אמר ה׳ צבאות
אלהי ישראל מה אני צריך והלא כבר נאמר הנה אני ה׳ אלהי כל בשר
both verses taken from Jeremiah. Cf. Introduction to *Ruth R.*, I 1. Cf. *Mechilta*, of R. Simon, p. 164.

(the *Shema*), which runs as follows: "He is *our* God by making his name particularly attached to us; but he is also the one God of *all* mankind. He is *our* God in this world, he will be the only God in the world to come, as it is said, And the Lord shall be King over all the earth; in that day there shall be one Lord, and his name one" (Zech. 14 9).[1] For, "in this world, the creatures, through the insinuations of the evil inclination, have divided themselves into various tongues, but in the world to come they will agree with one consent to call only on his name, as it is said, 'For then I will restore to the people a pure language, that they may all call upon the name of the Lord, to serve him with one consent'" (Zeph. 3 9).[2] Thus the *Shema* not only contains a metaphysical statement (about the unity of God), but expresses a hope and belief — for everything connected with this verse has a certain dogmatic value — in the ultimate universal kingdom of God.[3]

[1] See *Mechilta* and *Sifre*, *ibid*. I follow the reading of the לקח טוב to Deut. 6 4, which seems to me to be the best one, and is also supported by quotations in Mss. Cf. the commentaries of Rashi, Ibn Ezra, Nachmanides, and Bachye on this verse. See also *Mechilta*, 44 *a*, text and note 20.

[2] *Tan.*, רה, 19, and *Tan. B.*, 1 28 *b*, the source of which is the *Sifre*. See Rashi's commentary, just referred to, where also the verse in Zephaniah is cited.

[3] See *Rosh Hashanah*, 32 *b*., and *Tosefta*, *ibid*. 213, that the *Shema* is taken by the consent of the majority as implying מלכות. Cf. also below, p. 96, note 2, and p. 133, note 2.

V

THE KINGDOM OF GOD (INVISIBLE)

The concluding words of the last chapter, "The kingdom of God," derived from the *Shema*, have brought us to a theological doctrine described by some Rabbis as the very "Truth (or essence) of the Torah,"[1] or as another Rabbi called it, "The 'weighty' law." The typical expressions in the Bible, "I am the Lord your God," or "I am the Lord," are also thought by the Rabbis to suggest the idea of the kingship.[2] It is at once the centre and the circumference of Rabbinic divinity. God is king and hence claiming authority; the king is God, and therefore the manifestation and assertion of this authority are the subject of Israel's prayers and solicitations. The conception has, of course, its origin in the Bible, in which God appears so often as a king with his various attributes, but it is the Rabbinic literature where we first meet with the term "kingdom of heaven," a term, as it seems, less expressive of an accomplished fact than of an undefined

---

[1] See *Megillah*, 16 b, and the commentary of R. Chananel to that passage as reproduced by the *Tosafoth*, in *Gittin*, 6 b, and *Menachoth*, 32 b, which is accepted in the text here. Cf. Kohut, *Aruch*, s.v. אמת.

[2] See *Mechilta of R. Simon*, p. 30, and *Sifre*, 19 b.

and indefinable ideal, and hence capable of a wider interpretation and of varying aspects.

For our present purpose it will be best to view it from its two larger aspects, the invisible kingdom and the visible kingdom.

The invisible kingdom is mainly spiritual, expressive of a certain attitude of mind, and possessing a more individual character. "He who is desirous to receive upon himself the yoke of the kingdom of heaven let him first prepare his body,[1] wash his hands, lay his *Tephilin* (phylacteries), read the *Shema*, and say his prayers." Should he happen to be on a journey, then, for the purpose of receiving the yoke of the kingdom, he must "stop still and direct his heart to heaven in awe, trembling, and devotion, and (in the thought) of unifying the Name, and so read the *Shema*"; after which he may say the rest of the prayers on his way.[2] The worshipper is even bidden to dwell so long in his devotional attitude of mind when uttering the words "only one" (אחד) as to declare God king in all the four corners of the world.[3] Communion with God by means of prayer through the removal of all intruding elements between man and his Maker, and through the implicit acceptance of God's unity as well as an un-

---

[1] *Berachoth*, 14 *b*, 15 *a* The cleansing here has nothing to do with priestly ablutions; it means simply to prepare oneself in such a way as to be able to concentrate all one's mind during the prayer without any disturbance Cf. *Jer. Berachoth*, 4 *c*

[2] *Tan.* לך לך, 1. Cf. *Tan. B*, I 29 *a*, text and notes.

[3] *Berachoth*, 13 *b*.

conditional surrender of mind and heart to his holy will, which the love of God expressed in the *Shema* implies, this is what is understood by the receiving of the kingdom of God. "What is the section of the Law where there is to be found the acceptance of the kingdom of heaven" to the exclusion of the worship of idols? ask the Rabbis. The answer given is, "This is the *Shema*."[1] But under the word *idols* are included all other beings besides God. "Some nations confess their allegiance to Michael, others to Gabriel; but Israel chose only the Lord: as it is said, 'The Lord is my portion, saith my soul' (Lam. 3 24). This is the meaning of 'Hear, O Israel,'" etc.[2] The *Shema* also implies the exclusion of any human mediator, Israel desiring, whether on earth or in heaven, none but God.[3] It is in this sense that the scriptural words, "there is none else beside thee" (Deut. 4 35), and "The Lord, he is God, in heaven above and the earth beneath, there is none else" (Deut. 4 39), are declared to imply kingship.[4]

What love of God means we learn from the interpretation given to the words, "And thou shalt love the Lord with all thy heart, with all thy soul, and with all thy might" (Deut. 6 5). "Love God with all thy desires, even the evil *Yezer* (that is to say,

---

[1] *Sifre*, 34 *b* קיבול מ״ש ומיעט בה ע״ז. Cf. *Berachoth*, 13 *a*, and *Deut. R.*, 2 31, ואיזהו מלכות שמים ה׳ אלהינו ה׳ אחד. See also *Sifre*, 80 *a*, that this division of the *Shema* addresses itself to the individual, ליחיד.

[2] *Deut. R.*, 2 34. [3] *Deut. R., ibid.*, § 33. Cf. *Ag. Ber.*, ch. 27.
[4] *Rosh Hashanah*, 32 *b*.

make thy earthly passions and fleshly desires instrumental in the service of God), so that there may be no corner in thy heart divided against God." Again, "Love him with thy heart's last drop of blood, and be prepared to give up thy soul for God, if he requires it. Love him under all conditions, both in times of bliss and happiness, and in times of distress and misfortune.[1] For every measure he metes out to thee, praise and thank him exceedingly."[2] In a similar way the words, "To love the Lord your God" (Deut. 11 13), are explained to mean, "Say not, I will study the Torah with the purpose of being called Sage or Rabbi, or to acquire fortune, or to be rewarded for it in the world to come; but do it for the sake of thy love to God, though the glory will come in the end."[3] It is especially the love of self that is incompatible with the love of God or with the real belief in the unity. On this point the mediæval philosophers and mystics dwell with special emphasis, of which the following may serve as specimens: R. Bachye Ibn Bakudah, in his "Duties of the Heart": "The things detrimental to the (belief) in the Unity are manifold. . . . Among them is the disguised polytheism (or providing God with a companion), as, for instance, the religious hypocrisy of various kinds (being in reality worship of

[1] *Sifre*, 73 a. Cf. *Berachoth*, 61 b and parallels.
[2] *Mishnah Berachoth*, 9 b.
[3] *Sifre*, 79 b, to be supplemented and corrected by the parallel, 84 b. Cf. *Nedarim*, 62 a. See also Nachmanides' *Commentary to the Pentateuch* to Deut. 6 b. See also below, p. 162.

man instead of worship of God) or when man combines with the worship of God the devotion to his own gain, as it is said, 'There shall be no strange God in thee' (Ps. 81 10), on which our teachers remarked that it meant the strange god in the very body of man. . . ."[1] R. Meir Ibn Gabbai (born 1420), in commenting on Deut. 11 13, rightly remarks, "It is clear from these words that he who serves God with any personal object in view loves none but himself, the Most High having no share in his service; whilst the original design was that man should perform his religious duties only for God's sake, which alone means the establishing of the Unity of the Great Name both in action and in thought. . . . It is the man with such a purpose (aiming towards bringing about the perfect unity to the exclusion of all thought of self) who is called the lover of God."[2] Furthermore, R. Moses Chayim Luzzatto, a mystic of the seventeenth century, when speaking of the function of love in religion, says: "The meaning of this love is that man should be longing and yearning after the nearness of him (God), blessed be he, and striving to reach his holiness (in the same manner) as he would pursue any object for which he feels a strong passion. He should feel that bliss and delight in mentioning his name, in uttering his praises and in occupying himself with the words of the Torah which a lover feels towards the wife of his youth, or the father towards his only

[1] See פ״י שער היחוד חובות הלבבות.
[2] עבודת הקדש, Section יחוד ch. 28.

son, finding delight in merely holding converse about them. . . . The man who loves his Maker with a real love requires no persuasion and inducement for his service. On the contrary, his heart will (on its own account) attract him to it. . . . This is indeed the degree (in the service of God) to be desired, to which our earlier saints, the saints of the Most High, attained to, as King David said, 'As the heart panteth after the water brooks, so panteth my soul after thee, O God. My soul thirsteth for God, for the living God,' and as the prophet said, 'The desire of our soul is to thy name and to the remembrance of thee' (Is. 26 8). This love must not be a love 'depending on something,' that is, that man should not love God as his benefactor, making him rich and prosperous, but it must be like the love of a son to his father, a real natural love . . . as it is said, 'Is he not thy father who has bought thee?'"[1]

"Her yoke is a golden ornament," said Jesus, the son of Sirach, of Wisdom He considered it as a thing "glorious," and invited mankind to put their necks under her yoke. The Rabbis likewise looked upon the yoke of the kingdom of God and the yoke of the Torah as the badge of real freedom. "And if thou hast brought thy neck under the yoke of the Torah she will watch over thee," in both worlds.[2] The yoke of this kingdom was not felt as a burden. If the Rabbis

[1] See Luzzatto, מסילת ישרים, Warsaw, 1884, p. 27 b.
[2] See Ecclus 6 80, 51 17, and 26 b (Hebrew), and cf. *Kinyan Torah* 2; *Erubin*, 54 a; and *M. T.*, 2 11.

had any dread, it was lest it might be removed from them. "I shall not hearken unto you," said one of them to his disciples, who on a certain joyous occasion wanted him to avail himself of his legal privilege, and omit the saying of the *Shema;* "I will not remove from myself the yoke of the kingdom of heaven even for a single moment." [1] Even to be under the wrath of this yoke is a bliss. When one Rabbi quoted the verse from Ezekiel, "As I live, saith the Lord God, surely with a mighty hand, and with a stretched-out arm, and with fury poured out, will I be king over you" (20 33), his colleague answered to the effect, Let the merciful continue his wrath with us, and redeem (and reign over us against our will).[2] What the typical Rabbi longed for was that sublime moment when the daily professions of a long life might be confirmed by act. When R. Akiba, who died the death of a martyr, was in the hands of his torturers, he joyfully "received upon himself the yoke of the kingdom of heaven (by reciting the *Shema*). When asked why he did so, he answered, 'All my life I have recited this verse ('And thou shalt love,' etc.), and have longed for the hour when I could fulfil it. I loved him with all my heart, I loved him with all my fortunes. Now I have the opportunity to love him with all my soul. Therefore I repeat this verse in joyfulness.' And thus he died." [3]

[1] *Mishnah, Berachoth,* 2 5. Cf Rabbinowicz, *Varia Lectiones a l.*
[2] *Sanhedrin,* 105 a. Cf. Rashi, *a. l*
[3] See *Jer. Berachoth,* 14 *b* מיתרין means probably tortured, and has to be supplied by the parallel from Babli, *Berachoth,* 61 *b.*

There is no indication of despair in Akiba's death, but also no thought of a crown of martyrdom awaiting him for this glorious act.[1] He simply fulfils a commandment of love, and he rejoices in fulfilling it. It is "a love unto death,"[2] suffering no separation. "Though God," says Israel, "brings me into distress and embitters me, he shall lie betwixt my breasts,"[3] and to be always in contact with the object of his love is Israel's constant prayer. "Unite our hearts," runs an old Rabbinic prayer, "to fear thy name; remove us from all thou hatest, and bring us near to all thou lovest, and be merciful unto us for thy name's sake."[4] Even fear is only another expression with them for love. "I feared in my joy, I rejoiced in my fear, and my love prevailed over all."[5]

Still more distinctly, though not more emphatically, is this thought of the constant union with God and the constant love of God expressed in the later Jewish authors, with whom it takes a certain mystical turn. "What is the essence of love to God?" says R. Bachye

---

[1] The words in *Aboth.*, 4 7, "Make not (of the Torah) a crown," are explained by R. Samuel de Ozedo, to mean the crown of the saints in the after-life; any thought of reward, whether material or spiritual, whether in this world or in the next, being unworthy of the real worshipper of God. It may, of course, be questioned whether this was the real meaning of the Tanna's saying; but it is highly characteristic of the feelings of the Talmudical Jew in this respect.

[2] *Mechilta*, 37 a.

[3] See *Shabbath*, 88 b, on the interpretation of Song of Songs 1 18. Cf. *Cant R.* to this verse.

[4] *Jer. Berachoth*, 7 d.   [5] See *S. E.*, p. 3.

THE KINGDOM OF GOD (INVISIBLE)

Ibn Bakudah mentioned above. "It is the longing of the soul for an immediate union with him, to be absorbed in his superior light. For the soul, being a simple spiritual substance, is naturally attracted towards spiritual beings. And when she becomes aware of any being that could give her added strength and light, she devises means how to reach it, and clings to it in her thought . . . longing and desiring after it. This is the aim of her love. . . . And when the soul has realised God's omnipotence and his greatness, she prostrates herself in dread before his greatness and glory, and remains in this state till she receives his assurance, when her fear and anxiety cease. Then she drinks of the cup of love to God. She has no other occupation than his service, no other thought than of him, no other intent than the accomplishment of his will, and no other utterance than his praise. If he deal kindly with her she will thank him, if he bring affliction on her she will submit willingly, and her trust in God and her love of God will always increase. So it was told of one of the saints that he used to rise up in the night and say: My God, thou hast brought upon me starvation and penury. Into the depth of darkness thou hast driven me, and thy might and strength hast thou taught me. But even if they burn me in fire, only the more will I love thee and rejoice in thee. For so said the prophet, 'And thou shalt love thy God with all thy heart.'"[1]

[1] חובות הלבבות שער אהבת ה' פ"א. Of one of the exiles from Spain — who was exposed by the captain of the vessel, in which he

R. Eliezer of Worms writes to the effect: The meaning of this love is that the soul is full of the love of God and attached by the bonds of love in joyfulness and gladness of the heart. He is not one who serves his Master under compulsion. His love is burning in his heart urging him to serve God, and he rejoices so much to accomplish the will of the Creator even if they would seek to prevent him from it. . . . He does not serve him for his own profit or for his own glory. He says to himself, "How, was I chosen and created to be a servant to the King of Glory, I, who am despised and rejected of men, I, who am to-day here and tomorrow in the grave?" When the soul sinks in the depths of awe, the spark of the love of the heart breaks out in flames and the inward joy increases . . . the men of divine wisdom think with joy of the heart of accomplishing the will of their Creator, of doing all his commandments with all their hearts. Such lovers think not of the pleasures of the world, nor are they concerned in the idle pastimes of their wives and families. They desire only to accomplish the will of God and to lead others to righteousness, to sanctify his name and to deliver up his soul for the sake of his love as Abraham

had fled with his family, on a deserted island — something similar is reported. When his wife died from exhaustion, and his two children perished by famine, and he himself was in a fainting state, he exclaimed: "O Lord of the world, great are the afflictions thou hast brought upon me, tempting me to leave the faith. But thou knowest that I shall not solve thy covenant (with us) until death," שארית ישראל פכ״ג.

did. . . . They exalt not themselves, they speak no idle word, they see not the face of woman, they hear their reproach and answer not. All their thoughts are with their God. They sing sweet songs to him, and their whole frame of mind is glowing in the fire of their love to him.[1] An anonymous author (probably about the same period) says, "Those who believe that works are the main thing are mistaken. The most important matter is the heart. Work and words are only intended as preparatory actions to the devotion of the heart. The essence of all the commandments is to love God with all the heart. The glorious ones (*i.e.* the angels) fulfil none of the 613 commandments. They have neither mouth nor tongue, and yet they are absorbed in the glory of God by means of thought."[2] R. Meir Ibn Gabbai (quoted above) expresses the same thought in words to the effect: The love of the Only Name forms the highest attainment (in the scale) of the service of the Sanctuary. For the perfect adoration worship demanded of the true worshipper is the service of the Unity, that is, the unification of the glorious and the Only Name. But the essence of Love is the true Unity, and the true Unity is what is termed Love. . . . And behold, the soul comes into the body from the abode

[1] See R. Eliezer of Worms, רוקח שורש האהבה and ספר החסידים, Parma, § 300. The book רוקח is a casuistic book on questions of the Law. See also Dr. Gudemann, *Culturgeschichte*, I 160.

[2] Communicated by Dr. Gudemann, *Culturgeschichte*, I 160, from a Munich Ms., ספר החיים, emanating, as it seems, from the Franco-German school.

of Love and Unity, therefore she is longing for their realisation and by loving the Beloved One (God), she maintains the heavenly relations as if they had never been interrupted through this earthly existence.[1]

These instances, which could be multiplied by numerous other extracts from the later devotional literature and hymnology, suffice to show that there are enough individualistic elements in Judaism to satisfy all the longings of the religionist whose bent lies towards mysticism. And just as every Israelite "could always pour out his private griefs and joys before him who fashioneth the hearts," so was he able to satisfy his longing for perfect communion with his God (who is 'nigh to all them who call upon him') by means of simple love, without the aid of any forcible means.

It must, however, be remarked that this satisfying the needs of anybody and everybody is not the highest aim which Judaism set before itself. Altogether, one might venture to express the opinion that the now fashionable test of determining the worth of a religion by its capability to supply the various demands of the great market of the believers has something low and mercenary about it. Nothing less than a good old honest heathen pantheon would satisfy the crazes and cravings of our present pampered humanity, with its pagan reminiscences, its metaphysical confusion of

[1] והאהבה עניינה היחוד האמיתי ch. 28. יחוד Section, עבודת הקודש
.והיחוד האמיתי הוא הנקרא אהבה

languages and theological idiosyncrasies. True religion is above these demands. It is not a Jack-of-all-trades, meaning monotheism to the philosopher, pluralism to the crowd, some mysterious Nothing to the agnostic, Pantheism to the poet, service of man to the hero-worshipper. Its mission is just as much to teach the world that there *are* false gods as to bring it nearer to the true one. Abraham, the friend of God, who was destined to become the first winner of souls, began his career, according to the legend, with breaking idols, and it is his particular glory to have been in opposition to the whole world.[1] Judaism means to convert the world, not to convert itself. It will not die in order *not* to live. It disdains a victory by defeating itself in giving up its essential doctrines and its most vital teaching. It has confidence in the world; it hopes, it prays, and waits patiently for the great day when the world will be ripe for its acceptance.

Nor is the individual — the pet of modern theology — with his heartburnings and mystical longings, of such importance that Judaism can spend its whole strength on him. De Wette was certainly guilty of a gross exaggeration when he maintained "that all mysticism tends to a more refined lust, to a feasting upon the feelings" — something like our conceited culture dandy, who is eaten up with the admiration of his vague denials and half-hearted affirmations. For undoubtedly

[1] See *Gen R.*, 38 18, and 42 8 (the explanations of R. Judah to העברי); cf. Beer, *Leben Abrahams*, p 8 *seq.*

every religion can boast of saintly mystics who did much good service to their own creed and to the world at large. Indeed, no creed worthy of the name could or would ever dispense with that sprinkling of mystics representing the deeper elements of saintliness and religious delicacy. But they were of little use either to themselves or to the world when they emancipated themselves from the control of the law. For it cannot be denied that the mystic has not always shown himself very trustworthy in his mission. Instead of being absorbed by God, he has absorbed God in himself. His tendency towards antinomianism, and to regard law and works as beneath him, is also a sad historic fact. But the worst feature about him is his egoism, the kingdom of God within him never passing beyond the limits of his insignificant self, who is the exclusive object of his own devotions. The Rabbis often speak of the reward awaiting the righteous after their death as consisting, not in material pleasures, but in feeding on, or revelling in, the divine glory.[1] But such a vision "of the blissfulness of the spirit" is wisely confined to the next world, when the Great Sabbath will break upon us, when all things will be at rest. In this world, "the world of activity," the righteous have no such peace; they have to labour and to suffer with their fellow-creatures; and even such a sublime quietism as revelling in God may, without strong control, too easily degenerate into a sort of religious epicureanism. It

[1] See *Berachoth*, 17 *a* and parallels.

would seem as though it were with an eye to such "idle spirituality," that with reference to Deut. 6 5, "And thou shalt love the Lord thy God with all thy heart," the Rabbis make the remark, "I know not in which way they should love the Holy One, blessed be he," therefore the Scripture continues, "And these words which I command thee this day, shall be in thine heart" (Deut. 6 6), which means, "Place these words upon thy heart, for through them thou wilt learn to know the Holy One, blessed be he, and cleave unto his ways."[1] And "these ways," as we shall see, concern this world. The best control is thus to work towards establishing the visible kingdom of God in the present world. This, the highest goal religion can strive to reach, Judaism never lost sight of. It always remained the cherished burden of its most ardent prayers and the object of its dearest hopes.

[1] See *Sifre*, 74 *a*.

VI

THE VISIBLE KINGDOM (UNIVERSAL)

The visible kingdom may be viewed from two aspects, national and universal. An attempt will be made to give the outlines of these Aspects as they are to be traced in Rabbinic literature.

"Before God created the world," we read in the Chapters of R. Eliezer, "there was none but God and his great name." The great name is the tetragrammaton, the name expressive of his being, the "I am." All other names, or rather attributes, such as Lord, Almighty, Judge, Merciful, indicative of his relation to the world and its government, had naturally no meaning before the world was created. The act of creation again is a manifestation of God's holy will and goodness; but it requires a responsive goodness on the part of those whom he intends to create. For "whatever the Holy One, blessed be he, created in his world, he created but for his glory, for it is said, Every one that is called by my name: for I have created him for my glory. I have formed him; yea, I have made him (Is. 43 7), and again it is said, The Lord shall reign for ever and ever (Exod. 15 18)." "The Lord has made everything for himself" (Prov. 16 4),

THE VISIBLE KINGDOM (UNIVERSAL)

and heaven and earth, angels and planets, waters and herbs and trees and birds and beasts, all join in the great chorus of praise to God. But the attribute of kingship apparently does not come into full operation before the creation of man. Hence, "when the Holy One, blessed be he, consulted the Torah as to the creation of the world, she answered, 'Master of the world (to be created), if there be no host, over whom will the king reign, and if there be no peoples praising him, where is the glory of the king?' The Lord of the world heard the answer, and it pleased him."[1]

To effect this object, the angels already in existence did not suffice. "When God had created the world," one of the later Midrashim records, "he produced on the second day the angels with their natural inclination to do good, and an absolute inability to commit sin. On the following days he created the beasts with their exclusively animal desires. But he was pleased with neither of these extremes. 'If the angels follow my will,' said God, 'it is only on account of their inability to act in the opposite direction. I shall, therefore, create man, who will be a combination of both angel and beast, so that he will be able to follow either the good or the evil inclination.'"[2] His evil deeds will

---

[1] See *P.R E.*, ch. 3. The thought of the world, and especially man, having been created for God's glory, is very common in Jewish literature. Cf. *A. R. N.*, 67 b, text and notes at the end; *Tan.* בראשית, 1; *Exod. R.* 17· 1 and *M. T.*, 148 5.

[2] Quoted in the ספ״ק, § 53. Cf. *Tan. B.*, Introduction, 76 b. Cf. below, p. 261, note 1.

place him below the level of the brutes, whilst his noble aspirations will raise him above the angels.

In short, it is not slaves, heaven-born though they may be, that can make the kingdom glorious. God wants to reign over free agents, and it is their obedience which he desires to obtain. Man becomes thus the centre of creation, for he is the only object in which the kingship could come into full expression. Hence it is, as it would seem, that on the sixth day, after God had finished all his work, including man, that God became king over the world.[1]

Adam the First invites the whole creation over which he is master "to clothe God with majesty and strength," and to declare him King, and he and all the other beings join in the song, "The Lord reigneth, he is clothed with majesty," which forms now the substance of the 93d Psalm.[2] God can now rejoice in his world. This is the world inhabited by man, and when he viewed it, as it appeared before him in all its innocence and beauty, he exclaimed, "My world, O that thou wouldst always look as graceful as thou lookest now." "Beautiful is the world," a Rabbi exclaims, "blessed be the Omnipresent who shaped it and created it by his word. Blessed art thou (world) in which the Holy One, blessed be he, is king."[3]

[1] See *Rosh Hashanah*, 31 a, assuming, of course, that the words ומלך עליה on the second day came into the text by a clerical error. Cf. Rabbinowicz, *Variae Lectiones*, al. *A. R. N.*, Appendix 76 b, and the Mishna, ed. Lowe, 191 a.   [2] *P. R. E.*, ch 11.

[3] *Gen. R.*, 9 4   See also *Exod. R.*, 15 22.   Cf. also *Num. R.*, 10 1, that God longed to create the world.

This state of gracefulness did not last long. The free agent abused his liberty, and sin came into the world, disfiguring both man and the scene of his activity. Rebellion against God was characteristic of the generations that followed. Their besetting sin, especially that of the generation of the Deluge, which had to be wiped out from the face of the earth, was that they said, "There is no judge in the world," it being "an automaton."[1] They were the reverse of the faithful of later generations, that proclaimed God's government and kingship in the world every day.[2] They maintained that the world was forsaken by God, and said unto God, "Depart from us, for we desire not the knowledge of thy ways" (Job 21 14).[3] The name of God was profaned by its transfer to abominations (or idols), and violence and vice became the order of the day.[4] By these sins God was removed from the world in which he longed to fix his abode, and the reign of righteousness and justice ceased. The world was thus thrown into a chaotic state of darkness for twenty generations, from Adam to Abraham, all of them continuing to provoke God.[5] With Abraham the light returned,[6] for he was the first to call God master (אדון), a name which declares God to be the Ruler of the

[1] *A. R. N.*, 47 b and parallels. *M. T.*, 1 21.

[2] See *M. T.* ibid

[3] See *Sanhedrin*, 108 a. Cf also *P. R. E.*, ch 24, with special reference to the generation of Nimrod, who threw off the yoke of heaven.

[4] See *Mechilta*, 67 b. See also *Pseudo-Jonathan*, Gen. 4 26.

[5] See *Aboth*, 5 1, and commentaries.   [6] See *Gen. R.*, 3 8.

world, and concerned in the actions of men.¹ Abraham was also the first great missionary in the world, the friend of God, who makes him beloved by his creatures, and wins souls for him, bidding them, even as he bade his children, to keep the way of the Lord, to do righteousness and judgement.² It was by this activity that Abraham brought God again nearer to the world;³ or, as the Rabbis express it in another passage, which we already had occasion to quote: Before Abraham made God known to his creatures he had been only the God (or the king of the heavens), but since Abraham came (and commenced his proselytising activity) he has become also the God and the King of the earth;⁴ Jacob also is supposed by the Rabbis to have taught his children before his death the ways of God, whereupon they received the yoke of the kingdom of heaven.⁵ Hence the patriarchs (as models and propagators of righteousness) became, as mentioned above, the very throne of God, his kingdom being based upon mankind's knowledge of him, and their realisation of his nearness.⁶

But the throne of God is not secure as long as the recognition of the kingship is only the possession of a few individuals. At the very time when the patriarch

---

[1] *Berachoth*, 7 *b* See Edeles' Commentary to the passage.
[2] See *Sifre*, 73 *a* and parallels.
[3] *P. K.*, 1 *b*, and *P R*, 18 *b*.
[4] *Sifre*, 134 *b*, where the word מלך occurs
[5] See *Num. R.*, 2 8. See also *Gen. R.*, 93 8 and parallels.
[6] See above, p. 33.

THE VISIBLE KINGDOM (UNIVERSAL)

was teaching righteousness, there were the entire communities of Sodom and Gomorrah committed to idolatry and the basest vices,[1] whilst in the age of Moses, Pharaoh said, "Who is the Lord that I should obey his voice?"[2] The kingship is therefore uncertain until there was called into existence a whole people "which knows God," is sanctified unto his name, and devoted to the proclamation of his unity.[3] "If my people," God says to the angels, "decline to proclaim me as King upon earth, my kingdom ceases also in heaven." Hence Israel says unto God, "Though thou wast from eternity the same ere the world was created, and the same since the world has been created, yet thy throne was not established and thou wast not known; but in the hour when we stood by the Red Sea, and recited a song before thee, thy kingdom became firmly established and thy throne was firmly set."[4] The establishment of the kingdom is indicated in the eighteenth verse of the Song (*Shirah*), where it is said, "The Lord shall be king for ever and ever." But even more vital proofs of their readiness to enter into the kingdom, Israel gave on the day of "the glorious meeting" on Mount Sinai, when they answered in one voice, "All that the Lord hath said we will do, and be obedient" (Exod. 24. 7).[5] This unconditional surrender to the will of God in-

---

[1] *Sanhedrin*, 108 a and parallels.
[2] See Maimonides' *Mishneh Torah*, הלכות עכו״ם פ״א ה״י, which seems to be a paraphrase of some Midrash. Cf. *Num. R.*, 2 6.
[3] See *Agadath Shir Hashirim*, pp. 11, 53.
[4] See *Exod. R.*, 23 1.   [5] See *P. K.*, 17 a.

vested Israel, according to the Rabbis, with a special beauty and grace.[1] And by the manifestation of the knowledge of God through the act of the revelation the world resumes its native gracefulness, which makes it again heaven-like, whilst God finds more delight in men than in angels.[2]

There is a remarkable passage in the Mechilta, in which Israel is strongly censured because in the song at the Red Sea, instead of using the present tense, ה׳ מֶלֶךְ, "God *is* King," they said ה׳ ימלוך, "God *shall be* King," thus deferring the establishment of the kingdom to an indefinite future.[3] Israel had accordingly some sort of foreboding of the evil times to come, a foreboding which was amply justified by the course of history. Israel soon rebelled against the kingdom. There was the rebellious act of the Golden Calf, which took place on the very spot where the kingdom was proclaimed, and which was followed by other acts of

[1] See *Midrash Agadah*, ed. B. 171 a. Cf. the Targum to Song of Songs, 7 7.

[2] See *Exod R.*, 51 8, and parallels.

[3] See *Mechilta*, 44 a, in the name of R. Jose of Galilee. The text in the editions is corrupt. In the *M. H. G.* it runs. ה׳ ימלוך לעולם ועד · ר״ יוסי אומ׳ אלו אמרו ישראל ה׳ מלך עולם ועד לא שלטה בהם אומה ומלכות אלא ה׳ ימלוך לעולם ועד לעתיד לבוא · מפני מה כי בא סום פרעה מלמד שאף פרעה בכלל · וישב עליהם את מי הים · עליהם שב · אבל עמך וצאן מרעיתך ונחלתך בני אברהם אוהבך זרע יצחק ידידך משפחת יעקב בכורך · נפן שהסעת ממצרים וכנה שנטעה ימינך · ובני ישראל הלכו ביבשה בתוך הים. Cf. Targum Onkelos to this verse, whose paraphrase may have been intended to avoid the difficulty felt by R. Jose Cf, however, Nachmanides' commentary to this verse and his reference to Onkelos.

THE VISIBLE KINGDOM (UNIVERSAL) 87

rebellion against God.¹ "In the days of Joshua b. Nun, Israel received upon themselves the kingdom of heaven in love ... and their reward was that God regarded them as pupils in the house of their teacher and children gathered round the table of their father, and he apportioned to them a blessing."² Then came again continual relapses, and the sons of Eli were called בני בליעל, the sons of Belial, — men who threw off the yoke of God³ and denied the kingdom of heaven,⁴ but "in the times of the prophet Samuel, Israel (again) received upon themselves the kingdom of heaven in fear ... and their reward was that God came down from the upper heavens, the place of his glory ... and abode with them during the battle (with the Philistines), and apportioned to them a blessing."⁵ After David came the decay, and Solomon is described as one who threw off the yoke of God.⁶ The division of the ten tribes under Jeroboam was also regarded as a rebellion against the kingdom of God. The Rabbis interpreted 2 Samuel 20. 1, as if the original reading had been איש לאלהיו ישראל, "Every man *to his gods*, O Israel" (instead of to his *tents*).⁷ Even the princes

---

¹ See *Num. R.*, 7 2. ² *S. E.*, p 86. ³ See *Sifre*, 93 b.

⁴ See *Yalkut to Shemuel*, § 86, and *Midrash Shemuel*, B. p 31 b, from which the passage in question was taken. The marginal reference to *T. K.* (39 d) refers only to the first lines of the passage, which Schottgen (1149) confused. See *Eccles. R.*, 1 18.

⁵ *S. E.*, p. 86. ⁶ *Num. R.*, 4 10.

⁷ The rebellion of the Belial Sheba, the son of Bichri, is only a prelude to that effected by Jeroboam. See *Midrash Shemuel*, B. ch. 42 b, § 4, and notes, and *Mechilta*, 39 a, כיוצא בו אין לנו חלק בדוד, etc.

of Judah at a later time "broke the yoke of the Holy One, blessed be he, and took upon themselves the yoke of the King of Flesh and Blood." The phrase, "broke" or "removed" the yoke, is not uncommon in Rabbinic literature, and has a theological meaning. The passage just cited refers probably to some deification of Roman emperors by Jewish apostates, and not exactly to a political revolt.[1]

Yet, notwithstanding all these relapses, one great end was achieved, and this was, that there existed a whole people who did once select God as their king. Over the people as a whole, as already hinted, God asserts his right to maintain his kingdom. Thus the Rabbis interpret Ezekiel 20 33, "Without your consent and against your will I (God) shall be King over you;" and when the elders of Israel remonstrate, "We are now among the Gentiles, and have therefore no reason for not throwing off the yoke of his kingdom," the Holy One answers, "This shall not come to pass, for I will send my prophets, who will lead you back under my wings."[2] The right of possession is thus enforced by an inner process, the prophets being a part of the people; and so there will always be among them a remnant which will remain true to their mission of preaching the kingdom. The remnant is naturally small in number, but

[1] See *A. R. N.*, 36 *b*. See, however, Bacher, *Ag. Tan*, 1 58, note 1, and the reference there to Weiss דו"ר. Cf. *Beth Talmud*, 2, 333-334.

[2] See *T. K.*, 112 *b*. Cf. *Sanhedrin*, 105 *a* and parallels. Cf. also *Exod. R.*, 3 2, and above, p. 55, note 2.

is sufficient to keep the idea of the kingdom alive. "God saw," say the Rabbis, "that the righteous were sparse; he therefore planted them in (or distributed them over) all generations, as it is said (2 Samuel 1 8), 'For the pillars of the earth are the Lord's, and he has set the world upon them.'" The pillars, according to the Rabbinical explanation, are the righteous, who, by the fact of their being devoted to the Lord, form the foundation of the spiritual world.[1]

We will now try to sum up in some clearer way the results to which the preceding statements mostly consisting of Rabbinical quotations, may lead us. We learn first that the kingdom of God is in *this world*. In the next world, if we understand by it the heavens, or any other sphere where angels and ethereal souls dwell, there is no object in the kingdom. The term "kingdom of heaven" must therefore be taken in the sense in which heaven is equivalent to God, not locally, as if the kingdom were located in the celestial spheres. The term מלכות שדי in the Prayer Book,[2] the kingdom of the Almighty, may be safely regarded as a synonym of מלכות שמים.

This kingdom again is established on earth by man's consciousness that God is near to him; whilst nearness

---

[1] *Yoma*, 38 b.

[2] Beginning על כן נקוה, see below, p 94. Cf. *A. R. N.*, 36 b, where he speaks of עולו של הקב״ה, instead of which certain Mss. have all עול שמים. The mystical literature, it should be noted, speaks of angels "taking upon themselves the yoke of the kingdom of heaven." See Singer, p. 38 and Baer, p. 132.

of God to man means the knowledge of God's ways to do righteousness and judgement. In other words, it is the sense of duty and responsibility to the heavenly king who is concerned in and superintends our actions. "Behold thou art fair, my love," says God to Israel, "you are fair through the giving of alms and performing acts of loving-kindness; you (Israel) are my lovers and friends when you walk in my ways. As the Omnipresent is merciful and gracious, long-suffering and abundant in goodness, so be ye . . . feeding the hungry, giving drink to the thirsty, clothing the naked, ransoming the captives, and marrying the orphans. . . . They will behold the Right One, which is the Holy One, blessed be he, as it is said, 'A God of truth and without iniquity, just and Right is he'" (Deut. 32 4).[1] "The hill of the Lord," and "the tabernacle of God" in the Psalms, in which only the workers of righteousness and the pure-hearted shall abide, are kingdoms of God in miniature.

The idea of the kingdom may thus be conceived as ethical (not exactly eschatological) and it was in this sense perhaps that the Rabbis considered the patriarchs and the prophets as the preachers of the kingdom. It is not even exactly identical with the law or the Torah. Why do we read, ask the Rabbis, first the *Shema* (*i.e.* Deut. 6. 4-9), and afterwards the section Deut. 11 13, commencing with the words, "And it shall come to pass if ye will hearken diligently unto my command-

[1] See *Agadath Shir Hashirim*, p. 18, and p. 61.

ments"? This is done, say the Rabbis, to the end that we may receive upon ourselves first the yoke of the kingdom and afterwards the yoke of the commandments.[1] The law is thus only a necessary consequence of the kingdom, but not identical with it.[2]

Indeed, the Torah itself indicates its relation to the Kingdom; for the Rabbis say in allusion to Deut. 32 29, "Had Israel looked properly into the words of the Torah that were revealed to them, no nation would have ever gained dominion over them. And what did she (the Torah) say unto them? Receive upon yourselves the yoke of the kingdom of my name; outweigh each other in the fear of heaven, and let your conduct

[1] *Berachoth*, 13 *a*.

[2] In this connection reference may be had to the following Midrashic passage alluding to Zech. 99 · "Rejoice greatly, O daughter of Zion, . . . behold thy King is coming unto thee. . . ." God says to Israel. "Ye righteous of the world, the words of the Torah are important for me; ye were attached to the Torah, but did not hope for my kingdom. I take an oath that with regard to those who hope for my kingdom I shall myself bear witness for their good . . . These are the mourners over Zion who are humble in spirit, who hear their offence and answer not, and never claim merit for themselves." Lector Friedmann, in his commentary on the Pesikta, perceives in this very obscure passage the emphatic expression of the importance of the kingdom, which is more universal than the words of the Torah; the latter having only the aim of preparing mankind for the kingdom. See *P. R.*, 159 *a*, text and notes (especially note 23). To me it seems that the passage has probably to be taken in the sense of the text communicated from Friedmann's נספחים, below, p. 292. There are, also, very grave doubts as to the age and character of all these *Messianic Pesiktoth*. See Friedmann's interesting note, *ibid.*, p. 164 *a*, 164 *b*, though he defends their genuineness.

be mutual loving-kindness."[1] Among the features of the kingdom, the fear of God and the love of one's neighbor are thus found to be prominent.

Nor, again, is the kingdom of God political. The patriarchs in the mind of the Rabbis did not figure prominently as worldly princes, but as teachers of the kingdom.[2] The idea of theocracy as opposed to any other form of government was quite foreign to the Rabbis. There is not the slightest hint in the whole Rabbinic literature that the Rabbis gave any preference to a hierarchy with an ecclesiastical head who pretends to be the vice-regent of God, over a secular prince who derives his authority from the divine right of his dynasty.[3] Every authority, according to the creed of the Rabbis, was appointed by heaven;[4] but they had also the sad experience that each in its turn rebelled against heaven. The high priests, Menelaus and Alcimus, were just as wicked and as ready to betray their nation and their

---

[1] *Sifre*, 138 a. Perhaps we ought to read שמים instead of שמי. Cf. also *S. E.*, p. 143: "And thus said the Holy One, blessed be he, My beloved children, do I miss anything (which you could give me)? I want nothing but that you love each other, respect each other, and that no sin or ugly thing be found among you."

[2] There are some legends in which Abraham appears in the capacity of a prince, cf. *Gen. R.*, 42 5, but, it is not as a ruler, but as a teacher, that he figures mostly in Rabbinic literature.

[3] See Renan, *Hibbert Lectures*, p. 107, who has some apt remarks on this point, but which are at the same time greatly disfigured by his mania of generalising on Semitic religions.

[4] See *Berachoth*, 58 a. With regard to Rome in particular, see *Abodah Zarah*, 17 a, שאומה זו המליכוה מן השמים.

God as the laymen, Herod and Archelaus, who owed their throne to Roman machinations.

If, then, the kingdom of God was thus originally intended to be in the midst of men and for men at large (as represented by Adam), if its first preachers were, like Abraham, ex-heathens, who addressed themselves to heathens, if, again, the essence of their preaching was righteousness and justice, and if, lastly, the kingdom does not mean a hierarchy, but any form of government conducted on the principles of righteousness, holiness, justice, and charitableness, then we may safely maintain that the kingdom of God, as taught by Judaism in one of its aspects, is universal in its aims.

Hence the universal tone generally prevalent in all the kingship prayers (מלכיות). The foremost among these are the concluding lines of the kingship benediction recited on the New Year, running thus: "Our God and God of our fathers, reign thou in thy glory over the whole universe, and be exalted above all the earth in thine honour, and shine forth in the splendour and excellence of thy might, upon all the inhabitants of thy world, that whatsoever hath been made may know that thou hast made it, and whatsoever hath been created may understand that thou hast created it, and whatsoever hath breath in its nostrils, may say, the Lord God of Israel is King, and his dominion ruleth over all. . . . O purify our hearts to serve thee in truth, for thou art God in truth, and thy word is truth, and endureth forever. Blessed art thou, O Lord,

King over all the earth, who sanctifiest Israel and the Day of Memorial."[1] A later variation of this benediction, forming now a part both of the kingship prayers and of the daily prayer, is the passage referred to above, expressing the hope of Israel for the future, in the following exalted language: "We therefore hope in thee, O Lord our God, that we may speedily behold the glory of thy might, when thou wilt remove the abominations from the earth, and the idols will be utterly cut off, when the world will be perfected under the kingdom of the Almighty, and all the children of flesh will call upon thy name, when thou wilt turn unto thyself all the wicked of the earth. Let all the inhabitants of the world perceive and know that unto thee every knee must bow, every tongue must swear. Before thee, O Lord our God, let them bow and fall; and unto thy glorious name let them give honour; let them all accept the yoke of thy kingdom, and do thou reign over them speedily, and for ever and ever. For the kingdom is thine, and to all eternity thou wilt reign in glory; as it is written in thy Torah, the Lord shall reign for ever and ever."[2] One of the evening benedictions in the German ritual, which probably formed once the whole of the evening prayer, concludes with the following passages: "Our God who art in heaven, assert the unity of thy name, and

---

[1] See Singer, p. 249, and Baer, p. 399.
[2] Singer, pp. 76 and 247, and Baer, *ibid.*, pp. 132 and 398. See above, p. 89.

establish thy kingdom continually, and reign over us for ever and ever. May our eyes behold, our hearts rejoice, and our souls be glad in thy true salvation, when it shall be said unto Zion, Thy God reigneth. The Lord reigneth: the Lord hath reigned; the Lord shall reign for ever and ever: for the kingdom is thine, and to everlasting thou wilt reign in glory; for we have no king but thee. Blessed art thou, O Lord, the King, who constantly in his glory will reign over us and over all his works for ever and ever." [1] The Kaddish (the "Sanctification"), again, which is recited several times a day, in every synagogue, commences with the words: "Magnified and sanctified be his great Name in the world which he hath created according to his will. And may he establish his kingdom during your life and during your days," [2] etc. A variation of it is the prayer sung before the reading of the law on the Sabbath, after the declaration of the unity by the *Shema* and other verses, " Magnified and hallowed . . . be the name of the King of Kings of Kings, the Holy One, blessed be he, in the worlds which he hath created, — this world and the world to come." [3] The magnifying of God's name, as a consequence, both of his Unity and of his Kingship, finds also expression in the first line of an ancient prayer

---

[1] Cf. Singer, p. 101; Baer, p. 169

[2] Baer, *ibid.*, p. 129. See Singer, p. 75.

[3] See Baer, p. 224. Cf. Mueller, *Masechet Soferim*, ch. 25, and p. 196. See also Singer, p. 146.

known to the Geonim: "Our King, our God, assert the unity of thy name in thy world, assert the unity of thy kingdom in thy world."[1] In this connection it is worth noting that citations from the Scriptures embodied in the Kingship Benediction conclude with the verse from Deut. 6 4, "Hear, O Israel," etc., which proves again the close relation between the doctrine of the Unity and that of God's universal Kingdom,[2] which belief is among others well illustrated by the words of R. Bachye Ibn Chalwah, who says: "And it is well known that the real Unity (will only be realised in the days of the Messiah, for in the times of subjection of Israel) the signs of the Unity are not discernible (the worship of mankind being distributed among many unworthy objects), so that the denying of the truth is constantly in the increase. But with the advent of the Messiah all the nations will turn to one creed, and the world will be perfected under the Kingdom of the Almighty, all of them agreeing to worship the name and to call upon the name of God. Then only will the unity of God become common in the mouth of all the nations. This is the promise the prophet made for the future: "And the Lord shall be King over all the earth: in that day shall the Lord be One and his name One."[3]

[1] See *Seder Rab Amram*, p. 9 *a*.
[2] Baer, *ibid.*, p. 399, and cf above, p. 64, note 3.
[3] כד הקמח, end of the chapter יחוד.

VII

THE KINGDOM OF GOD (NATIONAL)

THE Kingship Prayer, just cited, is introduced by another group of prayers relating also to the kingdom of heaven, but containing at the same time emphatic references to Israel's connection with it. These prayers have for their burden the speedy advent of the day in which all creatures will form one single band to do God's will with a perfect heart, when righteousness will triumph, and the pious and the saints will rejoice; but also when God will give glory to his people, joys to his land, gladness to his city, and a clear shining light unto his Messiah, the son of Jesse. They conclude with the words, "And thou, O Lord, shalt reign, thou alone over all thy works on Mount Zion, the dwelling place of thy glory, and in Jerusalem, thy holy city, as it is written in thy Holy words, 'The Lord shall reign for ever, thy God of Zion, unto all generations. Praise ye the Lord'" (Ps. 146 10). The prayer of the Geonim also continues with the words, "Build thy house, establish thy Temple, bring near thy Messiah, and rejoice thy congregation." Indeed, the credit is given to Israel that they suppress the *Evil Yezer*, declare his (God's) unity, and proclaim him as king every day, and wait for his kingdom, and hope to see the building of his Temple, and say every day, "The Lord doth build up Jerusalem: he gathereth together the outcasts of Israel" (Ps. 147 2).[1] The idea of the kingdom is accordingly often so closely connected with the redemption of Israel from the exile, the advent of the Messiah, and the restoration of the Temple, as to be inseparable from it. This is its national aspect. "Israel are the people for whose sake (or *Zachuth*) the world was created; and it is on them that the world was based." Israel, again, as we have seen, are the people, who, by their glorious acts at the Red Sea, and especially by their readiness at Mount Sinai to receive the yoke of the kingdom, became the very pillars of the throne. To add here another passage of the same nature, the saying of R. Simon may be given, who expresses the idea in very bold language. Speaking of the supports of the world, and Israel's part in them, he says: "As long as Israel is united into one league (that is, making bold front against any heresy denying the unity or the supremacy of God), the kingdom in heaven is maintained by them; whilst Israel's falling off from God shakes the throne to its very foundation in heaven."[2] The banishment of Israel from the holy land has the same consequence.

---

[1] See Singer, p. 239 *seq.*; Baer, p. 395 *seq*; *Seder R. Amram*, 9 *a*; Friedmann, נספחים, p. 56.

[2] See Exod. R. 38 4. See also *Midrash Shemuel*, B. 5, 11 and references. Cf. Bacher, *Ag. Tan.* 2 140, note 1. See also above, p. 85.

Thus said the congregation of Israel before the Holy One, blessed be he, "Is there a king without a throne; is there a king without a crown; is there a king without a palace? 'How long wilt thou forget me, O Lord?'" (Ps. 13 2).[1] Jerusalem, which the Prophet (Jer. 3 17) called the throne of the Lord, becomes identified with it; and Amalek, who destroyed the holy city, is guilty of rebellion against God and his kingdom.[2] Therefore neither the throne of God nor his holy name is perfect (that is to say, fully revealed) as long as the children of the Amalekites exist in the world.[3] And just as Israel are the bearers of the name of God, so the Amalekites are the representatives of idolatry and every base thing antagonistic to God, so that R. Eleazar of Modyim thinks that the existence of the one necessarily involves the destruction of the other. "When will the name of the Amalekites be wiped out?" he exclaims. "Not before both the idols and their worshippers cease to exist, when God will be alone in the world and his kingdom established for ever and ever."[4] These passages, to which many more of a similar nature might be added, are the more calculated to give to the kingdom of heaven a national aspect, when we remember that Amalek is only another name for his ancestor Esau, who is the father of Edom, who is but a prototype for Rome. With this kingdom, represented in Jewish

---

[1] *M T.*, 13 1.   [2] *P. K.*, 28 a.
[3] *P. K.*, 29 a, *P. R*, 51 a and parallels.
[4] *Mechilta*, 56 a, 56 b. Cf. M. T. 97. 1 and 99: 1.

literature by the fourth beast of the vision of Daniel,[1] Israel according to the Rabbis is at deadly feud, a feud which began before its ancestors even perceived that the light of the world is perpetually carried on by their descendants, and will only be brought to an end with history itself.[2] The contest over the birthright is indicative of the struggle for supremacy between Israel and Rome. It would seem even as if Israel despairs of asserting the claims of his acquired birthright, and concedes this world to Esau. "Two worlds there are," Jacob says unto Esau, "this world and the world to come. In this world there is eating and drinking, but in the next world there are the righteous, who with crowns on their heads revel in the glory of the divine presence. Choose as first-born the world which pleases thee. Esau chose this world."[3] Jacob's promise to join his brother at Seir meant that meeting in the distant future, when the Messiah of Israel will appear and the Holy One will make his kingdom shine forth over Israel, as it is said (Obadiah 21): "And saviours shall come up on Mount Zion to judge the mount of Esau; and the kingdom shall be the Lord's."[4]

---

[1] See *Lev. R.*, 13 5 and parallels. Valuable information on this point is to be found in Senior Sachs's edition of the *Carmina Sancta Solomonis Ibn Gabirol*, pp. 70–100. Cf. also Zunz, *Synagogale Poesie*, p 437 *seq* See also A. Epstein, *Beitrage zur judischen Alterthumskunde*, p. 35.

[2] *Gen. R*, 61, §§ 6, 7, 9.

[3] See Friedmann, מספחים, 26 *b* and *P. K.*, 59 *b*.

[4] *Gen. R.*, 78 and parallels.

Thus the kingdom of heaven stands in opposition to the kingdom of Rome, and becomes connected with the kingdom of Israel, and it is in conformity with this sentiment that a Rabbi, picturing the glorious spring, in which the budding of Israel's redemption will first be perceived, exclaims: "The time has arrived when the reign of the wicked will break down and Israel will be redeemed; the time has come for the extermination of the kingdom of wickedness; the time has come for the revelation of the kingdom of heaven, and the voice of the Messiah is heard in our land."[1]

This is only a specimen of dozens of interpretations of the same nature, round which a whole world of myths and legend grew up, in which the chiliastic element, with all its excesses, was strongly emphasised. They fluctuate and change with the great historical events and the varying influences by which they were suggested.[2] But there are also fixed elements in them

---

[1] See *P K.*, 50 a, and *P. R*, 75 a, text and notes.

[2] Dr. Joseph Klausner's *Die messianischen Vorstellungen im Zeitalter der Tannaiten* is very instructive, though not all his results seem to me acceptable. See also Dr. Julius H Greenstone's *The Messiah Idea in Jewish History*, which gives also references to the latest literature on the subject, including the Rev Dr. R. H. Charles' *Eschatology*. On the whole I think that R. Isaac Abarbanel's noble משמיע ישועה contains still the best presentation of the Rabbinic belief in the Messiah, as entertained by the great majority of Rabbinic Jews (See especially in his fourteen articles, עיקרים.) The statement by some moderns, to the effect that Rabbinism did not hold the belief in a personal Messiah essential, is unscientific and needs no refutation for those who are acquainted with the literature.

which are to be found in the Rabbinic literature of almost every age and date. These are: —

1. The faith that the Messiah, a descendant of the house of David, will restore the kingdom of Israel, which under his sceptre will extend over the whole world. 2. The notion that a last terrible battle will take place with the enemies of God (or of Israel), who will strive against the establishment of the kingdom, and who will finally be destroyed. "When will the Lord be King for ever and ever? When the heathen — that is, the Romans — will have perished out of the land."[1] 3 The belief that the establishment of this new kingdom will be followed by the spiritual hegemony of Israel, when all the nations will accept the belief in the unity of God, acknowledge his kingdom, and seek instruction from his law. 4. The conviction that it will be an age of material happiness as well as spiritual bliss for all those who are included in the kingdom,[2] when further death will disappear and the dead will revive.

[1] See *M T.*, 10 7.

[2] It should however be noticed that the authorities are not quite in agreement as to the date of resurrection, not all of them making it a condition of the Messianic times Rabbi Hillel's (fl. 3ᵈ century) statement, "Israel has no hope for a Messiah" (*Sanhedrin* 99ᵃ), is entirely isolated It should further be noticed that in some sources the kingdom of the Messiah is to a certain extent a preparation for the time when God himself will reign. Indeed, all the versions of the well-known Midrash of the Ten Kings after the Messiah, the kingdom comes back to his first master, that is God, who was the first King after the creation of the world. The only place where the kingdom of Mes-

The two ideas of the kingdom of heaven, over which God reigns, and the kingdom of Israel, in which the Messiah holds the sceptre, became thus almost identical.

This identification has both narrowed, and to some extent even materialised, the notion of the kingdom. On the other hand, it also enriched it with certain features investing it with that amount of substance and reality which are most necessary, if an idea is not to become meaningless and lifeless. It is just this danger to which ideas are exposed in the process of their spiritualisation. That "the letter killeth, but the spirit giveth life," is a truth of which Judaism, which did depart very often from the letter, was as conscious as any other religion. Zerachya ben Shealtiel, in his Commentary to Job[1] 2 14, goes even so far as to say: "Should I explain this chapter according to its letter, I should be a heretic, because I would have to make such concessions to Satan's powers as are inconsistent with the belief in the Unity. I shall therefore interpret it according to the spirit of philosophy." But, unfortunately, there is also an evil spirit which sometimes possesses itself of an idea and reduces it to a mere

siah is identified with that of God is Pugio Fidei, by Raymundus, p. 397; but there is good reason to suppose that the text of Raymundus was tampered with for controversial purposes. See the literature on this point in the *Expositor*, vol. 7, 3d series, p. 108. Neubauer's remarks there are far from convincing. See also Cassel in his Commentary to Esther, p. 263, where he gives a reference to the New Testament, 1 Corinthians 15 23—28.

[1] Published in the תקות אנוש, a collection of commentaries to Job, by Schwartz.

phantasm. The history of theology is greatly haunted by these unclean spirits. The best guard against them is to provide the idea with some definiteness and reality in which we can perceive the evidence of the spirit.

This was the service rendered by the connection of the kingdom of Israel with the kingdom of God. It fixed the kingdom *in this world*. It had, of course, to be deferred to some indefinite period, but still its *locale* remained in our globe, not unknown regions in another world. It was extended from the individual to a whole nation, placing a whole people into its service and training it for this end, thus making the idea of the kingdom visible and tangible. A whole commonwealth, with all its institutions, civil and ecclesiastical, becomes part and parcel of the kingdom of God. The Lord has made all things for himself, for the glory of his kingdom, which includes all creation. But Israel understood their duty to the extent of giving in time of persecution their very lives rather than transgress the slightest law, as such a transgression at such a time involved the sin of profaning the Holy Name, and may be taken as a sign of apostasy or betrayal of the kingdom. For they are indeed the very legions of the kingdom.[1]

By this fact, it is true, the kingdom of God becomes greatly nationalised. But even in this case it loses nothing of its spiritual features. For even in its

---

[1] See *Tosephta Shabbath*, p. 134; *Agadath Shir Hashirim*, p. 34. See also above, p. 81, note 1.

identification with the nation, Israel is only the depository of the kingdom, not the exclusive possessor of it. The idea of the kingdom is the palladium of the nation. According to some, it is the secret which has come down to them from the patriarchs;[1] according to others, the holy mystery of the angels overheard by Moses, which Israel continually proclaims.[2] It has to be emphasised in every prayer and benediction,[3] whilst the main distinction of the most solemn prayers of the year on the New Year's Day consists, as we have seen, in a detailed proclamation of the kingdom of God in all stages of history, past, present, and future. "Before we appeal to his mercy," teach the Rabbis, "and before we pray for redemption, we must first make him King over us."[4] We must also remember that Israel is not a nation in the common sense of the word. To the Rabbis, at least, it is not a nation by virtue of race or of certain peculiar political combinations. As R. Saadya expressed it, כי אומתינו איננה אומה אם כי בתורותיה ("Because our nation is only a nation by reason of its Torah").[5] The brutal Torah-less nationalism promulgated in certain quarters, would have been to the Rabbis just as hateful as the suicidal Torah-less universalism preached in other quarters. And if we could imagine for a moment Israel giving up its allegiance

---

[1] See *Sifre*, 72 b, and the very instructive notes by the editor.

[2] *Deut. R.*, 2   [3] See *Berachoth*, 12 a

[4] See *Sifre*, 19 b, and *Rosh Hashanah*, 16 a. See also whole extract from the liturgy at the end of ch 5.

[5] אמונות ודעות, 3 : 7.

to God, its Torah and its divine institutions, the Rabbis would be the first to sign its death-warrant as a nation. The prophecy (Isa. 44 5), "Another shall subscribe with his hands unto the Lord," means, according to the Rabbis, the sinners who return unto him from their evil ways, whilst the words, "And surname himself by the name of Israel," are explained to be proselytes who leave the heathen world to join Israel.[1] It is then by these means of repentance and proselytism that the kingdom of heaven, even in its connection with Israel, expands into the universal kingdom to which sinners and Gentiles are invited. It becomes a sort of spiritual imperialism with the necessary accompaniment of the doctrine of the "Open Door" through which the whole of humanity might pass into the kingdom. "Open ye gates that the righteous people (*Goi*) which keepeth the truth may enter in" (Isa. 26 2). It is not said that the Priests or the Levites or the Israelites may enter, but *Goi* (Gentile). "Behold even one of other nations who fulfils (the laws of) the Torah is (as good) as the very high priest."[2]

The antagonism between the kingdom of God and the kingdom of Rome, which is brought about by the connection of the former with that of Israel, suggests also a most important truth: *Bad government is incompatible with the kingdom of God.* As already pointed

---

[1] *Mechilta*, 95 *b* and parallels.

[2] *T K.*, 86 *b*, taking the word גוי in the sense of heathen, non-Jew, and stranger. See also below, p. 133

out above, it is not the *form* of the Roman Government to which objection is taken, but its methods of administration and its oppressive rule. It is true that they tried "to render unto Cæsar the things that were Cæsar's, and unto God the things that were God's." Thus they interpreted the words in Ecclesiastes 8 2: "I counsel thee, keep the king's commandments and *that* in regard of the oath of God," in the following way: "I take an oath from you, not to rebel against the (Roman) Government, even if its decrees against you should be most oppressive; for you have to keep the king's commands. But if you are bidden to deny God and give up the Torah, then obey no more." And they proceed to illustrate it by the example of Hananiah, Mishael, and Azariah, who are made to say to Nebuchadnezzar, "Thou art our king in matters concerning duties and taxes, but in things divine thy authority ceases, and therefore 'we will not serve thy gods, nor worship the golden image which thou hast put up.'"[1] But compromises forced upon them by the political circumstances of the time must not be regarded as desirable ideals or real doctrine. Apart from the question as to the exact definition of things falling within the respective provinces of Cæsar and of God — a question which, after eighteen hundred years' discussion, is still unsettled — there can be little doubt that the Rabbis looked with dismay upon a government which derived its authority from the deification of

[1] See *Tan.*, נב, 10, and *Lev. R.*, 33 6. Cf. *Num. R.*, 14 6.

might, whereof the emperor was the incarnate principle. Edom recognises no superior authority, saying, "Whom have I in heaven?"[1] It represents iron (we would say blood and iron), a metal which was excluded from the tabernacle, the abode of the divine peace,[2] whilst its king of flesh and blood, whom Edom flatters in its ovations as being mighty, wise, powerful, merciful, just, and faithful, has not a single one of all these virtues, and is even the very reverse of what they express.[3]

But besides these differences the Rabbis held the Roman Government to be thoroughly corrupt in its administration; Esau preaches justice and practises violence. Their judges commit the very crimes for which they condemn others. They pretend to punish crime, but are reconciled to it by bribery. Their motives are selfish, never drawing men near to them, except in their own interest and for their own advantage. As soon as they see a man in a state of prosperity, they devise means how to possess themselves of his goods. In a word, Esau is rapacious and violent, especially the procurators sent out to the provinces, where they rob and murder, and when they return to Rome pretend to feed the poor with the money they have collected.[4] Such a government was, according

---

[1] Lev. *R*, 13 5.   [2] See *Exod R.*, 35 7.   [3] *Mechilta*, 35 *a*.
[4] See *Lev R.*, *ibid.*, *Aboth*, 2 8; *Exod. R.*, 31 11, *P. K.* 95 *b*.
Interesting is a passage in Mommsen's *History of Rome*, 4, which shows that the Rabbis did not greatly exaggerate the cruelty of the Roman

to the Rabbis, incompatible with the kingdom of heaven, and therefore the mission of Israel was to destroy it.[1]

Another essential addition made to the kingdom of God by its connection with the kingdom of Israel is, as already indicated, the feature of material happiness. Popular fancy pictured it in gorgeous colours: The rivers will flow with wine and honey, the trees will grow bread and delicacies, whilst in certain districts springs will break forth which will prove cures for all sorts of diseases. Altogether, disease and suffering will cease, and those who come into the kingdom with bodily defects, such as blindness, deafness, and other blemishes, will be healed. Men will multiply in a way not at all agreeable to the laws of political economy, and will enjoy a very long life, if they will die at all. War will, of course, disappear, and warriors will look upon their weapons as a reproach and an offence. Even the rapacious beasts will lose their powers of doing injury, and will become peaceful and harmless.[2] Such are the details in which the Rabbis indulge in their descriptions

Government. "Any one who desires," says our greatest historian of Rome, "to fathom the depths to which men can sink in the criminal infliction, and in the no less criminal endurance of an inconceivable injustice, may gather together from the criminal records of this period the wrongs which Roman grandees could perpetuate, and Greeks, Syrians, and Phœnicians could suffer." Cf. Joel's *Blicke*, I 109. How far matters improved under the emperors, at least with regard to the Jews, is still a question

[1] *Berachoth*, 17 a. See Rabbinowicz, *Variae Lectiones*, a.l.

[2] See, for instance, *Kethuboth*, 111 a, *Shabbath*, 63 a; *Gen R.*, 12 6; *M.H.G.*, 126 *seq.*; see also Klausner (as above, p. 101), p. 108 *seq.*

of the blissful times to come. We need not dwell upon them. There is much in them which is distasteful and childish. Still, when we look at the underlying idea, we shall find that it is not without its spiritual truth. The kingdom of God *is* inconsistent with a state of social misery, engendered through poverty and want. Not that Judaism looked upon poverty, as some author has suggested, as a moral vice. Nothing can be a greater mistake. The Rabbis were themselves mostly recruited from the artisan and labouring classes, and of some we know that they lived in the greatest want. Certain Rabbis have even maintained that there is no quality becoming Israel more than poverty, for it is a means of spiritual purification.[1] Still, they did not hide from themselves the terrible fact that abject poverty has its great demoralising dangers. It is one of the three things which make man transgress the law of his Maker.[2]

But even if poverty would not have this effect, it would be excluded from the kingdom of heaven, as involving pain and suffering. The poor man, they hold, is dead as an influence, and his whole life, depending upon his fellows, is a perpetual passing through the tortures of hell.[3] But it is a graceful world which God has created, and it must not be disfigured by misery and suffering. It must return to its perfect state when the visible kingdom is established. As we shall

[1] *Chagigah*, 9 *b*.   [2] *Erubin*, 41 *b*.
[3] *Nedarim*, 7 *b*, and *Berachoth*, 6 *b*.

see in the sequence,[1] Judaism was certainly not wanting in theories, idealising suffering and trying to reconcile man with its existence. But, on the other hand, it did not recognise a chasm between flesh and spirit, the material and the spiritual world, so as to abandon entirely the one for the sake of the other. They are both the creatures of God, the body as well as the soul, and hence both the objects of his salvation.

To a certain Jewish mystic of the last century, R. Moses Loeb, of Sasow, the question was put by one of his disciples to the effect, "Why did God, in whom everything originates, create the quality of scepticism?" The master's answer was, "That thou mayest not let the poor starve, putting them off with the joys of the next world, or simply telling them to trust in God, who will help them, instead of supplying them with food."[2]

We venture to maintain with the mystic that a good dose of materialism is necessary for religion that we may not starve the world. It was by this that Judaism was preserved from the mistake of crying inward peace, when actually there was no peace; of speaking of inward liberty, when in truth this spiritual but spurious liberty only served as a means for persuading man to renounce his liberty altogether, confining the kingdom of God to a particular institution and handing over the world to the devil.

[1] See below, p. 309.
[2] See מעשה צדיקים, Lemberg, 1897, p. 39, which differs somewhat from the version I have heard often told, and which is given in the text.

This is not the place to enter into the charity system of the Rabbis, nor to enlarge upon the measures taken by them so as to make charity superfluous. But having touched upon the subject of poverty, a few general remarks will not be out of place. In that brilliant essay known under the title of *Ecce Homo*, we meet the following statement: "The ideal of the economist, the ideal of the Old Testament writers, does not appear to be Christ's. He feeds the poor, but it is not his great object to bring about a state of things in which the poorest shall be sure of a meal." But it was just this which was included in the ideal of the Rabbis. They were not satisfied with feeding the poor. Not only did they make the authorities of every community responsible for the poor, and would even stigmatise them as murderers if their negligence should lead to starvation and death;[1] but their great ideal was not to allow man to be poor, not to allow him to come down into the depths of poverty. They say, "Try to prevent it by teaching him a trade, or by occupying him in your house as a servant, or make him work with you as your partner."[2] Try all methods before you permit him to become an object of charity, which must degrade him, tender as our dealings with him may be.

Hence their violent protests against any sort of money speculation which must result in increasing

---

[1] See *B. T. Sotah*, 38 *b*, and *Jer. Sotah*, 23 *d*.

[2] See *T. K.*, 109 *b*, and Maimonides' *Mishneh Torah*, הלכות מתנות עניים פ״י ה״ז וה׳ ח״ז. See also the older commentaries on *Aboth*, 1 5.

poverty : Thou lendest him money on the security of his estate with the object of joining his field to thine, his house to thine, and thou flatterest thyself to become the heir of the land; be sure of a truth that many houses will be desolate.[1] Those again who increase the price of food by artificial means, who give false measure, who lend on usury, and keep back the corn from the market, are classed by the Rabbis with the blasphemers and hypocrites, and God will never forget their works.[2]

To the employers of workmen again they say: "This poor man ascends the highest scaffoldings, climbs the highest trees. For what does he expose himself to such dangers, if not for the purpose of earning his living? Be careful, therefore, not to oppress him in his wages, for it means his very life."[3] On the other hand, they relieved the workman from reciting certain prayers when they interfered with his duty to his master.[4]

From this consideration for the employer and the employed a whole set of laws emanate which try to regulate their mutual relations and duties. How far they would satisfy the modern economist I am unable to say. In general I should think that, excellent as they may have been for their own times, they would not

---

[1] See Introduction to Midrash to *Lament. R.*, 22, on Isa. 5 8.
[2] See *A. R. N*, 43 *b*; *Baba Bathra*, 90 *a*.
[3] See *Sifre*, 123 *b*, and *B. Mezia*, and *Berachoth*, 16 *a*.
[4] *Berachoth*, 17 *a*.

quite answer to our altered conditions and ever varying problems. But this need not prevent us from perceiving, in any efforts to diminish poverty, a divine work to which they also contributed their share. For if the disappearance of poverty and suffering is a condition of the kingdom of the Messiah, or, in other words, of the kingdom of God, all wise social legislation in this respect must help towards its speedy advent.

It is this kingdom, as depicted in the preceding remarks in its larger features, with both its material and spiritual manifestations, that Israel is to express and establish. With this, it enters upon the stage of history. With its varying fortunes its own destiny is inseparably connected; and with Israel's final triumph, the kingdom will become fully effective. Or, as the Rabbis expressed it, it is only "with the redemption of Israel that the kingdom of heaven will be complete." Israel is the microcosm in which all the conditions of the kingdom are to find concrete expression. In the establishment of its institutions, in the reign of its law, in the peace and happiness of its people, the world would find the prototype and manifestation of these ideals in which universal holiness would be expressed. Not until these conditions were realised in Israel could like conditions obtain universally. The Rabbis have given expression to this correspondence of universalistic and national elements in the following statement: A solemn declaration has the Holy One, blessed be he, registered: I will not enter the heavenly Jerusalem until Israel shall come to the earthly Jerusalem. Thus Rabbinic Judaism does find a perfect consonance between Israel's establishment of the divine institutions in their full integrity in God's own land, and the triumph in all its glory of the kingdom of Heaven.[1]

[1] See *M. T.*, 99 1. See also *Taanith*, 5 *b*   The references speak of the oath.

VIII

THE "LAW"

THE Law derives its authority from the kingdom. For this, according to the Rabbis, is the meaning of the scriptural words, "I am the Lord thy God," or "The Lord your God," with which certain groups of laws are introduced (*e.g.* Exod. 22 2 and Lev. 18 2); that is, God makes his people conscious of the fact of his claims on them because of their having received his kingdom, saying unto them, "You have received my kingdom in love." "Aye" and "Aye" answers Israel, wherefore God says, "If you have received my kingdom, you receive now my decrees."[1]

Now the current notions about the Law or Torah are still so misleading that before entering upon the meaning and theological significance of the "decrees," a brief analysis of the term *Torah* seems most advisable. Even the hypothesis advanced by higher criticism, according to which it was just under the predominance of the Law that the Wisdom Literature was composed and most of the Psalms were written, had no effect on the general prejudice of theologians against the Torah. With a few exceptions our theo-

[1] *T. K.*, 85 *d*; *Mechilta*, 67 *a*, 67 *b*.

logians still enlarge upon the "Night of Legalism," from the darkness of which religion only emerges by a miracle supposed to have taken place about the year 30 of our era.[1]

An examination of the meaning of *Torah* and *Mizvoth* to the Jew will show that Legalism was neither the evil thing commonly imagined nor did it lead to the evil consequences assumed by our theologians. Nor has it ever constituted the whole religion of the Jew, as declared by most modern critics.

It must first be stated that the term *Law* or *Nomos* is not a correct rendering of the Hebrew word *Torah*. The legalistic element, which might rightly be called the Law, represents only one side of the Torah. To the Jew the word *Torah* means a teaching or an instruction of any kind. It may be either a general principle or a specific injunction, whether it be found in the Pentateuch or in other parts of the Scriptures, or even outside of the canon. The juxtaposition in which *Torah* and *Mizwoth*, Teaching and Commandments, are to be found in the Rabbinic literature, implies already that the former means something more than merely the Law.[2] Torah and Mitzvoth are a complement to each other, or, as a Rabbi expressed it, "they borrow from each other, as wisdom and understanding — charity and loving-

[1] See Mr. Israel Abrahams, *Jewish Quarterly Review*, 11: 626–642 See also Schechter, *Studies in Judaism*, p. 219 seq.

[2] See, for instance, *Berachoth*, 31 *a*; *Makkoth*, 23 *a*; *Aboth*, 3 11.

kindness — the moon and the stars," but they are not identical.¹ To use the modern phraseology, to the Rabbinic Jew, Torah was both an institution and a faith. We shall treat them separately: first Torah, and then the Mitzvoth.

It is true that in Rabbinic literature the term *Torah* is often applied to the Pentateuch to the exclusion of the Prophets and the Hagiographa.² But this is chiefly for the purpose of classification. It is also true that to a certain extent the Pentateuch is put on a higher level than the Prophets — the prophetic vision of Moses having been, as the Rabbis avow, much clearer than that of his successors.³ But we must not forget that for the superiority of the Torah, they had the scriptural authority of the Torah itself (Num. 12 6-8, Deut. 34 10), whilst on the other hand *they* could not find in the Prophets anything deprecatory of Moses' superior authority. They may, occasionally, have felt some contradictions between the Prophets and the Torah, but only in matters of detail, not in matters of principle.⁴

¹ See *Exod. R.*, 31 15.
² See, for instance, *Megillah*, 31 *a*; *Baba Bathra*, 13 *b*, and elsewhere
³ See *Jebamoth*, 49 *b*; *Lev. R.*, 1.
⁴ See the well-known passages about Ezekiel in *Shabbath*, 13 *b*, and *Menachoth*, 45 *a*. The contradictions are there reconciled to the satisfaction of the Rabbis at least. See also below, p 187 A contradiction which they did not try to reconcile was that between Isa. 6 1, "I saw the Lord sitting upon a throne," and Moses in Exod. 33 20, "For there shall no man see me, and live" (*Jebamoth*, 49 *b*). See

Of any real antagonism between Mosaism and "Leviticalism" and Prophetism, which modern criticism asserts to have brought to light, the Rabbis were absolutely unconscious. With the Rabbis, the Prophets formed only a complement or even a commentary to the Torah (a species of Agadah), which, indeed, needed explanation, as we shall see. Hence the *naïveté*, as we may almost call it, with which the Rabbis chose, for reading on the Day of Atonement, the 58th chapter of Isaiah — one of the most prophetic pieces of prophetism — as the accompanying lesson for the portion from the Pentateuch, Leviticus 16 — the most Levitical piece in Leviticalism.

But even the Pentateuch is no mere legal code, without edifying elements in it. The Book of Genesis, the greater part of Exodus, and even a part of Numbers are simple history, recording the past of humanity on its way to the kingdom, culminating in Israel's entering it on Mount Sinai, and their subsequent relapses. The Book of Deuteronomy, as the "Book containing the words of exhortation" (Tochachoth),[1] forms Israel's *Imitatio Dei*, consisting chiefly in goodness,[2] and supplying to Israel its confession of faith (in the *Shema*); whilst the Book of Leviticus — marvel

Jolowicz's *Himmelfahrt, etc., des Propheten Jesaiah*, p. 7, Leipzig, 1854. But it is significant that it is the wicked Manasseh who saw this contradiction.

[1] *Sifre*, 64 a.

[2] See *Sifre*, 74 a, 85 a; *Mechilta*, 37 a and parallels. See also below, p. 200.

upon marvel — first proclaims that principle of loving one's neighbour as one's self (Lev. 19 18) which believers call Christianity, unbelievers, Humanity.

The language of the Midrash would seem to imply that at a certain period there were people who held the narratives of the Bible in slight estimation, looking upon them as fictions (Piyutim) and useless stories. The Rabbis, however, reject such a thought with indignation. To them the whole of the Torah represented the word of God, dictated by the Holy Spirit, suggesting edifying lessons everywhere, and embodying even while it speaks of the past, a history of humanity written in advance.[1] "The Book of Generations of Adam," that is, the history of the Genesis, in which the dignity of man is indicated by the fact of his having been created in the image of God, teaches, according to Ben Azai, even a greater principle than that of Lev. 19, in which the law of loving one's neighbour as oneself is contained.[2] Another Rabbi deduces from the repetitions in Gen. 24 the theory that the conversation of the servants of the patriarchs is more beautiful than the laws even of later generations.[3] Another Rabbi remarks that the Torah as a legal code would only have commenced with Exod. 12, where the first (larger) group of laws is set forth, but God's object was to show his people the power of his work,

---

[1] See *Gen. R*., 85 2; *Sifre*, 33 a; *Sanhedrin*, 99 b; *M. T.*, 3 2.
[2] *T. K.*, 89 b, and parallels. Cf. Bacher, *Ag. Tan.*, I 720.
[3] *Gen. R.*, 60 8.

"that he may give them the inheritance of the heathen" (Ps. 111 6), and thus, in the end, justify the later history of their conquests.[1]

The Book of Genesis, which contains the history of this manifestation of God's powers, as revealed in the act of creation as well as in the history of the patriarchs, and leads up to the story of the Exodus from Egypt, is, according to some Rabbis, the book of the covenant which Moses read to the people (Exod. 24 7) even before the act of revelation. To come into the possession of this book (the Book of Genesis), which unlocked before them one of the inner chambers of the king (or revealed to them the holy mysteries of God's working in the world), was considered by the Rabbis one of the greatest privileges of Israel, given to them as a reward for their submission to God's will.[2]

Thus *Torah*, even as represented by the Pentateuch, is not mere Law, the Rabbis having discerned and appreciated in it other than merely legal elements. Moreover, the term *Torah* is not always confined to the Pentateuch. It also extends, as already indicated, to the whole of the Scriptures on which the Rabbis "laboured" with the same spirit and devotion as on the Pentateuch. For indeed "the Torah is a *triad*, composed of Pentateuch, Prophets, and Hagiographa." "Have I not written to thee the three things in counsels

---

[1] See *Tan. B.*, 1 4 *a*. Cf. Rashi to Gen. 1 1.
[2] See *Mechilta*, 63 *b*. Cf. *Cant. R.*, 1 4, on הביאני המלך חדריו.

and in knowledge?"[1] That lessons from the Prophets almost always accompanied those taken from the Pentateuch is a well-known fact,[2] as likewise that the Talmid Chacham, or the student, had to beautify himself with the knowledge of the twenty-four books of which the Bible consists, even as a bride adorns herself with twenty-four different kinds of ornaments.[3] That this injunction was strictly fulfilled by the student is clear from the facility and frequency with which the Rabbis quoted the Prophets and the Hagiographa. A striking instance may be seen in the *Mechilta*, a small work of not more than about seventy octavo pages when stripped from its commentaries; it has about one thousand citations from the Prophets and the Hagiographa.

"The sinners in Israel" (probably referring to the Samaritans), the Rabbis complain, "contend that the Prophets and the Hagiographa are not Torah, but are they not already refuted by Daniel (9 10), who said, 'Neither have we obeyed the voice of the Lord our God, to walk in his Toroth which he set before us by his servants the prophets.'" Hence, the Rabbis proceed to say, Asaph's exclamation in Ps. 78, "Give ear, O my people, to my Toroth."[4] Note, in

[1] See *Tan.*, B 2 87 a (§ 8), and *Midrash Prov.*, 22 19, text and notes, urging the שלישים.

[2] See Zunz, *Gottesdienstliche Vorträge*, p 3 (2d ed.), and Schürer's *Geschichte*, 2 880 f.   [3] See *Exod R.*, 41 5.

[4] See *M. T.*, 78 1, and *Tan.*, ראה, 1. Cf. Bacher, *Terminologie*, 2 81.

passing, that this Psalm, which claims to be Torah, is nothing but a *résumé* of Israel's history. With the Rabbinic Jews, the Hagiographa formed an integral part of their holy Scriptures. "The prophets of truth and righteousness" were, as can be seen from the benediction preceding the weekly lesson from the Prophets, God's chosen ones, in the same way as the Torah, as his servant Moses, and his people Israel — the depository of revelation.[1] In olden times they had even a special benediction before they began to read either the Prophets or the Hagiographa, running thus, "Blessed art thou, O Lord our God, who hast commanded us to read the holy writings."[2] This was quite in accordance with their principle regarding prophecy as "the word of God,"[3] and the continuation of his voice heard on Mount Sinai,[4] a voice which will cease only with the Messianic times, — perhaps for the reason that the earth will be full of the knowledge of God and all the people of the Lord will be prophets.[5]

[1] See Baer, p. 226. In *Masecheth Soferim*, ch. XIII, the words ובישראל עמו are omitted.

[2] See *Masecheth Soferim*, ch. XIV, and *Notes*, p. 188.

[3] *Shabbath*, 138 *b*.

[4] See *Sifre*, 92 *a*, and parallels given in the Notes. MHG., ובקולו סורר על דברי תורה ומורה על תשמעו בקול נביאיו. Cf. *ibid.* 114 *a*, רב״שע כבר כתבת הן ישלח אדם. See also *Sifre*, 135 *b*, דברי הנביאים. "Lord of the world, thou hast written, If a man put away his wife," etc., which is a verse in Jer 3 1. Cf. Blau, *Zur Einleitung in die Heilige Schrift*, p. 14. See also Bacher, *Terminologie*, 1 197; 2 229.

[5] See *Jer. Megillah*, 70 *d*, and the commentaries. Cf. also Maimonides' *Mishneh Torah*, הלכות מגילה וחנוכה, 2 18, and the השנת הרא״בד.

Says R. Isaac, "All that the Prophets will reveal in (succeeding) generations had been received by them on Mount Sinai." "And so he says, 'The burden of the word of the Lord to Israel by *the hand* of Malachi.' It is not said '*In the days of Malachi*,' for the prophecy was already in his hands (since the revelation) on Mount Sinai." And so Isaiah, "From the time that it (the Torah) was (revealed) I was there," and received this prophecy, "but it is now that the Lord God and his spirit has sent me."[1]

It is in harmony with this spirit — the Prophets and the Hagiographa being a part of Israel's Torah — that the former are cited in Rabbinic literature with the terms "for it is said" or "it is written" in the same ways as the Pentateuch. Again, in the well-known controversy about the scriptural authority for the belief in resurrection, both the Prophets and the

The special emphasis of the Jerushalmi of the Pentateuch's retaining its importance even after the Messiah has come, is, as is well known, the result of the opposition to sectarian teaching, demanding the abolition of the Law. The answer of the Rabbis was therefore that even the authority of the Messiah himself will not prevail against that of Moses. In this sense also — as opposition to this teaching — must be understood the passage in *Jer. Berachoth*, 3 *b* and parallels, where the prophet, so to say, is required to bring his imprimatur from the Torah, שלי וסמנטרין שלי חותם, the prophet without such a legitimation being very probably an antinomianist. Hence also the effort made by the Rabbis to prove that the Pentateuch already indicated the teachings of the *Kethubim*. See *Taanith*, 9 *a*.

[1] See *Lev. R.*, 28 6 and commentaries. Cf. Oppenheim in Geiger's *Judische Zeitschrift*, 11, p. 82 *seq*. See also Frankl in *Ersch und Gruber*, 2 sec., Bd. 33, pp. 15–34.

Hagiographa are quoted under the name of Torah; and the evidence brought forward by them seems to be of as much weight as that derived from the Pentateuch.[1] In the New Testament they also occasionally appear under the title of Nomos or Law. To the Jew, as already pointed out, the term *Torah* implied a teaching or instruction, and was therefore wide enough to embrace the whole of the Scriptures.[2]

In a certain manner it is extended even beyond the limits of the Scriptures. When certain Jewish Bos-

---

[1] *Sanhedrin*, 91 *b*; see also *Mechilta*, 34 *b*, 40 *b*. Cf. Blau, as above, pp. 16, 17. For more instances, see תורת נביאים by R. Hirsch Chajas, pp. 2 *a* and *b*, 5 *a*, 9 *a*, 10 *b*. This book contains the best exposition of the Rabbinical conception of the importance of the Prophets both from a Halachic and Hagadic point of view, and their relation to the Pentateuch. The student will find that a good deal that was written on the subject by other writers is mere talk due to the ignorance of Rabbinic literature.

[2] See Schurer's *Geschichte*, 2 253, note 17, for the references from the New Testament. Following Weber (p. 79), Schürer seizes the opportunity of making the remark that there is perhaps nothing more characteristic of the full appreciation of their importance on the part of the Jews than that they too (the Prophets and the Hagiographa) were not first of all to the Jewish conviction didactic or consolatory works, not books of edification or history, but were considered chiefly as Law, the substance of God's claim upon his people. So far Schürer, which of course only proves again to what misconception the rendering of Torah by Law must lead. Besides, we find that the Rabbis had such specification for the various books in the Bible as ספר יציאת מצרים for the Exodus (see Blau, as above), תוכחות for Deuteronomy (see above). The Psalms again are called the Book of Praises or Hymn Book, whilst the whole of the *Kethubim* are the Books of Wisdom (*P K.*, 158 *b*), and Isaiah was chiefly characterised as the "work of consolation" (*Baba Bathra*, 14 *a*).

wells apologised for observing the private life of their masters too closely, they said, "It is a Torah, which we are desirous of learning." [1] In this sense it is used by another Rabbi, who maintained that even the everyday talk of the people in the Holy Land is a Torah (that is, it conveys an object lesson). For the poor man in Palestine, when applying to his neighbour for relief, was wont to say, "Acquire for thyself merit, or strengthen and purify thyself" (by helping me); [2] thus implying the adage — that the man in want is just as much performing an act of charity in receiving as his benefactor in giving. In the east of Europe we can, even to-day, hear a member of the congregation addressing his minister, "Pray, tell me some Torah." The Rabbi would never answer him by reciting verses from the Bible, but would feel it incumbent on him to give him some spiritual or allegorical explanation of a verse from the Scriptures, or would treat him to some general remarks bearing upon morals and conduct.

[1] *Berachoth*, 62 a. See also Chajas, as above, 2 b.
[2] *Lev. R.*, 34 7.

IX

THE LAW AS PERSONIFIED IN THE LITERATURE

To return to Torah proper. It is the Torah as the sum total of the contents of revelation, without special regard to any particular element in it, the Torah as a faith, that is so dear to the Rabbi. It is the Torah in this abstract sense, as a revelation and a promise, the expression of the will of God, which is identified with the wisdom of Prov. 8, thus gaining, in the course of history, a pre-mundane existence, which, so to speak, formed the design according to which God mapped out the world. Said Rabbi Hoshayah, "It is written of Wisdom, 'Then (before the world was created) I was with him *amon*, and was daily his delight, rejoicing always before him.' The word *amon* is to be read *uman*, meaning architect. For as a king employs an architect when he proposes to build a palace, and looks into his plans and designs to know where the various recesses and chambers shall be placed, so did God look into the Torah when he was about to create the world."[1]

---

[1] See *Gen. R.*, 1 and parallels. Cf. Bacher, *Ag. Am.*, I 107, and his references to Freudenthal and the *Jewish Quarterly Review*, 3 857-860. See also Professor Cheyne, *Job and Solomon*, pp. 160–162 See also above, p. 13, note 4.

How far the idea is originally Jewish is not here the place to discuss. Nor is its meaning quite clear when subject to an analysis. One of the later commentators of the Midrash tries to connect it with the צמצום theory, that is, the limitation-mystery of the later cabalists, according to which the act of creation was an effluence of God's ineffable goodness and mercy — when he withdrew himself into himself, and thus revealed from himself the universe. But it is not quite clear what part the Torah plays in this mystical system.[1] As far as any definite meaning may be attached to such hazy and nebulous ideas, it may perhaps be reduced to this: that the Torah having been long destined to become a main factor in God's government of the world, its creation must have been predesigned by God before he called the world into existence. In this sense the Torah is classed with other creations of God which are endowed with pre-mundane existence, as Israel, the throne of God (kingdom?), the name of the Messiah, hell and paradise (or reward and punishment), and repentance.[2] With regard to repentance, the Chapters of Rabbi Eliezer teach, When God designed the world he found no firm basis for it until he created the quality of repentance.[3] The same thought of the impossibility of a world without a revelation may perhaps also have been present

---

[1] See פירוש מהר״זו to *Gen. R.*, 1.

[2] See *Gen. R.*, 1 4, and all the parallels given there, which are very varying. [3] See *P. R. E.*, 3. See also below, p. 314

to the mind of the Jew when he spoke of the pre-mundane existence of the Torah.

Plausible, however, as this explanation may be, it is a little too rationalistic and would hardly account for that exaltation of the Torah which is such a prominent feature in Jewish literature. As soon as the Torah was identified with the Wisdom of Proverbs, the mind did not rest satisfied with looking upon it as a mere condition for the existence of the world. Every connotation of the term *Wisdom* in the famous eighth chapter of Proverbs was invested with life and individuality. The Torah, by this same process, was personified and endowed with a mystical life of its own, which emanates from God, yet is partly detached from him. Thus we find the Torah pleading for or against Israel, as on the occasion of the destruction of the Temple, when the Torah was called to give evidence against Israel, but desisted from it at the instance of Abraham, who said unto her, "My daughter, were not my children the only ones who received thee, when thou wast rejected by other nations?"[1] Nay, even single letters of the alphabet are endowed with a separate life, enabling them to act the same part almost as the Torah.[2] The whole later mystical theory which degenerates into the combinations of letters to which the most important meaning is attached, takes its origin from these personifications.

[1] See *Lament. R.*, Introduction, I. See also *Lev R.*, 19 and parallels.
[2] See *Gen. R.*, I Cf *P. R.*, 109 a.

This notion of the personification of the Torah never hardened into an article of faith. Its influence is less felt in dogma than in literature, particularly in the legends and scriptural interpretations bearing on the subject of the revelation on Mount Sinai. We must, at least, consider them in their main features.

First, the day of revelation is considered as the day on which earth was wedded to heaven. The barrier between them was removed by the fact that the Torah, the heavenly bride, the daughter of the Holy One, was wedded to Israel on that day.[1] The simile is carried further, and even the feature of the capture of the bride is not missing, — the verse in Ps. 68 19, "Thou hast ascended on high, thou hast led captivity captive," being interpreted as referring to Moses, who ascended to heaven and captured the Torah, in spite of the resistance of the angels, who were most reluctant to allow the Torah, the desirable treasure, to be taken away from among them.[2] Our planet is in constant fear lest Israel should imitate the example of their heathen neighbours, which would signify its doom to destruction. Hence the attention of the whole universe is directed to this glorious act. When God gave the Torah we read that the creatures of the firmament paused in their flight, those of the earth ventured not to lift up their voices, the waves of the boisterous

---

[1] See *P. K.*, 104 b, and *Exod. R.*, 30 5, 33 7.
[2] See *Shabbath*, 89 b, *P. R*, 98 a, and b; and *Exod. R.*, 28 1 and parallels.

seas ceased to roll, and the angels interrupted their eternal song of "Holy, Holy, Holy," [1] — heaven and earth listening to the good message.

This listening of the universe suggests the universalistic feature of the Sinaitic revelation. Though magnifying Israel for their readiness to receive the Torah, and strongly blaming the gentiles who refused to subject themselves to the word of God, so that a certain animosity comes down from Mount Sinai against the worshipper of idols,[2] these legends still betray a universalistic tendency as to the real and original purpose of the revelation. Thus with reference to Isa. 45 19, God is supposed to have said: "I have not spoken (the word of the revelation) in secret. I did not reveal it in hidden places and in dark corners of the earth." Nor did God postpone the giving of the Torah till Israel should enter into the Holy Land, lest Israel might claim it for themselves and say that the nations of the world have no share in it (in other words, it was not God's intention to make it a national religion). He gave it in open places, in the free desert, so that every man feeling the desire might receive it. Nor did he say *first* to the children of Jacob, "Seek ye me."[3] For, as we read in other places, the Holy

---

[1] *Exod. R.*, 29 9.   [2] *Shabbath*, 89 a.

[3] See *Mechilta*, 62 a, 66 b, the whole passage beginning ויחנו במדבר. The text is not quite correct, but the drift of the thought is as we have it here. See Notes to the passage, and cf. Bacher, *Ag. Tan*, 2 164, note 1; and *Aruch*, ed. Kohut, s.v. פנגם. See also *Yalkut Machiri on Isa.*, p. 156, read פונגם instead of פנגם. The *MHG*. reads תהו בקשוני לא עשיתיה הפותיקי אלא נתתי מתן שכרה בצדה.

one, blessed be he, came first to the sons of Esau and offered to them the Torah. These asked, "What is written in it?" God answered, "Thou shalt not kill." "We cannot accept it," they rejoined, "killing being our profession." Other nations objected to it on account of the seventh and eighth commandments, immorality and the appropriation of other men's possessions being the purposes of their lives, and the motive-springs of their actions, and so they said, "For the knowledge of thy ways, we have no desire — give thy Torah to thy people."[1]

It is rather characteristic of these legends, which probably reflect the attitude of the Rabbis towards the missionary enterprises of their time, that it is chiefly the moral part of the decalogue to which the nations objected. Esau is broad enough for general principles and will admit the Jewish God into his pantheon, if he submit to the process of accommodation and evolution so that he can share his honours with other gods. Esau objected to the "Do nots." These were too definite to allow of a wide interpretation in which the wisdom of Edom excelled, and might thus interfere with Esau's calling, his gladiators, his legions, and the policy of his procurators.

Thus Mount Sinai becomes the place in which God reveals himself to the world, and Israel undertakes the terrible responsibility of bearing witness to this fact.

[1] See *Mechilta, ibid; Sifre,* 142 *b; Lament R.,* 31; *P. R. E.,* ch. 41; *P. R.,* 99 *b* and parallels.

"If you will not make known my divinity (divine nature) to the nations of the world, even at the cost of your lives, you shall suffer for this iniquity," said God.[1] Though, indeed, the whole of creation has the duty to join in his praise and to bear witness to his divinity (divine power), Israel is especially commanded to invite all mankind to serve God and to believe in him, even as Abraham did, who made God beloved by all the creatures. And so intensely should we love him that we should also make others love him. For those who make God beloved by mankind are much greater than the mere lovers.[2] By this acceptance of the Torah, Israel made peace between God and his world,[3] the ultimate end being that its influence will reach the heathen too, and all the gentiles will one day be converted to the worship of God;[4] for the Torah "is not the Torah of the Priests, nor the Torah of the Levites, nor the Torah of the Israelites, but the Torah of Man (Torath ha-Adam), whose gates are open to receive the righteous nation which keepeth the truth and those who are good and upright in their hearts."[5]

Another important feature in these legends and interpretations is the fact that the revelation was an act of grace and the effluence of God's goodness. When the princes of the world heard the thunders

---

[1] See *Lev. R.*, 6 5, and commentaries. Cf. also *M. T.*, 19 1.

[2] See Maimonides, ס׳היס מ׳ע א, ב. Cf. *M. T.*, 19 1, and *Midrash Tannaim*, ed Hoffmann, p. 40 See also *M. T.*, 18 7.

[3] *Gen. R.*, 66 2.   [4] See *Berachoth*, 54 b.   [5] *T. K.*, 86 b.

and lightnings which accompanied the revelation, they were frightened, thinking the world was to pass through another judgement as it did in the days of the deluge, whereupon they consulted their prophet Balaam. He calmed their fears, saying: "Fear not, ye kings, he who dwells in heaven has revealed himself to his children in his glory and his mercy. He has appeared, to give to his beloved people Torah, wisdom, and instruction,[1] and to bless them with strength and peace."[2] In another passage it is stated that God appeared on this occasion in the aspect of an instructing Elder, full of mercy.[3] Like rain and light, the Torah was a gift from heaven of which the world is hardly worthy, but which is indispensable to its maintenance.[4]

The gift was a complete one, without any reserve whatever. Nothing of the Torah, God assures Israel, was kept back in heaven.[5] All that follows is only a matter of interpretation. The principle held by the Rabbis was that the words of the Torah "are fruitful and multiply."[6] Thus the conviction could ripen that everything wise and good, be it ethical or ceremonial in its character, the effect of which would be to strengthen the cause of religion, was at least potentially contained in the Torah. Hence the famous adage, that everything which any student will teach at any future time, was already communicated to Moses on Mount Sinai, as also the injunction that any accept-

---

[1] See *P. R.*, 95 a.   [2] See *Sifre*, 142 b.   [3] See *Mechilta*, 66 b.
[4] *Gen. R.*, 64.   [5] *Deut. R.*, 8 6.   [6] See *Chagigah*, 3 b.

able truth, though discovered by an insignificant man in Israel, should be considered of as high authority as if it had emanated from a great sage or prophet or even from Moses himself.[1] It requires but an earnest religious mind to discover all truth there. For the Torah came down from heaven with all the necessary instruments: humility, righteousness, and uprightness — and even her reward was in her.[2] And man has only to apply these tools to find in the Torah peace, strength, life, light, bliss, happiness, joy, and freedom.[3]

The Torah was, in short, all things to all men. To the Theosophist, who had already come under the sway of Hellenistic influences, it was the very expression of God's wisdom, which he would, as far as it is consistent with Biblical notions, elevate into an emanation of God's essence, and endow with a pre-mundane existence, reaching almost to infinity. To the mystical poet, with his love for the picturesque, it was the heavenly bride adorned with all the virtues which only heaven could bestow on her, at whose presentation to Israel the whole universe rejoiced, for her touch with mankind meant the wedding of heaven to earth. What, then, could the poor mortal do better than to learn to know her and to fall in love with her?

To the great majority of the Rabbis who retained

---

[1] See *Sifre*, 79 b.   [2] *Deut. R., ibid*
[3] See *P. K.*, 105 b; *Mechilta*, 36 b, 47; *Sifre a*, 82 b, 83 b; *Exod. R.*, 36 a.

their sober sense, and cared more about what God requires us to be than about knowing what he is, the Torah was simply the manifestation of God's will, revealed to us for our good; the pedagogue, as the Rabbis expressed it,[1] who educates God's creatures. The occupation with the Torah was, according to the Rabbis, less calculated to produce schoolmen and jurists than saints and devout spirits. "Whosoever labours in the Torah for its own sake, merits many things ... he is called friend, beloved, a lover of God, a lover of mankind; it clothes him in meekness and fear (of God), and fits him to become righteous, pious, and upright; it keeps him far from sin, brings him towards the side of virtue, and gives him sovereignty and dominion and discerning judgement. To him the secrets of the Torah are revealed; he becomes a never failing fountain, he grows modest and long-suffering, forgives insults, and is exalted above all things."[2] On the other hand, his individualism does not make him exclusive, his freedom does not involve the subjection of others, the world rejoices in him, for he enriches it with sound knowledge, understanding, and strength.[3] His life is one even like that of Moses, a continuous mourning for the glory of God and the glory of Israel (at present obscured) and a con-

[1] See *Gen. R.*, 1. Cf. אבות עם תלמוד ירושלמי, etc., by R. נח חיים מקברין, *to Kinyan Torah*, 3 *b*, 4 *a*, the passage given there from the *Mechilta* of Ishmael, but not to be found there.

[2] See *Kinyan Torah* and Friedmann, נספחים, p. 15 *seq*.

[3] *Kinyan Torah, ibid.*

stant longing for their salvation,[1] whilst his activity (a continuation of the revelation) is making peace between heaven and earth.[2] In sooth, Israel has recognised the strength (or the secret) of the Torah; therefore, they said, "We forsake not God and his Torah, as it is said: 'I sat down under his shadow with great delight, and his fruit was sweet to my taste'" (Song of Songs 23).[3]

In fine, to the Jew the Torah was anything but a curse. He understood how to find out the sweetness and the light of it and of the Law which formed a part of it.

[1] See *S. E.*, pp. 17 and 63.   [2] See *Sanhedrin*, 99 *b*.
[3] See *Exod. R.*, 17 2.

X

THE TORAH IN ITS ASPECT OF LAW
(MIZWOTH)

R. SIMLAI, a well-known Agadic teacher and controversialist of the third century, said as follows: "Six hundred and thirteen commandments were delivered unto Moses on Mount Sinai; three hundred and sixty-five of which are prohibitive laws, corresponding to the number of days of the solar year, whilst the remaining two hundred and forty-eight are affirmative injunctions, being as numerous as the limbs constituting the human body."[1] This is one of the earlier comments on the number of the six hundred and thirteen laws, which are brought forward in many of our theological works, with the purpose of proving under what burden the scrupulous Jew must have laboured, who considered himself under the duty of performing all these enactments. The number is, by its very strangeness, bewildering; and the Pharisee, unable to rise to the heights above the Law, lay under

---

[1] *Makkoth*, 23 *b* and parallels, in the יפה עינים (where פדרי״א פמ״ח ought to be corrected into מ״א) Cf. Bacher, *Ag. Am.*, I 558, and notes. The earliest known source for this number is probably *Mechilta* 67 *a*. Cf. also Sifre, 90 *b*. See also Bloch, *Revue des Études Juives*, I 197 *seq*, and 209 *seq*.

TORAH IN ITS ASPECT OF LAW (MIZWOTH) 139

the curse of its mere quantity. A few words as to the real value of these statistics are therefore necessary, before we pass to other questions connected with our subject.

The words with which the saying of R. Simlai is introduced are,[1] "He preached," or "he interpreted," and they somewhat suggest that these numbers were in some way a subject for edification, deriving from them some moral lesson. The lesson these numbers were intended to convey was, first, that each day brings its new temptation only to be resisted by a firm Do not; and, on the other hand, that the whole man stands in the service of God, each limb or member of his body being entrusted with the execution of its respective functions.[2] This was probably the sentiment which the preacher wished to impress upon his congregation, without troubling himself much about the accuracy of his numbers. How little, indeed, we are justified in urging these numbers too seriously is clear from the sequel of R. Simlai's homily. It runs thus: "David came (after Moses) and reduced[3] them (the six hundred and

---

[1] דרש ר׳ שמלאי in most of the parallels.

[2] Cf. *P. K.*, 101 *a*, and Rashi to *Makkoth, ibid.* Cf. also *Tan.*, תצא, 2. There are, however, grave doubts whether the subdivision in 365 and 248 (the words in the Talmud from שם״ה to אדם) is not a later addition. Cf. Bacher, *ibid.*

[3] The word in the Talmud and in *Tan.*, שופטים end is והעמידן, which may mean "compressed" or "reduced." See Bacher, *ibid.* I take here the version of the Talmud, omitting the additional discussions. Cf. also *M. T.*, 15, end.

thirteen commandments) to eleven, as it is said: Lord, who shall abide in thy tabernacle? who shall dwell in thy holy hill? He that walketh uprightly, etc.[1] Then Isaiah came and reduced them to six, as it is said: He that walketh righteously, etc.[2] Then Micah came and reduced them to three: He hath shewed thee, O man, what is good; and what doth the Lord require of thee, but to do justly, etc.[3] Then Isaiah came again, and reduced them to two, as it is said: Thus saith the Lord, Keep my judgements, and do justice.[4] Then Amos came and reduced them to one, as it is said: Seek the Lord and live.[5] Whilst Habakkuk (also) reduced them to one, as it is said: But the just shall live by his faith.[6]" The drift of this whole passage shows that the homily was not so much intended to urge the necessity of carrying out all the commandments with their numerous details, as to emphasise the importance of the moral laws, which themselves, nevertheless, may be compressed into the principle of seeking God, or of faith in God.

Granted, however, that R. Simlai took it seriously with his number of six hundred and thirteen: granted,

---

[1] Ps. 15 2–5, which verses contain eleven moral injunctions. Cf. Kimchi's commentary to this chapter.

[2] Isa. 33 15, which verse contains six moral injunctions.

[3] Micah 6 8, where three moral injunctions are contained.

[4] Isa. 56 1.

[5] Amos 5 6. This was probably the original version of R. Simlai's words, notwithstanding the objections made there.

[6] Hab. 2 4.

again, that his enumeration rested on some old authority which may be regarded as a guarantee for its exactness,[1] this would prove nothing for the "burden theory." The only possible explanations of our Rabbi's saying are the lists of R. Simon Kiara and of Maimonides.[2] But even a superficial analysis will discover that in the times of the Rabbis many of these commandments were already obsolete, as, for instance, those relating to the arrangements of the tabernacle, and to the conquest of Palestine; whilst others concerned only certain classes, as, for instance, the priests, the judges, the soldiers and their commanders, the Nazirites, the representatives of the community, or even one or two individuals in the whole population, as, for example, the king and the high priest. Others, again, provided for contingencies which could occur only to a few, as, for instance, the laws concerning divorce or levirate-marriages. The laws, again, relating to idolatry, incest, and the sacrifices of children to Moloch, could hardly be considered as coming within the province of the practical life even of the pre-Christian Jew; just as little as we can speak of Englishmen being under the burden of the law when prohibited from burning their widows or marrying their grandmothers, though these acts would certainly be considered as crimes. A careful examination of the six hundred and thirteen laws will prove

[1] This seems to be the opinion of Maimonides.
[2] The former in the הלכות גדולות, the latter in the ספר המצות and the Introduction to the משנה תורה.

that barely a hundred laws are to be found which concerned the everyday life of the bulk of the people.[1] Thus the law in its totality, which by the number of its precepts is so terrifying, is in its greater part nothing else than a collection of statutes relating to different sections of the community and to its multifarious institutions, ecclesiastical as well as civil, which constituted, as I have already said, the kingdom of God.

And here lay the strength of Judaism. The modern man is an eclectic being. He takes his religion from the Bible, his laws from the Romans, his culture from the classics, and his politics from his party. He is certainly broader in his sympathies than the Jew of old; but as a composite being, he must necessarily be lacking in harmony and unity. His sympathies are divided between the different sources of his inspiration, — sources which do not, as we know, always go well together. In order to avoid collision, he has at last to draw the line between the ecclesiastical and the civil, leaving the former, which in fact was forced upon him by a foreign religious conqueror, to a separate body of men whose business it is to look after the welfare of his invisible soul, whilst reserving the charge of the body and the world to himself.

The Rabbinic notion seems to have been that "if religion is anything, it is everything." The Rabbi gloried in the thought of being, as the Agadic expression runs, "a member of a city (or community) which in-

[1] See Schechter, *Studies in Judaism*, p. 301.

TORAH IN ITS ASPECT OF LAW (MIZWOTH) 143

cluded the priest as well as the prophet, the king as well as the scribe and the teacher," all appointed and established by God.[1] To consider the administration of justice with all its details as something lying without the sphere of Torah would have been a terrible thought to the ancient Jew. Some Rabbis are anxious to show that the appointment of judges was commanded to Moses, even before Jethro gave him the well-known advice.[2] The Torah, they point out, is a combination of mercy and justice.[3] That the ways of the Torah "are ways of sweetness, and all her paths are peace" (Prov. 3 17. 18), was a generally accepted axiom,[4] and went without saying; what had to be particularly urged was that even such laws and institutions as appear to be a consequence of uncompromising right and of rigid truth, rather than of sweetness and peace, were also part and parcel of the Torah, with her God-like universality of attributes. Hence the assertion of the Rabbis that God threatens Israel with taking back his treasure from them should they be slow in carrying out the principle of justice (*dinim*).[5] "To the nations of the earth he gave some few laws; but his love to Israel was particularly manifested by the fulness and

---

[1] *Sifre*, 134 *a*. Cf. *Chullin*, 56 *b*. The passage in the text follows more the reading in the *MHG.*, ר״מ אומ׳ כרבא דכולא ביה ּ כהניו מתוכו לויו מתוכו מלכיו מתוכו נביאיו מתוכו חכמיו מתוכו סופריו מתוכו ומשניו מתוכו, etc. [2] See *Sifre*, 20 *a*.

[3] *Deut. R.*, 5 7.

[4] See, for instance, *Sukkah*, 32 *a* ; *Jebamoth*, 87 *b*, and elsewhere.

[5] *Exod R.*, 30 28.

completeness of the Torah, which is wholly theirs."[1] And in it they find everything. "If thou wantest advice," the Rabbis say (even in matters secular, or in questions regarding behaviour and good manners), "take it from the Torah, even as David said, From thy precepts I get understanding" (Ps. 119 104).[2]

As a fact, the old Rabbis hardly recognised such a chasm between the material and the spiritual as to justify the domain of religion being confined to the latter. The old Rabbinic literature is even devoid of the words *spiritual* and *material*. The corresponding terms, רוחני and גשמי, were coined by later translators from the Greek and Arabic philosophers, with whom the division between body and soul is so prominent. It is true that the Rabbis occasionally used such expressions as "things of the heaven" and "things of the world," or matters concerning "the eternal life" and matters concerning "the temporal life."[3] But apart from the fact that they were little meant to indicate a theological division between two antagonistic principles, the "things of the heaven" covered a much wider area of human life than is commonly imagined. Thus we hear of a Rabbi who remonstrated with his son for not attending the lecture of his friend R. Chisda. The son

---

[1] *Exod R*, *ibid.*, 9 and parallels.   [2] See *P. K.*, 105 *a*.
[3] מילי דשמיא — מילי דעלמא. See *e.g. Berachoth*, 7 *b*, v. *Shabbath*, 33 *b*. Interesting is the arrangement in the complete edition of the ספר יראים in which all the laws concerning conduct and morality are grouped under the heading of the duties towards God and man, whilst the ceremonial come under the heading of duties towards God alone.

apologised, and answered that he had once gone to the school of R. Chisda, but what he heard were "things of the world," the lecture having consisted in the exposition of a set of sanitary rules to be observed on certain occasions. Whereupon the father rejoined indignantly: "He (R. Chisda) is occupied with the life of God's creatures, and dost thou venture to call such matters 'things of the world'?"[1] Elsewhere we find the Rabbis deciding that to teach a child a trade or a handicraft is to be considered as one of the "delights of heaven," for which arrangements may be made even on the Sabbath.[2]

As a rule, the Rabbis spoke of sin and righteousness, a good action or a bad action, מצוה or עבירה, for each of which body and soul are alike held responsible. But no act is in itself the worse or the better for being a function of the body or a manifestation of the soul. When Hillel the Great, who, as it would seem, was the author, or at least the inspirer, of the saying, "Let all thy deeds be for the sake of Heaven," was about to take a bath, he said, "I am going to perform a religious act by beautifying my person, that was created in the image of God."[3]

R. Judah Hallevi, with the instinct of a poet, hit the

[1] *Shabbath*, 82 a. [2] חפצי שמים. *Shabbath*, 150 a.

[3] See *A. R. N.*, 33 b; *Lev. R.*, 34 8; and *P. R.*, 115 b. "The fourth degree of love," says St. Bernard somewhere, "is to love self only for God's sake." See also the passage from the *Yelamdenu* reproduced in Jellinek's *Beth Hammidrash*, 6: 85 where it is the נוי (or superior beauty) in which the צלם האל finds expression.

right strain when he said, in his famous Dialogue *Kusari*, "Know that our Torah is constituted of the three psychological states: Fear, love, and joy" (that is to say, all the principal emotions of man are enlisted in the service of God). "By each of these thou mayest be brought into communion with thy God. Thy contriteness in the days of fasting does not bring thee nearer to God than thy joy on the Sabbath days and on festivals, provided thy joy emanates from a devotional and perfect heart. And just as prayer requires devotion and thought, so does joy, namely, that thou wilt rejoice in his commandments for their own sake, (the only reasons for this rejoicing being) the love of him who commanded it, and the desire of recognising God's goodness towards thee. Consider these feasts as if thou wert the guest of God invited to his table and his bounty, and thank him for it inwardly and outwardly. And if thy joy in God excites thee even to the degree of singing and dancing, it is a service to God, keeping thee attached to him. But the Torah did not leave these things to our arbitrary will, but put them all under control. For man lacks the power to make use of the functions of body and soul in their proper proportions."[1]

The law thus conceived as submitting all the faculties and passions of man to the control of the divine, whilst suppressing none, was a source of joy and blessing to the Rabbis. Whatever meaning the words of the Apostle may have, when he speaks of the curse of the Law, it is

[1] *Kuzari* (ed. Sluzki, p. 45).

certain that those who lived and died for it considered it as a blessing. To them it was an effluence of God's mercy and love. In the daily prayer of the Jews the same sentiment is expressed in most glowing words. "With everlasting love thou hast loved the house of Israel, thy people; Torah, commandments, statutes, and judgements hast thou taught us. . . . Yea, we will rejoice in the words of thy Torah and thy commandments forever. . . . And mayest thou never take away thy love from us. Blessed art thou, O Lord, who lovest thy people Israel."[1] Beloved are Israel, whom the Holy One, blessed be he, surrounded with commandments, (bidding them) to have phylacteries on their heads and arms, a mezuzah on their door-posts, fringes on the four corners of their garments. . . . "Be distinguished," said the Holy One, blessed be he, to Israel, "by the commandments in order that ye may be pleasing unto me. Thou (Israel) art beautiful when thou art pleasing."[2] Indeed, there is not a single thing which is not connected with a commandment, be it the farm, or the home, or the garments of the man, or his flocks.[3] And it is on account of this fact that Israel considered themselves blessed in the city and in the field.[4] It is the very light sown for the righteous, God not having loved anything in the world which is not connected with a law.[5]

---

[1] See Singer, p. 69; Baer, p. 164. Cf. also Berachoth, 33 *b*; Singer, p. 227; and Baer, p. 347.   [2] *Sifre*, 75 *b* and parallels.
[3] *T. K.*, 42 *a*.   [4] *Tan.* תבא, 4.   [5] *Num. R.*, 17 5; cf. *Lev. R*, 6 8.

XI

THE JOY OF THE LAW

Law and commandments, or as the Rabbinic expression is, *Torah* and *Mizwoth*, have a harsh sound and are suggestive to the outsider of something external, forced upon men by authority from the outside, sinister and burdensome. The citations just given show that Israel did not consider them in that light. They were their very love and their very life. This will become clearer when we consider both the sentiment accompanying the performance of the Law and the motives urging them.

The שמחה של מצוה, the joy experienced by the Rabbinic Jew in being commanded to fulfil the Law, and the enthusiasm which he felt at accomplishing that which he considered to be the will of God, is a point hardly touched upon by most theological writers, and if touched upon at all, is hardly ever understood. Yet this "joy of the Law" is so essential an element in the understanding of the Law, that it "forms that originality of sentiment more or less delicate" which can never be conceived by those who have experienced it neither from life nor from literature.

How anxious a Jew was to carry out a law, and what joy he felt in fulfilling it, may be seen from the following story, which perhaps dates from the very time when the Law was denounced as slavery and as the strength of sin. According to Deut. 24 19, a sheaf forgotten in the harvest field belonged to the poor; the proprietor being forbidden to go again and to fetch it. This prohibitive law was called מצות שכחה, "the commandment with regard to forgetfulness." It was impossible to fulfil it as long as one thought of it. In connection with this we read in the Tosephta: "It happened to a Chasid (saint) that he forgot a sheaf in his field, and was thus enabled to fulfil the commandment with regard to forgetfulness. Whereupon he bade his son go to the temple, and offer for him a burnt-offering and a peace-offering, whilst he also gave a great banquet to his friends in honour of the event. Thereupon his son said to him: Father, why dost thou rejoice in this commandment more than in any other law prescribed in the Torah? He answered, that it was the occurrence of the rare opportunity of accomplishing the will of God, even as the result of some oversight, which caused him so much delight."[1]

This joy of the *Mizwah* constituted the essence of the action. Israel, we are told, receives especial praise for the fact that when they stood on Mount Sinai to receive the Torah, they all combined with one heart to accept

---

[1] *Tosephta Peah*, 22. Cf. *Midrash Zuta* (ed. Buber, 51 *b*). Of course, we must read there שלא בכונה for בעונה.

the kingdom of heaven in joy. The sons of Aaron, again, were glad and rejoicing when they heard words (of commandment) from the mouth of Moses. Again, "let man fulfil the commandments of the Torah with joy," exclaimed a Rabbi, "and then they will be counted to him as righteousness."[1] The words, "Moses did as the Lord commanded him" (Num. 27 22), are explained to mean that he fulfilled the Law with joy.[2] In a similar manner the words, "I have done according to all that thou hast commanded me" (Deut. 26 14), are interpreted to signify, I have rejoiced and caused others to rejoice.[3] Naturally, it is the religionist of high standard, or as the Rabbis express it, "the man who deserves it," who realises this joy in the discharge of all religious functions, whilst to him "who deserves it not" it may become a trial of purification.[4] But the ideal is to obtain this quality of joy, or "to deserve it." The truly righteous rejoice almost unconsciously, joy being a gift from heaven to them, as it is said, "Thou (God) hast put gladness in my heart."[5]

This principle of joy in connection with the *Mizwah* is maintained both in the Talmud and in the devotional literature of the Middle Ages. The general rule is: Tremble with joy when thou art about to fulfil a

---

[1] See *Mechilta*, 66 b; *T. K.*, 42 b. See also *S. E.*, p. 29. Cf. also *ibid.*, p 95.

[2] *Sifre*, 52 b.   [3] *Ibid.*, 129 a.

[4] *Yoma*, 72 b, זכה משמחתו לא זכה צורפתו.   [5] *S. E.*, p. 97.

commandment.[1] God, his Salvation, and his Law, are the three things in which Israel rejoices.[2] Indeed, as R. Bachye Ibn. Bakudah declares, to mention one of the later moralists, it is this joy experienced by the sweetness of the service of God which forms a part of the reward of the religionist, even as the prophet said, "Thy words were found, and I did eat them; and thy word was unto me the joy and rejoicing of mine heart" (Jer. 15 16).[3] R. Bachye Ibn Chalwah, again, declares that the joy accompanying the carrying out of a religious performance is even more acceptable to God than the *Mizwah* itself. The righteous, he points out, feel this ineffable delight in performing God's will in the same way as the spheres and planets (whose various revolutions are a perpetual song to God) rejoice in their going forth and are glad in their returning;[4] whilst R. Joseph Askari of Safed (sixteenth century) makes joy one of the necessary conditions without which a law cannot be perfectly carried out.[5] And I may perhaps remark that this joy of the *Mizwah* was a living reality even in modern times. I myself had once the good fortune to observe one of those old type Jews, who, as the first morning of the Feast of Tabernacles drew near, used to wake and rise soon after the middle of the night. There he sat, with

[1] *D E. Z.*, 2. [2] *P. K.*, 147 a, 194 a.
[3] חובות הלבבות עבודת האלהים פ״ט
[4] כד הקמח, ch. שמחה.
[5] See חרדים, Warsaw, 1879, p. 9. Cf. also Albo, *Ikkarim*, 3 88; also Luzzato, מסילת ישרים, 28 a.

trembling joy, awaiting impatiently the break of dawn, when he would be able to fulfil the law of the palm branches and the willows!

To give one or two further instances how many more things there are in the Synagogue and in the Law than are dreamt of by our divines, I shall allude to the Sabbath and to prayer.

The institution of the Sabbath is one of those laws the strict observance of which was already the object of attack on the part of the compilers of the Synoptic Gospels. Nevertheless, the doctrine proclaimed in one of the Gospels that the Son of man is the Lord of the Sabbath, was also current among the Rabbis. They too teach that the Sabbath is delivered into the hand of man (to break it when necessary), and not man into the power of the Sabbath.[1] And the Rabbis even laid down the axiom that a scholar living in a town, where there could be among the Jewish population the least doubt as to the question whether the Sabbath might be broken for the benefit of a person dangerously sick, was to be despised as a man neglecting his duty; every delay in such a case being fraught with grave consequences to the patient; for, as Maimonides points out, the laws of the Torah are not meant as an infliction upon mankind, "but as mercy, loving-kindness, and peace."[2]

The attacks upon the Sabbath have not abated. "The day is still described by almost every modern

[1] *Mechilta*, 104 a.
[2] *Jer. Yoma*, 45 b.   Cf. Maimonides, הלכות שבת פ״ב ה״ג.

writer in the most gloomy colours, and long lists are given of the minute observances connected with it, easily to be transgressed, which would necessarily make the Sabbath, instead of a day of rest, a day of sorrow and anxiety, almost worse than the Scotch Sunday, as depicted by continental writers." Even Hausrath[1] — who is something more than a theologian, for he also wrote history — is unable to see in the Rabbinic Sabbath more than a day which is to be distinguished by a mere non-performance of the thirty-nine various sorts of work forbidden by the Rabbis on Sabbaths, such as sowing, ploughing, reaping, winnowing, kneading, spinning, weaving, skinning, tanning, writing, etc., etc., — a whole bundle of participles, in the expounding of which the Pharisee took an especial delight.[2] Contrast this view with the prayer of R. Zadok, a younger contemporary of the Apostles, which runs thus: "Through the love with which thou, O Lord our God, lovest thy people Israel, and the mercy which thou hast shown to the children of thy covenant, thou hast given unto us in love this great and holy seventh day."[3] This Rabbi, clearly, regarded the Sabbath as a gift from heaven, an expression of the infinite love and mercy of God, which he manifested toward his beloved children. Thus the Sabbath is celebrated by the very people who observe

---

[1] See Schechter, *Studies in Judaism*, p. 297 *seq.*
[2] *History of the New Testament Times*, I 101.
[3] *Tosephta Berachoth*, 3 7.

it, in hundreds of hymns, which would fill volumes, as a day of rest and joy, of pleasure and delight, a day in which man enjoys some presentiment of the pure bliss and happiness which are stored up for the righteous in the world to come, and to which such tender names were applied as the "Queen Sabbath," the "Bride Sabbath," and the "holy, dearly beloved Sabbath." Every founder of a religion declares the yoke which he is about to put on his followers to be easy, and the burden to be light; but, after all, the evidence of those who *did* bear the Sabbath yoke for thousands of years ought to pass for something. The assertion of some writers that the Rabbis, the framers of these laws, as students leading a retired life, suffered in no way under them, and therefore were unable to realise their oppressive effect upon the great majority of the people, is hardly worth refuting. The Rabbis belonged to the majority, being mostly recruited, as already pointed out in another place, from the artisan, trading, and labouring classes.[1] This very R. Zadok, whom I have just mentioned, says: "Make not the Torah a crown wherewith to aggrandise thyself, nor a spade wherewith to dig;" whilst Hillel considers it as a mortal sin to derive any material profit from the words of the Torah.[2]

The prayers of the synagogue are another case in point. That Jews could pray, that they had, besides the Temple, a synagogue service, independent of sacri-

[1] See above, p. 110.   [2] *Aboth*, 4 7.

fices and priests, does not, as every student must have felt, fit in well with the view generally entertained of the deadly and deadening effects of the Law. The inconvenient Psalms of the later periods were easily neutralised by divesting them of all individualistic tendency, whilst the synagogue was placed under the superintendence of the Rabbis, "whose mechanical tendencies are well known." In their hands, we are told, prayers turn into rubrics, and it is with an especial delight that theologians dwell on the Rabbinical laws relating to prayer, as, for instance, how many times a day a man ought to pray, the fixed hours for prayer, in what parts of the prayer an interruption is allowed, which parts of the prayer require more devotion than others, and similar petty little questions of religious casuistry in which the Rabbi, as an expert, if I may call him so, greatly delighted. But these writers seem to overlook the fact that the very framers of these petty laws were the main composers of the liturgy. And who can say what the Rabbi's feelings were when he wrote, for instance, "Forgive us, our Father, for we have sinned"? The word "Father" alone suggests a world of such ideas as love, veneration, devotion, and childlike dependence upon God. It is easy enough to copy rubrics. They float on the surface of the so-called "Sea of the Talmud," and it requires only a certain indelicacy of mind, or what Renan would have called "the vulgarity of criticism," to skim them off, and pass them on to the world as samples of Jewish synagogue life. If Life and Times writers would only dip a little deeper into this sea, they would notice how easily the Rabbis could disregard all these rubrics. The subject of prayer is too wide to be dealt with here even in a perfunctory manner, but a few passages at least may be cited which will illustrate the sentiment of the Rabbis with regard to this topic. Thus we read, with reference to Jer. 14 8: "God is the *Mikweh* of Israel, which word the Rabbis take to mean "the source of purity" (Israel's purification being established by attachment to God). "God says to Israel, I bade thee read thy prayers unto me in thy synagogues; but if thou canst not, pray in thy house; and if thou art unable to do this, pray when thou art in thy field; and if this be inconvenient to thee, pray on thy bed; and if thou canst not do even this, think of me in thy heart."[1] Prayer is, indeed, as the Rabbis call it, "the service of the heart"; though man should praise the Holy One, blessed be he, with every limb in his body, even as David did who praised him with his head, with his eyes, with his mouth, with his ears, with his throat, with his tongue, with his lips, with his heart, with his reins, with his hands, with his feet, as it is said, "All my bones shall say, Lord who is like unto thee?" (Ps. 35 10); nay, with his soul and his breath.[2]

---

[1] *P. K.*, 157 *b*, 158 *a*, referring to the meaning "well" or "cistern" rather than "hope."

[2] *Taanith*, 2 *a*. Cf. *Sifre*, 80 *a*; *M T.*, 5 1, about the prayers of יחיד (individual). See *Mechilta of R. Simon*, p. 151. Cf. also above, p. 50, note 2.

THE JOY OF THE LAW

Prayer, and the recitation of the Shema, are among the things which keep the heart of Israel in exile awake,[1] and God requires of Israel that, at least in the time of prayer, they should give him all their hearts;[2] that is to say, that the whole of man should be absorbed in his prayer. "Prayer without devotion is like a body without a soul," is a common Jewish proverb. Indeed, he who prays should direct his heart to heaven, nay, he must consider himself as if the very Divine Presence is facing him.[3] God himself teaches Israel how to pray before him;[4] for nothing is more beautiful than prayer; it is more beautiful even than good works, and of more value than sacrifices.[5] It is the expression of Israel's love to God; God longs for it.[6] Prayer is Israel's chiefest joy.[7] When thou risest to pray, let thy heart rejoice within thee, since thou servest a God, the like unto whom there is none (Ps. 100 3). Hence the benediction in which Israel thank God that they are permitted to pray to him.[8]

And here I must again be allowed an allusion to personal reminiscences. The following passages in the

---

[1] See *Cant. Rabba*, 5: 2.   [2] *Tan.*, תבא 1, end.

[3] See *Berachoth*, 31 a, and *Sanhedrin*, 22 a.

[4] See *Rosh Hashanah*, 17 b. Cf. above, 37.

[5] See *Sifre*, 71 b, and *Tan.*, תבא 1.

[6] See *M. T.*, 116 1.

[7] See Yalkut to Ps 100. Cf. *M. T.* to this chapter.

[8] See *Jer. Berachoth*, 3 d (the first lines on the top). Cf. Baer's remarks to the מודים דרבנן, p 100.

Song of the Unity are recited in some congregations on the Eve of the Day of Atonement: —

We are thy people and thy sheep, who delight to obey thy will.

But how shall we serve, since our hand hath no power, and our sanctuary is burnt with fire?

How shall we serve without sacrifice and meat offering? for we are not yet come unto our rest,

Neither is there water to wash away defilement; lo! we are upon unpurified ground.

But I rejoice at thy word, and I am come according to thy bidding.

For it is written, I will not reprove thee for thy sacrifices, or thy burnt-offerings.

Concerning your sacrifices and your burnt-offerings I commanded not your fathers.

What have I asked, and what have I sought of thee but to fear me?

To serve with joy and a good heart?

Behold, to hearken is better than sacrifice,

And a broken heart than pure offering.

The sacrifices of God are a broken spirit.

In sacrifice and meat-offering thou delightest not; sin-offering and burnt-offering thou hast not asked.

I will build an altar of the broken fragments of my heart, and will break my spirit within me.

The haughty heart I will humble; yea, the haughtiness of mine eyes, and I will rend my heart for the sake of the Lord.

My broken spirit, that is thy sacrifice. Let it be
 acceptable upon thine altar![1]

But only one who has seen the deep despair reflected on the faces of the worshippers, as they repeat the first stanzas bewailing the loss of sacrifices as a means of atonement, and the sudden transition to the highest degree of joy and cheerfulness at the thought expressed in the last stanzas, that it is neither burnt-offering nor meat-offering which God requires, but that the heart is the real altar and the service of the heart the real sacrifice — only one who has witnessed such a prayer-meeting will be able to conceive how little the capacity of the Rabbi to pray, and to rejoice in prayer, was affected by the rubrics, and how superficial is the common conception of onlookers on this subject.

In the preceding remarks we had a reference to a saying of R. Zadok, prohibiting the making of the Torah a means of aggrandising one's self, and another saying of Hillel to the same effect.[2] The saying in question closes with the words, "Lo, whosoever makes profit from the words of the Torah removes his life from the world."[3] This brings us to the subject of לשמה (*Lishmah*), playing a very prominent part in Rabbinic literature. By *Lishmah* is understood the performance of the Law for its own sake, or rather

---

[1] שיר היחוד, first day. See *Service of the Synagogue*, Davis and Adler, London, 1906, vol I, p. 41.

[2] See above, p 145   [3] *Aboth*, 4 7.

for the sake of him who wrought (commanded) it, excluding all worldly intentions. Thus, with regard to sacrifices, the words of Lev. 1 9 (ריח ניחוח לה׳) are explained to mean that the sacrifice must be brought with no other intention but that of pleasing him who created the world.[1] The service of God should be as single-minded as he is single in the world, to whom this service is directed.[2] "It is pleasing unto me that I commanded and my will was done."[3] With reference to other laws, the injunction is, "Do the things (of the Torah) for the sake of him who wrought them, and speak in them for their own sake."[4] Indeed, the Torah is only then pure when man cleanses himself from all sin, and from every thought of profiting by it, so that he must not expect of mankind to serve him or maintain him, because he is a scholar.[5] Nay, it is only the occupation with the Torah for its own sake which is life, "but if thou hast not performed the words of the Torah in this manner, they kill thee."[6] It is just this purity of motive which forms the main difference "between the righteous and the wicked, between him that serveth God and

[1] *T. K.*, 7 *c* and 8 *c*. Cf. *Zebachim*, 37 *b*. See also below, pp. 297 and 298.

[2] *T. K.*, 43 *d*. See below, p. 258.   [3] *Sifre*, 39 *a* and 54 *a*.

[4] See *Nedarim*, 62 *a*, reading פועלם. See, however, *Sifre*, 84 *b*. *D. E Z* (ed. Tawrogi) has both readings. Cf. Bacher, *Ag. Tan.*, I 58. Duran in his commentary to אבות, 5 4, has the reading לשם פעלן ודבר בהם לשם שמים.

[5] *Mechilta of R Simon*, 98.

[6] *Sifre*, 131 *b*; *Taanith*, 7 *a* , cf Bacher, *Ag. Tan.*, 2 540.

him that serveth him not" (Malachi 3 18).[1] The same thing applies also to other laws. Two men feasted upon their Passover lamb. The one ate it for the sake of the *Mizwah*, the other devoured it in the manner of a glutton. To the former they apply the Scriptural words, "The righteous shall walk in them;" to the latter, "The transgressor shall fall therein" (Hosea 14 10).[2] This is of course the highest ideal of the religionist, though not everybody could attain to this high degree, and some concessions were made in this respect. Hence such statements as "Let a man be occupied in the study of the Torah and the fulfilling of commandments even in the case when they are not performed for their own sake;" but the statement closes with the words, "for this occupation will lead in the end to the desired ideal of the purer intention." This is in harmony with the sentiment expressed by another Rabbi, who was wont to pray, "May it be thy will that you bring peace . . . among those students who are occupied in the study of the Torah, both who do it for its own sake, and those who do not do it for its own sake. And that these latter may come to ultimately occupy themselves with it for its own sake."[3] In any case, this selfish occupation was considered as a Torah wanting in grace.[4]

---

[1] See *M. T.*, 31 9.
[2] See *Nazir*, 23 a. See also Albo, *Ikkarim*, 3 5 and 28.
[3] See *Berachoth*, 17 a.   [4] (חסד). See *Sukkah*, 49 b.

And let it be noticed that the notion of *Lishmah* excluded even the intention of fulfilling a law with the hope of getting such rewards as are promised by the Scriptures. Though the Rabbis never tired of urging the belief in reward and punishment, and strove to make of it a living conviction, they yet displayed a constant tendency to disregard it as a motive for action. The saying of Antigonos of Socho, "Be not like servants that serve their master with the view to receive reward," is well known.[1] All the commentators on the sayings of the Fathers explain this sentence as meaning that love pure and simple is the only worthy motive of the worshipper. But we must not look upon this saying of Antigonos as on one of those theological paradoxes in which divines of all creeds occasionally indulge. It is a sentiment running through the Rabbinic literature of almost every age. Thus the words in Deut. 11 13, "To love the Lord your God," are explained to mean: "Say not, I will study the Torah with the purpose of being called sage or Rabbi, or to acquire fortune, or to be rewarded for it in the world to come; but do it for the sake of thy love to God, though the glory will come in the end."[2] The words in Ps. 112 1, "Blessed is the man who delighteth greatly in his commandments," are interpreted to mean, that he is blessed who delighteth in God's commandments, but not in the reward promised for his commandments.[3] This proves, by

[1] *Aboth*, 1:3. [2] *Sifre*, 84 a. Cf. above, p. 68.
[3] *Abodah Zarah*, 19 a.

the way, that the Rabbis could depart from the letter of the Scripture for the sake of the spirit, the succeeding verses in this very Psalm being nothing else than a description of the reward awaiting the pious man who fulfils God's commandments. In another place, those who, in view of Prov. 3 16, look out for the good things which are on the left side of wisdom, namely, riches and honours, are branded as wicked and base.[1] And when David said, "I hate them that are of a double mind, but thy law do I love," he indicated by it, according to the Rabbis, his contempt for mixed motives in the service of God, as the Law should not be fulfilled either under compulsion or through fear, but only from the motive of love. Indeed, God bears evidence to the unselfishness of Israel and their full confidence in him, saying, " I gave them affirmative commands and they received them; I gave them negative commands and they received them, and though I did not explain their reward, they said nothing" (making no objection).[2] In the devotional literature of the Middle Ages there is hardly a single work in which man is not warned against serving God with any intention of receiving reward, though, of course, the religionist is strongly urged to believe that God does reward goodness and does punish wickedness.[3]

---

[1] See *Num. R.*, 22 9.   [2] *M. T.*, 119 46, and *ibid.*, 119 1.

[3] See ספר חסידים, Parma, p. 254   Cf also Azulai, מדבר קדמות, s.v., לשמה. See also above, pp 67 *seq* and 68 *seq*. Cf. also Schechter, *Studies in Judaism*, 2d series, the essay on *Saints and Saintliness*.

Nor does salvation exactly depend on the number of the commandments man accomplishes. It is true that every law gives Israel an opportunity of acquiring merit (*Zachuth*), and inheriting thereby the world to come; for which reason the Holy One, blessed be he, multiplied to them Torah and commandments.[1] But this multiplication only aims at an increase of opportunities enabling man to accomplish at least *one* law in a perfect manner, which alone possesses the virtue of saving. "Even he who has done *one* of those things (enumerated in the 15th Ps.) is valued as much as if he had done all those things and shall never be moved,[2] and only he shall not escape the mouth of Sheol who has not accomplished a single law." [3] But the accomplishment of this single law must be, as already indicated, in the most perfect way. As R. Saadya Gaon states on Talmudic authority, the worshipper (*Obed*) is to be considered the man who at least set one law apart for himself which he should never transgress, or fall short of in any way.[4]

[1] See *Makkoth*, 23 *b*, Mishnah. Cf. *Tan. B.*, 4 87 *a*, and *Num. R.*, 17 2, and Friedmann, נספחים, p. 23.

[2] See *Makkoth*, 24 *a*; *M. T.*, 16 7. Cf. also *Sanhedrin*, 81 *a*. It should be remarked that the paraphrase of the Rabbis of this Ps. and of Ez., 18 6 *seq.*, implies even a higher standard than suggested by the literal sense of the Biblical text

[3] See the statement of R. Jochanan in *Makkoth*, *ibid*. Cf. Rabbinowicz in *Variae Lectiones, a. l.*

[4] אמונות ודעות, 5 : 8. His authority is *Jer. Kiddushin*, 61 *d*. As an instance of such a law, the commandment of honouring father and mother is given there.

In conformity with this is the view of Maimonides, who declares that it is an essential belief of the Torah that if a man fulfils even (only) one of the six hundred and thirteen laws in a perfect manner, so that it is not accompanied by any worldly consideration but done for the sake of the love of God, he becomes thereby worthy of the life of the world to come.[1] Maimonides illustrates his point by the story of a Rabbi (of the Tannaitic age), who was about to die the death of a martyr, but shortly before he suffered, he discussed with his friend his prospects of sharing in the life of the world to come. The answer he received was to the effect that if ever there came "an action into his hands," he may hope for it; that is, if he ever met with a case requiring a special effort to carry the law into effect. The Rabbi then remembered that in his capacity as treasurer of the charities in his city such a case did occur, and that he performed his duty to the full. It is thus neither the martyrdom which he was to undergo nor the routine life in accordance with the law which may readily be expected of any Rabbi, but the accomplishment of one commandment in a perfect way that secures salvation.[2] Somewhat similar is the

[1] See Maimonides, Commentary to *Mishnah Makkoth*, 3 16. It is not impossible that both R. Saadya and Maimonides were also thinking of *Mechilta* 33 *b*, where we read in the name of R. Nehemiah, "He who receives upon himself (even) a single law, in faith, is worthy that the Holy Spirit should rest upon him."

[2] See Maimonides, *ibid*. See also *Abodah Zarah*, 18 *a*. Cf. Albo, *Ikkarim*, 5 29.

following story: A certain Rabbi who held communion with Elijah asked the prophet one day when standing in the market whether he could discover among the crowd there any person destined for the life of the world to come. "No," answered the prophet. Subsequently Elijah perceived a certain person, then he said to the Rabbi, "This is the man of the world to come." Upon inquiry by the Rabbi, it was found that he was a jailer, and that he possessed the merit of watching over the chastity of the daughters of Israel, whom misfortune brought under his authority. A little later, the prophet again pointed out two more individuals as men of the world to come. When the Rabbi asked after their profession they answered, "We are cheerful persons and cheer up the depressed ones. Again, when we see two persons quarrelling, we endeavour to make peace between them."[1]

It must further be noted that even mere negative virtues are not without a certain saving power. "He who refrains from committing a sin, they reward him as if he accomplished a commandment."[2] It should however be stated that this view is greatly modified by some other opinions that only admit the merit of this negative disposition when the temptation to sin was very great, or when the man out of conscientious scruples abstained from an action, the sinful feature of which

[1] See *Taanith*, 22 a and *Jer. Taanith*, 64 b. Cf. also Albo, *ibid*.
[2] See *Mishnah Makkoth*, 3 15. Cf. *Sifre*, 125 a, *Kiddushin*, 39 b, and *Jer. Kiddushin*, 61 d.

was not fully established.¹ It is further modified by the following statement: "A man might think," the Rabbis teach, "considering that he avoids every opportunity of sin and is on his guard against evil (with his tongue) and falsehood, he can now indulge in sleep (idleness), neither committing sin nor doing good; therefore it is said 'Depart from evil and do good,'" (Ps. 34 14). And by "good" is meant the occupation with the Torah.²

The real motive of this enthusiasm for the Law must be sought in other sources than the hope of reward. Those who keep the commandments of God are his lovers. And when the lover is asked, Why art thou carried away to be burned, stoned, or crucified? he answers, Because I have studied the Torah, or, Because I have circumcised my son, or, Because I have kept the Sabbath; but he considers the suffering as wounds inflicted upon him for the sake of his beloved one, and his love is returned by the love of God.³ The Law is thus a means of strengthening the mutual relations of love between God and his people.⁴ The fulfilment of the Law was, in the eyes of the Rabbis, a witnessing on the part of the Jews to God's relationship to the world. "Why does this man," they say, "refrain from work on the Sabbath? why does he close his business on the seventh day? He does so in order to bear

---

¹ See *Kiddushin*, 31 b, and *Jer. Kiddushin*, 61 d. Cf. also *M.T.*, 1 7.
² See *Abodah Zarah*, 18 b and 19 a, and *M. T.*, 1 6.
³ *Mechilta*, 68 b.   ⁴ See *Mechilta*, 98 a.

witness to the fact of God's creation of the world, and to his providence over it."[1] The Law, according to the Rabbis, was a source of holiness. Each new commandment with which God blesses Israel adds holiness to his people; but it is holiness which makes Israel to be God's own.[2] They deduce this doctrine from Exod. 20 22, 30, which verse they explain to mean that it is the fact of Israel being holy men אנשי קדש which gives them the privilege of belonging to God. Hence the formula in many benedictions: "Blessed art thou, O Lord our God, ... who hast sanctified us by thy commandments, and found delight in us."[3] Another version of the same sort is, "Beloved are the commandments by which the Holy One, blessed be he, exalted the seed of his friend Abraham and gave them unto Israel with the purpose of beautifying and glorifying them; whilst Israel, his holy people, and his inheritance, glorify his name for the commandments and statutes he gave them. And it is because of these commandments that Israel are called holy.[4] These reasons, namely, the motive of love, the privilege of bearing witness to God's relationship to the world, the attainment of holiness in which the Law educated Israel, as well as the other spiritual motives which I have already pointed out, such as the joy felt

---

[1] See *Mechilta*, 104 *a*   [2] *Ibid*, 98 *a*.   [3] Baer, p. 198
[4] See ספר המוסר, ed. Mantua, 126 *b*. The diction of the passage shows that it has been taken from some ancient Midrash. See also above, p. 147. and below, p. 209.

by the Rabbis in the performance of the Law and the harmony which the Rabbis perceived in the life lived according to the Torah, were the true sources of Israel's enthusiasm for the Law. At least they were powerful enough with the more refined and nobler minds in Israel to enable them to dispense utterly with the motives of reward and punishment; though, as in every other religion, these lower motives may have served as concurrent incentives to a majority of believers.

XII

THE *ZACHUTH* OF THE FATHERS

Imputed Righteousness and Imputed Sin

The last chapter having treated of the righteousness achieved through the means of the Law and the sin involved by breaking it, it will be convenient to deal here with the doctrine of the זכות אבות (the Merits of the Fathers), the merits of whose righteousness are charged to the account of Israel. This doctrine plays an important part in Jewish theology, and has its counterpart in the belief that under certain conditions one person has also to suffer for the sins of another person. We have thus in Judaism both the notion of imputed righteousness and imputed sin. They have, however, never attained such significance either in Jewish theology or in Jewish conscience as it is generally assumed. By a happy inconsistency, in the theory of salvation, so characteristic of Rabbinic theology, the importance of these doctrines is reduced to very small proportions, so that their effect was in the end beneficial and formed a healthy stimulus to conscience.

The term זכות (*Zachuth*) is not to be found in the

Bible, though the verb occurs in the sense of being pure or of being cleansed.[1] In the Rabbinic literature, the verb זכה is sometimes used as a legal term meaning to be acquitted, to be in the right, to have a valid claim; whilst the noun *Zachuth* means acquittal.[2] Occasionally it also means to be worthy of a thing, or to be privileged.[3] In the *pi'el* it means to argue, to plead for acquittal.[4] Further, in a theological sense, to lead to righteousness,[5] to cause one or to give one the opportunity to acquire a merit, while the noun *Zachuth* is used in the sense of merit, virtue, which under certain conditions have a protective or an atoning influence.[6]

For the sake of obtaining a clearer view of the subject, which is rather complicated, we shall treat it under the following headings: (1) The *Zachuth* of a Pious Ancestry; (2) The *Zachuth* of a Pious Contemporary; (3) The *Zachuth* of the Pious Posterity.

(1) The *Zachuth* of the pious ancestry may generally be described as the זכות אבות (the *Zachuth* of the Fathers), but the term *Fathers* is largely limited in Rabbinic literature to the three patriarchs, Abraham, Isaac, and Jacob, God's covenant with whom is so often ap-

---

[1] See Micah 6 11; Ps 119 9; Job 25 4.

[2] See *Baba Meziah*, 107 b; *Mishnah, ibid.*, 1 4; *Mishnah Sanhedrin*, 4 1. See Jastrow's *Dictionary*, s.v. See also Bacher, *Terminologie*, I 50.

[3] See *Sota*, 17 a; *Chagigah*, 5 b.

[4] See, for instance, *Mishnah Sanhedrin*, 3 5.

[5] See *Aboth*, 5 18.   [6] See *Jer. Kiddushin*, 61 d, and *P R*, 38 b.

pealed to already in the Bible. The Rabbinic rule is, "They call not Fathers but the three (patriarchs), and they call not Mothers but four" (Sarah, Rebeccah, Rachel, and Leah).[1] The last statement with regard to the Mothers suggests also that there is such a thing as the זכות אמהות (the *Zachuth* of the Mothers). This is in conformity with the Rabbinic statement in reference to Lev. 26 42 regarding God's remembering his covenant with the patriarchs, that there is also such a thing as the covenant with the Mothers.[2] In another place they speak even distinctly of the *Zachuth of the Mothers*, "If thou seest the *Zachuth* of the Fathers and the *Zachuth* of the Mothers, that they are on the decline, then hope for the grace of God."[3] And it would even seem that they would invoke the *Zachuth* of the Mothers together with the *Zachuth* of the Fathers in their prayers on public fasts prescribed on the occasion of general distress.[4] In connection with the same verse (Lev. 26 42), the Rabbis speak also of the covenant with the Tribes ("the servants of the Lord"), to whom God has also sworn as he did to the patriarchs,

[1] *Berachoth*, 16 b. See, however, *D. E. Z.*, ch. 1, where they speak of seven Fathers who entered into a covenant with God. In *Sirach* (heading to c. 44), the expression *Fathers* is even more extensive.

[2] *T. K.*, 112 c.

[3] See *Jer. Sanhedrin*, 27 d, and *Lev. R.*, 36 6. Cf. commentaries, and see also *Cant. R.*, 2 9.

[4] See Pseudo-Jonathan to Exod. 18 9 and *Mechilta*, 54 a. In our liturgy, the invocation to the *Zachuth* of the Mothers is very rare. A *Piyut* (hymn) by R. Gershom b. Judah, recited on the eve of the New Year, has a reference to the covenant of the Mothers.

and whose *Zachuth* Moses is also supposed to have invoked, as he did that of the Fathers.[1]

It is, however, the *Zachuth* of the Fathers which figures most prominently in Rabbinic literature. The thought of the creation of the Fathers preceded the creation of the world.[2] They are the rocks and the hills,[3] but also the foundations of the world, for it is on their *Zachuth* that the world is based.[4] Abraham is the very *petra* on which the Holy One, blessed be he, established the world,[5] as it is said, "For the foundations of the earth are the Lord's" (1 Sam. 2 8), whilst the *Zachuth* of the Fathers is also occasionally called "rock."[6]

It is true that the Fathers are not considered absolutely perfect. They could not, according to some authorities, stand the rebuke (or judgement) of God.[7] And though their position is so exalted that their abode would have been translated into the regions above had they wished it, nevertheless, they did not receive the epithet "Holy" until they died.[8] Yet, in general, they are considered as the greatest and

---

[1] *T. K.*, 112 *c*; *Exod. R.*, 44 9 and 10. Cf. Isa 63 17. See also *P. R.*, 191 *a*.

[2] *P. R. E.*, 3   Cf. *Gen. R.*, 1 4

[3] See *Mechilta*, 54 *a*, and *Sifre*, 140 *a*. Cf. also *Exod. R.*, 28 1.

[4] *Exod. R*, 15 6.

[5] See *Yalkut* to *Pent.*, § 766, reproduced from the *Yelamdenu.* Cf. above, p. 59.

[6] See *Yalkut* to *Pent.*, § 763, reproduced from the *Yelamdenu.*

[7] See *Arachin*, 16 *a*.   [8] *M. T.*, 16 2   See also commentary.

the most weighty among Israel,[1] except the King Messiah, according to certain Rabbis also except Moses.[2] It is because of the *Zachuth* of the Fathers, or the Covenant with the Fathers, that Israel was redeemed from Egypt.[3] That Moses was permitted to ascend Mount Sinai and to mingle there with the celestials and receive the Torah, was also for the sake of the *Zachuth* of the Fathers.[4] When Israel sinned in the desert (by the worshipping of the golden calf), Moses uttered ever so many prayers and supplications and he was not answered. Indeed, his pleading for Israel lasted not less than forty days and forty nights, but all in vain. Yet when he said, "Remember Abraham, Isaac, and Jacob thy servants" (Exod. 32 13), his prayer was heard at once.[5] One Rabbi gets so exalted at the thought of the *Zachuth* of the Fathers that he exclaims to the effect: Blessed are the children whose fathers have a *Zachuth*, because they profit by their *Zachuth;* blessed are Israel who can rely upon the *Zachuth* of Abraham and Isaac and Jacob, it is their *Zachuth* which saved them. It saved them on the occasion of the exodus from Egypt, when they worshipped the golden calf, and in the times of Elijah,

[1] See *Sifre*, 94 *a*.

[2] See *Tan B.*, I 70, text and commentary, and *Sifre*, 27 *b*.

[3] See *Exod. R.*, 1 36. See also *Mechilta*, 48 *a*, where the patriarchs are described as sinless. The opinions seem to have been divided. Cf. ספרי דאגדתא, ed. Buber, 25 *a*. See also Nachmanides' commentary to Exod. 12 10

[4] *Gen. R.*, 28 1 and 2.   [5] *Shabbath*, 42 *a*. Cf. *Exod. R.*, 44 1.

and so in every generation.[1] Indeed, Israel is compared to a vine, because as the vine is itself alive, but is supported by dead wood, so Israel is living and lasting, but is leaning upon the deceased Fathers.[2] It is by reason of this support, that the righteous deeds of the Fathers are remembered before God. "Who was so active before thee (God) as Abraham, the lover of God? Who was so active before thee as Isaac, who allowed himself to be bound upon the altar? Who was so active before thee as Jacob, who was so thankful to God?"[3] Therefore, whenever Israel comes into distress they call into remembrance the deeds of the Fathers.[4]

Besides the *Zachuth* of the Fathers, κατ' ἐξοχήν limited to the patriarchs, there is also apparently the *Zachuth* of every man's ancestry. The father, we are taught, transfers (זוכה) to his son the benefits of beauty, strength, wealth and wisdom and (old) age.[5]

---

[1] *Ag. Ber.*, ch. 10.   [2] *Exod. R.*, 44 1. Cf. *Lev. R.*, 36 2.

[3] See *Cant. R.*, I 4. The special activities here are supplied from *Sifre*, p. 73 *b*.

[4] *Aggadath Shir Hashirim*, p 14. With regard to the sacrifice of Isaac, playing such an important part in the liturgy, see *Midrashim* to Gen., ch. 22, *P. K.*, 154 *a* and *b*, text and notes, and *P. R.*, 171 *b*, and reference given there. Cf. also *MHG.*, 314 *seq.*, and Beer, *Leben Abrahams*, pp. 57 *seq.*, 175 *seq.*

[5] *Mishnah Eduyoth*, 2 9. Cf. *Tosephta, ibid.*, p. 456, and *Tosephta Sanhedrin*, 4 32, and *Jer. Kiddushin*, 61 *a*. See also 63 *c*, and references, and *Tan. B.*, I 64 *b*. Cf. also *Kinyan Torah*, *A. R. N.*, 55 *b*, note 11, and 60 *b*, note 24, and Friedmann, נספחים, pp. 19 and 20, text and notes.

Though these benefits are all personal and merely hereditary, it would seem that they were not quite dissociated in the mind of the Rabbis from the notion connected generally with *Zachuth* and its theological possibilities. This is the impression, at least, we receive from the remark of one of the ancient Rabbis, who declares that these benefits cease with the moment man has attained his majority, when he becomes responsible for his conduct, and that it depends upon his own actions whether these benefits should continue or not.[1] In the well-known controversy between the patriarch Rabban Gamaliel the Second and his opponents, the general opinion was that preference should be given to R. Eliezer b. Azariah, above other nominees, because he was a man who enjoyed the *Zachuth* of his fathers, having been a descendant of Ezra.[2] "The son of fathers" (that is, a man of noble descent) was generally respected, though some would place him below the scholar or "the son of the Torah."[3] Indeed, he who had *Zachuth* of his fathers was thought that he could with less risk expose himself to danger than any other man.[4] They were also considered fit to act as the representatives of communities. "Let all men," said a Rabbi, "who are

---

[1] See *Tosephta Eduyoth*, *ibid.*, and compare Maimonides' commentary to the *Mishnah*, *ibid*. From the references given in *A. R. N*, *ibid.*, and Friedmann, נספחים, *ibid.*, it is also evident that the transferring of benefits are a special privilege of the righteous. Cf. also the *Responsa of the Geonim*, ed. Harkavy, p. 176.

[2] *Berachoth*, 27 a. [3] See *Menachoth*, 53 a. [4] See *Shabbath*, 129 b.

labouring with a Congregation (that is, leaders of communities occupied in social duties), act with them in the name of heaven, for the *Zachuth* of the fathers sustains them." And the larger the number of these righteous fathers, the more effective is the *Zachuth* by which their children profit.[1]

All these statements, however, with their exaggerating importance of the *Zachuth* of a righteous ancestry, are greatly qualified by another series of Rabbinic statements, reducing the *Zachuth* to small proportions. With regard to the *Zachuth* of the Fathers (or patriarchs), we have the astonishing assertion by the Rabbis that this *Zachuth* was discontinued long ago. The passage in question begins with the words, "When did the *Zachuth* of the Fathers cease?" In a parallel passage, it runs, "How long did the *Zachuth* of the Fathers last?" Various dates are fixed by various Rabbis, but none of them is later than the age of the King Hezekiah. The Scriptural proofs adduced by these Rabbis are not very cogent. The way, however, in which the question is put impresses one with the conviction that this cessation of the *Zachuth* of the Fathers was a generally accepted fact and that the only point in doubt was the exact date when this cessation took place.[2] But when this date was reached, the Holy One, blessed be he, exclaimed, "Until now you possessed the *Zachuth* of the Fathers, but for the

[1] *Aboth*, 2 12. See also *M T.*, 59 1.
[2] See *Shabbath*, 55 a, *Jer. Sanhedrin*, 27 d; and *Lev. R.*, 39 6.

178 *SOME ASPECTS OF RABBINIC THEOLOGY*

future, every one will depend on his own actions. I shall not deal with you as I dealt with Noah (who, according to certain Rabbis, protected with his *Zachuth* his unworthy sons). Fathers will no longer save their children." [1] Of course, Israel need not despair, for when every *Zachuth* of the ancestral piety disappears, Israel can always fall back on the grace of God, never to be removed.[2] Thus on the day when the Holy One, blessed be he, will judge Israel, the latter will look at the Fathers that they should plead for them, but there is no father who can save his son, and no man can save his brother in this distress. Then they will lift up their eyes to their Father in Heaven. In another place, the same thought is expressed to the following effect: Those generations (who passed through distress) will say unto him, "Master of the World, those of yore had the Fathers, whose *Zachuth* stood by them, but we are orphans, having no father, but thou hast written, 'For in thee the fatherless findeth mercy'" (Hosea 14 4).[3] There is however one Rabbi who objects to all the dates given, maintaining that the *Zachuth*

---

[1] *Ag Ber.*, ch. 10. The authority of *Ag. Ber.* seems to be an old *Baraitha.* Cf *Midrash Tannaim*, p. 62, § 9, where it even seems that the *Zachuth* of Noah continued much longer than the *Zachuth* of the Fathers, Israel only living on the *Zachuth* of the commandments. See also *Tan.* ויצא, § 13, with reference to Gen. 31 42, where the remark is made that the *Zachuth* of (honest) handicraft is greater than the *Zachuth* of the Fathers. Cf. *Berachoth*, 8 a.

[2] *Lev R., ibid.* See above, p. 172, note 3, with regard to the *Zachuth* of the Mothers.

[3] See *M. T.*, 121 1; *Ag. Ber.*, ch. 83.

of the Fathers lasts forever, and that Israel can always appeal to it, as it is said, "For the Lord, thy God, is a merciful God; he will not forsake thee, neither destroy thee, nor forget the covenant of thy fathers which he sware unto them" (Deut. 4 31).[1] This, however, is more of an appeal to the covenant with the Fathers than to the *Zachuth*, the covenant being unconditional and everlasting, independent of Israel's actions.[2] "And the truth of God endureth forever" (Ps. 117 2), is the covenant which God has established with the Fathers.[3] This is in accordance with the remark of one of the mediæval commentators of the Talmud, who says, "Though the *Zachuth* of the Fathers has ceased, the covenant of the Fathers never ended." He points to the liturgy where we bring into remembrance the covenant, *not* the *Zachuth*, of the Fathers.[4] Another commentator, again, explains that it is only the very wicked who may not rely any longer

[1] *Jer. Sanhedrin*, 27 d. Cf *Lev. R.*, 39 6.

[2] Remarkable is the expression in the *Mechilta of R. Simon*, p. 94, ברית אבות וזכות בנים.

[3] *M. T.*, 117 2.

[4] See *Tosafoth Shabbath*, 55 a. The appeal to the *Zachuth* of the Fathers is hardly represented in the original prayers, except if we take as such the words, "who rememberest the pious deeds of the patriarchs," in the first benediction of the Eighteen Benedictions. These words, however, are omitted in the most ancient versions of the Eighteen Benedictions. To the *covenant* with the Fathers, however, we have a very emphatic appeal in the *Musaf* (Additional) Prayer of the New Year. It is in the later liturgy where the *Zachuth* of the Fathers plays such an important part. See Zunz, *Synagogale Poesie*, p. 455. Cf. Rev. S. Levy's *Original Virtue*, p. 7.

on the *Zachuth* of the Fathers, whilst the righteous still profit by it. He further suggests that together with prayer the *Zachuth* of the Fathers may prove efficacious even now. This opinion receives some support from a statement of an ancient Rabbi, who declares that the *Zachuth* of the Fathers, which was so potent a factor on the occasion of the exodus from Egypt, would have been of little use but for the fact that Israel did repentance in time, since there was against their account also the consideration that they were soon to commit the sin of the golden calf.[1] Generally, it may be stated that the *Zachuth* of the Fathers still retained its hold on Jewish consciousness, at least in its aspect of the covenant, if not directly, as a fountain of grace on which the nation can rely at all times. In fact, the two aspects are sometimes closely combined. Thus we are told that God removes the sin of Israel on account of the *Zachuth* of the conditions (or covenant) which he made with Abraham, their father (between the Pieces).[2] Again, "When Moses the Prophet began to say those words (the Curses of Deut. 28 15-68) . . . the Fathers of the World

---

[1] See the commentaries to *Lev. R.*, 36 6, and *Exod. R.*, 1 36. Cf. Beer, *Leben Abrahams*, p. 202 *seq.*

[2] See *Cant. R.*, 1 14. Cf. Gen. 15 10. Cf. also *Deut. R.*, 2 23, where the verse to prove the effect of the *Zachuth* of the Fathers upon the redemption is Deut. 4 31, "For the Lord . . . will not . . . forget the covenant of thy fathers which he sware unto them." See also *Deut. R.*, 6 4, where they speak of the *Zachuth* of the Fathers, the covenant and the oaths, which are afterwards reduced to the *Zachuth* of the Fathers alone.

(the patriarchs) lifted their voices from their graves . . . and said, 'Woe to our children when they are guilty, and all these curses come upon them. How will they bear them? Will he make an end of them, as our *Zachuth* will not protect them, and there will be no man who will pray for them?' Then there came a daughter voice from the high heavens, and thus she said, 'Fear not, ye Fathers of the World. Even if the *Zachuth* of the generations should cease, your *Zachuth* will never end, nor will the covenant I made with you be dissolved and (these) will protect them.'"[1]

It was different with the *Zachuth* of the fathers, or ancestral piety in general, where no such covenant exists. Various passages have also been reproduced in proof of the Rabbinic belief in this *Zachuth*.[2] It is hardly necessary to remind one of the Biblical authority for this belief, the very Decalogue containing the words, "For I the Lord thy God am a jealous God, visiting the iniquity of the fathers upon the children unto the third and fourth generations of them that hate me; and showing mercy unto thousands of them that love me, and keep my commandments" (Exod. 20. 5 and 6). Some Rabbis, urging the plural "unto thousands," (meaning at least two thousand), infer from this that the period of grace is to last five hundred times as long as that of punishment,[3] the visiting of iniquity extending only to the third and fourth generations.

[1] *Pseudo-Jonathan*, Deut. 28 15.   [2] See above, p. 175 *seq.*
[3] See *Tosefta Sotah*, 298; *Sotah*, 11 a.   Cf. *Yoma*, 76 a.

Other Rabbis explain these words to stand for generations of indefinite number and without end,[1] or, as it is expressed in another place, by the accomplishment of a religious act man acquires merit for himself and for his posterity, "until the end of all generations."[2] But this *Zachuth* experiences many limitations. Thus, with reference to Deut. 7 9, in which the extension of this *Zachuth* is confined to a *thousand* generations, and which the Rabbis took as contradicting the verse just quoted from Exodus (extending it to two thousand generations), the explanation is given that this former verse refers to cases in which those who transfer the merit serve God only through motives of fear; hence, their merit is not so enduring and is subject to limitations in time.[3] The *Zachuth*, thus to have a more lasting effect, has to be acquired by the highest degree of perfection in the service of God, which is that accomplished through the motive of love. But even of more importance are the limitations made on the part of those who are to profit by these merits. We are referring to the emphatic statement of Hillel, who said, "If I am not for myself, who is for me, and being for myself, what am I?" which is explained to mean, "I must work out my own sal-

---

[1] *Mechilta*, 68 *b*   Cf. also לקח טוב to Deut. 7 9.

[2] *T. K*, 27 *a*. Cf. also *Yoma*, 87 *a*, where it is stated that both *Zachuth* and guilt have their effect until the end of all generations.

[3] See *Sotah*, 31 *a*, See Rashi's commentary as to the meaning of fear and love.

vation, yet how weak are my unaided efforts!"[1] This interpretation is supported by a paraphrase given of it in an older source, "If I have not acquired merit for myself, who will acquire merit for me, making me worthy of the life of the world to come? I have no father, I have no mother, I have no brother" (upon whose merits I can rely).[2] A similar opinion of the Rabbis is expressed with reference to Deut. 32 39, "Fathers save not their children: Abraham saved not Ishmael, Jacob saved not Esau; brothers save not brothers, . . . Isaac saved not Ishmael, Jacob saved not Esau. All the money in the world established no ransom, as it is said, 'Surely a brother redeemeth not a man, nor giveth to God a ransom for him" (Ps. 49 8).[3] Again, "Let not a man say, my father was a pious man, I shall be saved for his sake. Abraham could not save Ishmael, nor could Jacob save Esau."[4] Indeed, it would seem as if this were a generally accepted axiom, expressed in the words, "A father cannot save the son."[5] In the face of such statements, some of which became almost proverbial, there can be no doubt that the *Zachuth* of the fathers in no way served to silence the conscience of the individual, relieving him from responsibility for his actions. What this *Zachuth*

[1] *Aboth*, 1 15. Cf. Taylor on this saying. See also *A. R. N.*, 27 b, note 58.

[2] *A. R. N.*, 27 b.

[3] See *Sifre*, 139 b. Cf. *Targum* to Ps. 49 8 and 10, authorised version. See also *A. R. N., ibid.*, and *Sanhedrin*, 104 a.

[4] *M. T.*, 46 2. [5] *Sanhedrin, ibid.*

served mostly to establish was the consciousness of the historic continuity, and to increase the reverence for the past which has thus become both foundation and inspiration. But this very idea brought Israel new duties. "We are thy people," runs an old prayer, "the children of thy covenant, the children of Abraham, thy friend . . . the seed of Isaac . . . the congregation of Jacob, thy first-born son. . . . Therefore it is our duty to thank, praise, and glorify thee, to bless, to sanctify, and to offer praise and thanksgiving unto thy name."[1] And it is in the end the grace of God himself to which the congregation of Israel appeals. The congregation of Israel says to the holy one, blessed be he: We have no salvation but in thee, we hope only in thee.[2] Again, when Israel comes into distress, they say unto the Holy One, blessed be he: Redeem us! but God says unto them: Are there among you righteous and God-fearing men (by whose *Zachuth* they could profit)? They answer: In the former times of our ancestors, the days of Moses, Joshua, David, Samuel, and Solomon, we had (such righteous men), but now, the longer the exile lasts, the darker it becomes. Then God says, "Trust in my Name, and my Name will save you."[3] Again, the congregation of Israel said before the Holy One, blessed be he, "It is not for the sake of our righteousness and the good deeds we possess, that thou wilt

---

[1] See Singer, p. 8; Baer, p. 45.   [2] See *M. T.*, 88 1.
[3] See *M. T.*, 31 1 and references.

save us, but whether to-day or to-morrow, deliver us for the sake of thy righteousness."[1] And indeed, it was for his Name's sake that he redeemed them from Egypt; that he brought them to the Holy Land was also for his Name's sake, not for the sake of Abraham, Isaac, and Jacob; and so will the future redemption from Edom be effected for his Name's sake.[2]

Corresponding to the ancestral piety is the ancestral sin, which is charged, as indicated above, to the account of posterity that it may be made to suffer for it. As in the case of imputed righteousness, so they had also for the belief in imputed sin Biblical authority in the words of the Decalogue, "Visiting the iniquity of the fathers upon the children unto the third and fourth generation of them that hate me" (Exod. 20 5). But it did not escape the Rabbis that this is in contradiction with the verse, "The fathers shall not be put to death for the children, neither shall the children be put to death for the fathers: every man shall be put to death for his own sin" (Deut. 24 16).

[1] *M. T.*, 71 2.
[2] See *M. T.*, 107 1. This is in contradiction to the statement made above, p. 174, that it was the *Zachuth* of the Fathers which was effective at the redemption from Egypt. According to other Rabbis at every redemption both in the past and in the future, various factors come into consideration, among them the *Zachuth* of the Fathers and repentance. See also *M. T.*, 114 5, and references given there, with regard to the *Zachuth* which was effective on the occasion of that redemption. Cf. *Jer. Taanith*, 63 *d*; *M. T.*, 106 9, *Deut. R.*, 2 28; *P. R* , 184 *b*. The last adds, "It is repentance which causes the mercy of God and the *Zachuth* of the Fathers (to be effective)."

They tried to meet this difficulty by explaining that children are made to suffer for the sins of their fathers only when they perpetuate the wicked deeds of their parents, in which case they are considered as identical with their parents, for whose sins they are thus punished in addition to their own.[1] Rather interesting is the way in which one of the Rabbis puts this contradiction: "When the Holy One, blessed be he, said unto Moses, that he was visiting the sins of the fathers upon the children, Moses answered, 'Master of the world, how many wicked people have begot righteous children? Shall they share in the sins of their parents? Terah worshipped images, and Abraham his son was righteous; Hezekiah was righteous, whilst his father Ahaz was wicked. . . . Is it proper that these righteous sons should be punished for the sins of their fathers?' Thereupon, the Holy One, blessed be he, said unto him, 'Thou hast instructed me well. By thy life, I shall remove my words and will establish thy words,' as it is said, 'Fathers shall not be put to death for their children,' etc. (Deut. 24 16). 'By thy life, I will ascribe (these words) to

---

[1] See *Onkelos* and *Pseudo-Jonathan* to the verse in Exodus. *Sanhedrin*, 27 b. Cf. also *Mechilta*, 78 b and 114 a, and *P. K.*, 167 b, as well as *T. K.*, 112 b, with reference to Lev 26 39. Nachmanides in his commentary to this passage in Exodus explains this contradiction that the visiting of the sins of the fathers takes place only in the case of idolatry, whilst in other sins the suffering or the punishment is confined to the individual who committed the crime. However, he gives no Rabbinical authority for this opinion. Perhaps he was thinking of *Mechilta* 68 a, which explains that it is only in the case of idolatry that he is an אל קנא, whilst in the case of other sins he is רחום וחנון.

thy name,' as it is said, 'But the children of the murderers he slew not: according unto that which is written in the book of the law of Moses, wherein the Lord commanded, saying, "The fathers shall not be put to death for the children,"'" etc. (2 Kings 14 6).[1] The same contradiction the Rabbis also saw between Exodus 20 5 and Ezekiel 18 20, "The soul that sinneth, it shall die. The son shall not bear the iniquity of the father, neither shall the father bear the iniquity of the son: the righteousness of the righteous shall be upon him, and the wickedness of the wicked shall be upon him," and tried to reconcile it in the following way: That in the case of a man who is righteous, his wicked posterity is not liable to suffer for their *own* sins so quickly, the punishment being suspended for a time by the merits of their fathers; but in the case that a man is wicked, the visiting of his sins upon his wicked posterity will hasten the judgement of God, so that his children will at once be punished for their *own* evil deeds. In no case, however, will they suffer for the sins of their fathers.[2] Other Rabbis, however, saw in this contradiction a direct prophetic improvement upon the words of the Torah. "Moses said, 'God visits the sins of the fathers upon the children,' but there came Ezekiel and removed it and said, 'The soul that sinneth, it shall die.'"[3]

[1] See *Num. R.*, 19 33.   [2] See *Mechilta of R Simon*, p. 106.
[3] *Makkoth*, 24 a. Cf also *Ag Ber*, ch. 10, where it would seem that there was a certain point in history when neither ancestral righteousness nor ancestral wickedness were of any consequence to the children.

The prophetic view is the one generally accepted by the Rabbis.[1] As an exception we may perhaps consider the sin of Adam, causing death and decay to mankind of all generations.[2] When the Holy One, blessed be he, created Adam, the first, he took him around all the trees of the Paradise and he said to him: "See my works, how beautiful and excellent they are. All that I have created I have created for thy sake. Take heed that thou sinnest not and destroy my world. For if thou hast sinned, there is none who can repair it. And not only this, but thou wilt also cause death to that righteous man (Moses). . . ." It is to be compared to a woman with child who was in prison. There she gave birth to a son, whom she brought up within the prison walls before she died. Once the King passed before the door, and the son began crying: "My master, the King! Here was I born, here was

[1] See ספר חסידים, Parma, pp. 32 and 39, for some interesting remarks and fine distinctions on this point. See also Schechter, *Studies in Judaism*, p 266 *seq*.

[2] See *Eccles. R.*, 7 18, but see also *Gen R.*, 14 6. Cf *T. K.*, 27 *a*. Cf. *Num R.*, 9 49. Cf. *Pugio Fidei*, p. 675 (865), who seems, however, to have tampered with the text. There can be little doubt that the belief in the disastrous effects of the sin of Adam on posterity was not entirely absent in Judaism, though this belief did not hold such a prominent place in the Synagogue as in the Christian Church. It is also thought that in the overwhelming majority of mankind there is enough sin in each individual case to bring about death without the sin of Adam. *See Tan. B.*, I 11 *a*, and Shabbath 52 *a* and *b*. The doctrine was resumed and developed with great consistency by the Cabalists of the sixteenth century. Cf. also Ginzberg, *Die Haggada bei den Kirchenvatern*, p. 46

I brought up; for which crime am I placed here?"
The King answered, "For the crime of your mother."
Likewise there are certain national sins, as, for instance,
the sin of the golden calf, in the expiation of which
each generation contributes its small share, at least in
the coin of suffering.[1]

(2) The *Zachuth* of a Pious Contemporary (and
Contemporary Sin). The most important passage to
be considered in this connection is that relating to the
scale of merit and the scale of guilt. Believing fully in
the justice of God, the Rabbis could not but assume
that the actions of man form an important factor in
the scheme of his salvation, whether for good or for
evil. Hence the statement that man is judged in accordance with the majority of his deeds, and the world
in general, in accordance with the number of the righteous or wicked men it contains.[2] In accordance with
this is the notion of the scale of merit (or *Zachuth*)
and the scale of guilt. Assuming a man to be neither
particularly righteous nor particularly wicked, and the
world in general to consist of an equal number of right-
ous and wicked men, the fate of the world may be
determined by a single action added to the scale which
outbalances the other, and so may the fate of the whole
world depend on it. "He performed one commandment, and bliss is unto him, for he may by this have
inclined the scales (הכריע) both with regard to himself

[1] See *Jer. Taanith*, 68 *c*, and *Sanhedrin*, 102 *a*.
[2] See *Tosephta Kiddushin*, 336. *Kiddushin*, 40 *b*, and *Eccles R*, 10 1.

and with regard to the whole world to the side of *Zachuth.* He committed one sin, woe is unto him, for he may by this have inclined the scales both with regard to himself and with regard to the whole world to the side of guilt."[1]

The protective power of the *Zachuth* of the pious contemporary not only turns the scales to the side of *Zachuth* but "even maintains the world that was created by Ten Sayings."[2] The authority for such a belief is given in the well-known dialogue between God and Abraham regarding the absence of the righteous men in Sodom and Gomorrah (Gen. 18 24 *seq.*). And it is with reference to this dialogue that we are told that Abraham received the good message that the world will never be lacking in a certain number of righteous men even like himself, for whose sake the world will endure.[3] This number is differently given in the various sources, ranking between fifty and one. "Even for the sake of one righteous man the world is maintained, as it is said, 'the righteous is the foundation of the world'" (Prov. 10 25). Indeed, every day a daughter-voice comes from Mount Horeb, that says, "The whole world is fed for the sake of my son Chaninah, but he himself lives the whole week on a *Kab* of carobs."[4]

---

[1] See *Kiddushin*, 40 *b*, and references.   [2] See *Aboth*, 5 1.
[3] See *Gen. R.*, 49 8 The number given there is thirty *Chullin*, 92 *a*, speaks of forty-five. *P. R. E.*, ch. 25, has fifty. Cf. *P. K.*, 88 *a*, and *MHG.*, 278 The statement given in the text is from *Yoma*, 38 *b*.
[4] *Berachoth*, 17 *b* See also *Tan. B* , 5 25 *a* For the contemporary *Zachuth* on a more limited scale, see among others, *Taanith*, 20 *b* and 21 *b* ; *Baba Mezia*, 85 *a* ; *Sanhedrin*, 114 *a* ; and *Chullin*, 86 *a*.

As to the effect of contemporary sin it is hardly necessary to point out that a difference is to be made between the punishment to be decreed by the worldly court and that inflicted by heaven. The court in Rabbinic notion is strictly confined in its dealings to the sinner himself. In the case of Achan, it is even declared against the literal sense of the Scriptures, that his children did not really suffer. According to the Rabbis, they were only made to be present at the execution of their father, in order to come under the deterring effect of the whole procedure.[1] The judgement of heaven, however, makes the community responsible for the sins of the individual. They indeed fall heavily into the scale, but not on the ground of imputation, but by reason of solidarity, which was very strongly felt in the ancient Jewish community. "Israel," an ancient Rabbi expressed himself, "is like one body and one soul.... If one of them sinned, they are all of them punished."[2] The great principle was, all Israel are surety one for another.[3] "You are all surety for each other. If there is one righteous man among you, you will all be sustained by his merit, and not only you alone, but also the whole world; and when one sins, the whole generation will be punished."[4] This responsibility affects

[1] See Joshua 7 24 and 25. Cf. *Targum* and commentaries to these verses, and *Sanhedrin*, 44 *a*. Against this is to be noticed *P. R. E.*, 38, text and commentaries.

[2] See *Mechilta of R. Simon*, p. 95. Cf. *Lev. R.*, 4 6. See also Lewy, *Ein Wort uber die Mechilta des R. Simon*, p. 25.

[3] See *Sanhedrin*, 27 *b* and references

[4] *Tan. B.*, 5 25 *a* and references.

the community differently with different sins. In the case of a false oath, not only the transgressor suffers, but also his family as well as the rest of the world are visited by the divine judgement. In lighter sins, the community is only made responsible in the case when they could have protested against the crime to be committed, but failed to do so.[1] The family of the criminal suffers, of course, in a higher degree than strangers.[2] It would seem, further, that, as far at least as the judgement of heaven was concerned, there was a tendency to consider the relatives of a criminal as a sort of accessories to the crime. Thus the question is put with reference to Lev. 20 5, "If he sinned, what crime did his family commit?" The answer given is, "There is no family counting among its members a publican in which they are not all publicans. There is no family counting among its members a highwayman in which they are not all highwaymen."[3] Little children seem to form almost a part of their fathers' selves and suffer on that account for the sins of their parents. They are not included in the classes of children exempt by the law of Lev. 24 16.[4] The elders

[1] See *Shebuoth*, 39 a. [2] See *Shebuoth*, 39 b. See, however, next note.
[3] See *T. K.*, 91 c, *Pseudo-Jonathan* to the verse in Leviticus, and *Shebuoth, ibid*. The comment of the *Gemara* seems to labour under the difficulty of reconciling various Rabbinic sayings. More probable it is that this heavy responsibility of the family refers on the whole to the sins of a very serious nature, such as a false oath, the worshipping of Moloch, etc.
[4] See *Sifre*, 124 a, and cf. below, p. 175, where the reason is given that they stand surety for their parents. From a Midrash quoted in

and leaders, again, of the community are burdened with a special responsibility, as it is assumed that their protest may, by reason of their authority, prevent crime.[1]

The Scriptural words, "Cursed be he that confirmeth not all the words of this law to do them" (Deut. 27 26), are interpreted to refer to the worldly tribunal which fails in its duty to enforce the law and to protest against crime.[2] Again, with reference to Prov. 6 1, the Rabbis remarked: This verse refers to the student. As long as one is a mere student, he is not concerned in the community and will not be punished for the sin of the latter. But when he is appointed at its head and has put on the gown (a special dress which the Rabbi used to wear in his judicial capacity) . . . the whole burden of the public is upon him. If he sees a man using violence against his neighbour or committing an immoral action and does not protest, he will surely be punished.[3] Indeed, he who has the power of protesting and does not protest, he who has the power to bring Israel back to the good and does not bring them back, is responsible for all the bloodshed in Israel, as though he would have com-

---

MHG., 4 6, MS., it would still seem that the loss of children is only another kind of punishment of the father. אבל הצלת הקטנים אינה מצלת אלא לאביהן הקרוב בלבד מפני שנתיסר בהן. See also *Midrash Zuta*, 47, that this death or suffering of children for the sin of their fathers is only up to the age of 13. After this age it is for the child's own sin. Cf also Low's *Lebensalter*, p. 411.

[1] See *Shabbath*, 55 a. Cf. *Tan. B.*, 3 21 a and references there.
[2] See *Jer. Sotah*, 21 d.   [3] *Exod. R.*, 27 9.

mitted the murder himself. For, as already stated, all Israel are surety one for another. They are to be compared to a company sailing in a ship, of whom one took a drill and began to bore a hole under his seat. When his friends protested, he said, "What does this concern you? Is not this the place assigned to me?" They answered him, "But will not the water come up through this hole and flood the whole vessel?" Likewise the sin of one endangers the whole community.[1]

The community, however, according to the majority of the Rabbis, is not responsible for the sins committed in secret. "When Israel stood on Mount Sinai they all made up one heart to receive the kingdom of heaven in joy, and not only this, they pledged themselves one for the other. When the Holy One, blessed be he, revealed himself to make a covenant with them which should also include the secret things, they said, 'We will make a covenant with thee for the things seen, but not for the things secret, lest one among us commit a sin in secret and the whole community be made responsible.'"[2] This condition of Israel was accepted by God. "Things hidden are revealed to the Lord, our God, and he will punish for them, but things seen are given over to us and to our children forever, to do

---

[1] See *S. E.*, p 56. Cf also *Lev. R*, 4 6.

[2] *Mechilta*, 66 b The reading there is not quite certain. Cf. commentary In the text the reading of the *Yalkut* was partly followed. For opposite views, see Friedmann, Introduction to *S E.*, p. 73, and references given there to *Sanhedrin*, 43 b.

judgement concerning them."¹ Quite isolated seems to be the opinion according to which this exemption from mutual responsibility extended after the Revelation on Mount Sinai also to things seen. It is expressed in the following way: From the moment that God gave the Torah, it is only he who sins that will be punished, though before that the whole generation was responsible for the sin of the individual. Thus there were many righteous men swept away with the deluge in the times of Noah.² On the other hand, we have also the view that this responsibility extended also to things secret with the moment all Israel passed the Jordan (and established there a proper commonwealth).³ It was only after the destruction of the Second Temple, when the Sanhedrin gathered in Jabneh, that they were relieved from this responsibility, a voice from heaven proclaiming, "You need not busy yourselves with things hidden;"⁴ that is to say, that with the loss of Israel's political independence, and proper jurisdiction of the community over all its members connected with it, the solidarity was also, partially at least, relaxed.

(3) The *Zachuth* of a Pious Posterity, or the sin of a wicked posterity which has a retroactive influence upon their progenitors. With regard to sin there is

---

¹ See *Pseudo-Jonathan* to Deut. 29 6. ² *Tan.*, ראה, 3.
³ See *Sanhedrin*, 43 b. The reading is uncertain. See commentaries. Cf. also *Sifre*, 18 a; *A. R. N.*, 50 a and b, and references.
⁴ *Jer. Sotah*, 22 a.

only a faint trace of such a belief left in the earlier Rabbinic literature. It is with reference to Deut. 21 8, where the statement is made that even the dead are in need of an atonement, but the context shows that such an atonement is only needed in case of murder, which is supposed to have a damaging effect upon the ancestors of the murderer. It is not impossible that this notion was suggested by Ezekiel 18 10, "And if he begat a son that is a robber or a shedder of blood." The murderer is thus born already with the taint of his subsequent sin. But, if the ancestor can be affected by a sin not committed by himself, it is only reasonable that he should secure pardon by an atoning action accomplished by posterity.[1] More ample are the references to the *Zachuth* of a pious posterity. Thus the Holy One, blessed be he, acts kindly with the first (fathers) for the sake of the *Zachuth* of the latter ones (descendants), as was the case with Noah, who was saved for the sake of his children.[2] Abraham, again, became worthy of taking possession of the land for the sake of the *Zachuth* attaching to the commandment of bringing the first sheaf of their harvest, which Israel will accomplish.[3] There was even a saying that a son can make his father acquire a merit,[4] "for so they said,

---

[1] See *Sifre*, 112 *b* (§ 110), text and commentary, especially note 6. The text is not quite certain. The Halachic point of view of this question is fully treated by Azulai, שער יוסף, p. 54 *seq*

[2] *Gen. R.*, 29 6.   [3] See *P. K.*, 71 *a* ; *Lev. R* , 28 6.

[4] See *Sanhedrin*, 104 *a*.

Children save their parents from the judgement of Gehenna." And so Solomon said, "Correct thy son and he shall give thee rest; yea, he shall give delight unto thy soul" (Prov. 29 17); that is, he will deliver thee from the judgement in the Gehenna, and will delight thy soul in Paradise with the righteous.[1]

This relief coming from the children is, according to the source of the statement just given, only for four generations, God suspending the judgement of the ancestors till their great-grandchildren are grown up, by whose righteousness they might be relieved. "And so Samuel said to Israel, 'But if ye will not obey the voice of the Lord, but rebel against the commandment of the Lord, then shall the hand of the Lord be against you and against your fathers' (1 Samuel 12 15). Be therefore careful that you do not provoke the wrath of God and receive punishment, so that even your fathers, whose sins were in suspense, who were hoping for your redeeming merits will now be judged according to their deeds."[2] The relief by

---

[1] *MHG.*, Num. Ms., 81 a.

[2] *MHG., ibid.* He derives this doctrine from Exod. 20 5, taking the word פקד in the sense of depositing or entrusting. See *Mechilta of R. Simon*, p. 106, text and notes, and cf. *P K.*, 167 a. This interpretation is preceded by a long argument ascribed to Tannaitic authorities in favour of this doctrine. Cf. *Reshith Chochmah*, Section גדול בנים, ed Cracow, pp. 332 b, 334 b, and 375 a and b, where the contents of these extracts from *MHG* are to be found, but in a rather corrupt text. Some reminiscence of it is to be found in *Eccles. R.*, 4 1. See also רב פעלים, by R. Abraham of Wilna, p. 34 b, and ספר הלקוטים by Grunhut, 3 a, seg Cf also ספר חסידים, Parma, pp. 76 and 261. See also Rashi and Kimchi to Samuel 12 15.

the posterity is extended from children to the general public, and a principle is laid down that the living redeem the dead,[1] and indeed we find cases in Rabbinical literature where prayers were offered for the benefit of the dead.[2] It does not seem, however, that the doctrine took root in Jewish conscience. The whole of the original liturgy has not a single reference to the dead, nor is there during the first ten centuries of our era to be found a single fixed prayer for the benefit of those departed. The first time we meet with the practical question of the use of offering alms or prayers for the dead is in the *Responsa* of a certain Gaon in the eleventh century, who was asked whether the offerings made for the dead can be of any advantage to them. He seems to have been quite astonished by this question, and confesses his ignorance of such a custom.[3]

[1] See *Tanchuma*, האזינו, I; *Tan. B.*, Introduction, 90 a.

[2] See *Gen. R.*, 98 2, and reference given there; *Chagigah*, 15 b; *Sotah*, 10 b; *Makkoth*, 11 b. Cf. also Friedmann's נספחים, p. 23 *seq.*;
[2] Maccabees, 13 48 *seq.*

[3] See קבץ על יד of the Mekize Nirdamim, Berlin, 1886, pp. 16 and 17, and cf. *Hechaluz*, 13 98. Cf. also הגיון הנפש by R. Abraham b. Chiya, p. 58 *seq.*, and 32 a.

XIII

THE LAW OF HOLINESS AND THE LAW OF GOODNESS

HOLINESS is the highest achievement of the Law and the deepest experience as well as realisation of righteousness. It is a composite of various aspects not easily definable, and at times even seemingly contradictory. But diverging as the ideals of holiness may be in their application to practical life, they all originate in the conception of the kingdom, the central idea of Rabbinic theology, and in Israel's consciousness of its close relation to his God, the King.[1] In its broad features holiness is but another word for *Imitatio Dei*, a duty intimately associated with Israel's close contact with God. The most frequent name for God in the Rabbinic literature is "the Holy One," occasionally also "Holiness,"[2] and so Israel is called holy.[3] But the holiness of Israel is dependent on their acting in such a way as to become God-like.[4] "Ye shall be

[1] See above, p. 65 *seq.*

[2] See Blau, *Zur Einleitung*, p. 13; Bacher, *Terminologie*, I 169. See also Friedmann. Introduction to נספחים, p. 20.

[3] See *Tan. B.*, 3 87 b; *P.K.* 111 a; *S.E.* 133. Cf. also *Shabbath*, 86 a, and references given there.

[4] See *Num. R.*, 9 4 and 17 6.

holy, for I the Lord am holy" (Lev. 19 2). These words are explained by the ancient Rabbinic sage Abba Saul to mean "Israel is the *familia* (suite or bodyguard) of the King (God), whence it is incumbent upon them to imitate the King." [1] The same thought is expressed in different words by another Rabbi, who thus paraphrases the verse from Leviticus which has just been cited. "Ye shall be holy, and why? because I am holy, for I have attached you unto me, as it is said, 'For as the girdle cleaves to the loins of a man, so I have caused to cleave unto me the whole house of Israel'" (Jer. 13 11).[2] Another Rabbi remarked, "God said to Israel, Even before I created the world you were sanctified unto me; be ye therefore holy as I am holy;" and he proceeds to say, "The matter is to be compared to a king who sanctified (by wedlock) a woman unto him, and said to her: Since thou art my wife, what is my glory is thy glory, be therefore holy even as I am holy." [3] In other words, Israel having the same relation to God as the *familia* to the king, or as the wife to the husband, or as children to the father,[4] it follows that they should take him as their model, imitating him in holiness.

Before proceeding to some analysis of this *Imitatio Dei*, or holiness, as suggested by the Rabbinic literature,

---

[1] *T K.*, 86 c. Cf Bacher, *Ag Tan.*, 2 867, and Lewy, *Ueber einige Fragmente aus der Mischna des Abba Saul*, p 23.

[2] *Tan. B.*, 3 87 b Cf also *P.K.*, 16 a.

[3] *Tan. B.*, 3 87 a.   [4] See *Lev. R.*, 24 4.

it must be remarked that the Hebrew term *Kedushah* does not quite cover our term *holiness*, the mystical and higher aspect of it being better represented by the Hebrew term *Chasiduth* (saintliness), for which Kedushah is only one of the preparatory virtues;[1] though the two ideas are so naturally allied that they are not always separated in Rabbinical texts. I shall, nevertheless, in the following pages classify my remarks under the two headings of *Kedushah* and *Chasiduth*. The former moves more within the limits of the Law, though occasionally exceeding it, whilst the latter, aspiring to a superior kind of holiness, not only supplements the Law, but also proves a certain corrective to it.

As we have seen, holiness, according to Abba Saul, is identical with Imitation of God. The nature of this imitation is defined by him thus: "*I and he*, that is like unto him (God). As he is merciful and gracious, so be thou (man) merciful and gracious."[2] The Scriptural phrases "walking in the ways of God" (Deut. 11 22), and "being called by the name of God" (Joel 3 5), are again explained to mean, "As God is called merciful and gracious, so be thou merciful and

---

[1] See *T B Abodah Zarah*, 20 *b*, and Rabbinowicz, *Variae Lectiones* to the passages. All the parables, however (given by Bacher in his *Ag. Tan.* 2, p 496, note 5, to which *Midrash Prov.*, 15, is also to be added), have חסידות close to רוה״ק

[2] *Mechilta*, 37 *a*, and *Shabbath* 133 *b* and parallels The interpretation of Abba Saul is based on the word ואנוהו in Exod. 15 2, which he divides into אני והו, meaning, "I (man) and he (God)." See also above, pp. 90 and 119.

gracious; as God is called righteous, so be thou righteous; as God is called holy, so be thou holy."[1] Again, as the way of heaven is that he is ever merciful against the wicked and accept their repentance, so be ye merciful against each other. As he bestows gifts on those who know him and those who know him not and deserve not his gifts, so bestow ye gifts upon each other.[2] "The profession of the Holy One, blessed be he, is charity and loving-kindness, and Abraham, who will command his children and his household after him 'that they shall keep the way of the Lord' (Gen. 18 19), is told by God: 'Thou hast chosen my profession; wherefore thou shalt also become like unto me, an ancient of days.'"[3] The imitation receives practical shape in the following passage: "The members of the house of Israel are in duty bound to deal with one another mercifully, to do charity (*Mizwah*), and to practise kindness. For the Holy One, blessed be He, has only created this world with loving-kindness and mercy, and it rests with us to learn from the ways of God." Thus said Rabbi Chama b. Chaninah, ". . . Walk in the attributes of God (or rather make his attributes the rule for thy conduct). As he clothes the naked (Gen. 3 21), so do thou clothe the naked; as he nurses the sick (Gen. 18 1), so do thou nurse the sick; as he comforts the mourners (Gen. 25 11), so do thou comfort the mourners; as he buries the dead

[1] *Sifre*, 85 *a* It seems that the Rabbis read in Joel יִקְרָא.
[2] *S.E.*, p 135. Cf. *Mechilta*, 59 *a*   [3] See *Gen R.*, 58, 9.

(Deut. 34 5), so do thou bury the dead." [1] Again, when R. Judah b. Ilai interrupted his lectures in order to join the bridal procession, he would address his disciples with the words, "My children! rise and show your respect to the bride (by joining the procession), for so we find that the Holy One, blessed be he, acted as best man to Eve." [2] Indeed, it is maintained that God himself observes the commandments, acting in this respect as an example to his children.[3] The imitation is further extended to mere good manners, in which God is also taken as a model. Thus, for instance, we are told by the Rabbis: Let man learn proper behaviour from the Omnipresent, who, though knowing the absence of righteous men from Sodom and Gomorrah, did not interrupt Abraham in his intercession for these cities, but waited until he finished his pleading and even took leave before parting with him.[4]

It is to be remarked that this God-likeness is con-

[1] *Sotah*, 14 *a*. The beginning of the passage is taken from the שאילתות פ׳ בראשית. According to the Agadic explanations Abraham was in an invalid state when God appeared to him in the plains of Mamre. The blessing, again, spoken of in Gen. 25 11, which took place after the death of Abraham, was meant as a message of condolence.

[2] See *A. R. N.*, 10 *a*. The words, "And he brought unto the man" (Gen. 2 28), are understood by the Rabbis that God took particular care to present Eve to Adam in the adorned state of a bride. See *Gen. R.*, 731.

[3] See *Jer. Bikkurim*, 66 *c*, and *Lev. R.*, 35 3.

[4] See *D. E.*, ch 5. I supplemented the passage with the parallel in *A. R. N.*, 56 *a*. Cf. also *Gen. R.*, 8 8; *Tan. B.*, I 28 *b*; and *Sukkah*, 30 *a*.

fined to his manifestations of mercy and righteousness, the Rabbis rarely desiring the Jew to take God as a model in his attributes of severity and rigid justice, though the Bible could have furnished them with many instances of this latter kind. Interesting in this connection is the way in which the commandment of the Imitation was codified by some of the later authorities: "The Holy One, blessed be He, ordained that man should cleave to his ways, as it is written, 'Thou shalt fear the Lord thy God, him shalt thou serve, and to him shalt thou cleave' (Deut. 10 19). But how can man cleave to the *Shechinah?* Is it not written, 'For the Lord thy God is a consuming fire, a jealous God'? (Deut. 4 24). But cleave to his ways: as God nurses the sick, so do thou nurse the sick, and so forth."[1] The feature of jealousy is thus quite ignored, whilst the attributes of mercy and graciousness become man's law. Indeed, it is distinctly taught that man should not imitate God in the following four things, which He alone can use as instruments. They are, jealousy (Deut. 6 5), revenge (Ps. 94 1), exaltation (Exod. 15 21, Ps. 93 1), and acting in devious ways.[2] The prophet Elijah, who said, "I have been very jealous for the Lord God of Hosts" (1 Kings 19 10), and even repeated the denunciation of Israel (*ibid.*

---

[1] R. Eliezer of Metz, ספר יראים, § 3. See also Maimonides, מ׳ה׳ס, מ״ע ח׳.

[2] *MHG.*, p 549; cf. פרקא דרבינו הקדוש, ed. Schonblum, § 34 in the Five Groups.

v. 14), was, according to the Rabbis, rebuked by God, who answered him, "Thou art always jealous," and was removed from his prophetic office, Elisha being appointed prophet in his stead.[1]

The second or negative aspect of holiness is implied in the Hebrew word *Kedushah*, the original meaning of which seems to be "separation" and "withdrawal."[2] So the Rabbis paraphrase the verse, "Sanctify yourselves, therefore, and be holy, for I am holy" (Lev. 11 44), with the words, "As I am separated, so be ye separated."[3] By the separateness of God is not meant any metaphysical remoteness, but merely aloofness and withdrawal from things impure and defiling, as incompatible with God's holiness, whence Israel should also be removed from everything impure and defiling.

Foremost among the things impure, which range very widely, are: idolatry, adultery, and shedding of blood. To these three cardinal sins the term *Tumah* (defilement) is especially applied.[4] The defiling nature of the second (including all sexual immorality) is particularly dwelt upon in Rabbinic literature. Thus

[1] See *S. E. Z.*, p. 187; and *Yalkut* to *Kings*, § 217. Cf. also *Cant. R.*, 1 6; *Agadath Shir Hashirim*, p 45. See also above, p. 52.

[2] See Robertson Smith's *Religion of the Semites*, p 140, about the uncertainty of the original meaning of the word.

[3] *T. K.*, 57 b Cf. *ibid.*, 86 c.

[4] See *Moreh Nebuchim*, 3 47. Maimonides' explanation was undoubtedly suggested to him by *T. K.*, 81 a (to Lev. 16 16). Cf below, p. 122 *seq*. See also *Sifre*, 113 a, where it is said of the daughters of Israel that they are קדושות וטהורות.

the Rabbis interpret the verse, "And ye shall be unto me a kingdom of priests and a holy nation" (Exod. 19 1), with the words, "Be unto me a kingdom of priests, separated from the nations of the world and their abominations."[1] This passage must be taken in connection with another, in which, with allusion to the scriptural words, "And ye shall be holy unto me ... and I have severed you from other people that you should be mine" (Lev. 20 26), the Rabbis point to the sexual immorality which divides the heathen from Israel.[2] In fact, all incontinence was called *Tumah* (impurity), indulgence in which disqualifies (or cuts man off from God); God says, "What joy can I have in him?"[3] but he who surrounds himself with a fence against anything unchaste is called holy,[4] and he "who shutteth his eyes from seeing evil (in the sense of immorality) is worthy of receiving the very presence of the *Shechinah*."[5]

The notion of impurity is further extended to all things stigmatised in the Levitical legislation as unclean, particularly to the forbidden foods "which

---

[1] *Mechilta*, 63 a. A few lines before these is given another explanation to the words וגוי קדוש, which was taken by the great master of the Agada, Lector Friedmann, to contain a protest against proselytising. The text, however, seems to be corrupt, and reads in the *MHG*.,

יכול מלכים בעלי מלחמה ת״ל כהנים אי כהנים יכול בטלנים
בענין שכ׳ ובני דוד כהנים היו ת״ל וגוי קדוש. Cf. *Mechilta of R. Simon*, p. 95.

[2] *T. K.*, 93 b. Cf. *Num. R.*, 9 7.
[3] *T. K.*, 86 d.
[4] *Lev. R.*, 26 8.
[5] See *Lev. R.*, 23, end.

make the soul abominable," the command being, "Be holy in your body." The observance of these laws the Rabbis seem to consider as a special privilege of Israel, marking the great distinction between them and the "descendants of Noah,"[1] whilst in the transgression of them they saw the open door leading to idolatry; in a word, to a deeper degree of impurity.[2]

The soul is also made abominable — and hence impure — according to the Rabbis, by doing anything which is calculated to provoke disgust, as, for instance, by eating from unclean plates or taking one's food with filthy hands.[3] In fact, to do anything which might have a sickening effect upon others is ranked among the hidden sins which "God shall bring into judgement";[4] but he who is careful to refrain from things filthy and repulsive brings upon himself a particular holiness purifying his soul for the sake of the holy one; as it is said, "Ye shall sanctify yourselves."[5]

---

[1] See *Exod. R.*, 30 9, and *ibid*, 31 9. Cf. *Tan. B.*, 3 14 b, and see also *Pseudo-Jonathan* to Lev. 20 7.

[2] This seems to me to be the meaning of the words in *D. E. Z.*, ch. 3, תחלת טומאות פתח לע״ז. See *T. K*, 57 b, ואם טמאים אתם בהם סופכם ליטמא בם and cf. the ראב״ד. The other explanation given there suggests our passage to be a parallel to that quoted in the preceding note from the *D. E. Z.* Perhaps we should read in *T. K.*, סופכם ליטמא בע״ז.

[3] See *T. B Makkoth*, 16 b, and Maimonides, הלכות מאכלות אסורות, § 17, the last five הלכות.

[4] See *T. B. Chagigah*, 5 a, the explanation of Rab. to Eccles, 12 14.

[5] Maimonides, *ibid*. Cf *T. B. Berachoth*, 53 b, the last line of the page.

Lastly, we have to record here that view which extends the notion of impurity to every transgression of Biblical law. Every transgression has the effect of stupefying the heart,[1] whilst the observance of the laws in the Torah is productive of an additional holiness.[2] According to this view, all the commandments, negative and affirmative, have to be considered as so many lessons in discipline, which if only as an education in obedience, result in establishing that communion between man and God which is the crowning reward of holiness. Thus the Rabbis say, with allusion to the verse, "That ye may remember and do all my commandments and be holy unto your God" (Num. 15 40), "Heart and eyes are the two middlemen of sin in the body, leading him astray. The matter is to be compared to a man drowning in water, to whom the shipmaster threw out a cord, saying unto him, Hold fast to this cord, for if thou permit it to escape thee, there is no life for thee. Likewise, the Holy One, blessed be he, said to Israel, 'As long as you cling to my laws, you cleave unto the Lord your God (which means life). . . . Be holy, for as long as you fulfil my commandments you

---

[1] See *T. B. Yoma*, 39 *a*, תני דבי ר שמטאל עבירה, etc. By עבירה in this passage is meant the transgression of any law.

[2] See *Mechilta*, 98 *a*, and *T. K.*, 35 *a*, and 91 *d*, קדושת כל המצות. The *MHG.* also seems to read in *T. K.* (to Lev. 11 44), והתקדשתם זו קדושת מצות; a reading which is confirmed by Maimonides when he says (*Moreh Nebuchim*, 3 88. 47), אמנם אמרו יתעלה והתקדשתם * * * ס׳ה׳מ, § 4. Cf. also his לשון ספרא זו קדושת מצות.

are sanctified, but if you neglect them, you will become profaned.'"[1]

Thus far holiness still moves within the limits of the law, the obedience to which sanctifies man, and the rebellion against which defiles. There is, however, another superior kind of holiness which rises above the Law, and which, as already indicated in the opening remarks of this chapter, should be more correctly termed *Chasiduth* (saintliness). The characteristic of the Chasid, as it is somewhere pointed out, is that he does not wait for a distinct commandment. He endeavours to be pleasant to his Maker, and like a good son studies his father's will, inferring from the explicit wishes of the father the direction in which he is likely to give him joy.[2] Hence the tendency of the Chasid to devote himself with more zeal and self-sacrifice to one law or group of laws than to others; just according to the particular bent of his mind, and the individual conception of the will of his father. Thus Rab Judah perceives the "things of *Chasiduth*" in paying particular attention to the tractate *Nezikin* (Damages), including the laws regarding the returning of lost goods, prohibition of usury, etc., and in avoiding anything which might result in injury to a fellow-man. Rabba again defines *Chasiduth* as carrying out the prescriptions in the tractate of *Aboth*; a tractate, be it observed, in which the ritual element is quite absent, as it is limited

---

[1] *Num R.*, 17 6. See also above, p. 168.
[2] See Luzzatto, מסילת ישרים, ed. Warsaw, p. 24 b.

to the moral sayings and spiritual counsels given by the ancient Jewish authorities. Another (anonymous) author thinks that *Chasiduth* consists in closely observing the laws prescribed in the (liturgical) tractate *Berachoth* (Benedictions), prayer and thanksgiving having been probably the particular passion of this Rabbi.[1]

The principle of *Chasiduth* is perhaps best summarised by the Talmudic formula, "Sanctify thyself even in that which is permitted to thee."[2] R. Eliezer, of Worms, who takes this saying as the motto to one of his chapters on the *Regulations of Chasiduth*, comments upon it to the effect: "Sanctify thyself and thy thoughts, reflect upon the unity (of God, and think of) whom thou art serving, who (it is that) observes thee, who (it is that) knows thy deeds, and who (it is) to whom thou wilt return. . . . Hence be (in ritual questions) stringent with thyself and lenient towards others. . . . The Torah in certain cases made concessions to the weakness of the flesh (hence the law cannot always be taken as the supreme standard of conduct). Take no oath even for the truth. . . . Keep thee from every wicked thing (Deut. 23 11), which means, among others, not to think even of the things impure," etc.[3] Impure thinking was, in the Rabbinic

[1] See *Baba Kama*, 30 a, text and commentaries, especially the ר"ן to their corresponding place in the רב אלפס. For the ten things of the *Chasiduth* which Rab is said to have observed (mixture of the ceremonial and moral) see *Sefer Ha-Orah*, ed. Buber, pp 3 and 4.

[2] See *Sifre*, 95 a; *T B. Jebamoth*, 20 a.

[3] See R. Eliezer of Worms, Introduction to the רוקח.

view, the antecedent to impure doing, and the ideal saint was as pure of heart as of hand, acting no impurity and thinking none.

Very expressive is Nachmanides, whose comments on the Rabbinic paraphrase of Lev. 11 44, "As I am separated so be ye separated," are to the following effect: —

According to my opinion, by the Talmudic term פרישות *separateness*, is not meant the abstaining from *Arayoth* (sexual intercourse forbidden in the Bible), but something which gives to those who practise it the name of Perushim. The matter (is thus): The Torah has forbidden *Arayoth* as well as certain kinds of food, but allowed intercourse between man and his wife as well as the eating of meat and the drinking of wine. But even within these limits can the man of (degenerate) appetites be drenched in lusts, become a drunkard and a glutton, as well as use impure language, since there is no (distinct) prohibition against these things in the Torah. A man could thus be the worst libertine with the very license of the Torah. Therefore the Scriptures, after giving the things forbidden absolutely (in detail), concluded with a general law (of holiness), to show that we must also abstain from things superfluous. As for instance, that even permitted sexual intercourse should be submitted to restrictions (of holiness), preserving it against degenerating into mere animal lust; that the drinking of wine should be reduced to a minimum, the Nazir being called holy because he abstains from drink; and that one should guard one's mouth and tongue against being defiled by gluttony and vile language. Man should indeed endeavour to reach a similar degree of holiness to R. Chiya, who never uttered an idle word in his life. The Scriptures warn us to be clean, pure, and separated from the crowd of men who taint themselves with luxuries and ugliness.[1]

It will be observed that this corrective of the Law is not considered by Nachmanides as a new revelation; according to him it is implied in the general scriptural rule of holiness, which, of course, considering the indefinable nature of holiness, can be extended to any length. Nor were the Rabbis conscious of any innovation in or addition to the Torah when they promulgated the principle of sanctifying oneself by refraining from things permitted; a principle which can be and was applied both to matters ritual as well as to morals and conduct.[2] As it would seem, they simply looked upon it as a mere "Fence" (*Geder*) preventing man from breaking through the limits drawn by the Torah itself. Very instructive in this respect is the conversation which the Talmud puts in the mouth of King David and his friend Hushai, the Archite. When David was fleeing before his rebellious son Absalom, he is reported to have been asked by Hushai, "Why hast thou married a cap-

[1] Commentary to the Pentateuch, Lev. 19 2.
[2] See רוקח, *ibid.*, where he deducts from it certain stringent rules, regarding the dietary laws as well as others bearing on conduct.

tured woman?" For, according to Rabbinic legend, Absalom's mother Maacah (2 Sam. 3 3) was a woman taken captive in war. Hushai thus accounted for the misfortune which had befallen David by this unhappy marriage. But David answered him, "Has not the Merciful allowed such a marriage?" (Deut. 21 10-13), whereupon Hushai rejoins, "Why didst thou not study the order of the Scriptures in that place?" In other words, the fact that the regulations regarding the woman taken captive in war are closely followed by the law concerning the stubborn and rebellious son (Deut. 21 18-21), indicates that the Torah, though not absolutely forbidding it, did not wholly approve of such a marriage, but foretold that its offspring was likely to prove a source of misery to his parents.[1] The corrective of the Law, for the neglect of which corrective David is so terribly punished, is thus effected, not by something antagonistic to or outside of it, but by its own proper interpretation and expansion. As another instance of this kind I quote the following, which, rendered in the old Rabbinic style, would run thus: "We have heard that it is written, 'Thou shalt not kill' (Exod. 20 13). We should then think that the prohibition is confined to actual murder. But there are also other kinds of shedding blood, as, for instance, to put a man to shame in public, which causes his blood to leave his face. Hence to cause this feeling is as bad as murder, whence he who is guilty of it loses his share in the world to come."[2] Again,

[1] See *T. B. Sanhedrin*, 107 a. [2] See *T. Z. Baba Mezia*, 59 a.

we have heard that it is written, 'Thou shalt not commit adultery' (Exod. 20 14). But the phrase in Job (24 15), 'The *eye* also of the adulterer waiteth for twilight,' teaches us that an unchaste look is also to be considered as adultery; and the verse, 'And that ye seek not after your own heart and your own eyes, after which ye used to go a whoring' (Num. 15 39), teaches us that an unchaste look or even an unchaste thought are also to be regarded as adultery."[1]

The law of goodness, closely connected with the law of holiness, is another corrective of the Law. It developed from such general commandments as the one in Deuteronomy, "And thou shalt do that which is right and good in the sight of the Lord" (6 18), which, as Nachmanides aptly remarked, means that the Torah bids man to direct his mind to do what is good and upright in the sight of God, seeing that God loves goodness and uprightness. He proceeds to say, "This is an important point, for it is impossible to refer in the Torah to all the relations between man and his neighbours, and his friends, his business affairs, and to all the improvements bearing upon one's community and one's

---

[1] See *Lev. R.*, 23 11. Cf. *P. R.*, 124 *b*, text and notes. See also *Mechilta* of R. Simon, 111, ר״א לא תנאף שלא ינאף ··· ולא בעין ולא בלב ומנין שהעין והלב מזנין דכתיב ולא תתורו אחרי לבבכם ואחרי עיניכם. Cf also New Testament, Matt. 5 21 and 27. I suspect that the expression in the N. T., "Ye have heard," had originally something to do with the Talmudic formula שומע אני ··· ת״ל, or ··· שמענו לא, or ··· ת״ל אלא, or במשמע ··· ת״ל (see *Mechilta*, 81 *b*, 82 *b*, and 84 *a*). Cf. also below, 224 *seq*.

country." But after the Torah had mentioned many such laws in another place (Lev. 19), it repeats in a general way that man has to do what is good and upright, which includes such things as arbitration (in the case of money litigations) and the not insisting upon the strict law. It further includes certain laws relating to neighbourly considerations as well as to kindly behaviour towards one's fellow-men.[1] Jerusalem indeed was destroyed only because of the sin that they insisted upon the law of the Torah,[2] thereby transgressing the law of goodness. According to others, this precept of not insisting upon the law of the Torah, and acting in a merciful way, is to be derived from Exod. 18 20, where Moses is asked to make Israel acquainted both with the Law and with the (merciful) actions going beyond the Law.[3] As a practical illustration of this law of goodness, we quote here the following case: Rabba Bar bar Chana had a litigation with carriers who broke (during their work) a cask of wine. He then took away their clothes; whereupon they brought to Rab a complaint against him. Rab

---

[1] See Nachmanides' commentary to Deut. 6 18. Cf. Deut. 12 28 and 14 19. See also *Sifre*, 91 *a* and 94 *a*, on these verses. Cf. also Maimonides, שכנים, 14 8, text and commentaries.

[2] *Baba Meziah*, 13 *b*.

[3] See *Mechilta*, 59 *b*, *Baba Meziah*, 30 *b*; cf. also *Pseudo-Jonathan* to this verse in Exod., where it is emphasised that this merciful treatment beyond the law should extend also to the wicked דין and לפנים משורת הדין correspond often with מדת הדין and מדת הרחמים, the quality of law or justice and the quality of mercy. See *Jer. Baba Kama*, 6 *c*. Note the use of these terms of men.

said to him, "Give them back their clothes." Rabba then asked, "Is this the law?" He said, "Yes (as it is said, 'Thou mayest walk in the way of the good' [Prov. 2 20])." He gave them back their clothes. The carriers then said, "We are poor men and laboured the whole day, and now we are hungry and have nothing to eat." Rab then said, "Pay them their wages." Whereupon Rabba again asked, "Is this the law?" He said, "Yes (as it is said), 'And keep the path of the righteous' [Prov. *ibid.*]."[1] A not less striking case is the following: The Roman army once besieged the town of Lydda, and insisted upon the delivering up of a certain Ula bar Koseheb, threatening the defenders with the destruction of the place and the massacre of its inhabitants in case of further refusal. R. Joshua ben Levi then exerted his influence with Ula, that he would voluntarily deliver himself to the Romans so that the place might be saved. Thereupon, the prophet Elijah, who often had communion with R. Joshua ben Levi, stopped his visits. After a great deal of penance, which the Rabbi imposed upon himself, Elijah came back and said, "Am I expected to reveal myself to informers?" Whereupon the Rabbi asked, "Have I not acted in accordance with the strict letter of the law?" "But," retorted Elijah, "this is not the law of the saints."[2]

---

[1] *Baba Meziah*, 83 *a*. See also Rabbinowicz, *Variae Lectiones*, *a.l.*
[2] See *Jer. Terumoth*, 46 *b*. Cf. Schechter, *Studies in Judaism*, Second Series, pp. 116 *seq.* and 166 *seq.*

The crowning reward of *Kedushah*, or rather *Chasiduth*, is, as already indicated, communion with the Holy Spirit, "Chasiduth leading to the Holy Spirit," or, as it is expressed in another place, "Holiness means nothing else than prophecy." [1] This superior holiness, which implies absolute purity both in action and thought, and utter withdrawal from things earthly, begins, as a later mystic rightly points out, with a human effort on the part of man to reach it, and finishes with a gift from heaven bestowed upon man by an act of grace.[2] The Talmud expresses the same thought when we read, "If man sanctifies himself a little, they (in heaven) sanctify him much; if man sanctifies himself below (on earth), they bestow upon him (more) holiness from above." [3] "Everything is in need of help (from heaven)." [4] Even the Torah, which is called pure and holy, has only this sanctifying effect, when man has divested himself from every thought of pride, when he has purified himself from any consideration of gold and silver, when he is indeed quite pure from sin." [5] Only Torah with holiness can bring about communion with God. Thus runs a prayer, or rather prophecy, by an ancient Rabbi: "Learn with

[1] ואת הקדוש והקריב אין קדושה אלא נבואה שנאמר אין קדוש כה׳, *Midrash* in Ms. Cf. also *Monatsschrift*, vol. 50, beginning of p. 410, given from the *Sifre Zuta*.

[2] ענין הקדושה ‥ ‥ תחלתו השתדלות וסופו מתנה, 36 *a*, מסילת ישרים

[3] *T. B. Yoma*, 39 *a*.

[4] *Midrash* to Ps. 20. Cf. *Tan* קדושים, 9.

[5] See *Mechilta of R Simon*, 98 Cf. above, p. 160.

all thy heart and all thy soul to know my ways, and to watch the gates of my Torah. Preserve my Torah in thy heart, and may my fear be present before thy eyes. Guard thy mouth against all sin, and make thyself holy against all sin and injustice, and I will be with thee."[1] Hence the prayer which so often occurs in the Jewish liturgy, "Sanctify us by thy commandments," for any thought of pride or any worldly consideration is liable to undo the sanctifying effect of the performance of any divine law.

[1] *T. B. Berachoth,* 17 a. See also Rabbinowicz, *Variae Lectiones,* to the passage.

XIV

SIN AS REBELLION

THE teaching of the Rabbis with regard to the doctrines of sin, repentance, and forgiveness is in harmony with their conception of man's duty towards the Law. This duty, as we have seen, is a result of the doctrine of God's Kingship.[1] As a consequence, sin and disobedience are conceived as defiance and rebellion. The root פשע, used in the confession of the High Priest on the Day of Atonement, denoting, according to the Rabbis, the highest degree of sin, is explained by them to mean rebellion, illustrating it by parallel passages in 2 Kings 1 1, 3 4 and 7.[2] The generation of Enosh, the generation of the deluge, and the generation which built the Tower of Babylon are described as *rebels* who transferred the worship of God to idols or to man and thus profaned the Holy Name.[3] The same remark is also made of Nimrod, who made man rebel against God, and of the people of Sodom and Gomorrah. These latter, and the generation of Enosh and the generation of the deluge, as well as the people of Egypt, are further described as those

---

[1] See above, p. 116. Cf. also *Pseudo-Jonathan*, Exod. 34 7, Lev. 16 21, and Num. 14 18.

[2] *T. K.*, 80 *d*. Cf. Lev. 16 16 and 21.

[3] See *T. K.*, 111 *b*, *Gen. R.*, 23 7 and 26 4.

who caused pains to the Holy One, blessed be he, and spited him by their wicked deeds.¹ As men spiting God, reference is also made to certain kings of Judah, as Ahaz, Amon, and Jehoiakim.² In the Halachic literature we meet also with the *spite apostate*, or the apostate out of spite, מומר להכעים, who commits sin, not for the sake of satisfying his appetite, but with the purpose of showing his rebellious spirit.³

Closely connected with rebellion is the *porek ol* (פורק עול), that is, he who throws off the yoke of the Omnipresent, or of heaven.⁴ The term *porek ol* is differently explained by various Rabbis, meaning according to some, the worshipper of idols,⁵ according to others, the man who treats the Torah as antiquated matter and declares its laws as abrogated.⁶ The throwing off of the yoke is classed together with the removing of the Covenant made by God with Israel on Mount Sinai,⁷ and the uncovering of faces,⁸ that is,

---

¹ *Gen. R*, 27 2. Cf. also *Sifre*, 136 a; *Mechilta*, 35 b and 36 a; and *Num R.*, 9 24.   ² *Sanhedrin*, 103 b.

³ See *Horayoth*, 11 a. See also Rabb. Dictionaries.

⁴ See *Sifre*, 93 a, and *Sanhedrin*, 111 b.

⁵ See *Sifre*, 31 b, with references to Num. 15 22.

⁶ See *Jer. Peah*, 16 b, and *Jer Sanhedrin*, 27 c. Cf. Friedmann's essay in the *Beth Talmud*, I 331–334.

⁷ See *Jer. Peah* and *Sanhedrin* as above; *Sifre*, 31 b and 33 a. According to others, by this Covenant is meant the Covenant of Abraham, see *Sifre*, 31 b, § 111 (to Num. 15 22), and the commentary of R. Hillel, quoted by Friedmann in his Notes (Note 3). Cf. also in Friedmann, *Beth Talmud*, I, p 334.

⁸ See *Sifre*, *ibid.* (to Num. 15 31). Cf. *Mishnah Aboth*, 3 13, and *A. R. N.*, I 41 b, text and Note 16 for other parallels. The best Mss.

SIN AS REBELLION

the treatment of the words of the Torah irreverently or ridiculing them, as Manasseh, the son of Hezekiah, did, when he preached "scandalous homilies, asking 'Could not Moses have written other things than, "And Reuben went in the days of the wheat-harvest," etc. (Gen. 30 14), or "And Lotan's sister was Timna" (Gen. 36 22)'?".[1] To both these classes, according to some Rabbis, the words of the Scriptures refer: "But the soul that does aught presumptuously . . ." or "who hath despised the word of the Lord and has broken His Commandments" (Num. 15 30 and 31).[2]

have not the words שלא כהלכה. Cf Bacher, *Ag. Tan.*, I 197; *Terminologie*, I 149. See also his *Die Bibelexegese Moses Maimonides*, p. 16, note 4. Cf. also *P. R. E.*, ch. 44, where this explanation of uncovering the faces is used of men in the sense of putting them to shame.

[1] This is the explanation of the *Sifre*, 33 a (to Num. 15 30), cf *Jer. Peah* and *Sanhedrin*, *ibid* Certain Rabbis of a later date think that the uncoverer of faces is he who denies revelation (cf *Sanhedrin*, 99 a) or "he who transgresses the word of the Torah in public, as the king Jehoiakim the king of Judah and his associates," while in the *Bab. Sanhedrin*, 99 b, the phrase is explained to mean he who despises the scholars. Cf. Friedmann, *ibid*, pp 334 and 335.

[2] *Sifre*, *ibid*. Cf. *Sanhedrin*, 99 b. See also Guttmann, *Monatsschrift*, 42, p. 337 seq He tries to justify the reading שלא כהלכה, explaining it to mean the allegoric interpretation of Scriptures, in opposition to its literal meaning (especially the legal portions), with the intention of abolishing the law. Dr Guttmann's explanation receives support from the fact that the interpretations of the Rabbis in the *Sifre* in the quoted places are undoubtedly strongly polemical, as may be seen from the following passage, forming a comment on Num. 15 22 and 23: "Where is it to be inferred from that he who believes in the worship of idols is as much as if he denied the Ten Words (the Decalogue)? . . . Where is it further to be inferred from that it is as much as if he would deny all that was commanded to Moses, . . that

Another expression suggesting rebellion is "stretching the hand into the root." By this is chiefly meant blasphemy and other sins punishable by stoning.[1] Blasphemers are sometimes classified together with those who commit sins in secrecy, and act insolently in public, and those who are men of strife. They will end as Korah and his congregation.[2]

The transgressions of which the most prominent of the rebels (especially the generations of the deluge, and the people of Sodom and Gomorrah) were guilty are the three cardinal sins[3] causing contamination and defilement[4] which the Jew is bound to undergo martyrdom for rather than commit.[5] These three things are:—

Idolatry. — "He who worships idols is called 'desolation, abomination, hateful, unclean, and iniqui-

was commanded to the Prophets, . . . that was commanded to the Patriarchs? . . . Thus, the Scripture teaches that he who believes in the worship of idols is as much as if he would deny the Ten Words, the commandments that Moses was commanded, the commandments that the Prophets were commanded, the commandments that the Patriarchs were commanded , and he who denies the worship of idols is as much as if he would confess the whole of the Torah."

[1] See *Jer. Sanhedrin*, 23 c.

[2] See *A. R. N.*, 2 85, *D. E.*, ch. 2, and *S. E.*, p. 77. It will be seen from these parallel passages that the reading is doubtful. Interesting is it that in the *S. E* and *D. E. R.*, the various groups of heavy sinners include both the heretic, the sectarian, and the apostate, as well as those who corner wheat, who lend on usury, and who gamble. Cf above, p 113.

[3] See *Gen. R* , 28 8 and 9; 31 6; 32 41; 41 27. Cf. *A. R. N.* 36 *b seq* , and *Sanhedrin*, 107 *b* and 109 *a*.

[4] See *T. K.*, 81 *c*, and *Num. R.*, 7, § 10.

[5] See *Sanhedrin*, 74 *a*. Cf. Graetz's *Geschichte d. Juden*, 3, pp 156 and 431.

tous, and causes five things: the contamination of the land, the profanation of the name of God, the removal of the Shechinah, the delivering of Israel to the sword, and the banishment of them from their land.'"[1] But the three cardinal sins have their appurtenances, of which a few will be given here. Thus, pride is another form of idolatry, and has the same grave results. "Moses was considered worthy to draw near the thick darkness (Exod. 20 21), because of his humility, as it is said, 'The man Moses was very humble' (Num. 12 3). The Scriptures teach that he who is humble will as a result make the Shechinah dwell with man on earth, as it is said, 'For thus said the high and lofty One that inhabiteth eternity, whose name is Holy, "I dwell in the high and holy place with him also that is of a contrite heart and humble spirit"'"[2] (Isa. 57 15). "But he who has a proud heart will bring defilement to the land and cause to remove the Shechinah, to remove as it is said, 'He who has a proud heart and high looks, with him I cannot be together' (Ps. 101 5).[3] Again, he who is proud of heart is called abomination (Prov. 16 5) as the idol is called abomination (Deut. 7 26), but as idolatry causes the defilement of the land and the removal of the Shechinah, so does he who is proud of heart" cause the same things.[4] It is only by forget-

[1] See *Sifre*, 104 *a*, text and Note 7. הסתר פנים=סילוק שכינה.
Cf. *Onkelos*, *Deut.* 31 · 18

[2] In the text are given also citations from Isa. 61 1, 66 2, Ps. 51 19.

[3] The Rabbis interpreted it as if they read אתו, "with him," instead of אותו. See *Arachin*, 15 *b*. [4] *Mechilta*, 72 *a*.

ting God that man's heart can be lifted up by conceit (Deut. 8 14).[1] There is no room for the Divine beside him, the Holy One saying, "He and I cannot dwell in the same place."[2] Something similar is said of the man who is wroth. The very Shechinah is not respected by a man in a violent temper.[3] Indeed, he sets up the strange god which is in himself which he worships.[4]

Adultery. — "All forbidden sexual relations are called contamination . . . (*Tumah*). If you pollute yourself by them (God says) you are hewn off (or cut off) from me; what joy have I in you? you have incurred the penalty of extermination.[5] As the idolater, the adulterer (or even the one who does any action which may lead to adultery) is also called desolation, abomination, hateful, unclean, and iniquitous.[6] Again, before they sinned, the Shechinah was dwelling with every one of Israel, as it is said, "The Lord, thy God walketh in the midst of thy camp" (Deut. 23 15), but after they sinned (abandoning themselves to immorality), the Shechinah was removed, as it is said, "that he see no unclean thing in thee, and turn away from this" (Deut. *ibid.*).[7] The sin of adultery further involves the sin of heresy, or that of denying God's knowledge of the secret actions of man. Thus, with reference to Job 24 15,

---

[1] See *Sotah*, 4 b.
[2] *Sotah*, 5 a   Cf also *Berachoth*, 43 a.
[3] *Nedarim*, 22 b.
[4] *Shabbath*, 105 b.
[5] *T. K.*, 86 d.
[6] *Sifre*, 115 b.
[7] See *Sotah*, 3 b; cf. *Sifre*, 120 b and 121 a; *A. R. N.*, 1, 58 a

the Rabbis paraphrase it in the following way: "The eye also of the adulterer waiteth for the twilight, saying, No Eye (that is, the Eye of the Above) shall see me."[1] For so the adulterer says, no creature knows it. But the eyes of the Holy One, blessed be he, run to and fro through the world. . . . Grave is (the case of) the adulterer, and that of the thief, both causing the removal of the Shechinah. . . . Is not the Holy One, blessed be he, everywhere? Can any one hide himself in secret places that I shall not see him? saith the Lord. Do I not fill heaven and earth? saith the Lord (Jer. 23 24). But the adulterer acts in such a way (as if) he said to God, "Remove thyself for a short while, and make room for me."[2] But adultery includes every unchaste action or unchaste thought, the Biblical prohibitions extending to all kinds of unchastity, whether in action or in thought.[3] Heresy is also considered an unclean thought and comes also under the heading of the commandment, "Then keep thee from every wicked thing" (Deut. 23 10).[4] The *Olah* (burnt-offering), though belonging to the voluntary offerings, is declared to have

---

[1] See *Num. R.*, 9, 1.

[2] *Tan. B.*, 4 14 b, 15 a. Cf. Zach. 4 10. Cf also *Tan. B., ibid.*, 13 b and 14 a, and *Num. R.*, 9 12; where it is maintained that adultery means a breach of all the Ten Commandments. The breach with the first commandment is proved from *Jeremiah* 5 12.

[3] For references, see above, p 214, note 1, to which are to be added *Sifre*, 35 a; *Berachoth*, 12 b. Cf. Maimonides, מליית ומ, סהיימ.

[4] See *Sifre*, 120 b, and *Abodah Zarah*, 20 b.

the function of atoning for the (sinful) meditations of the heart, as it is even said of Job: "And (Job) offered burnt-offerings, according to the number of them all: for Job said, It may be that my sons have sinned, and cursed God in their hearts. Thus did Job continually" (Job 1 5).[1] The uttering of obscene words brings distress and death into the world.[2] In fact, he who uses foul language is included among these wicked, of whom it is said, "Behold the day cometh, that shall burn as an oven, and . . . shall burn them up" (Mal. 3 19), whilst he who indulges in impure thought is not admitted into the presence of God.[3]

Shedding of Blood also has the effect of contaminating the land and removing the Shechinah, besides that of leading to the destruction of Israel's sanctuary.[4] He who commits murder acts like one who overturns the statue of the king, destroys his image, and mutilates his impress (on the coins). "For in the image of God made he man" (Gen. 9 6).[5] "But he who transgresses a light commandment will end in violating the more heavy one. If he neglected (the injunction of) 'Thou shalt love thy neighbour as thyself' (Lev. 19 18), he will soon transgress the commandment of 'Thou

[1] See *Tan. B.*, 3 9 a. See below, p. 300, note 2.
[2] See *Shabbath*, 33 a.
[3] See *Niddah*, 13 b. Cf. English version, Mal. 4 1. Cf. above, pp. 207 and 214.
[4] *T. K.*, 62 a; cf. *Shabbath*, 33 a.
[5] See *Mechilta*, 70 b. Cf. *Mishnah Sanhedrin*, 4 5, and *Exod. R.*, 30 16.

shalt not hate thy brother in thine heart' (*ibid.*, v. 17), and that of 'Thou shalt not avenge or bear grudge against the children of thy people' (*ibid.*, v. 18), which, terminating in acting against 'And thy brother shall live with thee' (*ibid.*, 25 36), will lead to the shedding of blood."[1] In fact, "wanton hatred" is as great a sin as idolatry, adultery, and shedding of blood, all combined.[2] Likewise the sin of slander and backbiting is even worse than the three cardinal sins,[3] for man would never make these utterances unless he "denied the root"[4] (the existence of God), and they have the effect of removing the Shechinah from the world.[5]

Again, he who robs his neighbour, even if the goods robbed do not amount to more than the value of a Perutah, is as much as if he murdered him.[6] Some Rabbis maintain the sin of the generation of the deluge to have consisted in robbery (גזל), that is, the appropriation of wealth by violence and other unlawful means. "Behold," says Rabbi Jochanan, "how terrible are the effects of robbery, for, though the generation of the deluge transgressed everything, their verdict (of extermination) was not sealed till they stretched forth their hands to acquire wealth by un-

---

[1] See *T. K.*, 108 *b*, cf. *D E.*, ch. 11.   [2] *Yoma*, 9 *b*.
[3] *M. T.*, 52 2. Cf. also *ibid.*, 39 1, and *Arachin*, 15 *b*.
[4] *Jer. Peah*, 16 *a* Cf. *M. T*, 52 2.
[5] *Jer. Peah*, *ibid*, and *P. K*, 31 *b*, and *M T*, 7 7.
[6] *Baba Kama*, 119 *a*. Cf. *Lev. R.*, 22 16.

lawful means."[1] Again, the prophet Ezekiel in his exhortation (c. 22 3-12) enumerated twenty-four sins, but wound up with the words, "And thou hast greedily gained of thy neighbours by extortion, and hast forgotten me, said the Lord God."[2] Nay, God calls him "wicked" even after he made restitution.[3]

Sacrifices brought by the man who is not quite free from the sin of robbery are rejected. "If thou dost wish to bring an offering, rob no man first, for I, the Lord, love judgement, 'I hate robbery for burnt-offering' (Isa. 61 8). I shall only accept it when thou wilt have cleansed thy hands from plunder."[4] Something similar is said of charity: Here is a man who committed an immoral action, on which he spent his money, but he hardly left the place when a poor man met him and addressed him for alms. This man thinks that God put this poor man in his way with the purpose of making him find pardon through the alms he gave, but the Holy One, blessed be he, says: Wicked man, think not so. The hand which gives alms will not cleanse the other from the evil which it did by paying the wages of sin.[5] Indeed, the prayers of the man whose hands are tainted by robbery are not answered, for his supplication is turbid, being under transgression. Therefore man is bound to

---

[1] *Sanhedrin*, 108 a. Cf. *Tanhuma Noah*, 4.
[2] See *Lev. R.*, 33 8; *MHG.*, p 143.
[3] *Yalkut* to *Ezekiel*, § 782, reproduced from *Yelamdenu*.
[4] *Tan. B.*, 3 7 a.   [5] See *Midrash Prov.*, ch. 11.

SIN AS REBELLION

cleanse his heart (from every covetousness) before he prays, as it is said, "No robbery in mine hands, and my prayer is clean" (pure) (Job 16 17).[1]

The wrong administration of justice may also be classified under this heading: The Holy One, blessed be he, does not cause his divine presence to rest upon Israel, until the false judges and bad officers shall have disappeared from their midst.[2] "When three establish a court, the Shechinah is with them,"[3] and God says to the judges, "Think not that you are alone, I am sitting with you,"[4] but when they are about to corrupt judgement, that is, to give a false verdict, God removes his Shechinah from among them, as it is said, "For the oppression of the poor, for the sighing of the needy (caused by injustice), now I will rise (to leave the Court), saith the Lord."[5] The same thought is expressed elsewhere as follows: "When the judge sitteth and delivereth just judgement, the Holy One, blessed be he, leaves — if it were possible to say so — the heaven of heavens and makes his Shechinah dwell on his side, as it is said, 'And when the Lord was with the judge' (Judg. 2 18), but when he sees that the judge is a respecter of persons, he removes his Shechinah, and returns to heaven. And the angels say unto him, 'Master of the world, what hast thou done?' (what is the reason for this removal), and he answers, 'I have found that the judge is a respecter of persons,

---

[1] See *Gen. R.*, 22 8.   [2] See *Shabbath*, 139 a.
[3] See *Berachoth*, 6 a.   [4] *M. T.*, 82 1.   [5] *M. T.*, 12 2.

and I rose from there.'"[1] For, the respecters of persons are men "who have thrown off the yoke of heaven and loaded themselves with the yoke of men."[2] But it is written, "Ye shall do no unrighteousness in judgement, in meteyard," etc. (Lev. 19 35), which teaches "that he who is occupied in measuring, weighing, performs the function of judge, but if he gave false measure, he is called iniquitous, etc., . . . and causes the Shechinah to be removed from the earth."[3] Israel, indeed, was brought out of the land of Egypt, on the condition that they accept the fulfilment of the commandment relating to just measure, and he who denies this commandment "denies also the exodus from Egypt" (that is, God's special relation to Israel in history).[4]

Something similar is remarked of usury. The Rabbinic interpretation is in reference to the commandment: "Thou shalt not give him thy money upon usury, nor lend him thy victuals for increase. I am the Lord your God which brought you out of the land of Egypt" (Lev. 25 37-38). Whereupon, the Rabbis from the proximity of the two verses infer, "That he who receives upon himself the yoke of the commandment of usury receives upon himself the yoke of heaven, and he who removes the yoke of the commandment of usury removes from himself the yoke of heaven." And they then proceed to comment on the latter verse:

---

[1] See *Exod R.*, 30 24.
[2] *Sotah*, 47 b.
[3] *T. K.*, 91 a.
[4] *T. K., ibid.*

"Upon that condition I brought you forth out of the land of Egypt 'that you will receive upon yourselves the commandment regarding usury.' Because he who confesses this commandment acknowledges the fact of the exodus from Egypt, and he who denies it denies also the fact of the exodus from Egypt."[1] It is evident from this interpretation of the Scriptures that the Rabbis thought that each *Mizwah*, that is, the fulfilment of a commandment, had also a certain doctrinal value, bearing evidence to God's relation to man in general and his historic relation to Israel in particular.

The act of lending upon usury, which is also said to weigh as heavily as murder,[2] was, as it seems, considered as containing also an ironic implication directed by the man of affairs against the man of religion. He thereby declares Moses untrue and his Law false, saying, "If Moses would have known that there was so much profit in it, he would never have written it."[3] Hence to witness a bill in which interest of money is promised, is as much as to give evidence that the lender has denied the God of Israel.[4] It is probably for the same reason that the Rabbis say in another place, "Be careful not to be unmerciful, because he who keeps back his compassion from his neighbour is to be compared to the idolater and to the one who throws off the

---

[1] *T. K.*, 109 *c*   Cf. *Exod.*, 20 2.
[2] See *Baba Mezia*, 60 *b*.   [3] See *Baba Mezia*, 75 *b*.
[4] *Baba Mezia*, 71 *a*. See also *Rashi* to that passage.

yoke of heaven from himself," [1] since he could not act cruelly without considering the laws commending charity and charitableness impracticable, and devoid of all divine authority. Indeed, the notion is that no man betrays the confidence put in him by his neighbour until he has first denied the root (God); that no man engages in sin until he has first denied him who forbade it.[2]

The three cardinal sins, as well as blasphemy and slander, are called the evil things.[3] An impure thought is also described as evil.[4] All of these cause separation between man and God (as it is said), "Neither shall the evil dwell with thee" (Ps. 5 5). The scoffers, the liars, the hypocrites, are also excluded from the Divine Presence.[5] Every deed, again, implying a certain disrespect for those who deserve to be honoured on the ground of their being the teachers of Israel, as well as the showing impatience with the performance of religious actions, have the effect of the divine presence being removed from Israel.[6] This punishment of separation, as it would seem, is extended to sin in general. "Blessed be the man," says a Jewish teacher, "who is free from transgression, and possesses no sin or fault, but is devoted to good actions, to the study of the Torah, is low of knee (meek) and humble.

---

[1] *Sifre*, 98 b.   [2] See *Tosephta Shebuoth*, 4 50.   Cf. *T. K.*, 27 d.
[3] *Sifre*, 120 b.   [4] See *Niddah*, 13 b.
[5] *Sanhedrin*, 103 a   See also above, p. 33 *seq*.
[6] *Berachoth*, 17 b and 5 b.

The Holy One, blessed be he, says this is the man who dwells in heaven with him" (Isa. 57 15). The wise man said, "Thy deeds will bring thee near, and thy deeds will remove thee." How is this? If a man performed ugly deeds and unworthy actions, his deeds removed him from the Shechinah, as it is said, "But your iniquities have separated between you and your God, and your sins have hid his face from you, that he will not hear" (Isa. 59 2).[1]

From the preceding remarks it is clear that sin is conceived as an act of rebellion, denying the root, that is the existence of God, or his providence, or his authority, indeed, excluding him from the world. This extends also, as we have seen, to a sinful thought, in fact from the moment that a man thinks of sin it is as much as if he would commit treason against God.[2] It is also described as contamination and contaminating. The favourite expression for sin of the *Seder Elijah* is "ugly things and ugly ways."[3] This term is occasionally used also by older Rabbis. "Remove thyself," said "the wise men," in speaking of sin, "from ugliness and from that which is like ugliness."[4] Another similar expression is "dirt." Thus, Abraham is commanded to leave the land of his birth which is "dirtied" by idolatry.[5] The man, again, whose hands are "dirtied"

---

[1] *S. E.*, p 104. See above, p. 33.

[2] *Sifre Zuta*, as communicated by *Num. R.* 8 5. Cf. also *Yalkut* to *Pent.* § 701. [3] See Friedmann's Introduction, ch. 10 (p 105).

[4] *Chullin*, 44 b, *A. R. N.*, 5 a I, text and note 22.

[5] *MHG.*, p. 201. See also *Aruch Completum*, s.v. מנף.

by robbery is bidden not to pray, or is warned that his prayers will be of no avail.[1] In another passage, the Rabbis speak of the effect of the Day of Atonement, which is to purify Israel who are "dirty" by sin, throughout the whole year.[2] The verse in Proverbs, "As a jewel of gold in a swine's snout, so is a fair woman which is without discretion" (11 22) is illustrated by the Rabbis, "If thou puttest a vessel of gold into the nose of a swine, he will 'dirty' it with mire and refuse;" so is the student of the Torah if he abandon himself to immorality, he makes his Torah "dirty."[3] More frequent, we have the term of putrefaction and offensive smell, in connection with sin. The sin of the golden calf is described as a putrefaction. Song of Songs 1 12, is paraphrased in the Targum as follows: "And whilst their master Moses was still in heaven to receive the two tablets of stone, and the Torah, and the Commandments, there arose the wicked men of that generation and made a calf of gold. . . . And their deeds became putrefied, and their evil fame spread in the world."[4] The expression seems especially connected with rebellion and disobedience. Thus, the parable of a later Rabbi who began a sermon with the words, "And it came to pass, when the flock gave an offensive smell and obeyed not the words of its master, they hated the shep-

[1] *Exod. R.*, 22 8.

[2] See *M. T.*, 15 5. The right reading is from *Yalkut Machiri*, 42 b. See also *Tan* בשלח, 28.

[3] *Yalkut* to *Prov.*, § 14.   [4] *Targum*, Song of Songs, 1 12.

SIN AS REBELLION

herds and the good leaders, and went away far from them."[1]

Sin is thus a symptom of corruption and decay in the spiritual condition of man. He who committed a transgression is as one who was defiled by touching the corpse of a dead man.[2] The thoroughly wicked man is therefore even in life considered as dead.[3] Nay, the sin becomes also a part of himself and clings to him and appears with him together on the Day of Judgement.[4] The presence of the man of sin has, so to speak, a sickening and offensive effect upon everything pure and holy, so that he has to be removed from its neighbourhood. With reference to the scriptural words, "Ye shall therefore keep all my statutes, and all my judgements, and do them: that the land, whither I bring you to dwell therein, spew you not out" (Lev. 20 22), the Rabbis remark, "The land of Israel (by reason of its holiness) is not as the rest of the world. It cannot tolerate men of transgression. It is to be compared to the son of a King, whom they made to eat food that was coarse (that is, indigestible), which he is compelled (by reason of his delicate constitution) to vomit out."[5] The voice of God, which gave Adam delight and enjoyment, became a terror to him,[6] whilst he lost also his power over the lower creation which before his

---

[1] *P. R.*, 128 b. Cf. also *Aruch Completum*, s.v. םרח.
[2] *M. T.*, 51 2.
[4] *Sotah*, 3 b.
[3] *Berachoth*, 18 a and b.
[5] *T. K.*, 93 a.
[6] *P. K.*, 44 b, and *P. R.*, 68 b; see notes for parallels.

sin stood in awe and fear of him. His very stature was diminished, and instead of longing after, he feared the nearness of the Divine Presence.[1] His face, originally bearing the image of God, became disfigured and hateful.[2] Before Israel sinned (by worshipping the golden calf) their eyes saw the glory of God which was surrounded by (seven) walls of fire, and they feared not, as it is said, "And the sight of the glory of the Lord was like devouring fire on the top of the Mount in the eyes of the children of Israel" (Exod. 24 17); but after they sinned they could not even bear to look at the face of the middleman (Moses), as it is said, "And when Aaron and all the children of Israel saw Moses, behold, the skin of his face shone; and they were afraid to come nigh him" (Exod. 34 30).[3]

As in the Bible, sin is described in Rabbinic literature also as folly. The Rabbinic expression שפט, fool, like the Biblical term כסיל, has the original meaning of being fleshy and fat. They who know not God are טפשים, "fools."[4] By the act of sinning, man becomes a fool,[5] whilst the neglect of the Torah was the cause of Israel's becoming stupid and fools.[6] But more frequent is the expression of שוטים, fools, or שטות, folly. Thus, we read, "he whose heart is arrogant in decision is a fool (שוטה), a wicked man and puffed up in spirit."[7]

---

[1] *P. K.* and *P. R.*, *ibid.* See also *Eccles. R*, 8 1.
[2] *P K.*, 37 d; *P R*, 62 a; and *Gen. R*, 11 2.
[3] *P. K* and *P. R*, *ibid*   [4] See *Agadath Shir Hashirim*, p. 90.
[5] See *Targum* to 1 Kings 8 47.
[6] *Sifre*, 132 b.   [7] *Aboth*, 4 11.

SIN AS REBELLION

Again, a discussion as to God's suffering the sin of idolatry, considering that he could easily destroy the objects of the heathen's worship, the Rabbis answered, "Shall God cause his world to perish because of the fools (שוטים), who worship also the sun and the moon?"[1] The sin of idolatry is also described as folly. The word שטים in Num. 25 1 is held to indicate that Israel abandoned themselves there to folly (שטות).[2] But it must be remarked that the word שוטה, or שטות, implies also madness. "No man," the Rabbis say, "would ever commit a sin but for the fact that there came unto him a spirit of שטות,"[3] whilst in another place we read that no man abandons himself to immorality if he were in his right sense.[4] Similarly, it is said of the suspected woman, that her fall could only be explained as the effect of madness.[5]

The effects of sin extend even further. It has, apparently, a blighting influence upon the world, under which even the righteous suffer. The light which the Holy One, blessed be he, created on the first day was such that a man could see from one end of the world to the other, but it was concealed because of the sin of Adam; according to others, because of the future corrupt actions of the men of the deluge and of the men of the Tower of Babel.[6] Moses, who before Israel

---

[1] *Aboaah Zarah*, 54 *b*.
[2] *Bechoroth*, 5 *b*; *Num R.*, 20 22.
[3] *Sotah*, 3 *a*.
[4] *Num R.*, 9 6.
[5] *Num. R., ibid.*, reading in Num. 5 12 תשטה instead of תשטה, "she went mad."
[6] *Gen. R.*, 11 2, and *P. R.*, 107 *a*.

sinned could not be approached even by the archangels Michael and Gabriel, is after that in fear of the angels of destruction, Anger and Wrath.[1] Hillel and Samuel Hakaton were both worthy that the divine presence should rest upon them, but they were deprived of this gift because of the unworthiness of the generations in which they lived.[2] In another passage we read that it is sin which made Israel deaf so that they could not hear the words of the Torah, and blind so that they could not see the glory of the Shechinah.[3] The exodus from Babel (in the time of Ezra) was of such importance that such miracles could have been performed for it as at the exodus from Egypt, but sin made such a manifestation of the divine power impossible.[4]

More emphatically this doctrine is taught in the following words: "He who committed one sin, woe is unto him, for he inclined the balance both with regard to himself and with regard to the whole world toward the side of guilt," as it is said, "But one sinner destroys much good" (Eccles. 9 18). Thus by a single sin which man committed he deprived himself and the world from much good.[5] But the most bitter result of sin is that they (the sinners) are, as the Rabbis express it, "weakening the Power of the Above"; that is, that they prevent the channels of

---

[1] *P. K.*, 45 *a* and 45 *b*; *P. R.*, 69 *a*.
[2] *Sotah*, 48 *b*.
[3] *Ag. Ber.*, ch. 69.
[4] *Berachoth*, 4 *a*
[5] *Tosephta Kiddushin*, I , Cf. also *Eccles. R.*, 10 1. See also above, p. 191.

grace to flow so freely and fully as intended by the Merciful Father. "As often," says God, "I desired to do good unto you, you weaken the power from above by your sins. . . . You stood at Mount Sinai and said, 'all that the Lord hath said we will do and be obedient' (Exod. 24 7), and I desired to do you good, but you altered your conduct and said to the golden calf, 'These be thy gods, O Israel, which have brought thee out of the land of Egypt' (Exod. 32 8), and thus weakened the Power."[1] In another place, the same thought is expressed in somewhat different language. When Israel accomplishes the will of God, they add Power to Might (גבורה), as it is said, "And now let the power of the Lord increase" (Num. 14 17). According to another Rabbi, this is to be inferred from Ps. 60 14, which he translates, "*In* God we shall make our power."[2] If they act against the will of God (one might almost apply to them), "And they are gone without Power" (Lam. 1 6).

It is in harmony with this conception that the Rabbis exclaim, Woe unto the wicked who turn the attribute of mercy into that of strict judgement! for everywhere the Tetragrammaton is used it implies the attribute of mercy (as we can learn from Exod. 34 6, "The Lord, the Lord God, merciful and gracious"); but the same name of God is used in connection with the destruction of the men of the generation of the deluge, where we

[1] *Sifre*, 136 *b* and 137 *a*.
[2] *P. K.*, 166 *b*. See also above, p. 34.

read, "And God saw the wickedness of man was great in the earth" (Gen. 6 5).[1] In another place we read, "This is what Isaiah said, 'A sinful nation ... they have forsaken the Lord' (Isa. 1 4), they have made me forsake myself; I am called the 'merciful and gracious,' but through your sins I have been made cruel and I have converted my attribute (of mercy) into that of strict judgement; as it is said, 'The Lord was an enemy' (Lam. 2 5); and so he says also in another place, 'But they rebelled and vexed his Holy Spirit; therefore he was turned to be their enemy'" (Is. 63 10).[2]

It is further to be remarked that this abhorrence of sin is not entirely confined to sins committed wilfully. It extends also to sins committed unintentionally, as it is said, "Also that the soul be without knowledge is not good, and he who is hasty with his feet sinneth" (Prov. 19 2). Again, with reference to Eccles. 12 14, "For God shall bring every work into judgement, with every secret thing, whether it be good or it be evil," a Rabbi exclaimed in tears, "What hope is there for a slave whose master reckons unto him the unintentional sins as the intentional?"[3]

They took it as a sign of carelessness, which might have more serious consequences. "Men," they say, "need not feel distressed on account of an unintentional sin,

[1] *Gen. R.*, 33 8.
[2] *Tan. B.*, 3 55 a. Cf. *Yalkut Machiri* to Isaiah, p. 7.
[3] *Tan. B.*, 3 8 b. Cf. *Chagigah* 5 a. The Rabbis interpret the word נעלם in Eccles. 12 14, that the sin was concealed even from the man who committed it.

SIN AS REBELLION

except for the reason that a door to sin is thus opened to them, leading both to more unintentional and even intentional sins."[1] They even expressed their wonder that a soul coming from a place of righteousness, free from sin and transgression, shall sin through ignorance. "The soul," they say, "is the child coming from the palace above," knowing all the etiquette of the court, therefore sin should be impossible to it, and if it does sin even through ignorance, it is also considered a transgression.[2] The same thought takes a deeper aspect with the mystics. Thus Nachmanides, in alluding to Lev. 4 2, "If a *soul* shall sin through ignorance," remarks, "Since thought concerns only the soul, and it is the soul which is ignorant, the Scripture mentioned Soul here (in contradistinction to Lev. 1 2, where it speaks of *Man*), and the reason for bringing a sacrifice for the ignorant soul is because all sin leaves a taint in her, causing her to have a blemish, and she will not be worthy to face the Presence of the Maker, but when she is free from all sin."[3] The later mystics dwell on this thought at great length: the soul, they say, is an actual part of the divine, as it is said, "For the Lord's portion, is his people" (which they interpret to mean that his people are a portion of the Lord). Every sin, therefore, taints the divine in man, breaking all communion with heaven.[4]

[1] *Tan. B., ibid.* [2] *Tan. B.*, 3 4 *a* and *b*.
[3] Nachmanides, *Commentary to the Pentateuch*.
[4] See *Reshith Chochmah*, Section יראה, 9 and 10.

XV

THE *EVIL YEZER:* THE SOURCE OF REBELLION

Sin being generally conceived as rebellion against the majesty of God, we have now to inquire after the source or instigator of this rebellion. In Rabbinic literature this influence is termed the יצר הרע (*Yezer Hara*). This is usually translated "evil imagination," but the term is so obscure and so variously used as almost to defy any real definition.[1]

The term יצר הרע was probably suggested by Gen. 6 5 and *ibid*. 8 21, where the noun יצר is followed by the predicate רע, *evil*. Deut. 31 21 is also another case in point. After predicting that Israel will turn to strange gods and worship them, and provoke God to break his covenant, the Scriptures proceed to say: "For I know his *Yezer* (יצרו)," etc. It is thus the *Yezer* generally which is represented as something unreliable, and made responsible for Israel's apostasy. And it is in accordance with this notion that Pseudo-Jonathan renders it "their *Evil Yezer*," though the Hebrew original has not the word רע in this place. A parallel to this we have in Ps. 103 14, "For he knows our

[1] See on this subject Dr. F. C. Porter's article, *The Yeçer Hara*, in *Yale Biblical and Semitic Studies*, 1901, pp. 91–156.

Yezer," which the Targum renders, "the *Evil Yezer* that causes to sin." [1] 1 Chron. 28 9 and 29 18, in which the expression יצר מחשבות occurs, are generally understood to mean simply imagination, or desire, whatever the nature of this desire may be, good or evil. But it is to be remarked that the word לבבות in 28 9 is explained by some Rabbis to mean two hearts and two *Yezers*: the bad heart with the *Evil Yezer*, the good heart with the *Good Yezer*.[2]

The more conspicuous figure of the two *Yezers* is that of the *Evil Yezer*, the יצר הרע. Indeed, it is not impossible that the expression *Good Yezer*, as the antithesis of the *Evil Yezer*, is a creation of a later date.[3]

The names applied to the *Evil Yezer* are various and indicative both of his nature and his function. R. Avira, according to others R. Joshua b. Levi, said: "The *Evil Yezer* has seven names. The Holy One, blessed be he, called him *Evil* (Gen. 8 21); Moses called him *uncircumcised* (Deut. 10 16); David called him *unclean* (Ps. 51 12); Solomon called him *fiend* (or *enemy*) (Prov. 15 31); Isaiah called him *stumbling-block* (Isa. 57 14); Ezekiel called him *stone*

[1] See, however, English versions to this verse and Baethgen in his commentary to the Ps., *ibid*.

[2] See *M. T.*, 14 1. Cf. notes for another reading: "These are two hearts: the *Good Yezer* and the *Evil Yezer*." See also below, 255, note 2, and 257, note 2

[3] See, however, *Mishnah Berachoth*, 9 5, *Sifre*, 73 *a*; *A. R. N.*, 47 *a*, *Berachoth*, 61 *b*; where it is clear that the Tannaim were already acquainted with this expression.

(Ezek. 36 26); Joel called him the *hidden-one* (צפוני) in the heart of man (Joel 2 20).[1]

Other names applied to this *Yezer* are: the *foolish old king* who accompanies man from his earliest youth to his old age, and to whom all the organs of man show obedience;[2] the *spoiler* who spares none, bringing man to fall even at the advanced age of seventy or eighty;[3] and the *malady*.[4] He is also called the *strange god*, to obey whom is as much as to worship idols, and against whom Scripture warns, "There shall be no strange god in thee" (Ps. 81 10), whilst the words, "Neither shalt thou prostrate thyself before a strange god" (Ps., *ibid.*), are taken to mean "appoint not the strange god to rule over thee."[5]

The activity of the *Evil Yezer* is summed up by R. Simon b. Lakish, who said, "Satan and *Yezer* and the Angel of Death are one,"[6] which view is confirmed

---

[1] *Sukkah*, 52 a. Cf. also the כבוד חופה by Horwitz, p. 55, where Ezekiel is cited before Isaiah, thus agreeing with the ancient order of the Prophets given in *Baba Bathra*, 14 b. It has also the additional words to "Zephoni": זה יצר הרע שהוא צפון בלבושו את פניו ("The *Evil Yezer* who is hidden when disguising his face"). With reference to the name *stone*, see *Gen. R.*, 89 1, where it would seem the *Evil Yezer* is (with allusion to Job 28 3) identified with "the stone of darkness and the shadow of death"

[2] See *Eccles. R.*, 4 13, and *M. T.*, 9 5 and ref.

[3] See *P. K.*, 80 b; *Gen. R.*, 54 1; *M. T.*, 34 2.

[4] See *Lev R.*, 16 7.

[5] See *Jer. Nedarim*, 41 b, and *Shabbath*, 105 a.

[6] *Baba Bathra*, 16 a. See *Targum* to *Zechariah*, ch. 3, where *Satan* is rendered with חטאה

by the statement of an earlier anonymous Tannaitic authority: "He cometh down and leadeth astray; he goeth up and worketh up wrath (accuses); he cometh down and taketh away the soul."[1] His rôle as accuser is described in another place with the words, "The *Evil Yezer* persuades man (to sin) in this world, and bears witness against him in the future world;"[2] whilst his function as Angel of Death is expressed in the words, "He accustoms (or entices) man to sin and kills him."[3] Some modification of this thought we may perceive in another statement of R. Simon b. Lakish, who says, "The *Yezer* of man assaults him every day, endeavouring to kill him, and if God would not support him, man could not resist him; as it is said, 'The wicked watcheth the righteous and seeketh to slay him' (Ps. 37 32)."[4]

The identification of the *Evil Yezer* with the Angel of Death is sometimes modified in the sense of the former being the cause of death consequent upon sin rather than of his performing the office of the executioner. This is the impression, at least, one receives from such a passage in the *Mishnah* as the following: "The evil eye (envy), the *Evil Yezer*, and the hatred of one's fellow-creatures put man out of the world."[5] According to an ancient paraphrase of this passage, the rôle of the *Evil Yezer* who accosts man from the very moment of his birth, is of a passive nature, neglecting

---

[1] *Baba Bathra, ibid.* [2] *Sukkah,* 52 *b.* [3] *Exod. R.,* 30 18.
[4] *Sukkah,* 52 *b.* Cf. also *Kiddushin,* 30 *b.* [5] *Aboth,* 2 16.

to warn him against the dangers following upon the committing of such sins as profaning the Sabbath, the shedding of blood, and the abandoning of oneself to immorality.[1] A close parallel to the passage quoted above, likewise found in the *Mishnah*, is the following saying, in which the same expression is used with regard to the consequence of sin. It reads: "Envy, lust, and conceit put man out of this world."[2] "Lust" here apparently corresponds to *Evil Yezer*, and as the context shows, can only mean that it is the cause of death. In another place, these three evil impulses are said to have incited the serpent to his invidious conversation with Eve, resulting in her transgressing the first commandment given to man and finally in death.[3] The identification in the *Zohar* of Samael with the *Evil Yezer* is probably in some way connected with the given Rabbinic passages,[4] since in another place the tempting serpent is said to have been Samael in disguise, originally a holy angel, but who through his jealousy of man, determined to bring about the latter's fall.[5]

The *Evil Yezer* is also credited with inflicting other kinds of punishment upon man besides death, as, for instance, in the story of the Men of the Great Assembly in their effort to destroy the *Yezer*. When, perceiving

[1] *A. R. N.*, 31 *b*.   [2] *Aboth*, 4 28. Cf. *Aboth*, 3 14.
[3] See *P. R. E.*, ch. 13.
[4] See *Zohar*, Gen. 41 *a*. On page 248, *ibid.*, the *Evil Yezer* is identified with the Angel of Destruction אנירוסן.
[5] See *P. R. E.*, *ibid.*, and *Pseudo-Jon.*, Gen. 3 6.

the *Evil Yezer*, they exclaimed: "Here is the one who has destroyed the sanctuary, burned the Temple, murdered our saints, and driven Israel from their country."[1]

But it must be noted that in other places it is sin itself that causes death. "See, my children," said the saint R. Chaninah b. Dosa to his disciples, "it is not the ferocious ass that kills, it is sin that kills."[2] Again, with allusion to Prov. 5 22, the Rabbis teach, "As man throws out a net whereby he catches the fish of the sea, so the sins of man become the means of entangling and catching the sinner."[3] It must be further noticed that both the function of the accuser and witness are sometimes ascribed to God himself: "He is God, he is the Maker, he is the Discerner, he is the Judge, he is the Witness, he is the Complainant."[4] Again, with allusion to Mal. 3 5, an ancient Rabbi remarked, "What chances are there for a slave whose master brings him to judgement and is eager to bear witness against him?"[5] In another passage, the function of bearing witness is ascribed to the two angels accompanying man through life, whilst others think that it is the soul of man or his limbs that give evidence. Nay, the very stones of man's abode and the beams in it cry out against man and accuse him, as it is said, "For the stones shall cry out of the wall and the beam out of the timber shall answer it" (Hab. 2 11).[6]

[1] *Yoma*, 69 b.
[2] *Berachoth*, 33 a.
[3] *Midrash, Prov.*, ch. 5.
[4] *Aboth*, 4 29.
[5] *Chagigah*, 5 a. Cf. *P. K.*, 164 b.
[6] *Chagigah*, 16 a.

Neither the function of bearing witness against man and accusing him, nor that of executing the judgement, can thus be exclusively ascribed to the *Evil Yezer*. His main activity consists in seducing and tempting. His ways are of the insinuating kind, appearing first to the man as a modest traveller (הלך), then as a welcome guest (אורח), and ending in exacting obedience as the master of the house (איש).[1] He shows himself also more as an effeminate being with no capacity for doing harm, but afterwards overwhelms with masculine strength.[2] The snares in which the *Evil Yezer* entangles man are at first sight as insignificant and vain as the thin thread of the cobweb, but take soon the dimensions of the rope, making it impossible for man to free himself from it.[3] In another place this treachery of the *Evil Yezer* is compared with that of the dogs in the city of Rome: they lie down before a baker's shop and simulate sleep; but when the baker in his security allows himself to take a nap, they quickly jump up, snatch away a loaf, and carry it away. The *Evil Yezer* deals with man in the same way, feigning weakness and helplessness, but as soon as man is off his guard, he jumps on him and makes him sin.[4]

The man who is most exposed to the allurements of

---

[1] *Sukkah*, 52 a. Cf *Gen. R*, 22 6.   [2] *Gen. R*, ibid.

[3] See *Sukkah, ibid., Sanhedrin*, 99 b. Cf. *Gen. R*, ibid. and Rabb. Dictionaries, s.v. בוביא. *Sifre*, 33 a, this simile is made of sin itself.

[4] See *Gen. R.*, 22 6.

the *Evil Yezer* is the vain one. "*Yezer*," the Rabbis say, "does not walk in retired places. He resorts to the middle of the highroads. When he sees a man dyeing his eyebrows, dressing his hair, lifting his heels, he says, 'That is my man!'"[1] Again, when Simon the Just asked a Nazarite of stately appearance, beautiful eyes, and curly hair, "My son, why didst thou choose to have thy beautiful hair destroyed?" (the Nazarite having, according to Num. 6 18, to have his hair shaved when the days of his separation are fulfilled), he answered, "I acted as father's shepherd in my town. Once, I went to fill the casket from the well; but when I saw the image reflected in the water, my *Yezer* grew upon me and sought to turn me out from the world. Then I said to him, 'Thou wicked one! why dost thou pride thyself with a world which is not thine; thou, whose destiny is to become worm and maggots? I take an oath that I will have thee shaved in the service of heaven!'"[2] It is interesting to notice in passing that this instantaneous resistance to the *Evil Yezer* is also recommended in another place. "He that spoils his *Yezer* by tender and considerate treatment (that is, allows him slowly to gain dominion over himself without rebuking him) will end in becoming his slave."[3]

[1] *Gen. R.*, 22 6. Cf. *MHG*, p. 119, reading ממסמם for ממשמש. Cf. also *Zohar*, I 190 (Gen 39 12), where the vanity of fine clothes is added.

[2] *Sifre*, 9 b; *Nedarim*, 9 b; *Num. R.*, 10 7 and references. Cf. also *Yoma*, 35 b   [3] *Gen. R., ibid.* Cf. *Rashi* to Prov. 29 21.

The two great passions which the *Yezer* plays most upon are the passions of idolatry and adultery. The latter is called the יצרא דעבירה, the passion of sin; just as מצוה in many places means charity, so does עבירה in a large number of passages refer to immorality.[1] The passion of idolatry, though once more general and more deeply rooted in the nature of man than any other passion, is stated, however, to have already disappeared from the world through the work of the Men of the Great Assembly who prayed for its extinction.[2]

Of the two passions, it is pointed out that the passion of idolatry was (once) even stronger than that of adultery; the former having such a power over man as to induce him to have his sons and daughters sacrificed to idols. It knows no shame, performing its office both in public and in private, and sparing no class of society, enlisting in its service both small and great, old and young, men and women.[3] It is worth noting that the desire for acquiring wealth is not counted by the Rabbis among the grand passions, though it is stated in another place that it is the sin of dishonesty in money transactions under which the great majority of mankind is labouring. It is there further remarked that the sin of immorality involves only the minority, whilst none escape the sin of slander-

---

[1] See Levy's Rabb. Dictionary, *s.v.*

[2] See *Yoma*, 69 *b*   See also *Midrash Cant.*, 7 8.   Cf. also *Jer. Abodah Zarah*, 40 *c*.

[3] *MHG.*, p. 120.

EVIL YEZER: SOURCE OF REBELLION

ing, or at least of invidious talk against their neighbours.[1] Scepticism is another means by which the *Evil Yezer* reaches man. Sometimes he questions the nature of the Deity, ascribing to God corporeal qualities, such as to be in need of food;[2] at others, his attacks are directed against the Biblical precepts relating to the dietary laws, and certain ritual observances known under the name of חוקים (statutes), the reason for which is unknown.[3] The *Yezer* is especially anxious to show him that the ceremonies and the cult of other religions are more beautiful than those of the Jew.[4] Sometimes he even deigns to bring evidence from Scripture, as in the case of Abraham. When Abraham was on his way to Mount Moriah to sacrifice his son Isaac, Satan met him and said, "Old man, where art thou going?" He answered, "I am going to fulfil the will of my Father in Heaven." Then Satan said unto him, "What did he tell thee?" Abraham answered, "To bring my son to him as a burnt-offering." Thereupon Satan said, "That an old man like thee should make such a mistake! His attention was only to lead thee astray and to tire thee! Behold, it is written, 'Whoso sheds man's blood, by man his blood shall be shed' (Gen. 9 6). Thou art the man who bringest mankind under the wings of the Shechinah.

[1] *Baba Bathra*, 165 *a*.
[2] See *Tan. B.*, 4 48 *b*. See also below, p. 298.
[3] See *T. K*, 86 *a*. See also *P. R.*, 64 *a*, text and notes.
[4] *T. K.*, *ibid.*, שלהם נאים משלנו, apparently relating to matters of cult.

If thou wilt sacrifice thy son, they will all leave thee and call thee murderer."[1] The name Satan here is identical with the *Evil Yezer*, who, as in the case of Job, performs the office of the informer against Abraham. *Yezer*, indeed, shows special anxiety for man's duty to his family. Thus when man "loves in his heart" to do a מצוה (give charity), the *Evil Yezer* in him says, "Why should you do a מצוה and diminish thy property? Rather than to give to strangers, give to thy children."[2] Sometimes he appeals to his vanity, telling man, for instance, not to pay a visit of condolence, because he is too great a man.[3] When all fails, he will appeal to the mercy of God, saying to man, "Sin and the Holy One, blessed be he, will forgive thee."[4]

The beginning of the association of the *Evil Yezer* with man is a controverted point among the Rabbis. According to some, the *Evil Yezer* arises with the act of cohabitation. Thus R. Reuben b. Astrobolis expresses himself to the effect: How can man keep aloof from the *Evil Yezer* considering that the very act of generation came through the strength of the *Evil Yezer*, constantly gaining in strength till the time of his birth arrives? The *Evil Yezer* dwells at the opening of his heart.[5] This is in accordance with the view of R.

---

[1] *MHG.*, pp. 304 and 305. Cf. notes 3 and 4.
[2] *Exod. R.*, 36 8.   [3] *P. R.*, 150 a.   [4] *Chagigah*, 16 a.
[5] *A. R N.*, 32 b, according to the text given in the Note 22. Cf. *MHG.*, p. 106.

Acha, who, with reference to Ps. 51 7, expressed himself to the effect that in sexual intercourse even the saint of saints cannot well escape a certain taint of sin, the act of cohabitation being performed more with the purpose of satisfying one's animal appetite than with the intention of perpetuating the human species.[1] Very near to this notion, though not quite identical, is that which teaches that the *Evil Yezer* enters into man when he is still in the embryonic state; but this seems to have been an isolated opinion, having been abandoned by the very authorities who taught it first. This can be seen from the following passage, which is to the effect that Antoninus put the question to R. Judah the Saint, "When does the *Evil Yezer* begin his rule over man: from the moment of his formation into bones, muscles, and flesh, or from that of his birth?" R. Judah was inclined to the former view, to which Antoninus objected on the ground that we have no proof of any malign tendency on the part of the embryo. Thereupon R. Judah declared himself in favour of the latter view, and in a public lecture made the statement, "This fact Antoninus taught me, and Scripture is in his support; as it is said, 'At the door (of man's entering the world) the sin lieth.'"[2] Likewise isolated is another opinion, which is to the effect: that the child

---

[1] *Lev. R.*, 14 5. The sense of the passage is not very clear. See also *Yalkut Machiri. Ps.* to this verse and cf. Bacher, *Ag Am*, 3 144

[2] See *Sanhedrin*, 91 b. Cf. *Gen. R*, 34 6, and *Jer Berachoth*, 6 d. Cf. Löw's *Lebensalter*, p 64 *seq*

of six, seven, eight, and nine years sins not; only from
the age of ten he begins to grow (or perhaps to magnify,
or to cultivate) the *Evil Yezer*.[1] The general notion
seems to be the one accepted by R. Judah, which is
that the *Evil Yezer* accompanies man from his earliest
childhood to his old age, by reason of which he enjoys
a priority of not less than thirteen years over the *Good
Yezer*, who only makes his appearance at the age of
puberty.

It is on account of this seniority that he establishes
a certain government over man and is thus called "the
old foolish king."[2] It is true that children enjoy a
certain immunity from sin, on account of their unde-
veloped physical condition, so that the Rabbis speak
of the breath of the school children, in which there is
no (taint of) sin. Indeed, the death of children is
mostly explained as an atonement for the sins of
their parents or their grown-up contemporaries.[3]
Yet, they are, as already indicated, not quite free
from the *Evil Yezer*, who, as we have seen, accosts
man from his earliest childhood. "Even in his state
as minor, man's thoughts are evil."[4] As it would seem,

[1] See *Tan.* בראשית, 7.

[2] See *A. R. N.*, 32 *b*; *Eccles. R.*, 4 18 and 9 15; *Nedarim*, 32 *b*;
M., T. 9 5, and *Tan. B.*, I, 102 *a* and *b*. From *Tan. B*, I 68 *a*, it would
seem that it is at the age of fifteen that the effects of the *Evil Yezer*
become visible. The reading is, however, not certain. See Note 5,
ibid, on the various parallel passages and the different readings.

[3] See *Shabbath*, 119 *b* and 33 *b*. Cf. *Gen. R.*, 58 2 and commentaries. See also above, p 193, below, p 311.

[4] *Jer. Berachoth*, 6 *b*.

it is in the aspect of "fool" (stupid and wanting in caution and foresight) that the influence of the *Evil Yezer* makes itself felt in the child. "From the moment man is born, the *Evil Yezer* cleaves to him." And this is illustrated by the following fact: If a man should attempt to bring up an animal to the top of the roof, it will shrink back; but the child has no hesitation in running up, with the result of tumbling down and injuring himself. If he sees a conflagration, he will run to it; if he is near burning coals, he will stretch out his hands to gather them (and be burnt). Why (this audacity and want of caution), if not because of the *Evil Yezer* that was put in him?[1]

The seat both of the *Evil* and the *Good Yezer* is in the heart, the organ to which all the manifestations of reason and emotion are ascribed in Jewish literature.[2]

---

[1] See *A. R. N.*, 32 *a*, 32 *b*, text and notes.

[2] The importance of this organ in Rabbinic literature will be more clearly seen by the reader through reproducing here the following passage in *Eccles. R.*, 1 16, omitting such clauses as seem to be mere repetition, as well as the Scriptural verses cited there in corroboration of each clause. Cf. *P. K.*, 124 *a* and *b*, text and notes: "The heart sees, the heart hears, the heart speaks, the heart walks, the heart falls, the heart stops, the heart rejoices, the heart weeps, the heart is comforted, the heart grieves, the heart is hardened, the heart faints, the heart mourns, the heart is frightened, the heart breaks, the heart is tried, the heart rebels, the heart invents, the heart suspects (or criticises), the heart whispers, the heart thinks, the heart desires, the heart commits adultery, the heart is refreshed, the heart is stolen, the heart is humbled, the heart is persuaded, the heart goes astray, the heart is troubled, the heart is awake, the heart loves, the heart hates, the heart is jealous, the heart is searched, the heart is torn,

It is in this heart, with its manifold functions, that the *Evil Yezer* sets up his throne. The *Evil Yezer* resembles a "fly" (according to others, a "wheat" grain), established between the two openings (valves) of the heart.[1] More minute are the mystics, who describe the heart as having two cavities, the one full of blood, which is the seat of the *Evil Yezer;* the other empty, where the *Good Yezer* dwells.[2] Somewhat different is the statement, "Two reins are in man: the one counsels him for good, the other for evil," and they proceed to say it is evident the former is on the right side, the latter on the left side; as it is said, "The heart of the wise man is on his right, the heart of the fool is on his left" (Eccles. 10 2).[3] The reins in this case seem to have an auxiliary function. "The reins counsel and the heart understands (to decide for action)." It should, however, be noted that in another place, this very verse is

the heart meditates, the heart is like fire, the heart is like stone, the heart repents, the heart is warned, the heart dies, the heart melts, the heart accepts words (of comfort), the heart accepts the fear (of God), the heart gives thanks, the heart covets, the heart is obstinate, the heart is deceitful, the heart is bribed, the heart writes, the heart schemes, the heart receives commandments, the heart does wilfully, the heart makes reparation, the heart is arrogant "

[1] *Berachoth*, 61 a The first view, which is that of Rab, is derived from Eccles 10 1, " Dead flies cause the precious oil of the apothecary to become stinking and foaming ; so doth a little folly, him that is valued for wisdom and honour " The second, ascribed to Samuel, is a play on the word חטאת (Gen. 4 7) = חטה This latter interpretation is probably connected with the legend maintaining that the Tree of Knowledge grew wheat (*Berachoth*, 40 a).

[2] *Zohar, Exod*, 107 a.   [3] See *Berachoth, ibid*

interpreted to mean that the wise man's heart on the right is the *Good Yezer*, which is placed on the right of man; and the fool's heart to his left is the *Evil Yezer*, which is placed to his left.[1] We are thus brought to the notion identifying the two *Yezers* with the two hearts, of which the Rabbis speak occasionally. What is the meaning, they say, of the verse, "For the Lord searcheth all the hearts"? (1 Chron. 28 9). These are the two hearts and the two *Yezers:* the bad heart with the *Evil Yezer*, and the good heart with the *Good Yezer*.[2] Indeed, the angels, who have only one heart, are free from the *Evil Yezer*, a blessing to which Israel will attain only in the Messianic times.[3] Therefore, man is bidden not to have two hearts when he prays, one directed to the Holy One, blessed be he, and the other occupied with worldly thoughts; just as the priests are bidden not to have two hearts, one directed to the Holy One, blessed be he, and the other directed to something else, when they are performing their sacrificial rites.[4] Indeed, the pious generation of the prophetess Deborah had only one heart, directed towards their Father in Heaven.[5] The same thought is expressed in different words in another place: Moses

---

[1] *Num. R.*, 22 9.

[2] See above, p. 243, note 2 and reference there to a differing reading. To this should be added *Midrash Prov.*, 12, where, with reference to Ps. 7 10, it is distinctly remarked, "Has a man two hearts? But by these are meant, the *Good Yezer* and the *Evil Yezer*."

[3] *Gen. R.*, 48 11.

[4] *Tan.*, תבא, 1 and 2.   Cf. *Tan. B.*, 5 28 b.   [5] *Megillah*, 14 a.

said to Israel, "Remove the *Evil Yezer* from your hearts, so that ye may be all in one fear of God and in one counsel to serve before the Omnipresent. As he is alone in this world, so shall your worship of him be only to him (single-hearted)," as it is said, "Circumcise therefore the foreskin of thy heart." [1]

The loose manner in which heart and *Evil Yezer* are interchangeably used in the foregoing passage, suggest the close affinity between the two, as indeed, heart sometimes stands for *Yezer*.[2] "The eyes and the heart are the agents of sin," but as it is pointed out by an ancient Rabbi, the first impulse comes from the heart, the eyes following the heart.[3] There is a clean heart for which the Psalmist prays (51 12), and there is the contaminated heart to which the *Evil Yezer* owes the name of "unclean." [4] Again, it is the heart that brings the righteous to Paradise, it is the heart that hurls down the wicked to Hell, as it is said, "Behold, my servants shall sing for joy of *heart*, but ye shall cry for sorrow of *heart*" (Is. 65 14).[5] We must, however, not press this point too much so as to identify the heart with the *Evil Yezer*, for not only have the Rabbis, as we have

---

[1] *T. K.*, 33 d. See above, 160.

[2] See *Sukkah*, 52 a (heart of stone), and cf above, 243. In *Pseudo-Jonathan* the לב is in most cases rendered with יצרא Cf. Exod. 4 21; 7 8; 13 and 14; 8 15. 28, 9 7. 84; 10 1. 20. 27; 11 10. Deut. 5 26; 11 16; 29 25; 30 6.

[3] See *Jer. Berachoth*, 3 c; *Sifre*, 35 a, and *Num R.*, 17 6.

[4] See above, p. 243, and reference given there to *Sukkah*, 52 a.

[5] *M T.*, 119 6 (146 b)

seen, assigned to it the seat of the *Good Yezer*, but they have even declared it as the abode of wisdom.[1] The good heart, again, is the most desired possession.[2] In the later literature, the heart is described as outweighing all the other organs of man, hatred and love having their seat in the heart; as it is said, "Thou shalt not hate thy brother in thine heart" (Lev. 19 17), whilst it is also said, "And thou shalt love the Lord, thy God, with all thy heart" (Deut. 6 5).[3] It is also maintained that the heart is purer than anything else, and that everything good proceeds from it.[4] All that the heart is accused of is inconsistency. God says, "Two hundred and forty-eight organs have I created in man; all of these keep in the same manner as I have created them, except the heart;" (and) so said Jeremiah, "The heart changeth from moment to moment. It alters itself and perverts itself."[5] These changes apparently depend upon the nature of the tenant who gets possession of the heart. "As often as the words of the Torah appear and find the chambers of the heart free, they enter and dwell therein. The *Evil Yezer* has no dominion over these, and no man can remove them."[6]

The heart is thus not in itself corrupt; at least, not more corrupt than any other organ. Indeed, when

---

[1] *Midrash Prov.*, ch. 1.
[2] See *Aboth*, II 9.
[3] אותיות דר"ע אות ל"י.
[4] *Zohar, Num.*, 225 a.
[5] See *Ag. Ber.*, ch. 2. Cf. Jeremiah, 17 19.
[6] *A R. N.*, 15 b, *Midrash Prov.*, ch. 24.

man is under the incitement of sin, all his members are obedient to the *Evil Yezer*, who is king over man's two hundred and forty-eight members; whilst when he makes an effort to perform good work, they all show laziness and reluctance.[1] Again, when the *Evil Yezer* lays siege to man, it is all the members, not the heart in particular, that act as auxiliaries.[2] It is only because of the heart's various functions, as pointed out above, that it is more often liable to be enlisted in the service of the *Evil Yezer* than any other organ, and therefore more blamed than any other part of the human body, but not on account of a special depravity attaching to it. As a matter of fact, the heart in this respect is only synonymous with soul in the Bible, where it is the נפש which commits sin, and even the Rabbis occasionally speak of the "soul of man," with its greed after wealth (even when acquired by dishonest means) and its tendency towards lust.[3] Indeed, according to the Rabbis, Scripture is astonished that the soul coming from a place where there is no sin should sin, but nevertheless, the fact is accepted that it shares in sin as much as the body, though the body comes from a village and the soul comes from the court and is well acquainted with the etiquette of the court. But it is this very fact which makes this sin of the soul less excusable; and the Holy One, blessed be he, says

---

[1] *A. R. N.*, 32 a; *MHG.*, p. 109.
[2] *Nedarim*, 32 b.
[3] *Mishnah Makkoth*, end. See also *Sifre*, 125 a.

to the soul, "All that I have produced in the first six days of creation I have produced for thy sake, but thou didst rob, sin and commit violence. . . ." "But it is impossible for the body to be without the soul, and if there is no soul there is no body, and if there is no body there is no soul; they sin together; (hence) 'the soul that sinneth, it shall die' (Ezekiel 18 20)."[1]

The passages indicating a tendency to identify the heart (or the soul) with the *Evil Yezer* have further to be qualified by other Rabbinic statements looking for the source of sin to some force outside of man. For

[1] See *Tan. B*, 3 4 *a* and *b*, and *Eccles. R*, 6 6. The simile of the villager and the courtier will be better understood by the following Rabbinic passages, on which it was probably based: *Mechilta* 36 *b* and *Mechilta of R. Simon*, p. 59, where Antoninus asks Rabbi, "Considering that the man is dead and the body in a state of decay, whom does God bring to judgement?" Whereupon Rabbi answered him, "*Before thou asketh me about the body which is impure, ask me about the soul which is pure.*" This is followed by the well-known parable of the blind and the lame, who robbed the garden of the king, etc. "Pure" and "impure" apparently stand here for lasting and decaying. It should be remarked that the words in italics are missing in the parables of *Sanhedrin*, 91 *a* ; *Lev. R.*, 4 5 ; *Tan B.*, 3 4 *b*, and *Tan* ויקרא 6. In *Sifre*, 132 *a*, man is defined as the only creature whose soul is from heaven and his body from the earth. If he obeyed the Torah and performed the will of his father in heaven, he is like one of the creatures above ; if he did not obey the Torah and the will of his father in heaven, he is like one of the creatures below. Closely corresponding with it is the passage in *Gen. R* , 8 11, where also man is described as a combination of those above (angels) and those below (animals). See also *Gen R.*, 14 2 and 27 4 ; *Chagigah*, 16 *a* ; and *A. R. N.*, 55 *a*, text and notes See also *Tan. B.*, 1 15 *b*. Cf. also above, 81 and 241, and below, 285.

apart from what we may call the mythological view, identifying the *Evil Yezer* with the serpent, or Samael, and of which some other names of the *Evil Yezer* in Rabbinic literature are to be considered as reminiscent at least,[1] the comparison of the *Yezer's* visitations to man with the passing traveller and other similar passages[2] point also to the fact that the Rabbis did not entirely view man in the light of a corrupt being. We have further to note that the *Evil Yezer* is, as indicated above, more conspicuous in the Jewish literature than the *Good Yezer*, whilst by *Yezer*, without any further specification, is often meant the *Evil Yezer*.[3] This would suggest that there is in fact only one *Yezer*, the *Evil Yezer*, and we may further conclude that it is man himself, by his natural tendency, that represents the *Good Yezer*. Accordingly, when he commits evil, he acts under certain impulses not exactly identical with his own natural self. The Rabbis further speak of the *leaven in the dough*, preventing man from doing his (God's) will.[4] This metaphor is taken by some as indicating some inner physical defect in human nature, but in another place forming a parallel passage to the one just quoted, the leaven in the dough appears together with the subjection to foreign governments that make compliance with God's

---

[1] See above, p. 243.   [2] See above, p. 248.

[3] See *e.g. Sukkah*, 52 *b*; *Gen. R.*, 59 6; *Aboth*, I 4; *Sifre*, 74 *a*; *Targum* to Ps. 4 6.

[4] *Jer. Berachoth*, 7 *d*. See below, p. 265, where the passage is given.

will hard, if not impossible.[1] It is thus a certain quasi-external agency which is made responsible for sin, whilst man himself, by his spontaneous nature, is only too anxious to live in accordance with God's commandments.

[1] *Berachoth,* 17 a.

XVI

MAN'S VICTORY BY THE GRACE OF GOD, OVER THE *EVIL YEZER* CREATED BY GOD

The opinions recorded in the preceding chapter, some of which suggest the placing of the *Evil Yezer* outside of man, and the further fact that he is described as the source of rebellion, must, however, not be pressed to such an extent as to give the *Evil Yezer* an independent existence, representing a power at warfare with God. As is so often the case in Jewish theology, the Rabbis, consciously or unconsciously, managed to steer between the dangerous courses, never allowing the one aspect of a doctrine to assume such proportions as to obscure all other aspects. First, it must be noted that the *Evil Yezer*, whatever its nature, is, as is everything else in the universe, a creature of God. Thus with reference to Gen. 2 7, a Rabbi interprets the fact of the word וייצר being written with two *Yods* to indicate that God created man with two *Yezers:* the *Good Yezer* and the *Evil Yezer*.[1] For "God hath also set the one against the other" (Eccles.

---

[1] *Gen. R.*, 14 7; *Berachoth*, 61 *a* and references. Cf. also *Pseudo-Jonathan*, Gen. 2 14. Cf. also below, p. 313, the quotation given there from *M. T.*, 32 4.

7:14), which verse Rabbi Akiba explains to mean that God created the righteous and God created the wicked.[1] In a later semi-mystical Midrash, the same thought is repeated, "God created the world in pairs, the one in contrast to the other," as life and death, peace and strife, riches and poverty, wisdom and folly, the righteous and the wicked.[2] This thought was so familiar to the people that the Rabbis tell a story of one of their colleagues who overheard a young girl praying thus: "Lord of the universe! Thou hast created paradise, thou hast created hell, thou hast created the righteous, thou hast created the wicked. May it be thy will that the sons of men should not be ensnared by me!" that is, that she might not prove the opportunity for the wicked.[3]

We have already referred to the metaphor of the *leaven in the dough* as applied to the *Evil Yezer*. The metaphor occurs in a Rabbinic prayer running thus: "May it be thy will, O my God, and the God of my fathers, that thou breakest the yoke of the *Evil Yezer* and removest him from our hearts; for, thou hast created us to do thy will, and we are in duty bound to do thy will. Thou art desirous and we are desirous. But who prevents it? The leaven in the dough. It is revealed and it is known before thee that we have not the strength to resist him; but may it be thy will,

[1] *Chagigah*, 15 a.   [2] See *Midrash Temurah*.
[3] See *Sotah*, 22 a. Cf. Edeles. The parallel, however, in *Baba Bathra*, 16 a (cf. below, p. 273), shows that by creation of the wicked is meant creation of *Evil Yezer*.

O Lord my God, and the God of my fathers, that thou wilt remove him from us, subject him, so that we may do thy will as our will, with a perfect heart." But this leaven is a creation of God, which fact called forth the remark (with reference to Gen. 8 21), "How wretched must the leaven be, that he who has created it bears witness" (that it is bad)![1] More emphatically the same thought is expressed in another place with reference to Gen. 6 6. The Holy One, blessed be he, said, "It is I who put the leaven in the dough; but for the *Evil Yezer* which I have created in him, he (man) would have committed no wrong."[2]

But the leaven, evil as it is, has, according to the Rabbis, its good purpose and its proper place in the universe, as anything created by God, indeed, cannot be entirely evil. Thus, the Scriptural words, "And God saw everything that he had made and behold, it was very good" (Gen. 1 31), are explained among other things to refer to the *Evil Yezer;* whereupon the question is put, "Indeed, can the *Evil Yezer* be considered as very good?" The answer given is that but for the *Evil Yezer* a man would neither build a house, nor marry

---

[1] See *Jer Berachoth*, 7 d, *Gen. R*, 34 10. Cf. ריד״ל, note 12. Cf. above, p 145, note 6 It should be noticed that *Gen. R*, 34 10, has also one opinion to the effect " How poor must the dough be, that the baker bears witness against it." This would, acccording to some commentators, include the whole of man and the condemnation of his all being bad, but this opinion seems to be isolated, and is not reproduced in the parallel passages, such as the *MHG.*, p 132, and *Tan. B.*, 1 15 b, which has also שאור רע.

[2] See *MHG.*, p. 132. Cf. *Gen. R.*, 27 4, and *T. B.*, 1 15 b.

a wife, nor beget children, nor engage in commerce. As further proof of this is given the verse, "Again I considered all travail, and every right work, that for this a man is envied of his neighbour" (Eccles. 4 4).[1] Envy itself, which is one of the ugliest qualities, can thus be made serviceable for a good purpose. This corresponds with another statement, according to which the three things upon which the world is based are: envy, lust, and mercy. In another version the same statement is paraphrased in the following way: "Three good qualities, the Holy One, blessed be he, created in this world, namely, the *Evil Yezer*, *Envy*, and *Mercy*."[2] The *Evil Yezer* has thus little in common with the evil principle of theology, but is reduced to certain passions without which neither the propagation of species nor the building up of the proper civilisation would be thinkable. They only become evil by the improper use man makes of them. It is probably in this sense that the *Evil Yezer* is called once the servant of man. "The Holy One, blessed be he, said: 'See what this wicked people do. When I created them I gave to each of them two servants, the one good and the other evil. But they forsook the good servant and associated with the evil one.'"[3] But even the *Evil Yezer* in his aspect of

[1] *Gen. R.*, 9 7. Cf. also *Eccles. R.*, 3 11.

[2] *A. R. N.*, 9 *a*, text and note 9.

[3] *Ag. Ber.*, 1 4. Cf. *Tan. B*, 1 18 *a*. The latter reads, "Two creations I made in man: the *Good Yezer* and the *Evil Yezer*." But a comparison of the two texts shows that in this case the *Ag. Ber.* pre-

adversary and enemy of man, as his identification with Satan suggests, is not supposed to be entirely evil. Thus Satan is said to have had godly intentions in his denunciation of Job. His purpose was that the merit of Abraham should not be entirely obscured by that of Job. Satan proved himself so grateful for this appreciation of his nature, that he is reported to have kissed the Rabbi on his knees, who thus interpreted his intentions in this generous way.[1] One Rabbi went even so far as to make man responsible for the wickedness of *Yezer*. This opinion is expressed in connection with the verse, "Lo, this only have I found, that God hath made man upright" (Eccles. 7 29), on which the Rabbi remarked: The Holy One, blessed be he, who is called righteous and upright and created man in his image, did this only with the intention that man should be as righteous and upright as he himself. If man will argue, why did he then create the *Evil Yezer* of whom it is written that he is evil from the very youth of man? If God described him as evil, who then could make him good? God's answer is, "Thou (man) hast made him bad." As a proof is given that

served the better reading. Cf also *S. E. Z*, p. 176, about the two angels or three, and יפה תואר to *Gen. R.*, 34 10. Cf. also R. Simon Duran's commentary (אוהב משפט) to Job (ed. Venice), 29 *b* and 47 *b*. It is interesting to see there how the rationalistic school, taking its clew from non-Jewish philosophy, insists upon making the body (or the flesh) responsible for the *Evil Yezer*, maintaining the dualism of flesh and spirit in the most positive manner, whilst the mystical school objects to it and endeavours to ascribe all evil to powers outside of man.

[1] *Baba Bathra*, 16 *a*.

little children commit no sin, and as it is man who breeds the *Evil Yezer* it is thus with the growth of man that sin comes. God further reproaches man, saying, that there are many things harder and bitterer than the *Evil Yezer*, but man finds the means to sweeten them. If man succeeds in making things palatable that are created bitter, how much more could he succeed in tempering the *Evil Yezer* who is delivered into the hands of man?[1]

By making him "bad" is meant, the abuse of those passions which are in themselves a necessity. The same question as to why God has created the *Evil Yezer* is answered in another place to the following effect: The matter is to be compared to a king who had slaves separated from him by an iron wall. The king proclaimed, "He who loves me shall climb this wall and come up to me. He will prove by this effort that he fears the king, and loves the king."[2] The text is not quite clear, but the general drift is that the *Yezer* who forms such an obstacle on the path of righteousness was created with the purpose that man should make a strong effort to overcome him, thereby testifying his loyalty and devotion to the King God, and increasing his reward when all the obstacles have been overcome.

Though these two opinions differ as to the nature and purpose of the *Evil Yezer*, they both agree that he

[1] *Tan.*, בראשית, 7.
[2] *S. E. Z.*, p. 193.

is in the hands of man, who is able to overcome him with a strong effort. Man is warned not to be intimidated by the fact that the *Evil Yezer* is a creation of God, and say that he has no authority over him, for it is written in the Torah, "And unto thee shall be his desire, but thou shalt rule over him" (Gen. 4 7).[1] This verse is paraphrased, "If thou wilt mend thy actions in this world, everything shall be forgiven and pardoned in the world to come. But if thou wilt not mend thy deeds in this world, thy sin will be preserved for the great Day of Judgement. And at the door of thy heart he lies, but in thy hand I have given the *Evil Yezer*, and thou shalt rule over him both for good and for evil."[2] Man has the power in his own hands,[3] and it is only by man's own neglect and weakness that the *Evil Yezer*, who appears first quite effeminate and powerless, gains masculine strength, enabling him to dictate to man. If man does well, he finds forgiveness; but if he does not well, he is delivered into the hands of the *Evil Yezer* who lies at the door.[4]

The difference between the wicked and the righteous is that the wicked are in the power of their hearts, while the righteous have the heart in their power.[5] Indeed, it would seem as if everything depended upon man. Either Satan enters into his body and gains dominion

---

[1] *Gen. R.*, 22 6. Cf. the commentary of מהרז״ו.
[2] *Pseudo-Jonathan*, Gen 4 7. [3] See *MHG.*, p. 109.
[4] See *MHG.*, p. 107. See above, p. 249.
[5] See *Gen. R.*, 34 10. By "heart" is of course meant here the *Yezer*.

over man and sin becomes his master, or man gains mastery over Satan and he suppresses him.[1] Nay, man has in his power not only to resist the *Evil Yezer*, but to turn his services to good purpose. At least the wicked are reproached for their failing to make the *Evil Yezer* good.[2] It is simply a question of choice, the wicked preferring the *Evil Yezer*, while the righteous decide for the *Good Yezer*.[3] Again, the men of the deluge are described as those who themselves made the *Evil Yezer* rule over them, by following his devices.[4] On the other hand, Abraham is said to have had dominion over the *Evil Yezer*,[5] whilst all the patriarchs are recorded to have enjoyed the blessing that the *Evil Yezer* had no dominion over them.[6] Joseph, again, is called the ruler over his *Evil Yezer*.[7] When the *Evil Yezer* is about to overpower man, the righteous will resist him with an oath, as we find in the case of Abraham, Boaz, David, and Elijah, who all conjured their *Yezer* to desist from his evil intentions, while the wicked will conjure their *Yezer*, urging him to commit the evil deed, as in the case of Gehazi.[8] Counsel is given to man that he should prove himself higher and above his sin, not allowing himself to become its slave and be buried under

---

[1] See Wertheimer, לקט מדרשים, p. 4 *b*.
[2] See *Ag. Ber.*, ch 1.
[4] *MHG.*, p. 131.
[3] *Eccles. R.*, 9 1.
[5] *MHG.*, p. 354.
[6] See *Baba Bathra*, 17 *a*.
[7] *Num. R.*, 14 6 Cf. *Deut. R.*, 2: 33.
[8] See *Sifre*, 74 *a*; *Gen. R.*, 87 5; *Lev. R.*, 23 11; and references given there. Cf. also *MHG.*, p. 585, text and note 31.

its heavy burden.[1] If man has to make a goad to direct the animal, which he uses for the purpose of ploughing, etc., how much more should he be careful to use the goad for the purposes of directing his *Yezer*, who can by his seduction remove him from this world and the world to come?[2]

Man is further advised to stir up (to war) the *Good Yezer* against the *Evil Yezer*.[3] In this war, man is not supposed to be neutral. It is his duty not only to assist the *Good Yezer* and save him from his enemy, the *Evil Yezer*, but he should also make an effort to establish the kingdom of the *Good Yezer* over the *Evil Yezer*.[4] As an instance of such a victory of the *Good Yezer* over the *Evil Yezer* the following story may be given: The Saint, Abba Tachna, returned to his village on the eve of the Sabbath, when darkness was about to set in. He had his pack on his shoulders, but there he found at the crossroad a leper, lying, who said unto him, "Rabbi, do with me a righteousness (or act of mercy), and carry me to the town." Abba Tachna said, "If I leave here my pack (which contained all his earnings) how shall I and my family maintain ourselves? But if I leave here this leper, I forfeit my soul." But he declared the *Good Yezer* king over the *Evil Yezer*, and carried the leper to the town, and then came back and took

---
[1] See *Gen. R*, 22 6. It is with allusion to Ps. 32 1.
[2] See *Lev R*, 29 17; *Eccles. R.*, 2 11.
[3] *Ber.*, 5 a. Cf. *P K.*, 158 a.
[4] *Lev. R.*, 34 1, See also *M. T*, 41 2, text and notes.

his pack and arrived at the town again just about sunset. They all wondered and said, "Is this the Saint Abba Tachna?" He himself had some regrets in his heart about it, fearing that he had profaned the Sabbath, but just at this time the Holy One, blessed be he, caused the sun to shine.[1]

The weapons used in this war against the *Evil Yezer* are mainly: occupation with the study of the Torah and works of loving-kindness. "Blessed are Israel," the Rabbis say; "as long as they are devoted to the study of the Torah, and works of loving-kindness, the *Evil Yezer* is delivered into their hands." [2]

It is especially the Torah which is considered the best remedy against the *Evil Yezer*. When Job remonstrated with God, "Thou hast created Paradise, thou hast created Hell, thou hast created the righteous, and thou hast created the wicked. Who prevented thee (from making me righteous?)," he sought by this argument to release the whole world from judgement, seeing that they sin under compulsion. — But his friend answered him, "If God has created the *Evil Yezer*, he also created the Torah as a spice (remedy) against him." [3] To the same effect is another passage, "My son, if this ugly one (the *Evil Yezer*) meets you, drag him into the schoolhouse (Beth-Hammidrash). If he is a stone, he will be ground (into powder); if he is iron, he will be broken into pieces; as it is said, 'Is not my word like

[1] See *Eccles. R*, 9 7.   [2] *Abodah Zarah*, 5 *b*.
[3] *Baba Bathra*, 16 *a*.

unto a fire? saith the Lord, and like a hammer that breaketh the rocks in pieces?'" (Jer. 23 29).[1]

The words in the Psalms, "Order my steps in thy word, and let not any iniquity have dominion over me" (Ps. 119 133), are paraphrased in the following way: "David said, 'Allow not my feet to go where they wish, but let them go all the time to thy Torah in the Beth-Hammidrash, for the *Evil Yezer* does not enter the Beth-Hammidrash. He may pursue man all the way, but as soon as they reach the Beth-Hammidrash, Satan must abandon the race.'"[2] Again, he whose heart is absorbed in the words of the Torah removes thereby from himself all idle thoughts as well as the thoughts insinuated by the *Evil Yezer*.[3] The name *stone* given to the *Evil Yezer* suggested also the following allegorical explanation of Gen. 29 2: "*And Jacob looked, and behold there were three flocks of sheep.* By these are meant the three masters of the Synagogue; *For out of this well they watered the flocks;* by this is meant the Torah; *but the stone is great;* this is the *Evil Yezer*, who can only be removed by the efforts of the whole congregation; *who rolled the stone from the well's mouth*, by means of their listening to the Torah. But as soon as they left the Synagogue, the *Evil Yezer* reasserted himself."[4] The fact, however, that a part of the Torah, or rather the Decalogue, was written on stone or

---

[1] *Kiddushin*, 30 b.   [2] *M T*, 119 62.   [3] *A. R. N.*, 35 b.
[4] *Gen. R.*, 70 8. The word קרואים is doubtful, and still requires a proper explanation. See above, p. 244, note 1.

on "tablets of stone" (Exod. 24 22), suggested the following explanation: "Since the *Evil Yezer* is also called *stone*, as it is said, 'And I will take away the stony heart'" (Ezek. 36 26), "it is only proper that stone should watch over stone." [1] The effects of the Torah in this battle with the *Yezer* seem to be differently understood by the different authorities, for while one Rabbi gives as advice, "If the *Yezer* come to make you merry (or frivolous), then kill him (or throw him down) by the word of the Torah," the other Rabbi counsels us "to rejoice the *Yezer* with the words of the Torah"; that is, to use the inclination of man towards joy and cheerfulness for the joy and the happiness which man should find in accomplishing the will of God.[2] The killing of the *Evil Yezer* is further recommended in the following words, "To him who kills his *Yezer* and confesses upon it, it is reckoned as if he would have honoured the Holy One, blessed be he, in two worlds, this world and the world to come." [3] But it would seem that this is not considered as the highest attainment of man; for it is said of Abraham, that he made the *Evil Yezer* good. Indeed, the *Evil Yezer* compromised with him, entering into a covenant that he would not make Abraham sin, whilst David, who could not resist the *Evil Yezer*, had to slay him in his heart.[4]

[1] *Lev. R*, 35 5; cf. also *Num. R.*, 14 4, and *Cant. R.*, 6 11.
[2] See *Gen. R.*, 22 6, text and commentaries. Cf. *MHG.*, p. 110, for varying readings. Cf. Theodor's ed. of *Gen. R.*, p 212.
[3] *Sanhedrin*, 43 b. Cf *Lev R.*, 9 1. See also below, p. 335 *seq.*
[4] *Jer. Berachoth*, 14 b. See also above, p. 67

Another means of defeating the machinations of *Yezer* is the contemplation of death.[1] This can be best illustrated by the following passage of Akabiah b. Mahalaleel, "Consider three things, and thou wilt not come into the hands of sin. Know whence thou comest, and whither thou art going, and before whom thou art to give account and reckoning."[2] Another version of the same saying is, "He who thinks of the following four things will never sin again: that is, from whence he comes, where he is destined to go, what will become of him, and who is his Judge."[3] Sin or the *Evil Yezer* in this case is chiefly representative of the passion of vanity. These passages could be multiplied to any extent, but they are all to the effect that man, meditating upon his lowly origin and his sad end, will not be slow to give up all pretensions that come from pride and conceit. Sometimes, the remembrance of death serves also as a damper to man's tendency towards excess. An instance of this we have in the following: "At the wedding of the son of Rabina, the students there present said unto Rab Hamnuna Zuta, 'Let the master sing a song unto us,' whereupon he began to sing, 'Woe unto us that we shall die! Woe unto us that we shall die!' When they asked for the refrain, he gave the words, 'Where is the Torah, and where are the good works that will protect us?'"[4]

---

[1] *Berachoth*, 5 a.   [2] *Aboth*, 3 1.
[3] *D. E.*, p. 3. Cf. *A. R. N.*, 35 a, text and notes.
[4] *Berachoth*, 31 a.

There may further be brought together under this category other remedies against the *Evil Yezer* which are of an ascetic nature. The story of the Nazarite who had his hair cut off with the purpose of subduing his *Yezer* has already been referred to.[1] A certain Rabbi, again, is recorded to have prayed for the death of his nearest kin, when he was under the impression that she would become the cause of sin.[2] The later Jewish moralists prescribed a whole set of regulations, which are more or less of an ascetic nature, and calculated to make a fence against transgression. But the underlying idea of all of them is that all opulence, wealth, gluttony, and other opportunities of satisfying one's appetite are so many auxiliaries to the *Evil Yezer*. Thus the Scriptural verses in Deut. 11 15–16 are paraphrased, "Moses said unto Israel, 'Be careful that you rebel not against the Holy One, blessed be he, because man does not enter upon this rebellion, but when he is full,'" that is, revelling in food and other luxuries.[3] The proverb was, "A lion does not roar from the midst of a heap of straw, but from the midst of a heap of meat." Another proverb was, "Filled stomachs are a bad sort (or plenty is tempting)."[4] Hence the homily of the Rabbi with reference to the verse, "Behold, I have refined thee, but not with silver; I have chosen thee in the furnace of poverty" (Isa. 48 10), that it teaches that the Holy One, blessed be he, searched all good

---

[1] See above, p. 249.
[2] *Taanith*, 24 a.
[3] *Sifre*, 80 b. Cf. *ibid.*, 136 a.
[4] *Berachoth*, 31 a.

things but found nothing better for Israel than poverty.[1]

It should, however, be remarked that even the Torah is not an all-powerful remedy in itself without the aid of heaven, which gives the Torah its real efficiency. Thus with reference to the verse, "Let my heart be sound (תמים) in thy statutes, that I be not ashamed" (Ps. 119, 80), the Rabbis remark, "David said, 'Master of the world, when I am occupied in Thy Law, allow not the *Evil Yezer* to divide me . . . that the *Evil Yezer* may not lead me astray . . . but make my heart one, so that I be occupied in the Torah with soundness (perfection or fulness).'"[2] Again, with reference to another verse, "Make me understand the way of thy precepts" (Ps. 119 27), it is remarked that David said, "My Master, say not unto me, behold they (the words of the Torah) are before thee, meditate upon them by thyself. For if thou wilt not make me understand them, I shall know nothing."[3] The Torah by itself is thus not sufficient to defeat the *Evil Yezer*. The conquest comes in the end from God. We are thus brought to the necessity of grace forming a prominent factor in the defeat of the *Yezer*. Hence, the various prayers for the removal or the subjugation of the *Evil Yezer*. Specimens of such prayers have already been given.[4] Here we might further refer to the

[1] See *Chagigah*, 9 b.

[2] *Exod. R.*, 19 2. The reading is not quite clear. I have adopted the reading suggested by רד״ל, note 8

[3] *M. T.*, 119 16. See also *ibid.* to verse 33. [4] See above, p. 265,

individual prayer of R. Judah the Saint, in which he supplicates that God may save him from the *Evil Yezer*.[1] A similar prayer we have from another Rabbi of a later date.[2] Other Rabbis, again, put their prayers in a more positive form, as, for instance, those who prayed that God would endow them with a *Good Yezer*.[3] Sometimes neither the *Evil Yezer* nor the *Good Yezer* is mentioned, the prayer being more directed against sin, as for instance, the one running, "May it be thy will that we shall not sin, and then we shall not be put to shame."[4] The heart plays a special part in these prayers, as for instance the one which is to the effect, "May our heart become single in the fear of thy name. Remove us from all thou hatest. Bring us near to all thou lovest, and do with us a righteousness for thy Name's sake." Another similar prayer is, "May it be thy will, Lord God, and the God of our fathers, that thou put into our hearts to do perfect repentance."[5] As typical in this respect we may perhaps mention the lines in the daily prayer-book, "Make us cleave to the *Good Yezer* and to good deeds; subjugate our *Evil Yezer* so that it may submit itself unto thee."[6] A prayer fairly combining all these features is the one repeated several times on the Day of Atonement, running thus: "Our God and God of our

---

[1] *Berachoth*, 16 b.   [2] *Berachoth*, 17 a.

[3] See *Berachoth*, 17 b, and *Jer. Berachoth*, 4 c.

[4] *Berachoth*, 17 b.   [5] *Jer. Berachoth*, 7 d.

[6] See *Berachoth*, 60 b, the text of which differs in some minor points from that in our prayer-books. Cf. *Singer*, p. 7, Baer, p. 43.

fathers, forgive and pardon our iniquities on this Day of Atonement. . . . Subdue our heart to serve thee, and bend our *Yezer* to turn unto thee; renew our reins to observe thy precepts, and circumcise our hearts to love and revere thy Name, as it is written in thy Law: And the Lord thy God will circumcise thy heart and the heart of thy seed, to love the Lord thy God with all thine heart and with all thy soul, that thou mayest live."[1] The underlying idea of these passages, which can be multiplied by any number of parallel passages, is man's consciousness of his helplessness against the powers of temptation, which can only be overcome by the grace of God. The oldest prayer of this kind, of course, is the one in the Eighteen Benedictions, praying for God's help to bring man back unto him or his Torah and to his service, as well as the one for repentance.[2]

A special feature about the Rabbinic passages emphasising the necessity of grace in the struggle with the *Evil Yezer*, is the implication of God's responsibility for the existence of the *Evil Yezer*. The pleading of Job and his insistence upon God's power to prevent sin has already been quoted, but there Job is censured for it.[3] Indeed, he was considered as an heretic for making this plea. A similar case we have with Cain. When reproached for murdering his brother, he is described as saying, "Master of the world, if I have

[1] See Festival Prayers, Day of Atonement, Part II, pp. 14, 185, 234.
[2] See below, p. 341.   [3] See above, p. 273, note 3.

killed him, it is thou who hast created in me the *Evil Yezer*. Thou watchest me and the whole world. Why didst thou permit me to kill him? It is thou who hast killed him ... for if thou hadst received my sacrifice, as thou didst receive his (Abel's) sacrifice, I would not have become jealous of him."[1] But of course Cain represents the bad type of humanity. Yet it is not to be denied that the Rabbis themselves sometimes employed similar arguments. Thus, with reference to the verse, "O Lord, why hast thou made us to err from thy ways, and hardened our heart from thy fear?" (Isa. 63 17), the Rabbis plead in favour of the brothers of Joseph, "When thou (God) didst choose, thou didst make them love; when thou didst choose, thou didst make them hate."[2] Something similar is hinted about the affair of Cain and Abel. R. Simon b. Jochai said, "It is a thing hard to say, and it is impossible for the mouth to utter it. It is to be compared to two athletes who were wrestling in the presence of the king. If the king wills, he can have them separated; but the king wills not; (in the end) one overwhelmed the other and killed him. And (the dying) man shouted: 'Who can now demand justice for me (seeing that the king was present and could have prevented it)?'"[3] In another place we read with reference to the verses in Micah 4 6, Jer. 18 6, and Ezek. 36 26, that but for such statements as these, implying the pos-

[1] See *MHG.*, p. 112, and note 36.
[2] *Gen. R.*, 18 20.   [3] *Gen. R.*, 22 9.

sibility of God's power to exterminate the *Evil Yezer*, there would be no hope for Israel, such a possibility serving in extenuation of their guilt.[1] Again, with reference to the verse, "For he knoweth our frame (יצרנו); he remembereth that we are dust," we are told that this fact will save Israel from seeing Hell. So Israel will plead before the Holy One, blessed be he, "Master of the world, thou knowest the *Evil Yezer* who seduces us."[2] It is with reference to the same verse, that we read as stated in another place, "Wretched, indeed, must be the leaven, if he who has created it declares it as evil."[3] The "whisper from above" (heaven) makes the serpent (or the *Evil Yezer* whose creation God regrets) bite or commit violence on earth; because of which fact "a door of mercy is opened to the sinners in Israel that they may be received as penitents; as they will plead before him, Master of the world: it is revealed and known unto thee that it is the *Evil Yezer* that incites us. In thy great mercy receive us in perfect repentance."[4]

More emphatic, even, is another remark on the verse of Jer. 18 6, "Israel said, 'Master of the world . . . even when we sin and make thee angry, be not removed from us, for we are the clay, and thou art the potter! . . .' Israel said, 'Thou hast created in us the

[1] *Berachoth*, 32 a, and *Sukkah*, 52 b.

[2] *A. R. N.*, 32 a and b. Cf. *Sanhedrin*, 105 a, homily on Isa. 28.26.

[3] *Gen R.*, 34 10. Cf. *M T.*, 103 14, text and Note 55. See above, 266.

[4] See *S. E.*, p 63 a, text and notes. Cf. *Eccles. R.*, 10 1.

Evil Yezer from our very youth. It is he who causes us to sin before thee, but thou dost not remove from us the sin. We pray thee, cause him to disappear from us, so that we may do thy will.' Whereupon God says, 'So I will do in the world to come.'"[1] Nay, there are recorded cases of men belonging to the best type of humanity, who make the same plea as Job and Cain, though in somewhat more modest terms. Thus, Moses is said to have "knocked words against the height" (reproached God), arguing it was the gold and silver which he gave to Israel that was the cause of their making the golden calf.[2] Again, Elijah "knocked words against the height," saying to God, "Thou hast turned their heart back again" (1 Kings 18 37). And the Rabbis proceed to say that God confessed that Elijah's contention was right.[3]

For, indeed, God sometimes does make sin impossible, as in the case of Abimelech, to whom God said, "For I also withheld thee from sinning against me: therefore suffered I thee not to touch her" (Gen. 20 6). The Rabbis illustrate this in the following way: "It is to be compared to a strong man riding on a horse. But there was a child lying on the road which was thus in danger of being run over. But the man drove the horse so that it avoided the child. The praise in this case is certainly due to the rider, not to the horse. In a similar way Abimelech claimed a special merit for not having sinned. But God said unto him, 'The

[1] *Exod. R.*, 46 4. [2] *Berachoth*, 32 a. [3] *Berachoth, ibid.*

Yezer who causes you to sin is in my power, and it was I who drew thee away from sin.' "[1]

This direct interference, however, with the *Evil Yezer* seems exceptional. What was prominent in the mind of the Jew was first, that God, "who is a law unto himself," does not choose to make use of this prerogative of his, though the *Evil Yezer* evidently belongs to this class of creation which the Holy One, blessed be he, regrets to have called into existence, if one can say so.[2] "There is astonishment before me" (God says), "that I have created in man the *Evil Yezer*, for if I would not have created in man the *Evil Yezer*, he would not have rebelled against me."[3] This regret of God is expressed by another Rabbi in the following way: "After the Holy One, blessed be he, created this world he regretted the creation of the *Evil Yezer*, as it is said, ' O that there were such an heart in them that they would fear me and keep my commandments always' (Deut. 5 29). This teaches that God longs that Israel should labour in the Torah. From this thou inferrest that the authority (choice) of man is given unto him; therefore if he does what he is commanded, he merits to receive reward, as it is said, ' That it might be well with them and their children for ever' (Deut. 5 26)."[4] Apparently, the world is so constituted that man should be a hybrid of angel and beast with the

[1] *Gen. R.*, 52 7. Cf *Exod. R* 21, and *P. K.*, p. 176 *b*.
[2] *Sukkah*, 52 *b*. Cf. *S E.*, p 63.
[3] *Gen. R.*, 27 4.   [4] *MHG.*, Deut., p. 46 *b*, Ms.

possibility of sin, which spells death, and that of conquering sin, which means life.[1] Angels have no *Evil Yezer* and are thus spared from jealousy, covetousness, lust, and other passions, but those who dwell below are under the temptation of the *Evil Yezer*, and therefore require a double guard of holiness to resist him.[2] This double guard they have in the Torah, as indicated above; otherwise man is a free agent. To secure this freedom, it would seem that God has even foregone his prerogative in respect of preventing sin, so that the bold statement of the Rabbi that everything is in the power of God except (the forcing upon man of) the fear of God, has become a general maxim, though, as is well known, this maxim is not without its difficulties.[3] All that God does is only in the way of warning, and reminding man that there is an Eye watching him, and that he will be responsible for his choice. "Everything is seen, and freedom of choice is given . . . the shop is open; and the dealer gives credit; and the ledger lies open; and the hand writes; and whosoever wishes to borrow may come and borrow."[4] In another place,

[1] See *Gen. R.*, 14 8. See above, p. 261, note 1, and below, 292.
[2] See *Shabbath*, 89 a; *Gen. R.*, 48 11; *Lev. R.*, 24 8 and 26 5.
[3] See *Berachoth*, 33 b, *Megillah*, 25 a; *Niddah*, 16 b; *Tan.* פקודי, 3. Cf. *Tosafoth* to the passages in the Talmud.
[4] See *Aboth*, 3 15. Cf Taylor, 3 24, and Bacher, *Ag. Tan.*, I 282. See also *A R.N.*, 58 b. According to the version given there of this saying of R. Akiba, it is altogether very doubtful whether the Rabbi really meant to emphasise the antithesis of predestination and free will. Cf. Commentaries to *Aboth*. See also *A.R.N.*, 75 a and 81 b, suggesting that the צפוי refers to man.

the responsibility for his choice is expressed in the following words: "As it was said, 'I have set before you life and death, blessing and cursing' (Deut. 30 19), Israel might perhaps say, 'Considering that the Holy One, blessed be he, placed before us two ways, the way of life and the way of death, we might go in any of these which we like,' therefore it is further said, 'Choose life, that both thou and thy seed may live' (Deut., *ibid.*)."[1] Life is identical with the good way. Deut. 30 15 is paraphrased, "Behold, I have set before you this day the way of life, which is the good way, and the way of death, which is the bad way."[2] The sin of Adam, indeed, consisted in the fact that he made choice of the evil. The Omnipresent placed before him two ways, the one of death and the one of life, and he (Adam) chose the way of death.[3] The same complaint is made of other transgressors in history, of whom it is said, "He setteth himself in a way that is not good" (Ps. 36 5). They walk in iniquity and meditate iniquity: they have two ways, the one for good and the one for evil. And so Solomon said, "Who leave the paths of uprightness to walk in the ways of darkness." For indeed the heart was created to speak truth, but your heart works wickedness; the hands were created to accomplish goodness and righteousness, and you do violence and robbery, and so the

---

[1] See *Sifre*, 86 a. Cf. *Tan.*, ראה, § 3.
[2] See *Pseudo-Jonathan* to this verse.
[3] *Mechilta*, 33 a. Cf. *Gen. R.*, 20 5 and references.

blind walk in the evil way and the open-eyed ones walk in the way of good.¹

The verse, again, "Surely he scorneth the scorners; but he giveth grace unto the lowly" (Prov. 3 34), is interpreted, he who desires to contaminate himself they open unto him, he who desires to purify himself they aid him (from heaven). "For indeed things defiling do not come upon man unless he turned his mind to them and became defiled by them," whilst God increases the strength of the righteous that they may do his will, but he that guards himself against sin for three times, has the promise that henceforth God will guard him ² In different words, the same thought is expressed in another place, "In the way in which a man chooses to walk, they guide him (or allow him to walk). This is to be derived from the Torah, where it is written (with regard to Balaam), first, 'Thou shalt not go with them' (Num. 25 12), and then, 'Rise up and go with them' (*ibid.* 20); from the Prophets, where it is said, 'I am the Lord, thy God, which teacheth thee to profit, which leadeth thee by the way that thou shouldst go' (Isa. 48 17); and from the Hagiographa, where it is said, 'Surely, he scorneth the scorners; but he giveth grace unto the lowly' (Prov. 3 35)." ³

A peculiar paraphrase of the verses quoted above from

---

¹ *M. T*, 36 8 and 58 2; *Exod. R* , 30 20.
² *Shabbath*, 104 a. See also *T. K.*, 91 a; *P K* , 161 a, and *Jer. Kiddushin*, 61 d.   ³ *Makkoth*, 10 b.

Deuteronomy (30 15), we have in the following passage
taken from a later Midrash: "Rabbi Eliezer said, 'I
heard with my ears the Lord of Hosts speaking. And
what did he say? "Behold, I have set before you this
day the life and the good, death and the evil."
The Holy One, blessed be he, said, "Behold, these
two ways I have given to Israel, the one for good and
the one for evil: that of good is of life, that of evil
is of death." That of good branches off in two ways:
of righteousness and of loving-kindness: Elijah is
placed in the middle. And when a man is about to
enter upon them, he exclaims and says, "Open ye the
gates, that the righteous nation . . . may enter in"
(Isa. 26 2). . . . But that of the evil has four doors:
upon each door seven guardians are seated: four
within and three without. Those outside are merciful
angels. . . . And when he is about to enter in the
first door, the merciful angels meet him first and say
unto him, "Why dost thou want to enter into this
fire, among the wicked and the coals? Listen unto
us and do repentance. . . ." When he comes to the
second door, they say unto him, "Behold, thou hast
already passed in through the first door, do not enter
into the second! Why dost thou want to be removed
from the Torah of God, that they call thee 'unclean,'
and flee from thee?" . . . When he comes to the third
door, they tell him, "Thou hast already passed the
second door! Why come into the third? Why wilt
thou be wiped out from the book of life? . . .

Listen unto us and return!" When he reaches the fourth door, they say unto him, "Thou hast passed already the third door! do not come into the fourth door! ... Thou hast not listened and stayed thy steps hitherto ... the Holy One, blessed be he, forgives the sins and pardons, and says every day, 'Return, ye backsliding children!'" If he listens unto them, well; if not, woe unto him and to his star.'"[1]

The quoted passage, with the constant reminder coming from the angels of mercy, brings us back to the idea of grace, or the thought of man standing in need of the aid of heaven in his struggle with *Yezer*. Besides the passages given above, we may add here the following statement, "Every day the *Yezer* of man assaults him and endeavours to kill him, and but for the Holy One, blessed be he, who helps man, he could not resist him."[2] It may be that it was this feeling of man's comparative helplessness in such a condition which wrung the cry from the Rabbi, "Woe unto me of my (*Evil*) *Yezer* and woe unto me of my *Yozer* (Creator)."[3] But man has to show himself worthy of this grace, inasmuch as it is expected that the first effort against the *Evil Yezer* should be made on his part, whereupon the promise comes that *Yezer* will be finally removed by God. Thus with reference to the

---

[1] *P. R. E.*, ch. 15. Cf. the commentary of רד״ל. Cf. Mr. C. G. Montefiore, *Rabbinic Conception of Repentance, Jewish Quarterly Review*, v 16, pp. 209–257.

[2] *Sukkah*, 52 b.   [3] See *Berachoth*, 61 a.

Scriptural verse, "O Israel, return unto the Lord thy God; for thou hast stumbled by thine iniquity" (Hos. 14 1), the Rabbis remark that it is to be compared to a huge rock that was placed on the crossways, on which men used to stumble; whereupon the king said unto them, "Chip it off little by little until the hour comes when I will remove it altogether."[1] Another version of the same saying is, "Israel said before the Holy One, blessed be he, 'Master of the world, thou knowest the power of the *Evil Yezer*, which is very hard.' Whereupon the Holy One, blessed be he, said unto them, 'Move the stone a little in this world, and I will remove it from you in the next world, as it is said, "Cast up, cast up the highway; gather out the stones" (Isa. 62 10), whilst in another place it is said, "Cast ye up, cast ye up, prepare the way, take up the stumbling-block of my people"' (Is. 57 14)."[2]

The struggle with the *Evil Yezer* will cease with the advent of the Messiah, "when the Holy One, blessed be he, will bring the *Evil Yezer* and kill him in the presence both of the righteous and of the wicked." To the righteous he will appear in the shape of a big mountain, and they will cry and will say, "How were we able to subdue such an obstacle?" In the eyes of the wicked, he will resemble a thin hair, and they will cry and say, "O that we were not strong enough to defeat such an insignificant impediment!"[3] In another

---

[1] *P. K*, 165 a.   [2] *Num. R.*, 15 16   Cf. *Tan. B.*, 4 28 a.
[3] *Sukkah*, 52 a.   Cf. also *Gen. R*, 48 11 and 89 1; *Exod. R.*, 41 7 and 46 4, and *Num R.*, 17 6, *Deut R.*, 2 30 and 6 14, *P R.*, 29 a.

place, the removal of the *Yezer* from the world is described as follows: "If your scattered ones will be in the end of the heaven, from there the word of the Lord your God will gather you through Elijah the High Priest, and from there he will bring you near through the hands of the King Messiah. And the word of the Lord your God will bring you to the land which your fathers inherited, and you shall inherit it; and he will do you good, and multiply you above your fathers. And the Lord your God will remove the folly of the hearts of your children, for he will make the *Evil Yezer* cease from the world, and will create the *Good Yezer*, who will counsel you to love the Lord your God with all your hearts, and all your souls, that your lives may last forever." [1]

Only once in history Israel had a presentiment of these Messianic times. When Israel (on the occasion of the Revelation on Mount Sinai) heard the commandment "Thou shalt have no other gods before me" (Exod. 20 3), the *Evil Yezer* was uprooted from their hearts; but when they came to Moses and said unto him, "Our master Moses, become thou the messenger between us (Israel and God), as it is said, 'Speak thou with us . . . but let not God speak with us lest we die' (Exod. 20 19), the *Evil Yezer* came back at once in his place." They came again to Moses and said, "Our master Moses, we wish that he (God) should reveal himself again unto us." He answered them,

[1] *Pseudo-Jonathan*, Deut , 30 4.

"This is impossible now (but it will take place in the future to come)."[1] Every separation from God, though not with the intention of sin, but with the purpose of establishing an intermediary, is, as we see, considered as the setting up of another God, who is the cause of sin; whilst on the other hand, it is suggested that it is by the conquering of the *Evil Yezer* that man enters into close communion with God. Thus Lev. 9 6 is paraphrased, "Remove the *Evil Yezer* from your heart and the Divine Presence will at once be revealed to you."[2] But it is this struggle on the part of man which places him above the angels. "The angels said in the presence of the Holy One, blessed be he, 'Master of the world, why are we not allowed to intone our song here in heaven (in the praise of God) before Israel sing their song below on earth?' And the Holy One, blessed be he, answered to them, 'How shall you say it (the song) before Israel? Israel have their habitation on earth; they are born of women, and the *Evil Yezer* has dominion among them, and nevertheless they oppose the *Yezer* and declare my unity every day, and proclaim me as King every day, and long for my Kingdom and for the rebuilding of my Temple.'"[3]

[1] *Cant. R*, 1 2.   [2] *Pseudo-Jonathan*, Lev. 9 6.
[3] See Friedmann, נספחים, p. 56. See above, p. 91, note 2.

XVII

FORGIVENESS AND RECONCILIATION WITH GOD

THE various aspects of the doctrine of atonement and forgiveness as conceived by the Rabbis may be best grouped round the following Rabbinic passage: "They asked Wisdom (Hagiographa), 'What is the punishment of the sinner?' Wisdom answered, 'Evil pursues sinners' (Prov. 13 21). They asked Prophecy, 'What is the punishment of the sinner?' Prophecy answered, 'The soul that sinneth, it shall die' (Ezek. 18 4). They asked the Torah, 'What is the punishment of the sinner?' Torah answered, 'Let him bring a guilt-offering and it shall be forgiven unto him, as it is said, "And it shall be accepted for him to make atonement for him"' (Lev. 1 4). They asked the Holy One, blessed be he, 'What is the punishment of the sinner?' The Holy One, blessed be he, answered, 'Let him do repentance and it shall be forgiven unto him, as it is said, "Good and upright is the Lord: therefore will he teach sinners in the way"' (Ps. 25 8) — that is, that he points the sinners the way that they should do repentance."[1] It need hardly be remarked that to the Rabbi the whole of the Bible was the word of God, and he could not thus fairly have seen a contradiction between the dictum of the Holy One, blessed be he, and the dicta of the Torah and those of the "Prophets of truth and righteousness." Besides, it could not have escaped the Rabbi that both the Torah and the Prophets have passages enough insisting upon the importance of repentance. Again, sacrifices, as we shall see presently, according to the Rabbis are always accompanied by repentance, whilst the chief function of repentance is limited to such cases as those in which sacrifices are of no avail. What the Rabbi really meant is, that forgiveness is achieved in various ways, through suffering and death, through atonement of sacrifices, but more prominently through repentance, which latter is the most divine aspect of the three. It should be premised that the prerogative of granting pardon is entirely in the hands of God, every mediator being excluded from this prerogative; "for he will not pardon your transgressions," being a mere messenger to accomplish what he is bidden to do. And so David said, "Master of the world, wilt thou deliver me into the hand of an angel who wilt not lift up his countenance? Forgiveness is with

[1] See *Jer. Makkoth*, 31 *d*, and *P K.*, 158 *b*. The texts are in both places defective, but they supplement each other. Cf. *Yalkut Machiri* to Ps. 25 8, reproducing the passage from *Jer. Makkoth* in the order of Torah, Prophecy, Hagiographa, and God, adding also between Prophets and Hagiographa David, with a reference to Ps. 104 85.

thee (God), as it is said, 'But there is forgiveness with thee' (Ps. 130 4)."[1] David also prayed, "Let my sentence come from thy Presence (Ps. 17 1); do thou judge me, and deliver me not into the hands of an angel, or a seraph, or a cherub, or an *ofan*, for they are all cruel," as indeed they do object to the acceptance of the penitents altogether.[2] Indeed, God is desirous of acquitting his creatures and not of declaring them guilty. When the Holy One, blessed be he, said unto Moses, "What is my profession (אומנות)?" he answered, "Thou art merciful and gracious and long-suffering and abundant of goodness."[3] When they sin and provoke his anger, the Holy One, blessed be he, seeks for one to plead on their behalf and paves the way for him.[4]

As sacrifice as a means of atonement is a prominent feature both in the Torah and in Rabbinic literature, it will perhaps be best here to treat first of this aspect. It should be remarked that sacrifices are, as just hinted at, very limited in their efficacy as a means of atonement and reconciliation. Thus with reference to Lev. 4 1, "If a soul shall sin through igno-

[1] See *Tan. B.*, 2 44 *b*, text and notes. Cf. *Sanhedrin*, 38 *b*, the references there to Exod 23 21. Cf. above, p. 41, text and notes.

[2] See *Ag. Ber.*, ch. 9. See also below, pp. 319 and 321. Cf *S. E.*, p. 109. See also Hoffmann's remark, *Das Buch Leviticus*, 1186, that whilst it is the priest who atones, וכפר הכהן, the pardon comes from God, ונסלח

[3] See *Yalkut* to Num. 14 8 and Job, § 907, reproduced from the *Yelamdenu*.

[4] *Tan.*, וירא, 8. Cf. *P. R., ibid.*

rance," the general rule is laid down, "One brings a sin-offering for sins committed in ignorance, but brings no sin-offering for sins committed wilfully," which rule is also applied to sin-offerings.[1] In another place, with reference to Prov. 21 2, it is pointed out that the superiority of practising the works of charity and justice over sacrifices consists in this, that whilst the atoning effect of the former extends also to the sins committed wilfully, that of the latter is confined only to sins committed unintentionally.[2] It is further to be noticed that the great majority of sacrifices are largely confined to matters ritual and ceremonial, and certain other transgressions relating to Levitical impurity; whilst all those sins which concern a person and which fall mostly under the heading of moral laws could not be atoned without proper restitution.[3] Lastly, it is to be remarked, that sin- and guilt-offerings, according to the opinion of the majority of the Rabbis, are accompanied by repentance and by a confession of sins on the part of the man who brings the sacrifices.[4] The injunction is, "Be not like the fools who bring a sacrifice for their offences, but turn not from

---

[1] See *Kerithoth*, 9 a; *T. K.*, 15 b, *Sifre*, 32 b.

[2] *Deut. R.*, 5 3. See commentaries.

[3] See Maimonides, הלכות שגגות, ch. 1 and 9, regarding the cases in which a sin- or guilt-offering is brought.

[4] See *Shebuoth*, 13 a; *Kerithoth*, 7 a; *Tosephta Yoma*, p. 190 (§ 9) Cf. also *Sifre*, 2 a, with regard to Confession. See also Maimonides, תשובה, I., and Hoffmann, *Das Buch Leviticus*, I., p. 202 Cf. also below, p. 337, note 1.

the evil deeds which they have in their hands, and are not accepted in grace." [1]

A main condition in the sacrificial service aptly described sometimes in contradistinction to prayer as the "service of deeds" is the purity of intention and the singleness of purpose with which the sacrifice is brought. It has to be brought with the intention "of giving calmness of spirit for the sake of him who created the world." Quantity is of no consideration, considering that both the burnt-offering of an animal and the burnt-offering of a mere bird form a sweet savour unto the Lord (Lev. 1 9 and 17). "This is to teach," as the Rabbis proceed to say, "that both he who increases (his offering) and he who diminishes his offering are alike pleasing unto the Lord, provided each directs his mind toward heaven." [2] From another place, it would almost seem as if it were the less costly sacrifice that is the more acceptable. It is with reference to the circumstance that the term והקריב used of the sacrifice consisting in a ram (Lev. 1 13) is omitted at the sacrifice consisting of a bullock (Lev. *ibid.*, 9). On this the Rabbis remark, "Let no man think, 'I will do things ugly and things unworthy, but will afterwards bring a bullock which has much flesh and cause it to be brought upon the altar.' How! will God respect per-

---

[1] *Targum*, Eccles. 4 17; cf. *Berachoth*, 23 a.

[2] See *T. K*, 8 *b* and 9 *b*. See also *Zebachim*, 46 *b*. Cf. Hoffmann as above, p. 92. The words "calmness of spirit" are a sort of paraphrase of the Hebrew equivalent, ריח ניחח, usually rendered into English by "sweet savour." Cf. above, p. 160.

sons? 'But let man do good deeds and devote himself to the study of the Torah and bring the lean ram . . . and I shall have mercy with him and accept his repentance.'"[1] If the sacrifice is not brought with the intention of pleasing God, it is reckoned unto them as if they have brought it only for their own purposes.[2] Indeed, it would seem that according to the Rabbis the only *raison d'être* for sacrifices is man's compliance with God's will, who prescribed this order of service. Thus, with reference to Num. 28 2, it is remarked, "It is a calmness of spirit for me, I, who commanded it and my will was done." The Rabbi proceeds then to prove that the sacrifices have not the purpose of providing the Holy One, blessed be he, with food, and quotes the well-known verses of the 50th Psalm, and concludes to the effect: "But why did God say sacrifice unto him, in order to accomplish his will?"[3]

[1] See *S. E*, pp. 36 and 38, and *Lev. R.*, 2 12. The term והקריב (to bring near) is interpreted to mean the closer communion with God which is to be established by the sacrifice in question. See the commentary, יפה תואר, to this passage in *Lev. R.*

[2] See *T K.*, 12 c. Cf , however, the commentary of R. Abraham b. David to this passage.

[3] See *Sifre*, 54 a. Cf. *P. K.*, 56 *seq* , and *P. R.*, pp. 80, 194 a *seq.*, and references, given there in the commentaries. See also *Yalkut Machiri* to Ps 50 4–14. It ought to be remarked that the reading in the concluding sentence of our passage in the *Sifre* is not certain According to the *Machiri*, this sentence reads to the effect that, "Indeed, God is in no need of sacrifices, but only told man to sacrifice unto him in order to do his (man's) will," which reading received some support from *P. R.*, 195 a, where it reads that "the sacrifices were only instituted for thy (man's) atonement and honour." Neverthe-

The atoning effect of sacrifices differs with the various sacrifices. The sin-offering brings complete reconciliation, whilst others have only the power of partial atonement or of suspending the judgement of God.[1] Interesting is the following controversy between the School of Shammai and the School of Hillel with reference to the "continual burnt-offering" consisting of two lambs (Num. 28 3, *seq.*). According to the School of Shammai, "they only subdue the sins of Israel," as it is said, "He will subdue our iniquities; and thou wilt cast all their sins into the depths of the sea" (Micah 7 19), but the School of Hillel teaches that, "Everything which is subdued (or sunk) may, in the end, come to the surface," but the name of this sacrifice means that the two lambs have the effect to wash away the sins of Israel.[2] It is in this way, it is

less I am not inclined to think that the Rabbis entertained any such rationalistic views as those with regard to sacrifices Excepting the well-known passage in *Lev. R.*, 22 8, the meaning of which is, however, very doubtful, there is nothing to prove that they in any way deprecated it. Cf Hoffmann, *Das Buch Leviticus*, pp. 79–92. On the other hand, the facility with which the Rabbis adapted themselves after the destruction of the Holy Temple to the new conditions must impress one with the conviction that the sacrificial service was not considered absolutely indispensable.

[1] Cf. Hoffmann, *ibid*, pp. 79–92. About sacrifices atoning only partially or having only suspending power, תולה, see *Yoma*, 85 b, text and commentaries.

[2] *P. K.*, 61 b; *P. R.*, 84 a and commentaries. The *Beth Shammai* take the word כבשים as if it were written with a שׁ, thus meaning "suppressing" or "subduing," and corresponding to יכבש of Micah The *Beth Hillel* take the word כבשים as if it would have a ס instead of a שׁ, which would thus mean "washing" and refer to Jeremiah, 4 14.

pointed out, that the man living in Jerusalem could be considered as righteous, considering that the continual offering of the morning atoned for the transgressions of the night, and the continual offering of the afternoon atoned for the transgressions of the day.[1]

The continual offering was a communal offering, nor is there in the Bible ascribed to it any atoning power; but there is a marked tendency in Rabbinic literature to bestow on all sacrifices, even such as the burnt-offering and the peace-offering, some sort of atoning power for certain classes of sins, both of commission and omission, for which the Bible ascribes no sacrifice at all.[2] We find, further, that they ascribed an atoning power to the vestments of the high priests. All such passages have to be taken *cum grano salis;* they are in no way meant to relieve the individual from his duty to perform or to refrain from certain actions, nor from any punishment or fine connected with the transgression in question, be it of a prohibitive or affirmative nature. Such atonements, especially those connected with the vestments of the high priests or with communal offerings, extend chiefly to the community, which, in accordance with the Rabbinic high conception of the close solidarity

[1] See *Pseudo-Jonathan* to Num. 28 4; *P. K*, 55 *b*; and *P R.* 78 *b*.

[2] See above, p. 226, with regard to the function of the burnt-offering, which atones for the evil meditations of the heart. According to others, it atones for failing to accomplish the affirmative laws of the Bible. See *Arachin*, 16 *a*, with regard to incense. See also *Tan.* תצוה, 15.

of Israel, was greatly responsible for the sins of the individual, but practically helpless to prevent them. Following, as it seems, the precedent of the expiatory ceremony of the heifer beheaded in the valley in the case of unknown murder (Deut. 21 1–9), they also came to perceive in almost every object connected with the sanctuary or the high priest as many symbolic atonements protecting the community against the consequences of sins beyond its ken and its power to interfere.[1]

The Day of Atonement, with its various atoning functions, is also, as is well known, largely the means of protection for the community, and is chiefly concerned with sins connected with Levitical impurity. According to the Rabbis, the atoning effect of the scapegoat (Lev. 16 21) extends also to the individual, and expiates also for other "transgressions of the Law, the light and the heavy ones, committed intentionally or unintentionally, knowingly or unknowingly, of an affirmative or prohibitive nature, punished by excision from the community or even by capital punishment."[2] It is

---

[1] See *J. T. Yoma*, 44 *b*; *Arachin*, 15 *a*, *Zebachim*, 88 *b*, text and commentaries, *Lev. R*, 10 6, and *Cant. R.*, 4 4. Some sort of a precedent is given in the diadem on the forehead of the high priest, to which an atoning efficacy is ascribed in the Scriptures. See Exod 28 88 Cf also Epstein's commentary, תורה תמימה, to Exod. 29 1. The explanation given in the text here is that suggested by certain commentators of the Talmud, which is undoubtedly the only true one, though the Agadic expressions are very vague and not always consistent.

[2] See *Shebuoth*, 2 *b*, *Mishnah* and *Gemara*, 2 *b* and 6 *b* to 14 *a*. Cf. *Yoma*, 85 *b*, *Mishnah*, *T. K*, 82 *b*. The distribution of the vari-

further to be noticed that, according to the Rabbis, it is the *Day* of Atonement that atones "even when there is no sacrifice and no goat," it being the day itself which has this efficacy, independent of the sacrificial worship.[1] But, on the other hand, this efficacy is subject to the following two important conditions: first, that it has to be accompanied by repentance on the part of those who are meant to profit by it;[2] and, further, that in matters between man and man the

ous atonements over the various sacrifices brought on the Day of Atonement and other festivals and the particular function of each sacrifice is one of the most complicated subjects in Rabbinic literature, and is discussed at great length by different schools both in the Talmud of Babylon, and the Talmud of Jerusalem of the Tractates just named. Briefly stated, it comes to this, that all the sacrifices brought by the congregation (צבור) on new moons and the various festivals which the Scriptures describe as a sin-offering or as intended to make atonement (cf Lev. 23 19, and Num. 28 15. 22. 29, 29 4. 9. 16. 19. 22. 25. 28. 31. 34 38) are limited in their efficacy to Levitical impurity. This is also the case with the various sin-offerings brought on the Day of Atonement, as detailed in Lev, ch 16 An exception is made with reference to the scapegoat, whose atonement extends to all possible cases. See especially *Tosephta Shebuoth*, p. 445, where the importance of Levitical purity is proved by the fact that any breach against it was atoned for by not less than thirty-two sacrifices every year Cf. also Maimonides, שגגות, 3 9 and 11 9. See also Maimonides, תשובה, 1 2 For the statement of Maimonides, that the scapegoat atones in lighter transgressions even without repentance, see טורי אבן by R. Eleazar Rokeach (in *Mishneh Torah*, ed. Warsaw, 1900), that it refers only to cases when the person remained ignorant of his sin, לא הודע.

[1] See *T. K.*, 83 a. Cf also *Jer Yoma*, 45 c

[2] This is the general opinion of the Rabbis. See *T. K.*, 102 a; *Jer. Yoma*, 45 b, and *B T.*, *ibid.*, 85 b. Cf. Maimonides, תשובה, ch. 3. The contrary opinion of R Judah, the Patriarch, forms the only exception and stands entirely isolated.

Day of Atonement loses its atoning power until proper restitution is made to the wronged person. "Matters between thee and the Omnipresent they forgive thee; matters between thee and thy fellow-man they forgive not until thou hast appeased thy neighbour."[1] In such matters touching one's fellow-man God neither respects persons nor will he by any means clear the guilty.[2] But apparently, in wronging one's fellow-man, there is also an offence against the majesty of God. Whence the formula in the case of asking forgiveness for the injury done to a man who died before satisfaction could be given him is, "I have sinned against the Lord, the God of Israel, and against the man I have injured."[3] Man is thus also in need of the pardon of heaven, besides the achieved reconciliation from his fellow-man or through the worldly tribunal. Through these conditions, the Day of Atonement becomes practically the great Day of Repentance, the culmination of the Ten Days of Repentance. It brings with itself purification, the Father in Heaven making white the sin committed by the son, by his forgiveness and pardon.[4] "It is the Day of the Lord, great and very terrible," inasmuch as it becomes a day of judgement,[5] but also the Day of Salvation.[6]

---

[1] *T. K.*, 83 a; *Yoma*, 85 a.

[2] See *Sifre Zuta* as reproduced by *Yalkut* to *Pent.*, § 711, and *Num R.*, 11 6. Cf. *Rosh Hashanah*, 17 b The Rabbinic interpretation deals there with the seeming contradiction between Num. 6 26 and Deut. 10 17.

[3] See *Yoma*, 87 a. See also *Mishnah, Baba Kama*, 8 7.

[4] *M. T.*, 9 4.   [5] See *Tan*, וישלח, 2.   [6] *P. R.*, 175 b.

"Israel is steeped in sin through the *Evil Yezer* in their body, but they do repentance and the Lord forgives their sins every year, and renews their heart to fear him."[1] "On the Day of Atonement I will create you a new creation."[2] It is thus a penitential day in the full and in the best sense of the word.

Death and suffering may be viewed either as a punishment satisfying the claims of justice or as an atonement, bringing pardon and forgiveness and reconciling man with God. The first aspect finds its most emphatic and most solemn expression in the following Tannaitic statement: The born are to die; and the dead to revive; and the living to be judged; for to know, and to notify, and that it may be known, that he is the framer, and he the creator, and he the discerner, and he the judge, and he the witness, and he the complainant, and he is about to judge, with whom there is no iniquity, nor forgetfulness, nor respect of persons, nor taking of bribe, for all is his, and know that all is according to reckoning. Let not thine *Yezer* assure thee that the grave is a place of refuge for thee; for perforce thou wast framed, and perforce thou wast born, and perforce thou livest, and perforce thou diest, and perforce thou art about to give account and reckoning before the King of the king of kings, the Holy One, blessed be he.[3] But "the judgement (to proceed with another Tannaitic statement of R. Akiba) is a

---

[1] *Exod. R.*, 1 6. [2] *P. R*, 169 a.
[3] *Aboth*, 4 22. Cf. *Taylor*, 4 81-82; Bacher, *Ag. Tan.*, 2 502.

judgement of truth."[1] And when Pappos, on the authority of Job 23 13, expressed views implying a certain arbitrariness on the part of God because of his being One (alone), he was severely rebuked by R. Akiba, the latter Rabbi interpreting the meaning of the verse mentioned, "There is nothing to answer to the words of him by whose word the world was called into existence, for he judges all in truth and everything in judgement (justice)."[2] The same thought is somewhat differently expressed by another Rabbi, in allusion to Deut. 32 4: "'He is the Rock, his work is perfect: for all his ways are judgement: a God of truth and without iniquity, just and right is he.' His work is perfect towards all who come into the world (mankind), and none must allege that there is the slightest injustice. Nobody must brood upon and ask, why was the generation of the deluge swept away by water; why was the generation of the Tower of Babel scattered over all the world; why were the generations of Sodom and Gomorrah consumed by fire and brimstone; why was Aaron found worthy to be endowed with the priesthood; why was David worthy to be presented with the kingdom; and why were Korah and his congregation swallowed up by the earth? . . . He sits in judgement against every

---

[1] *Aboth*, 3 15.

[2] See *Mechilta*, 33 a; *Cant. R.*, 1 9. The parallel in *Tan. B.*, 2 4 b, to the effect that God occupies only the position of the president of the heavenly court composed of angels, seems to be a younger paraphrase of the statement of R. Akiba. See *Exod. R.*, 6 1. Cf. Bacher, *Ag. Tan.*, 3 26.

one and gives every one what is due to him."[1] It is with reference to the same verse (Deut. 32 4) that a later Rabbi makes the remark to the effect: He who says the Holy One, blessed be he (or the Merciful One), is loose (or lax) in his dealing out justice, let his life become loose. He is long-suffering but collects his (debt) in the end.[2] In another place the same thought is expressed in the words: God says, "I am the merciful one, but also a judge to punish."[3]

It should, however, be remarked that the same R. Akiba, who insists on the strict (true) judgement of God, teaches also that the world is judged by grace.[4]

---

[1] See *Sifre*, 133 a. Cf. also לקט מדרשים, ed. Werthheimer, p. 6 b, with reference to Job 11 7.

[2] See *Baba Kama*, 50 a; *Jer. Shekalim*, 48 d; M. T., 10 8, text and notes.

[3] *Gen. R.*, 16 6.

[4] *Aboth*, 3 15. Cf. Taylor, 3 24. It should be remarked that this sentence is followed in the editions by the words והכל לפי רוב המעשה ("everything is according to the majority of the actions"). This reading receives some support from *Kiddushin*, 40 a, and *Eccles. R.*, 10 1, that both the world and the individual are judged according to the majority of good actions. Cf. Bacher, *Ag. Tan.*, I 282. But there are also other readings, as "But not everything is according to the majority of deeds;" or merely, "But not according to the deed." Cf. Taylor, *ibid*, and his Appendix, p. 153. From *Jer Kiddushin*, 61 d, it would seem that this insistence upon a majority of good actions applies only to the judgement in the next world, but in this world even one good action can save a man. If we should assume that this represents also the opinion of R. Akiba, there would be no real contradiction. Cf. *A. R. N.*, 81 b, and the commentary to *Aboth* in *Machsor Vitri*, p. 514, where *Aboth* 3 15 is explained in the way just indicated. Cf. above, p. 15, note 1.

But it would seem that this grace is only confined to this world. In the next world there is only strict justice prevailing. Even Israel, apparently, enjoying otherwise so many privileges, is not exempt from the punishment awaiting the sinners in the next world. When Moses ascended from hell, he prayed, "May it be thy will . . . that thou savest thy people Israel from this place." But the Holy One, blessed be he, said unto him, "Moses, there is not with me respect of persons, nor taking of bribe. He who will do good will be in the Paradise, he who will do evil will be in hell, as it is said, 'I the Lord search the heart, I try the reins, even to give every man according to his ways, and according to the fruit of his doings' (Jer. 17 10)."[1] But even in this world, "when man sees that suffering comes upon him, he has to examine his actions," to see whether it has not come as a punishment for his sins. Likewise is death considered, in the majority of cases at least, as a punishment for the sin of the individual. For God is not suspected to execute judgement without justice.[2]

But besides satisfying the claims of a just God or of justice, death and suffering also atone and reconcile

---

[1] See בתי מדרשות, ed. Werthheimer, 4 29 a. Against this view are *Cant. R.*, 8 8 ; *Exod R* , 30 16. Cf. also *M.T.*, 15 24, text and notes, but the view given in the text appears to be the older one. Cf. *Sifre*, 12 b, text and notes 5 and 6, and *Num. R.*, 11 7.

[2] See *Berachoth*, 5 a and b. For the difficulties in the way of this theory and the manner in which the Rabbis tried to solve it, see Schechter, *Studies in Judaism*, Essay on Retribution, p. 259 *seq.*

man with God. They form, according to the Rabbis, two of the four (or the three) kinds of atonement taught by the Scriptures.[1] Self-inflicted suffering, such as fasting, assumes naturally the aspect of sacrifices. Hence the prayer of a Rabbi after a fast that the fat and blood which he lost through the fast should be accounted to him as a sacrifice on the altar, and have the same effect as the sacrifice in the days of yore when the Holy Temple was in existence.[2] This was considered as a kind of self-sacrifice, or rather sacrifice of his soul,[3] but this notion was not entirely limited to voluntary suffering. Every loss of property sustained by man, as well as every kind of physical suffering which he happens to undergo, are considered an atonement. "A man stumbled in a transgression, and became guilty of death by heaven (in contradistinction of the worldly tribunal). By what means shall he atone? His ox died, his chickens went astray, or he stumbled on his finger so that blood came out — by these losses and suffering, his debts (to the account of heaven against him) are considered paid."[4] Indeed, the loss of blood

---

[1] See *Mechilta*, 68 b and 69 a. *A. R. N.*, 44 b, text and notes for other references. The other kinds of atonement are the Day of Atonement and Repentance, but since they are all accompanied by repentance, there are practically only three kinds. The Scriptural references are Lev. 16 30, for the Day of Atonement, Isa. 22 14, for death, Jer. 3 22, for repentance, and Ps. 89 33, for suffering.

[2] See *Berachoth*, 17 a. Cf *M T.*, 25 3.

[3] See *Lev. R.*, 3 4 and commentaries.

[4] See *Jer. Sotah*, 17 a; *Eccles. R.*, 7 27; *Pesachim*, 118 a.

through any accident atones as the blood of a sacrifice.[1]

It is further maintained that the appearance of leprosy on the body of a man is the very altar of atonement.[2] Hence the dictum, "Beloved is suffering, for as sacrifices are atoning, so is suffering atoning." Nay, suffering has even a greater atoning effect than sacrifice, inasmuch as sacrifice affects only man's property, whilst suffering touches his very self.[3] "Who caused the son to be reconciled to his father (in heaven), if not suffering?"[4] "Therefore, let man rejoice in suffering more than in prosperity," for it is suffering through which he receives pardon and forgiveness.[5] "If thou seekest for life, hope for suffering," as it is said, "And reproof of chastisement (is) the way of life" (Prov. 6 3).[6] Indeed, the good son does not even pray that the suffering should cease, but says, "Father, continue thy chastisement."[7] This suffering has to be a sacrifice accompanied by repentance. The sufferer has to accept the suffering prayerfully and in a spirit of submission, and has to recognise that the visitation of God was merited by him. Man knows well in his heart when weighing his deeds with the suffering which came upon him that he was dealt with mercifully.[8] Indeed, the great difference between Israel and

---

[1] See *Chullin*, 7 b.
[2] See *Berachoth*, 5 b.
[3] See *Sifre*, 73 b and reference given there.
[7] See Minor Tractate, *Semachoth*, 8.
[4] *Sifre, ibid.*
[5] *Sifre*, 73 b.
[6] *M. T*, 16.
[8] *Sifre, ibid.*

the gentiles, is that the gentiles rebel when suffering comes upon them, and curse their gods; but Israel becomes humble and prays, as it is said, "I found trouble and sorrow. Then called I upon the name of the Lord," etc. (Ps. 116 34).[1]

The atonement of suffering and death is not limited to the suffering person. The atoning effect extends to all the generation. This is especially the case with such sufferers as cannot either by reason of their righteous life or by their youth possibly have merited the afflictions which have come upon them. The death of the righteous atones just as well as certain sacrifices.[2] "They are caught (suffer) for the sins of their generation. If there are no righteous, the children of the schools (that is, the innocent young children) are caught for the sins of their generation."[3] There are also applied to Moses the Scriptural words, "And he bore the sins of many" (Isa. 53 12), because of his offering himself as an atonement for Israel's sin with the golden calf, being ready to sacrifice his very soul for Israel, when he said, "And if not, blot me, I pray thee, out of thy book (that is, from the Book of the Living), which thou hast written" (Exod. 32 32).[4] This readiness to sacrifice oneself for Israel is characteristic of all the great men of Israel, the patriarchs and the Prophets

---

[1] See *Mechilta*, 72 *b* and reference given there. Cf. *T. B.*, 5 24 *b*.
[2] See *Moed Katon*, 28 *a*.
[3] See *Shabbath*, 32 *b*.
[4] *Sotah*, 14 *a*, and *Berachoth*, 32 *a*.

acting in the same way, whilst also some Rabbis would, on certain occasions, exclaim, "Behold, I am the atonement of Israel." [1] This sacrifice is, of course, voluntary. But this is also the case with the sacrifice on the part of the children who in some mystical way are made to take upon themselves this surety. When God was about to give the Torah to Israel, Rabbinic legend relates that he asked for some guarantee that Israel will on its part fulfil the obligations which the Revelation will devolve upon them. Then Israel offered as such the patriarchs and the Prophets, but they were not found sufficiently free from debt (faultless) to be worthy of this confidence. At last they offered their children, and the Holy One, blessed be he, accepted them willingly. But he first asked them, "Will you serve as surety for your parents, that they fulfil the Torah which I am about to give them, and that you will suffer in case they do not fulfil it?" They said, "Yes." Then the Act of Revelation began, which also the children witnessed, even those who were still in the embryonic state, when they gave their consent to each commandment revealed. This is what is said, "Out of the mouths of babes and sucklings hast thou ordained strength" (Ps. 8 2).[2]

[1] See *Mechilta*, 2 a; *Mishnah Negaim*, 2 1. Cf. Introduction to S. E., 127. By patriarchs is understood in that place, David. Cf. 2 Samuel 24 17. Cf above, p 52 *seq*.

[2] See *M T*, 8, *Midrash Cant.*, 1 8 and references given there. Cf. also above, pp. 193 and 254.

Atoning power is also ascribed to Torah and charity. The descendants of Eli could find no atonement by sacrifice and meat-offering, but they might receive pardon through the occupation with the study of the Torah and acts of loving-kindness.[1] Indeed, the Holy One, blessed be he, foresaw that the Holy Temple would be destroyed and promised Israel that the words of the Torah, which is likened unto sacrifices, will, after the destruction of the Temple, be accepted as a substitute for sacrifices.[2] Something similar is maintained with regard to acts of loving-kindness, which take the place of sacrifice, atoning for the sins of Israel after the destruction of the Temple; nay, it is even maintained that acts of loving-kindness or charity are more important than sacrifices.[3] Reference may be made here also to the atoning effect ascribed to the dining-table in the household of a man, which is considered, by reason of the hospitality offered on it to the poor, as the altar in the Temple, on which the sacrifices were brought.[4] The chaste woman is also likened to the altar; as the altar atones (for the sins of Israel), so she atones for her house.[5]

[1] *Rosh Hashanah*, 18 a.

[2] *Tan.*, אחרי, 10. Cf. *Tan B.*, 3 85 a.

[3] See *A. R. N.*, 11 a and b, text and notes, and *Sukkah*, 49 b. See above, p. 308.

[4] *Berachoth*, 55 a. See, however, A. Epstein, אלדד הדני, p. 117, note 126.

[5] *Tan.*, וישלח, 6.

XVIII

REPENTANCE: MEANS OF RECONCILIATION

THE prayer of the Psalmist, "Be merciful unto me, O God" (Ps. 56 2), is paraphrased by the Rabbis in the following way, "Be merciful unto me that I shall not be brought to fall by sin, but when I have sinned (God forefend) be merciful unto me that I may return in repentance." In another place the same thought is expressed in the following way: The Holy One, blessed be he, says (unto man), "I made the *Evil Yezer*. Be careful that he should not make thee sin; but if he did make thee sin, be eager to do repentance, then I will forgive thy sins." And as we have seen, repentance is the remedy offered by the Holy One, blessed be he, himself.[1] As it must further be clear from the preceding remarks, it is practically considered a necessary accompaniment of all other modes of atonement. Indeed, it would seem as if repentance is the only means of cleaning the guilty, though God is long-suffering, and forgiving iniquity and transgressions.[2] Its im-

[1] *M. T.*, 57 1. See also *ibid.*, 32 : 4. See Montefiore (as above, p 289, note 1) on the subject.

[2] See *Sifre Zuta* as communicated in the name of Ben Azai in *Num. R.*, 11 7 Cf. *Yoma*, 86 *a*, and *Midrash Prov* , 10 The interpretation is based on Exod. 34 7, where the Rabbis, in a homiletical way, separated the infinitive of ונקה from the verb לא ינקה.

portance is so great that it forms one of the things which preceded creation,[1] as a preliminary condition to the existence of the world. "When he drew the plan of the world he found that it could not stand (endure) until he had created repentance," since, as the early commentators explained it, the nature of man is so constituted that he cannot well escape sin. His existence would therefore have proved impossible without the remedy of repentance.[2] In agreement with this explanation is another passage from a semi-mystical book, running thus: "Rabbi Ishmael said, 'The world could never have existed but for the fact that repentance was created (first), and the Holy One, blessed be he, stretches out his right hand to receive penitence every day.' The sages said, 'After God thought to create the *Evil Yezer* he began to regret it, but prepared the cure before the affliction, and created repentance.'"[3]

God not only created repentance, but he continues to instruct mankind in repentance. "Good and upright is the Lord, therefore will he teach sinners in the way" (Ps. 25 8). This way is, as the Rabbis explained, the way of repentance which God points out to the

[1] See *Gen. R.*, 1 4, and *Pesachim*, 54 *a*, and references, especially *M. T.*, 9 11, text and note 69.

[2] See *P. R. E.*, 11; cf. *MHG.*, p. 8, and the commentary on the *Sefer Yezirah*, of R. Jehudah Barzillai of Barcelona, pp. 88 and 96. Cf. also above, p. 128.

[3] Quoted by a commentary to *Aboth* in Ms (in the Library of the Jewish Theological Seminary) forming a kind of *Yalkut* to this Tractate (22 *a*). The use of the word אלהים in the text would point to the *Yelamdenu* as the original source.

sinner.¹ In other places, the Rabbis speak of the "doors of repentance," or "the gates of repentance," which are likewise opened by God himself.² Such a "door" God opened to Adam after his fall, saying unto him, "Do repentance," but of this offer he did not avail himself; whereupon he was expelled from Paradise.³ Adam only learned the force of repentance from his son Cain, whom God established as a "mark" (or standard, example) for penitence.⁴ He then submitted to a course of repentance and prayed, "Lord of the world, remove my sin from me and accept my repentance, so that all generations should learn that there is repentance and that thou hast accepted the repentance of those who return unto thee."⁵ It is further recorded that God gave warning (by certain phenomena in nature) and opportunity for repentance to the generation of the deluge,⁶ the generation of the Tower of Babel,⁷ as well as to the men of Sodom⁸ in

---

¹ See *Jer. Makkoth*, 31 *d*; *P. K.*, 158 *b*; *M. T.*, 25 10; and *Yalkut Machiri* to this verse. Cf. *Sanhedrin*, 105 *a*, on Isa. 28: 26, יורנו.

² See *P. K.*, 157 *a*; *Deut. R.*, 2 12 and references. See also M. Grünbaum, *Gesammelte Aufsatze*, etc., pp. 505 *seq.* and 510 *seq.*

³ See *Gen. R.*, 21 6; *P. R.*, 26 *b*, text and notes.

⁴ See *Gen. R.*, 22 12 and 13.

⁵ See *P. R. E.*, ch. 20; cf *Erubin*, 18 *b* and *Tan.*, תזריע, § 9. This is in contradiction with another Agadic statement which describes Reuben, the first-born of Jacob, as the first man to do repentance. Cf. *Gen. R.*, 82 11 and 84 19.

⁶ See *A. R. N*, I 82 and reference given there.

⁷ See *Gen. R.*, 38 9.

⁸ See *Gen. R.*, 49 6; cf. also *Tan.* נח, 18, and בשלח, 15.

spite of their open rebellion against God. A similar opportunity was given to Korah, Moses deferring the action of offering the incense which brought about the catastrophe until "to-morrow," for the purpose of giving him and his adherents time to reconsider their evil behaviour and to repent.[1] With regard to Israel, it is stated that the Divine Presence tarried, before the destruction of the Temple, on the Mount of Olives for not less than thirteen and a half years (after it removed from the Temple), proclaiming three times a day, "Return, ye backsliding children, and I will heal your backslidings" (Jer. 3 22).[2] When the Temple was destroyed, God prays, "May it be my will that I exterminate the *Evil Yezer* that brings my children to sin, so that they do repentance and I hasten the rebuilding of my house and my sanctuary."[3] But this mercy of God is not confined to Israel, the Holy One, blessed be he, hoping for the nations of the world that they might do repentance that he should bring them near under his wings (by becoming proselytes).[4] The example set by God (in praying for the regeneration of the sinner) is imitated both by Moses and by Aaron, who prayed for the sinners in Israel that they might become penitents.[5] It is also narrated that

---

[1] See *Num. R.*, 18 7; cf. Deut. 16 5 *seq.*

[2] See *P. K.*, 115 *a*, text and notes; and *Lament. R.*, ed. Buber, 15 *b*, text and notes.

[3] *M. T*, 76 8. See text and notes.

[4] See *Num R.*, 10 1; *Cant. R.*, 61 1 (§ 5).

[5] See *Sotah*, 14 *a*, and *T. K.*, 46 *a*.

the Saint Abba Hilkia had certain outlaws in his neighbourhood for whose death he prayed, but his wife prayed that they might return to repentance, and that her actions were approved by signs from heaven.[1]

It is further assumed that great moral catastrophes were almost providentially brought about with the purpose of setting the good example to sinners that no sin is so great as to make repentance impossible. As such examples, are cited: David, who committed the sin of adultery; and the whole congregation of Israel, the contemporaries of Moses, who worshipped the golden calf. Neither David nor Israel, considering their high moral standing, were, the Rabbis declare, capable of such crimes, but it was brought about against their own will, as just stated, to give a claim for repentance in the future both in the case of the individual, as David, and in the case of the whole community, as that of the golden calf, in which the whole of Israel was involved, and thus showing that there is no room for despair of reconciliation with God, be the sin never so great and all-embracing.[2] Indeed, David became a "witness to the people," bearing evidence to the power of repentance, for "he who is desirous to do repentance has only to look at David." Hence, he

[1] See *Taanith*, 23 b. Cf. *Berachoth*, 10 a, the story of R. Meir and Berurya.
[2] See *Abodah Zarah*, 4 b and 5 a, text and commentaries; cf *Shabbath*, 65 a.

is called the man that established the sublimity of repentance.[1]

The encouragement of mankind to repentance is carried so far on the part of heaven that the "door" is opened even when this repentance is not entirely the expression of real remorse and regret, having been brought about only by pressure, and furthermore meant to atone for crimes of a most revolting kind. Such a case is particularly that of Manasseh, the son of Hezekiah, the wicked King of Judah, whose reign was, according to the testimony of the Scriptures, one long series of the most atrocious crimes" (2 Kings 21 2 *seq.* and 2 Chron. 33 2 *seq.*). "When he found himself during his captivity in Babel, in real distress, there was no idol he failed to invoke. . . . But when he saw that they were of no help to him, he said, 'I remember that my father made me read, "When thou art in tribulation, and all these things are come upon thee, even in the latter days, if thou turn to the Lord, thy God, and shalt be obedient unto his voice: For the Lord thy God is a merciful God; he will not forsake thee, neither destroy thee" (Deut. 4 30. 31). I will now invoke him. If he will answer me, well; if not, I will declare that all Powers are alike.' The angels thereupon shut the openings of heaven and said before the Holy One, blessed be he, 'Shall repentance avail

[1] See *M. T.*, 40 2 and 51 3. Cf Isa. 55 4. See also *Moed Katon*, 16 *b*, and Rashi's commentary as given in the עין יעקב to this passage. Cf. also *Num. R.* 18 21, text and reference given there.

for a man who placed an image in the very *Hechal* (sanctuary)?' (2 Kings 21 7 and 2 Chron. 33 7). Then the Holy One, blessed be he, said, 'If I accept not his repentance, I thereby shut the door against all other penitents.' He then dug for Manasseh's repentance a special passage from below the Throne of Glory (over which the angels have no control) and through this was heard Manasseh's supplication."[1] "Thus, if a man would tell thee that God receives not the penitents, behold Manasseh, the son of Hezekiah, he will bear evidence that no creature in the world ever committed before me so many wicked deeds as he did, yet in the moment of repentance I received him."[2] Some Rabbis even resented the apparently ancient tradition excluding Manasseh from the bliss of the world to come, inasmuch as it may have the effect to "weaken the hand of penitence," that is, to make sinners despair of the efficacy of repentance.[3]

Of Jeroboam it is said that the Holy One, blessed be he, laid hold of him and said, "Return (in repentance), and I and the son of Jesse and thou shall walk together in Paradise." The conceit of Jeroboam, however,

[1] See *P. K.*, 162 a and b; cf. *Jer. Sanhedrin*, 78 c, and *B. T. Sanhedrin*, 103 a; *Lev. R*, 30 8, *Deut R*, 2 20; *Ruth R*, 5 14; *P. R. E*, ch. 43; and *Targum* to *Chron.*, a l See also *Ag Ber.*, ch. 9, and *Sifre*, 144 b. Cf also *M T.*, 4 5, where the statement is more general, but is based on the Manasseh legend.

[2] See *Num. R.*, 14 1 and references. Cf also *Gen. R.*, ed. Wilna, Appendix on the Blessing of Jacob, p. 376, col. 2, the story there about Cain. [3] *Sanhedrin*, 103 a.

made him refuse God's offer, as he was not willing to be second to the son of Jesse.[1] Naturally such a *Teshubah* as that of Manasseh, undertaken amidst suffering and through fear of punishment, is not considered the highest degree of repentance, leaving man in a state of slavery, whilst the repentance undertaken through the motive of love reestablishes man's child-like relations to his Father in Heaven.[2]

This consideration, that nothing should be said or done which might lead to the discouragement of the penitent, had also an influence on certain ordinances of the Rabbis which were introduced for the special benefit of those who "returned." Thus, in certain cases, the restitution of the article appropriated in a dishonest way was not insisted upon, the robber being allowed to repay its value in money. It seems that even for the cattle-drivers and the tax-gatherers and the publicans, whose repentance meets with difficulties (because of their plundering the community at large, so that they are not in a condition to make restitution to the wronged person), certain provisions were made to make their repentance possible.[3] The rule was also that they would accept sacrifice from sinners in Israel in order that they might return as penitents.[4]

---

[1] See *Sanhedrin*, 102 b.

[2] See *Yoma*, 86 a. See also Rabbinowicz, *Variae Lectiones, a.l.*

[3] תקנת השבים. See *Eduyoth*, 7 9. See *Baba Kama*, 94 b and 95 a. Cf. also Maimonides, ה׳ גזלה ואבדה, I 13.

[4] See *Chullin*, 5 a, and Maimonides, מעשה הקרבנות, 3 4, about the various modifications of this law. Cf. also *P. R.*, 192 a.

We find even that friendly relations were entertained with sinners in the hope that intercourse with saintly men would engender in them a thought of shame and repentance. Thus it is said of Aaron the High Priest, who "did turn many away from iniquity" (Mal. 2 6), when he met a wicked man he would offer him his greetings. When the wicked man was about to commit a sin, he would say to himself, "Woe unto me, how can I lift my eyes and see Aaron? I ought to be ashamed before him who gave me greetings." And he would then desist from sin.[1] It was also forbidden to say to the penitent, "Remember thy actions of former days," such a reference to the former depraved life of the penitent being considered an oppression and coming under the Scriptural prohibition of, "Ye shall therefore not oppress one another: but thou shalt fear thy God: for I am the Lord, your God" (Lev. 25 17).[2]

The objection of the angels to the admittance of repentance is not confined to such extraordinary cases as the one of Manasseh. As it would seem, they oppose repentance in general. "When a man commits a transgression, the angels come and denounce him, and say, 'Master of the Universe, bow down thy heavens, O Lord, and come down: touch the mountains and they shall smoke,' etc. (that is, they demand immediate

[1] *A. R. N.*, 24 b. Cf. *Sanhedrin*, 37 a, the story of R. Zera, who entertained certain relations with the outlaws in his neighbourhood for the same purpose.

[2] See *Baba Mezia*, 58 b

satisfaction). But the Holy One, blessed be he, says, 'Man may be hard for the time, but if he will do repentance, I will receive him.'"[1] But it should be remarked that in other places this opposition to the admittance of repentance is ascribed to the Divine attribute of strict justice, which is overruled by the Divine attribute of mercy.[2] Nay, repentance is so beloved by the Holy One, blessed be he, that he is ready to overrule his own Law for its sake. It is written in the Torah, "When a man hath taken a wife and married her, and he has found some uncleanness in her, then let him write a bill of divorcement. . . . And if the later husband hate her, and write her a bill of divorcement, . . . her former husband which sent her away cannot take her again to be his wife, after she is defiled" (Deut. 24 1, 3, and 4). But this is not so with the Holy One, blessed be he, for though they have forsaken him and worshipped another, he said unto them, "Do repentance and come back unto me and I will receive you."[3] It is the right hand of God which is stretched out to receive penitence, against the pleading of angels, and as we may add also against

---

[1] See *M. T.*, 94 4; see also *Yalkut Machiri Ps.*, *a. l.*, who gives a better reading, which is reproduced here.

[2] See *Sanhedrin*, 103 a, and *Pesachim*, 119 a. See also *Pseudo-Jonathan S. E Z.*, p. 37. This is an interesting case of hypostatised attributes, to which others might be added. The subject is still in need of a good monograph.

[3] *P. R.*, 184 a. Cf. *Yoma*, 86 b. This homily forms a paraphrase of Jer. 3 1.

the view of the Prophets demanding punishment by death, and the decision of the Torah, demanding at least a sacrifice. The "right hand" represents the attribute of mercy, which is also called "the strong hand," inasmuch as it has to repress the attribute of strict justice.[1] This suggests that the admittance of repentance is an act of grace on the part of God, as forgiveness in general is. "There is no creature which is not in debt (or rather guilty) to God, but he is merciful and gracious and forgives the sins of the past," when succeeded by repentance.[2] When the Holy One, blessed be he, said to the Torah, "Let us make man in our image after our likeness," the Torah answered, "Master of all worlds, the world is thine, but the men thou desirest to create are 'of few days and full of trouble' and will fall into the power of sin, and if thou wilt not defer thy anger, it is better for him (man) that he should not come to the world." Then the Holy One, blessed be he, said to her, "Is it for naught that I am called long-suffering and abundant in goodness?"[3] "I am," says God, "the same (in my attribute of mercy) before man sins and (the same in my attribute of mercy) after man has sinned, if he will do repentance."[4] Indeed,

---

[1] See *Sifre*, 50 b.   [2] See *Exod. R.*, 31 1.

[3] See *P. R. E.*, ch. 12, text and notes of Loria, especially his reference to ch. 3, *ibid.* The connection of the attribute of long-suffering with repentance is also given in *P.K.*, 161 b, with allusion to Joel 2 18. Cf Gen. 1 26; Exod. 34 7; Job 8 1.

[4] See *Rosh Hashanah*, 17 b; cf. *P.R*, 145. The text forms an interpretation to Exod. 34 6, referring to the two mentions of the Tetra-

repentance is described as the good portion which God assigned to his world, which proved effective even in the case of an Ahab,[1] and the call to repentance embodied in the words of Amos, "Seek ye me and ye shall live" (5 4), is considered as the sweet message.[2] The sinner even receives the promise that after a sincere repentance entered upon through the motive of love (of God) his very intentional sins during his unregenerated life will be charged unto him as so many merits.[3]

The verse from Amos just quoted is paraphrased, "My children, what do I ask of you but seek me and you shall live."[4] It is, as we have just seen, the sweet message; but it assumes an endeavour on the part of man to break with his sinful past.[5] For, though repentance is, as just pointed out, an act of grace, there is, as in other such cases, a certain initiative and co-operation expected on the part of man.[6] Every encouragement is given to the penitent. No false shame should stand in the way of the repentant in seeking reconciliation with God. "Said the Holy One, blessed be he,

grammaton in that verse, which Divine Name represents, in Rabbinic literature, the attribute of mercy.

[1] See *Jer. Sanhedrin*, 78 b. I am inclined to think that the word מנה should be amended to מתנה. The sense then would be that repentance is one of God's good gifts to the world.

[2] See *Cant. R.*, 6 1

[3] See *Yoma*, 86 b. Cf. *Cant. R.*, 6, *ibid.*

[4] See *P. R.*, 158 b; cf. also *ibid*, 157 a.

[5] See *Cant. R., ibid.*   [6] See above, 289.

to Jeremiah, 'Go and bid Israel to do repentance.' He went and delivered his message. Thereupon they said to him, 'With what face can we enter before his presence? Have we not made him angry; have we not provoked his wrath? Are not those mountains and hills on which we worshipped the idols, still existing? We lie down in our shame and our confusion covers us.' He came back to the Holy One, blessed be he, and said so (repeating their answer). Then God said to him, 'Go back and tell them, "If you return to me, is it not to your Father in Heaven to whom you come? For I am a Father to Israel, and Ephraim is my firstborn."'" [1] Nor must man despair because of the quantity of his sins. When David, and after him Ezra, said, "Our iniquities are increased over our heads and our trespass is grown up to the heavens," the Holy One, blessed be he, answered, "Fear not because of this thing, even if they (the sins) reached the very heaven, and if you do repentance, I will forgive; and not only the first heaven . . . but even if they reached the very Throne of Glory, and if you will do repentance, I will receive you at once (as it is said): 'O Israel, return unto the Lord thy God' (Hos. 14 1)." [2] In another place, the words "unto thy God" are interpreted to refer to the *quality* of sins, be they even of such a nature that they touched the very Deity itself, as, for instance, when man

---

[1] See *P. K*, 165 *a*; cf. also Jer. 3 25, 31 9, and Hosea 4 18. See also *Tan B*., Introduction, 68 *b* and 69 *a*.

[2] See *P. R.*, 155 *a*; cf. Ps. 38 5; Ezra 9 6.

denied the very root (the existence of God) or committed blasphemy. It is customary, the Rabbis say, when a man insults his neighbour in public and after a time he seeks for reconciliation with him that the latter insist that he should ask for his pardon in public. "But with the Holy One, blessed be he, it is not so. Man rises and blasphemes in the market-place. But the Holy One, blessed be he, says unto him, 'Do repentance between thee and me and I will receive thee.'"[1] And when Israel, under the heavy burden of sin, says, "Master of the world, wilt thou receive us if we shall do repentance?" God answers them, "I have received the repentance of Cain . . . the repentance of Ahab . . . the repentance of the men of Anathoth . . . the repentance of the men of Nineveh . . . the repentance of Manasseh . . . the repentance of Jehoiachin, against all of whom there were ordained heavy decrees, shall I not receive your repentance?"[2] indeed, even as David said, "Master of the world, thou art a great God and my sins are also great. It is only becoming for the great God that he should forgive the great sins."[3]

Thus neither the quantity of sins, nor the quality of sins, need make man hesitate to follow the Divine call to repentance. He has only to approach, so to speak, the "door" with the determination of repentance, and

[1] See *P. K.*, 163 *b*; see also *S. E.*, p. 189.
[2] See *P K.*, 160 *a* to 163 *b*.
[3] See *Lev. R.*, 5 8, text and commentaries.

it will be widely opened for his admittance. Thus said the Holy One, blessed be he, to Israel, "Open unto me the door of repentance, be it even as narrow as the sharp point of a needle, and I will open it so wide that whole wagons and chariots can pass through it."[1] Indeed, it would seem that this Divine call of repentance implies also a certain mutual repentance, so to speak, or returning on the part of God, who meets Israel halfway. "It is to be compared to the son of a king who was removed from his father for the distance of a hundred days' journey. His friends said to him, 'Return unto your father,' whereupon he rejoined, 'I cannot.' Then his father sent a message to him, 'Travel as much as it is in thy power, and I will come unto you for the rest of the way.' And so the Holy One, blessed be he, said, 'Return unto me and I will return unto you' (Mal. 3 7)."[2] In another place, with reference to a Korahite's Psalm (55 7), we read, "The sons of Korah said, 'How long will you say, "Turn, O backsliding children"?' (Jer. 3 14) whilst Israel said, 'Return, O Lord, how long?' (Ps. 90 15). . . . But neither thou (God) wilt return by thyself, nor will we return by ourselves, but we will return both together as it is said, 'Turn us, O God of our salvation.

---

[1] See *Cant. R.*, 5 2 and 6, and *P K.*, 163 *b*, text and notes. See also *Targum a. l.*

[2] See *P. R.*, 184 *b* and 185 *a*; see also *ibid*, 144 *a*, the comparison with the sick prince, where it would seem that God takes the initiative of returning to Israel on his part.

... Wilt thou not come back and revive us?' (Ps. 85 4,5 and 6). As Ezekiel said, 'Behold, O my people, I will open your grave . . . and shall put my spirit in you, and ye shall live' (Ezek. 37 12-14)."[1]

The statement that neither the quantity nor the quality of sins can prevent repentance is subject to certain modifications in Rabbinic literature. The most important, though somewhat obscure, passage is the following: "Five are exempt from forgiveness: He who repeatedly does repentance and repeatedly sins; he who sins in a righteous generation; he who sins with the intention to repeat; and he who has in his hands (on his conscience) the sin of the profanation of the Name of God."[2] The passage is, as just stated, obscure and undoubtedly corrupt, but as with all these groups of numbers, it probably forms only a résumé of Tannaitic statements, scattered over the Rabbinic literature, bearing on the subject of the efficacy of repentance. As such, the following may be cited, in illustration and elucidation of the text just given: He who says, "I will sin and repent, I will sin and repent," they do not make it possible for him to repent.[3] As a reason is given in the Talmud the psychological fact that when a man has committed the same sin twice it becomes to him a thing permitted (that is, he ceases to consider it a sin), and he is therefore unable any more to repent and

[1] See *M. T.*, 85 3; cf. *Lament. R.*, 5 21.
[2] See *A R. N.*, 58 b.
[3] See *Mishnah Yoma*, 85 b.

to leave off doing it.¹ The same sentiment is expressed elsewhere in the following words, "Let not a man say, 'I shall commit ugly deeds and things unworthy and will then bring a bull that has much flesh which I will sacrifice upon the altar and then God will have mercy upon me and accept me as a penitent.'"² In another place, we read, "He who causes the multitudes to sin, they do not make it possible for him to do repentance."³ As to the profanation of the Name of God, we have the statement that "for him who has committed this sin, there is no power in repentance to suspend (the punishment), nor in the Day of Atonement to atone, nor in suffering to purify," full forgiveness only being obtained when the sinner dies.⁴ For the whole of the Torah was only given with the purpose to sanctify his Great Name.⁵ From these illustrating passages it will be readily seen that the statement that certain transgressions are excluded from forgiveness means in most cases that these transgressions are of such a nature that man is not likely to enter upon a course of real repentance such as would be followed by forgiveness. Some-

---

[1] See *Yoma*, 87 a.

[2] See *Lev. R.*, 2 12. See also commentaries. See also *S.E*, p. 36.

[3] See *Aboth*, 5 18. See also *A. R. N*, 60 b, *Yoma*, 87 a, and *Tosephta Yoma*, 4. See also *Sotah*, 47 a. This may perhaps be the meaning of the clause in *A. R. N.*, "He who sins in a righteous generation," that is, the generation by itself is righteous, but is caused to sin by his criminal example.

[4] See *Mechilta*, 69 a; *Yoma*, 86 a.

[5] See *S. E.*, p. 74.

times the two expressions occur together. Thus we read, "He who is confirmed (מוחלט) in transgressions (that is, a confirmed or inveterate sinner) cannot repent, and there is never forgiveness for him."[1] Indeed, there is a class of sinners who, at the very door of Gehenna, continue their rebellion and never repent.[2]

This is even more distinctly seen from another group of numbers commencing with the words, "Twenty-four things prevent repentance," which include also some of those just mentioned. They are: "He who is accustomed to slander; he who indulges in anger; he who entertains evil thoughts; he who associates with the wicked; he who looks at women; he who shares with thieves; he who says I will sin and repent, I will sin and repent; he who exalts himself at the disgrace (expense) of his neighbour; he who separates himself from the community; he who slights his masters;[3] he who curses the many;[4] he who prevents the many from doing charity; he who causes his neighbour to leave the good way for the evil way; he who makes use of the pledge of the poor;[5] he who receives bribery with the purpose of making others act unjustly; he who finds lost goods and does not return it to its owner;

---

[1] See *M. T.*, 1 22; cf. *Yoma*, 86 *b*. See also *A. R. N.*, 62 *a*.

[2] See *Erubin*, 19 *a*, and *M. T.*, *ibid.*

[3] Reading רבותיו instead of אבותיו.

[4] Perhaps we should read המכשיל instead of המקלל, meaning, "he who puts a stumbling-block in the way of the many." Cf. the expression: המביא תקלה לרבים.

[5] See *Deut.* 24 12.

he who sees his children embracing a depraved life and does not protest; he who eats the plunder of the poor and the widows;[1] he who criticises the words of the wise man; he who suspects upright men; he who hates admonition; and he who scoffs at the commandments. Of these the Scripture says, 'Make the heart of the people fat, and make their eyes heavy, and shut their eyes; lest they see with their eyes, and hear with their ears, and understand with their heart, and convert, and be healed'" (Is. 6 10).[2] But as it is rightly pointed out by the authorities, it is not because real repentance is unacceptable, but because the nature of these sins is such that they are so habitual, or so little conspicuous, that man hardly looks upon them as sins; or because of the difficulties in the way of making proper restitution. Maimonides, who in his Law of Repentance gives the above passage with some comments, distinctly adds that though these things delay repentance, they do not make it impossible. "If a man does return, he is considered a penitent, and has a share in the world to come."[3]

[1] Reading שׁוּר instead of שׁוֹר (ox). There is, however, some justification for this latter reading. See Job 24 8. 4.

[2] See Maimonides, תשובה, ch. 4. This group is also known to many of the earlier post-Talmudic authorities, such as *Alfasi*, the *Machsor Vitri*, and others. The original source is unknown, but there can be but little doubt that it formed once a part of the Minor Tractate. See Friedmann, נספחים pp. 7 and 8, and his remarks there, on which the reader will find the authority for the corrections given in the text. See also Friedmann, *ibid*., p. 8, for the expression cited in note 47. [3] See Maimonides, *ibid.*, at the end of the chapter.

The "fattening" of the heart referred to above, which makes man impervious to the thought of repentance, has a close parallel in the "hardening" of the heart used in connection with Pharaoh.[1] But there it is God himself who hardens the heart of Pharaoh (Exod. 10 1). And the Rabbis felt the difficulty, since under these conditions Pharaoh had it no longer in his power to do repentance. The answer given is that "after the Holy One, blessed be he, has given man warning three times (to do repentance) and he did not return, God shuts his heart against repentance in order to punish him for his sins."[2] "After the Holy One, blessed be he, hoped (waited) for the wicked that they will do repentance, if they do not, then he takes away their heart so that they cannot return even if they want to. Nay, he makes it impossible for them to pray."[3] This is in agreement with another statement of the Rabbis, according to which pardon is only granted for three times, but there is no forgiveness for the fourth time,[4] and cases are recorded where men hear voices from heaven giving them the sad message that there is no hope for them. Others, again, feel themselves such outcasts that they appeal to heaven and

---

[1] See Exod 7 3, 10 1, and 11 10. [2] See *Exod. R.*, 13 8 and 11 6.

[3] See *Exod. R.*, 11 1. This homily seems to be based on Job 36 9-13. It is to be noted that according to other interpretations God gave to Pharoah the opportunity of repentance to the very last. See *Exod. R.*, 12 1 and especially 13 4.

[4] See *Yoma*, 86 *b*, in the name of R. Jose b Judah Cf Job 33 29; *Amos* 2 4. 6. The sense of the passage is not clear. Cf. Edeles, *a. l.*

earth, to mountains and hills, to sun, moon, and planets, to pray for them, which, however, decline.[1] Legend also records that the Prophet Elisha made a special journey to Damascus to cause Gehazi (who is supposed to have stirred up people to worship idols) to do repentance, but that Gehazi referred him to a tradition which he had from the Prophet himself, that they do not make it possible for him to do repentance who causes others to sin.[2] It seems also that where reparation was impossible, repentance was also regarded as unacceptable. Such cases are: the robbery of the public, as for instance, the man who gives a false measure, since he cannot well reach those whom he cheated,[3] and murder[4] and adultery,[5] since the wrongs resulting from these sins can never be rectified.

All these qualifications, however, have to be taken as mere hyperboles, emphasising and intensifying the evil consequences of sin, and the difficulty of doing real repentance. The general rule is that accepted by all authorities, that there is nothing which can stand in the way of the penitent, be the sin ever so great,[6] or as

[1] See *Chagigah*, 25 *a*, and *Abodah Zarah*, 17 *a*.

[2] *Sotah*, 47 *a*

[3] *Baba Bathra*, 88 *b*, and *Jebamoth*, 21 *a*

[4] *Sanhedrin*, 7 *a*.

[5] See *Chagigah*, 9 *a* and *b*, and *Jebamoth*, 22 *b*.

[6] *T J Peah*, 17 *b*, R. Saadya Gaon, אמונות ודעות, 5 6. See also Maimonides, *Teshubah*, 33 14 Cf *Sefer Chasidim*, Parma, p. 38 See also the *Responsa* of R David b Zimra, 2 45, in the section on Maimonides. A peculiar case is that given in the *Responsa* of R Joseph

the outcasts above mentioned said after all intercession was declined, "The matter is only depending on me." Man has only to determine and he may be sure of acceptance. Let not man say, "I have sinned and there is no hope (of restoration or mending) for me," but let him put his confidence in the Holy One, blessed be he, and he will be received.[1] Rather bold but true is the assertion of the mystic that even a voice from heaven telling man that he is excluded from repentance should not be obeyed, it being the will of God himself that man should become importunate with his prayers and supplications, and persist in his entreaties until he finds admittance through the door of repentance.[2]

As to the nature of repentance, it is as the word תשובה suggests, first of all the returning from the evil ways, that is, a strong determination on the part of the sinner to break with sin. To enter upon a course of repentance and not to leave off sinning is compared to the man who enters a bath with the purpose of cleansing himself of a Levitical impurity, but still keeps in his hands the dead reptile which is the cause of all this

Trani (2:8), where the sinner confesses to have been especially guilty of the three cardinal sins, — idolatry, adultery, and the shedding of blood, and the Rabbi nevertheless prescribes for him a course of repentance

[1] See *M. T.*, 40 s. See also *Abodah Zarah*, 17 a, with reference to the outcasts.

[2] See *Reshith Chochmah*, Section קדושה 17. See also *Responsa* of R. Joseph Trani, 2 s.

impurity. "What shall he do? Let him throw away the thing impure and then take the bath and he shall be purified."[1] In the addresses to the people on fast days, the elder would say, among other things, "My brethren, it is not sackcloth and fasts which cause forgiveness, but repentance and good deeds: for so we find of the men of Nineveh, that it is not said of them that God saw their sackcloth and fasts, but that 'God saw their works that they turned from their evil way' (Jonah 3 10)."[2]

Repentance begins in thought, and its effect is instantaneous.[3] But it is further followed up by words of confession. As Maimonides puts it, "Repentance means that the sinner gives up the sin, removing it from his mind, and determining in his heart not to repeat the evil action again; and so also he must regret his past . . . he must also confess with his lips and give expression to the thoughts which he determined in his heart."[4] The regret includes the feeling of shame, for "to him who commits a transgression and

[1] See *P. R.*, 182 *b*. The simile with the reptile occurs first in *Tosephta Taanith*, 1. Cf. *Jer. Taanith*, 65 *b*; *Lament R.*, 3 8; and *B. T. Taanith*, 16 *a*.

[2] *Taanith*, 16 *a*.

[3] See *P R.*, 185 *a*; *P. K.*, 163 *b*; cf. *Kiddushin*, 49 *b*, and *Gittin*, 57 *b*. Cf *M T.*, 45 · 4. The Rabbinic expression is, "He thought (or conceived) the thought of repentance in his heart (or in his mind)." See above, p. 31.

[4] See Maimonides, תשובה, 2 2, and *ibid*, 1 1. Cf. also *Chagigah*, 5 *a*, that forgiveness depends on regret on the part of the sinner. Cf. Dan. 7 7 and 8; Ezra 9 6.

afterwards is ashamed of it, they forgive all his sins."[1] Indeed, God asks nothing more of man but that he shall say before him, "I have sinned."[2] And the judgement which he brought on Jerusalem was because she said, "I have not sinned."[3] But when man says, "I have sinned," no angel (of destruction) can touch him.[4] That David (after his sin) became worthy of eternal life was because he said, "I have sinned."[5] For he who knows that he sins and prays against the sin and fears the sin and argues (pleads or confesses) it between him and the Holy One, blessed be he, shall receive forgiveness.[6] And so it is with Israel in general, upon whom God will have mercy as soon as they will have confessed their sins (as repentants).[7] At the waters of Marah, Israel was supplicating and praying to their Father in Heaven, as a son who implores his father, and a disciple who beseeches his master, saying unto him, "Master of the world, we have sinned against thee when we murmured on the sea."[8] Confession thus becomes an essential feature of repentance, preceding

---

[1] See *Berachoth*, 12 b.
[2] See *Jer. Tanith*, 65 d. Cf. *Midrash Shemuel*, ch. 13.
[3] See *Tan. B.*, 2 91 b; cf. Jer. 2 35.
[4] See *Tan B*, 4 70 a.
[5] See *M. T.*, 51 1.
[6] See *M. T.*, 51 2.
[7] See *T. K*, 112 b; cf. Lev 26 40.
[8] See *Mechilta*, 45 b. Cf. Exod. 14 11. Cf. Jastrow's Dictionary, p. 273, col. 1, about the correct reading of this passage. See also above, 34.

the various kinds of atonements,[1] at the same time expressive of the determination of man to leave off sin-

[1] The most important Halachic aspect of this institution is given in Maimonides, *Teshubah*, 1 1. "If a person has transgressed any law in the Torah, be it affirmative or prohibitive, whether intentionally or unintentionally, he is under the obligation of confession before the Lord, blessed be he; as it is said, When a man or a woman commit any sin, etc., 'then they should confess their sin' (Num. 5 6 and 7), by which is meant the confession in words This confession is an affirmative command. How do they confess? One says, 'O God, I have sinned, I have perverted, I have rebelled against thee. I have committed such and such an action, and behold, I regret it and am ashamed of my deeds and never will I return to that thing.' These are the contents of confession. . . . Likewise, those who bring a sin-offering or a guilt-offering (for sins) committed, intentionally or unintentionally, are not atoned for by their sacrifices until they have done repentance and uttered confession; as it is said, 'And he shall confess that he has sinned' (Lev. 55 5) Likewise, those who are under the sentence of death or of receiving thirty-nine lashes are not atoned for by their execution or by the fact of their having received the lashes, unless they have first done repentance and confessed. Likewise, he who injured his neighbour (bodily) or damaged him in money matters, though he made restitution for what he owed him, is not atoned for until he confessed and determined never to repeat the offence." The statement in Maimonides is based on *Sifre Zuta*, reproduced in the *Yalkut*, 1. § 701, and partially also in *Numb. R.*, 8 5. Cf. also Friedmann, *Mechilta*, 121 *b*, the quotation given there from Maimonides, ספר המצות, and Horowitz, *Monatsschrift* (1906), pp. 76 and 77. See also *T. K.*, 24 *b*; *Sanhedrin*, 43 *b*, and *Sifre*, 2 *a*. Whether those who are about to die a natural death are also included in the duty of confession as derived by the Rabbis from Num. 5 6, depends largely on the reading מומתים (killed) (executed) or מתים (dying) in the *Sifre* and *Sifre Zuta*, referred to, which is difficult to determine, though there is good authority for the latter reading. Cf. R. Isaac Ibn Guiath, מאה שערים, 2 28 *b*. In any event, the institution of confession before death (even natural) is very ancient. See *Shabbath*, 32 *b*; Tractate *Semachoth Zutarti*, ed. C. M. Horowitz, pp 30–31, text and the reference

z

ning.¹ "He that covers his sins shall not prosper, but whoso confesses (on the condition) with the determination to forsake his sin, shall receive mercy."² It is in this sense that confession is regarded as a means of killing the *Yezer*,³ and effects a reconciliation with God. "Take with you words and turn to the Lord" (Hos. 14 2). This verse is paraphrased, "The Holy One, blessed be he, said unto Israel, 'My children, I will accept from you neither burnt-offerings nor sin-offerings nor guilt-offerings nor meat-offerings, but (I expect from you) that you will be reconciled unto me by prayer and supplication and by the direction of your heart . . . with confession and prayers and tears.'"⁴ It is probably prayer of this kind, asking for forgiveness and acknowledging the sin, which is occasionally quoted together with repentance;⁵ this being one of the features of repentance,

given there in the notes. See also *N. T.*, James 5 16, which, as may be seen from the contents, relates to the sick on the death-bed, and apparently is an echo of Ecclus. 38 9-10. Ancient is also the confession on the Day of Atonement (see *Yoma*, 87 *b*), taken over probably from the Temple. (See Lev. 16 21; and cf. *T. K.*, 82 *a*; *Yoma*, 66 *a*; and *Jer. Shebuoth*, 1 5) It is then extended to other fasts. See *M. T.*, 141 · 2. Cf. also *Yoma*, 87 *b*, about the confession of Raba throughout the whole year.

¹ About the various formulas of confession, see *Jer. Yoma*, 87 *b*, and *Lev. R.*, 3 8; *P. R.*, 160 *b*, text and notes. Cf. also Landshut and Baer in their edition of the Prayer Book.

² See *P. K.*, 159 *a*, paraphrasing Prov. 28 13.

³ See *Lev. R.*, 9: 1. ⁴ See *P. R.*, 198 *b*.

⁵ See *Rosh Hashanah*, 16 *b*; cf. *P. K.*, 191 *a*; *P. R.*, 200 *b* and references given there.

as Maimonides explains it, that the penitent should constantly cry before God with tears and supplication.¹

Neither, however, the determination to leave off sin nor the regret of the past and the shame and confusion of sin expressed in confession and prayer seem to have been deemed a sufficient guarantee against a relapse into the former habits of sin. As R. Saadya Gaon remarks, we may fairly rely on the great majority of our people that during their prayer and fast they do really mean to forsake sin and regret it, and seek atonement; but what the Gaon is afraid of is, repetition, that is, relapse into sin. The Rabbis, therefore, think that this claim to real exemption from any particular sin can only be maintained after the penitent had twice at least the full opportunity to commit the sin under which he was labouring during his unregenerate life, and escaped from it.² Fasting is also mentioned together with repentance, indeed, following closely upon repentance; as it is said, "Therefore also now, saith the Lord, turn ye even to me with all your heart, and with fasting, and with weeping, and with mourning"³ (Joel 2 12), but they deal treacherously who fast without doing repentance, and shall be put to shame.⁴ It is in conformity with

¹ See Maimonides, תשובה, 2 4.

² See *Yoma*, 86 *b* Some of the best authorities omit the word "twice." See above, p. 333, note 6, the reference to R. Saadya.

³ *M. T.*, 25 5, with allusion to Ps. 25 8.

⁴ *Midrash Prov* , 6: 4. There can be little doubt that the copyist shortened the quotation from the Bible, omitting verse 12, on which the interpretation of the *Midrash* is based. See also above, p. 308, for

this sentiment, for which there is abundant authority both in the Scriptures and in the Talmud, that ascetic practices tending both as a sacrifice and as a castigation of the flesh, making relapse impossible, become a regular feature of the penitential course in the mediæval Rabbinic literature.[1]

But repentance is not confined to the habitual sinner nor to a particular time. True, the Rabbis admit repentance on the death-bed. If a man was absolutely wicked all his days and did repentance in the end, God will receive him.[2] "For as long as man lives, the Holy One, blessed be he, hopes for his repentance; when he dies his hope perishes: as it is said, 'When a wicked man dies his hope shall perish' (Prov. 11 7),"[3] denying the possibility of repentance to the wicked after their death even if they desire to do it.[4] For indeed this world is like the vestibule before the hall, and he who has not prepared himself in the vestibule, how shall he come into the hall? And when the wicked say, "Leave us, and we shall do repentance," the Holy

the quotation given there with reference to fasting, to which any number of references might easily be added.

[1] See *Sanhedrin*, 25 a; cf. Saadya, *ibid.;* Bachye, חובות הלבבות, section תשובה. See especially Introduction to רוקח, by Rabbi Eleazar of Worms, with his four kinds of repentance, which is reproduced by any number of moralists writing on this subject

[2] See *Kiddushin*, 40 b; cf. *Gen R*, 65 22, the case of *Joseph*, משיתא, and of *Yakum*, איש צרורות; *Ruth R*, 6 4, the case of Elisha b Abuyah; and *Abodah Zarah*, 17 a, the case of Eleazar b. Durdaya

[3] See *Eccles. R.*, 7 15

[4] See *Eccles Targum*, 1 15 and 3 20. Cf. *P. R.*, 184 a and b.

One, blessed be he, says unto them, "Repentance is possible only before death."[1]

But this death-bed repentance is not regarded as repentance of the highest order, though it may secure final salvation. "Blessed be he who does repentance when he is still a man" (possessing still his manly vigour).[2] The saying of the sage was, "Repent one day before thy death," but when his disciples asked him, "How does man know which day he will die?" he answered, "The more reason that he should repent every day lest he shall die on the following day, so that all his life is spent in repentance."[3] Hence, the benedic-

---

[1] See *Midrash Prov.*, ch. 6; *Eccles. R.*, 1:15 and 7:15, and *P. R. E.*, ch. 43, text and commentaries. This is the generally accepted view by almost all Jewish moralists. Cf. commentaries to *Aboth* 4.16 and 17, and the *Books of Discipline* (*Sifre Mussar*) generally. There is, however, a statement in the name of R. Joshua b. Levi, according to which the wicked will do repentance in the Gehenna and justify upon themselves the judgement of God, which repentance will contribute to their salvation in the end. As it is clear, however, from other Talmudic passages, this promise does not extend to all classes of sinners. See *Tosafoth and Edeles, a. l.* The saying of R. Joshua b. Levi may also have some connection with the Purgatory state after the wicked have already suffered for a time. There is also a whole circle of later Agadoth in which the wicked in the Gehenna secure a release by their answering "Amen" after the *Kaddish*, to be recited by Zerubbabel on the Day of Judgement succeeding the Resurrection. (?) See Friedmann, נספחים, pp. 32, 33, text and notes and reference given there to *Yalkut* and *Beth Hammidrash*, ed. Jellinek. Cf the controversy between the Schools of Hillel and Shammai, *Rosh Hashanah*, 17 a. See also Nachmanides' *Shaar Haggemul*.

[2] See *Abodah Zarah*, 19 a.

[3] See *Aboth*, 2 10 Cf *Shabbath*, 153 a, and *Eccles. R*, 1 7.

tion in the daily prayer for repentance, running originally, "Turn thou us unto thee, O Lord, and we shall be turned; renew our days as of old. Blessed art thou, O Lord, who delightest in repentance."[1] This is an answer to the call coming daily from heaven, exclaiming, "Return, ye backsliding children."[2] The call, however, seems to have been especially heard on the nine days forming a preparation to the Day of Atonement, which, including this latter day, constitute the Ten Penitential Days. It is on the first of these (New Year's Day — the first of *Tishri*), on which the "Lord shall utter his voice" through the sound of the *Shofar*, which is an invitation to repentance;[3] whilst all the Ten Penitential Days are considered as an especial time of grace "to seek the Lord while he may be found."[4] The Day of Atonement forms the climax, but it would have no atoning efficacy without repentance. These Ten Penitential Days are distinguished by special liturgies and by special ascetic practices.[5]

---

[1] See Schechter, *J. Q. R.*, 10 654 *seq.*; cf. Dalman, *Die Worte Jesu*, p. 299. Cf. Lam. 5 21. The text in our prayer-books omits the verse, and substitutes for it, "Cause us to return, O our Father, unto thy Law; draw us near, O our King, unto thy service, and bring us back in perfect repentance unto thy presence. Blessed, etc. . . ." See Singer, p. 46; Baer, p. 90.

[2] See *P. R. E.*, ch. 15 and 43 and commentaries.

[3] See *Tan.*, וישלח, 2; cf *P K.*, 187 *b*. Cf Joel 2 11

[4] See *Rosh Hashanah*, 18 *a*, and *P. R.*, 155 *b* Cf. Isa. 55 6. Cf. also *Jer. Bikkurim*, 64 *d*

[5] See *Tur Orach Chayim*, par 602 and 603, and the commentaries given there. See above, p. 303 *seq.*

But they are only set apart, as already indicated, as a special time of grace, but not as the only days of repentance. For repentance is as wide as the sea, and as the sea has never closed and man can always be cleansed by it, so is repentance, so that whenever man desires to repent, the Holy One, blessed be he, receives him.[1]

[1] See *P. K.*, 157 *a*, and *M. T.*, 65 4 and references.

ADDITIONS AND CORRECTIONS

Page 21 *seq*, and p 49, Note 2 In connection with the contents of the 2d chapter, and p 49, Note 2, see Dr N I Weinstein's *Zur Genesis der Agada*, Frankfurt, 1901. More important in connection with these contents is Dr David Neumark's learned *Geschichte der Judischen Philosophie des Mittelalters*, Berlin, 1907, especially the first chapters of this volume, which only appeared recently, when our text was nearly finished in press

Page 26 Cancel "stay of the world," and corresponding note.

Page 55, Note 1. See *Sifre*, 113 a, and *Jebamoth*, 48 b, with reference to Deut 21.13, where the words את אביה ואת אמה are explained to mean ע"ז (her former idols) As a proof is given Jer. 2 27, "Saying to a stock, thou art my father, and to a stone, thou hast brought me forth" If this explanation reflected the pagan usage of the Tannaitic time, which is not impossible, we might easily explain the fact that some Rabbis, at least, were sparing with the epithet Father in reference to the Deity.

Page 57, Note 1. See also R Joseph Ibn Yachya in *Torah Or*, ch 77, where he speaks of two fundamental doctrines, האמונה בה׳ שהוא אלהינו ואין זולתו מהאלוהות ושאנחנו ישר׳ עמו ולא זולתנו מהאומות.

Page 100, Note 1 Attention should be called to the statement of R Simon b Lakish, in which the מלכות שמים is contrasted with the מלכות הארץ, and the compliment is even paid to the latter that it establishes order and law. See *Gen R* 9 13, and *Gen R*, ed Theodore, p 73. The context makes it clear that by the Kingdom of the Earth is meant Rome, but this favourable estimation of the Roman Government does not represent the general opinion of the Jews. I found also these terms in a Genizah fragment from an unknown *Mechilta* to Deuteronomy In connection with this, the following extract from another Genizah fragment is instructing. It forms the conclusion of the third benediction in the *Grace After Meals* in the House of Mourning, and read thus·
ברוך אתה ה׳ הבונה ברחמיו את ירושלים אמן כחיינו אמן במהרה בימינו תבנה ציון ברנה ותכון עבודה בירושלים וארמון על משפטו ורומי הרשעה תפול

Page 101, Note 2, and 102, Note 2 It is suggested by various writers that the saying of R Hillel was directed against Chris-

345

tianity, which gave undue emphasis to the belief in the Messiah at the expense of the Law R Hillel in a certain measure found a follower a thousand years later in R. Joseph Albo, who was prompted probably by the same tendency (See *Ikkarim* 4 · 42) And something similar may be observed of R Moses Sofer of the nineteenth century (Responsa II, par 356), who likewise protested against Maimonides, who includes the belief in the Messiah among the *fundamental* doctrines of Judaism, though his protest was, as it seems, less directed against Christianity than against the antinomian tendencies of his time It is hardly necessary to say that both Albo and Sofer considered the belief in the advent of Messiah an essential Jewish doctrine, though not a fundamental doctrine. Rashi explains the saying of Hillel to the effect that the future redemption of Israel will not be by the Messiah, but by God himself. This explanation, though seeming a little far-fetched, becomes plausible by similar statements of other Rabbis. Thus, with reference to Isa 35 · 10, "And the redeemed of the Lord shall return," a Rabbi remarks, "They are the redeemed of the Lord, and not the redeemed of Elijah, nor the redeemed of the King Messiah." (See *M. T.* 106 . 1.) Again, with reference to Deut 17 : 14, we are told that after the sad experience Israel had with their various kings, they began to exclaim. "We have no desire for a King any longer. We want back our first King, God, as it is said, 'The Lord is our King, he will save us'" (Isa. 33 : 22) Thereupon, the Lord said, "By your life I will do so, as it is said, 'And the Lord shall be King over the earth, etc'" (Zech. 14 · 9) (*Deut R.* 5 . 11) The Wilna edition is mutilated by the censorship. (Cf also *S E*, Introduction, p 26) It is, however, not impossible that these passages and similar ones were provoked by polemics with Christians

Page 165, Note 1. See דרוש להראי״ש in the *Hildesheimer Jubelschrift*, p 92, Note 3 The author evidently confuses there the words of Maimonides with those of R. Saadya, quoted in our text

Page 192–193, Note 1 The statement of the *Midrash Zuta* is probably based on an older Tannaitic interpretation of Deut 24 · 16. Cf. Hoffmann, לקוטי בתר לקוטי of the *Mechilta to Deut.*, p. 31, text and notes.

Page 305, Note 2. This later version of the statement of R. Akiba has a parallel in the saying of R Jochanan. (See *Jer. Sanhedrin*, 18 a.) Cf. *Exod. R* 6 1 See Bacher, *Ag Tan* 3 26 These bold statements (all in contradiction to *Aboth*, 4 . 8) have the

ADDITIONS AND CORRECTIONS

purpose of refuting the tendency of making God's judgement arbitrary and despotic

Page 324, Note 3. Cf also *Berachoth*, 34 *b*, the well-known statement of R Abahu with reference to the high position to be occupied by the penitents, even higher than that of the perfect righteous. See also Dr Ginzberg's *Genizah Studies*, p. 377, reproducing the following extract from an unknown Sheelta: —

ופליגא דר׳ אבהו מקום שבעלי תשובה עומדין אין צדיקים
גמורים עומדים והאיך דומים בעלי תשובה למלך שהיו לו שני
בנים אחד הלך בטוב ל   ואחר יצא לתרבות רעה שני שלום
שלום לרחוק ולקרוב מאי רחוק.

The text is defective, but it can hardly be doubted, as Dr Ginzberg points out, *ibid*, p 351, that in its completeness the comparison represented the well-known parable of the prodigal son in the *N T*. Cf. *Num. R*, 8 2

Page 331, Note 2. Instead of "Note 47," read "p 330, Note 4"

Page 333, Note 6 See *Meor Enaŷim*, by R. Azariah de' Rossi, p. 235, ed. Cassel. (Wilna, 1866.)

LIST OF ABBREVIATIONS AND BOOKS NOT QUOTED WITH FULL TITLE

Abarbanel, Isaac, משמיע ישועה, Konigsberg, 1860

Ag Ber = *Agadath Bereschith*, ed Buber, Cracow, 1902, quoted by chapters

Agadath Shir Hashirim, ed Schechter, Cambridge, 1896

Albo, *Ikkarim*, Pressburg, 1853, quoted by book and chapter

A R N = *Aboth de Rabbi Nathan recensiones duas*, ed S Schechter, Vienna, 1887, quoted by chapter or folio

Azulai, מדבר קדמות, Leghorn, 1793, printed together with the same author's יעיר אזן

Azulai, שער יוסף, Leghorn, 1757

Bacher, *Ag P Am* = *Die Agada der Palaestinensischen Amoraer*, I, Strassburg, 1892, II, ib, 1896, III, ib, 1899

Bacher, *Ag Tan* = *Die Agada der Tannaiten*, I, Strassburg, 1884, II, ib, 1890

Bacher, *Terminologie* = *Die exegetische Terminologie der jud Traditionsliteratur*, I–II, Leipzig, 1899–1905

Bachye ibn Bakudah, חובות הלבבות ed Sluzki, Warsaw, 1870

Bachye ibn Chalwah, כד הקמח, ed Breit, Lemberg, 1880–92

Baer, עבודת ישראל, Roedelheim, 1868

Berliner, *Targum* = *Targum Onkelos*, I–II, Berlin, 1884

Beth Talmud, Periodical ed. Friedmann and Weiss, I–V, Vienna, 1880–89.

Blau, *Zur Einleitung in die Heilige Schrift*, Budapest, 1894.

DE = *Derek Erez Rabba* in the Talmud, at the end of the fourth order

DEZ = *Derek Erez Zutta*, ed A J Tawrogi, Konigsberg i Pr, 1885

Duran, Simon, *Magen Aboth*, commentary to Aboth, Leipzig, 1855

Edeles, חידושי מהרש״א, commentary to the Talmud, ed Wilna

Epstein, אלדד הדני, Pressburg, 1891

Friedmann, הציון, commentary to Ezekiel, ch 20, Vienna, 1888

Friedmann, נספחים לסדר = נספחים אליה זוטא *Pseudo-Seder Eliahu Zuta*, Vienna, 1904.

Ginsburger, *Das Fragmententargum (Thargum Jeruschalmi zum Pentateuch)*, Berlin, 1899

Grunhut, ספר הלקוטים, I–VI, Jerusalem, 1898 seq

Gudemann, *Culturgeschichte* = *Geschichte des Erziehungswesens und der Cultur der abendlaendischen Juden*, I, Vienna, 1880

Hechaluz XIII by Osias H Schorr, Vienna, 1889

Jellinek, *Bet ha-Midrasch*, I–IV, Leipzig, 1853–57, V–VI, Vienna, 1873–77

Jer = Talmud of Jerusalem quoted by treatise, folio, and column of ed Krotoschin, 1866, corresponding to ed Venice, ca 1523.

Joel, *Blicke* = *Blicke in die Religionsgeschichte zu Anfang des zweiten christlichen Jahrhunderts*, I–II, Breslau and Leipzig, 1880–83

LIST OF BOOKS NOT QUOTED IN FULL TITLE

Judah Hallevi, *Kuzari*, ed Sluzki, Leipzig, 1864.

Kinyan Tora, Sixth chapter of *Aboth*, being an appendix.

Landshut, מקור ברכה in Edelmann, סדור הגיון לב, Konigsberg, 1845

Luzzatto, מסילת ישרים, Warsaw, 1889 An excellent edition with German translation by I. Wohlgemuth appeared lately, Berlin, 1906.

Machzor Vitry, ed S Hurwitz, Berlin, 1889–93.

Maimonides, *Mishneh Torah*, Wilna, 1900, quoted by book, chapter, and paragraph

Maimonides, *Moreh Nebuchim*, Warsaw, 1872; quoted by book and chapter

Maimonides, ספר המצות = סה"מ with many commentaries, Warsaw, 1891, quoted by the number of the precepts (מצות עשה = מ"ע) or prohibitions (מצות לא = מל"ח תעשה)

Mechilta = *Mechilta de-Rabbi Ismael*, ed Friedmann, Vienna, 1870, quoted by folio

Mechilta of R Simon = *Mechilta de-Rabbi Simon b Jochai*, ed Hoffmann, Frankfurt a M, 1905, quoted by folio; often also the number of the verse is given

Meir ibn Gabbai, עבודת הקדש, Warsaw, 1883

M H G = *Midrash Hag-gadol*, ed S Schechter, I, *Genesis*, Cambridge, 1902 The other volumes are quoted from Mss in the possession of the author

Midrash Agadah ed B = *Agadischer Commentar zum Pentateuch*, ed Buber, Vienna, 1894

Midrash Prov = *Midrasch Mischle*, ed Buber, Wilna, 1893, quoted by chapter

Midrash Shemuel B = *Midrasch Samuel*, ed Buber, Cracow, 1893, quoted by chapter and paragraph

Midrasch Suta, ed Buber, Berlin, 1894, quoted by folio

Midrasch Tannaim zum Deuteronomium, excerpted from the *M H G* by D Hoffmann, I, Berlin, 1908.

Mishna, quoted by treatise, chapter, and paragraph Occasionally *ed Lowe* = The Mishnah on which the Palestinian Talmud rests, ed. by W H Lowe, Cambridge, 1883, is referred to

M T = *Midrasch Tehillim* (*Schocher Tob*), ed. Buber, Wilna, 1891, quoted by chapter and paragraph

Nachmanides, *Shaar Haggemul*, Ferrara, 1556.

Pentateuch with *Targum Onkelos, Pseudo-Jonathan and Jerushalmi* and the commentaries of Rashi, Ibn Ezra, Nachmanides, etc, ed. Netter, Vienna, 1860.

P K = *Pesikta von Rab Kahana*, ed Buber, Lyck, 1868, quoted by folio

P. R *Pesikta Rabbati*, ed Friedmann, Vienna, 1880, quoted by folio

PRE = *Pirke Rabbi Eliezer* with commentary of R David Loria (רד"ל), Warsaw, 1852, quoted by chapter

Pseudo-Jonathan (*Targum Jonathan ben Usiel zum Pentateuch*), ed Ginsburger, Berlin, 1903

Pugio Fidei by Raymundus Martini, ed Carpzov, Leipzig, 1687

LIST OF BOOKS NOT QUOTED IN FULL TITLE 351

R after the books of the Pentateuch or the Five Scrolls means *Midrash Rabba* with many commentaries, Wilna, 1878, quoted by chapter and paragraph of this edition, except for *Cant R*, where the numbers refer to chapter and verse of the Biblical book The introductions in the beginning of *Lament R* are quoted with their respective numbers

R Rabbinovicz, *Variae lectiones in Mischnam et in Talmud Babylonicum*, I-XV, Munich, 1877-86, XVI, Przemysl, 1897

Reshith Chochmah by R Elijah de Vidas, Cracow, 1593

Responsa of R David b Zimra = שו״ת הרדב״ז, II, Venice, 1749

Responsa of the Geonim, ed Harkavy, Berlin, 1887 (*Studien und Mittheilungen aus der Kaiserlichen Oeffentlichen Bibliothek zu*, St Petersburg, IV)

Responsa of R. Isaac b Sheshet = שו״ת הריב״ש, Constantinople, 1547

Responsa of R Josef Trani = שו״ת מהרי״ט, Furth, 1768

Saadya, אמונות ודעות, Josefow, 1885

S E = Seder Eliahu rabba und Seder Eliahu zuta (Tanna d'be Eliahu), ed Friedmann, Vienna, 1900 Introduction, *ib*, 1902

Seder Rab Amram, Warsaw, 1865

Semachoth Zutarti in C M Horowitz, Uralte Tosefta's, II-III, Frankfurt a M, 1890, pp 28-40

Semachoth in the Talmud at the end of the fourth order

S E.Z = Seder Eliahu zuta, see S E

Sifre = Sifre debê Rab, ed Friedmann, Vienna, 1864, quoted by folio

Sifre Zuta, a Tannaitic commentary on Numbers known through quotations in Yalkut and *M H G*. and a fragment ed Schechter (*Jewish Quarterly Review*, VI, 656–63) A collection of these quotations was begun by Konigsberger, Frankfurt a M, 1894 and 1907, and by S Horovitz in *Monatsschrift f Geschichte und Wissenschaft des Judentums*, 1905 seq

Simon Kiara, הלכות גדולות, ed Traub, Warsaw, 1874 A different version, ed Hildesheimer, Berlin, 1888–92

Singer, *The Authorised Daily Prayer Book with a New Translation*, London, 1890

Talmud, ed. Wilna, 1880–86, contains the commentaries of R Chananel, R Gershom, etc ; quoted by treatise and folio, all editions having the same pagination

Tan = Tanchuma, quoted by section of the Pentateuch and paragraph of ed Lublin, 1879, with commentary עץ יוסף

Tan B = Midrasch Tanchuma, ed by S Buber, Wilna, 1885, 5 vols, quoted by volume (book of the Pentateuch) and folio

T K = Torat Kohanim, called also Sifra, ed with the commentary of R. Abraham b David (ראב״ד), by I H Weiss, Vienna, 1862, quoted by folio and column.

T Muller, *Masechet Soferim*, Leipzig, 1878

Tosephta, quoted by folios of ed M. S Zukermandel, Pasewalk, 1881. Occasionally A *Schwarz*, Tosifta juxta Mischnarum ordinem recomposita, I, Ordo Seraim, Wilna, 1890, is referred to.

Tur Orach Chayim by R Jacob b Asher, Konigsberg, 1861

Weiss, דור דור ודורשיו = דו״ד *Zur Geschichte der jüdischen Tradition*, I–V, Vienna, 1871–91.
Wertheimer, בתי מדרשות, I–IV, לקט מדרשים Jerusalem, 1903
Wertheimer, Jerusalem, 1893–97

Yalkut = *Yalkut Shimeoni*, Frankfurt a M, 1687, Part I to Pentateuch, Part II to Prophets and Hagiographa, quoted by paragraphs
Yalkut Machiri on Isa = The Yalkut on Isaiah of Machir b Abba Mari, ed Spira, Berlin, 1894
Yalkut Machiri = *Jalkut Machiri zu den Psalmen*, ed Buber, Berdyczew, 1899
Yelamdenu, lost Midrash to the Pentateuch, frequently excerpted by the Yalkut and others Quotations are collected by L Grunhut, ספר הליקוטים, IV seq, Jerusalem, 1900 seq

Zohar, Krotoschin, 1844–45, 3 vols

אותיות דרבי עקיבא = אותיות דר״ע in Jellinek, Bet ha-Midrasch, III, pp 12–64
בחיי, commentary to the Pentateuch by Bechaye Ibn Chalwa, Amsterdam, 1726
ס׳ חסידים, Parma = *Das Buch der Frommen nach Cod De Rossi*, No 1133, ed Wistinetzki, Berlin, 1891
יפה עינים, R Arje Loeb Jellin's glosses to the Talmud, Wilna, 1880–86
ל״ב מדות of R Eleazar b Jose of Galilee Rules of interpretation printed in the first volume of the Talmud and in the introduction to *M H G*. Separate edition under the title נתיבות עולם, with commentary by Katzenellenbogen, Wilna, 1858.
לקח טוב, *Lekack-Tob*, commentary by R Tobia b Eliezer Genesis and Exodus, ed Buber, Leviticus, Numbers, and Deuteronomy, ed Padua, Wilna, 1880.
מורינו הרב רבי זאב וואלף = מה״רזוו איינהארן, author of a commentary to Midrash Rabba, ed Wilna, 1878.
מסכת אבות עם תלמוד בבלי וירושלמי, by Noah Chajjim of Kabrin, Warsaw, 1878
ספר מצוח קטן = סמ״ק, by R Isaac of Corbeil, also called עמודי גולה, Cremona, 1556
ספר המוסר, by R Jehuda Kalaz, Mantua, 1560
וספר יראים by R Eliezer of Metz, Warsaw, 1881.
ספרי דאגדתא, *Sammlung agadischer Commentare zum Buche Esther*, ed Buber, Wilna, 1886
עין יעקב, by R Jacob ibn Chabib, Wilna, 1883, 3 vols.
פרקי דרבי אליעזר = פדר״א
פרקא דרבינו הקדוש in Schoenblum, שלשה ספרים נפתחים, Lemberg, 1877
פרקי היכלות, Jellinek, Bet ha-Midrasch, III, pp 83–108, from a different Ms ed, Wertheimer, Jerusalem, 1890.
רבי דוד לוריא = רד״ל, author of notes to Midrash Rabba, ed Wilna, 1878, and a commentary to *PRE*
רוקח, by R Eleazar of Worms, Warsaw, 1880
שאלתות, by R Achai Gaon, with commentary by R Isaia, Berlin, Dyhernfurt, 1786
שארית ישראל, Amsterdam, s. a
תנא רבי אליהו = תדב״א, title of the old editions of S E

INDEX

Aaron, prays for the regeneration of the sinner, 316, encourages sinners to repent, 321.

Abba Hilkia, wife of, prays that outlaws may repent, 317

Abba Saul, Rabbi, on *Imitatio Dei*, 200, 201–2

Abba Tachna, illustrates the victory of the *Good Yezer* over the *Evil Yezer*, 272–3

Abimelech, protected by the grace of God against the *Evil Yezer*, 283–4

Aboth, Mishnic tractate, and *Chasiduth*, 209–10

Abraham, God pays a sick visit to, 37, God argues with, 37, the rock, 59, as proselytiser, 77, 84, 93, the friend of God, 84, and the kingship of God, 83–4, testifies for Israel against the Torah, 129, the world established on, 173, and the *Zachuth* of posterity, 196, attacked by the *Evil Yezer*, 251–2, the merits of, guarded by Satan, 268 has dominion over the *Evil Yezer*, 271, 275

See also Fathers, the, Patriarchs, the

Absalom, alluded to, 213

Abuhah, Rabbi, as a geologist, 19

Accuser, the. See Satan

Acha, Rabbi, on the taint of sin in sexual intercourse, 253

Achan, and the doctrine of imputed sin, 191

Adam, God at the wedding of, 37, 203; acknowledges God as king, 82, 93; and the doctrine of imputed sin, 188; corrupting effect of sin on, 235–6, the sin of, conceals the light of the first day, 237, urged by God to repent, 315.

Admonition, hating, prevents repentance, 331

Adulterer, the, names for, 224

Adultery, a cardinal sin, 205, extended meaning of, 214, penalty for, 224–5, removes the Shechinah, 224–5, what is included under, 225, heresy a form of, 225–6, and the *Evil Yezer*, 250, forced upon David, to make him an example of repentance, 317–18; not subject to repentance, 333.

Affirmative injunctions, the number of, 138

Agadah, the, character of, 3, retells the Bible stories with application to later conditions, 24–5, and corporeal terms applied to God, 35

See also under Rabbis, the.

Agadic saying, on the Mizwoth, 138–40.

Ahab, the repentance of, 324, 326.

Ahaz, spites God, 220

Akabiah ben Mahalaleel, on the contemplation of death as a remedy against the *Evil Yezer*, 276

Akiba, Rabbi, on justification by grace or works, 15–16, considers the paternal relation between God and Israel unconditional, 54, rejoices in the yoke of the kingdom of heaven, 71–2, on the justice of God, 304–5, on the grace of God, 306

INDEX

Alcimus, high priest, alluded to, 92
Allegoric interpretation of Scripture, prejudice against, 4
Allegorising method, the, and the Rabbis, 39–44
See also Corporeal terms
Alphabet, the, endowed with life, 129.
Amalekites, the, impair the perfection of the kingdom of God, 99–101; identified with Esau and Rome, 99.
Amon, spites God, 220.
Amos, the Book of, cited, in connection with the Mizwoth, 140, with repentance as a sweet message, 324
Anathoth, the repentance of the men of, 326
Ancient One of the world, epithet for God, 26
Angel of Death, the, identified with the *Evil Yezer*, 244–5.
Angels, the, surrounding God, 28, 32; lower than Israel, 49, incapable of sin, 81; object to the removal of the Torah from heaven, 136, free from the *Evil Yezer*, 257, 285, object to the repentance of Manasseh, 318–19, oppose repentance in general, 321–2
Anger, akin to idolatry, 224; habitual, prevents repentance, 330
Antigonos of Socho, on purity of motive in performance of the Law, 162
Antinomian influence of the Apostle Paul, 4.
Antinomianism, and the mystic, 78
Antoninus, on the time the *Evil Yezer* takes possession of man, 253
Apocalyptic works, not useful as a source of Rabbinic theology, 5
Apocryphal works, not useful as a source of Rabbinic theology, 5.

Apologetics, and Rabbinic theology, 18–19
Apostasy, changes the relation of Israel to God, 55 n.
Apostate, spite, 220.
Apostles, the, meagreness of Rabbinic literature contemporary with, 8
Araboth, the seventh heaven, the abode of God, 28–9, 30–1, 32.
Arayoth, forbidden sexual intercourse, 211.
Arbitration of disputes, a law of goodness, 215.
Archelaus, king, alluded to, 93.
Ascetic practices, to guard against relapsing into sin, 340; connected with the Ten Penitential Days, 342
Ascetic remedies, against the *Evil Yezer*, 277–8
Askari *See* Joseph Askari.
Astruc, alluded to, 19
Atonement, needed by the dead, 196, through sacrifices limited in efficacy, 295–7, resides in sacrifices, 300–1, by sacrifices intended for the community, 300–1, through death and suffering, 304, 307–8; Scriptural kinds of, 308, through children and the righteous, 310–11, through the Torah and charity, 312, repentance must accompany all kinds of, 313
See also Forgiveness; Reconciliation
Atonement, the Day of, Scriptural and Prophetical portions for, 119; purifies Israel, 234, prayer on, for grace to conquer the *Evil Yezer*, 279–80, atones for the community and the individual, 301 n ; repentance on, 302–4, inefficacious without repentance, 34^
Attributes, of God, 38
See also Mercy, Justic

INDEX

Avira, Rabbi, enumerates seven names for the *Evil Yezer*, 243-4

Azariah, justified in rebelling against Nebuchadnezzar, 107

Bachye Ibn Bakudah, on love of God, 68-9, 72-3, on the joy of the Law, 151

Bachye Ibn Chalwah, on the unity and the kingdom of God, 96, on the joy of performing the Mizwoth, 151

Backbiting, a form of bloodshed, 227

Balaam, and the grace of the revelation, 134

Benaha, Rabbi, as the forerunner of Astruc, 19

Ben Azai, on "The Book of Generations of Adam," 120

Benedictions, the, preceding the Prophets and Hagiographa, 123, convey the idea of holiness through commandments, 168

Berachoth, Talmud tractate, and *Chasiduth*, 210

Beth-Hammidrash (schoolhouse), the, a refuge from the *Evil Yezer*, 273, 274

Blasphemy, a sin of rebellion, 222; called an evil thing, 232; repentance possible for, 326

Bloodshed, a cardinal sin, 205; different kinds of, 213, the consequences of, 326-7, slander, a form of, 227, robbery, a form of, 227-9, bad administration of justice, a form of, 229-30, due to the *Evil Yezer*, 246.

See also Murder

Boaz, banishes the *Evil Yezer*, 271

Body, the, liable to sin, 260-1

"Book of Generations of Adam, The," on the dignity of man, 120

Bribery, prevents repentance, 330.

Bride, term for the relation between God and Israel, 47, term applied to the Sabbath, 154

Brother, term for the relation between God and Israel, 47, 56

Burnt offering, the, instituted for heresy, 225-6, the continual, controversy on the atoning power of, 299-300

Cabalists, the, and the creation of the world, 128

See also under Mystic

Cain, makes the *Evil Yezer* responsible for his crime, 280-1, an example of penitence, 315; repentance of, acceptable, 326

Captives, objections to marriage with, 213

Cardinal sins, the, enumerated, 205-6

See Sins, the cardinal.

Catastrophes, to teach that repentance is possible for the greatest sins, 317

Chama ben Chaninah, Rabbi, quoted, on the imitation of God, 202-3

Chambers, Chapters of the, mystical description of the heavens, 29

Chaninah ben Dosa, Rabbi, miracle-worker, lacks influence on Jewish thought, 7, on sin as the cause of death, 247.

Chanukah Candles, the Lighting of the, as a command, 13.

Chapters of the Chambers, mystical description of the heavens, 29

Charity, invalidated by robbery, 228, disparaged by the *Evil Yezer*, 252, superior to sacrifices as a means of atonement, 296, 312, the atoning power of, 312, preventing, makes repentance impossible, 330.

Charity system, the, of the Rabbis, 112.
Chasiduth, saintliness supplementing the Law, 201, 209, discriminates between one and another group of laws, 209, various definitions of, 209-10, summarised in a Talmudic formula, 210, Eliezer of Worms on, 210, abstention from superfluous things, according to Nachmanides, 211-12, a corrective of the Law, 212-14, the reward of, 217-18.
See also Holiness
Chasiduth, *Regulations of*, by Eliezer of Worms, quoted, 210
Chaste women, the, the atoning power of, 312.
Chayoth, the, surrounding God, 28
Cheating, not subject to repentance, 333
Cherubim, the, surrounding God, 32
Children, term for the relation of Israel to God, 46, 49 (*bis*), not saved by their fathers, 178, and the doctrine of imputed sin, 191, 192-3, the *Evil Yezer* in, 253-5, the death of, an atonement for the sins of adults, 254, are without sin, 269, the atoning power of, 310-11
See also Zachuth, the, of a pious posterity
Chisda, Rabbi, criticised by a pupil, 144-5
Chiya, Rabbi, the holiness of, 212
Choni Hammaagel, miracle-worker, lacks influence on Jewish thought, 7.
Chosen ones, a term applied to Israel by God, 47
Christianity, the essential principle of, in the Book of Leviticus, 120
Chronicles (I), the Book of, cited, in connection with the uniqueness of Israel, 48, with the *Evil Yezer*, 243 (*bis*), with the heart as the seat of the *Yezers*, 257.
Chronicles (II), the Book of, cited, in connection with the repentance of Manasseh, 318, 319
Civil law, in the Mishnah, 2.
Commandment, the performance of one, and the salvation of the world, 189-90
Commandments, the, kept by God, 203
See Mizwoth, the
Communion, with the Holy Spirit, brought about by *Chasiduth*, 217; with God, follows the banishment of the *Evil Yezer*, 292
Community, the, responsibility of, and the doctrine of imputed sin, 191-5, and the atoning power of sacrifices, 300-1, and the Day of Atonement, 301, separation from, prevents repentance, 330.
See also Solidarity.
Compilation, a, inadequate as a theologic source, 3-5.
Conceit, causes death, 246.
See also Pride
Conduct, determines man's nearness to God, 33
Confession of sins, the, accompanies certain sacrifices, 296, a part of repentance, 335-8.
Contamination, description of sin, 233-4
Corporeal terms applied to God, mitigated, 35-6, exaggerated, 40.
See also Allegorising method, the
Corrective of the Law, *Chasiduth*, 212-14, the law of goodness, 214-16
Corruption, sin a symptom of, 235
Court of justice, the, duties of, and the doctrine of imputed sin, 191, 192, 193-5.
Covenant, the, of God with Israel and the *Porek ol*, 220 and n

Covenant with the Fathers, the, unlimited, 179
  See also Zachuth, the, of the Fathers
Creation, Master of all, epithet for God, 22
Creation of man, the, subject of controversy, 8
Creation of the world, the, a glorification of God, 80-1, man the centre of, 82, and wisdom, 127-8, according to the Cabalists, 128, repentance indispensable to, 128, 314
Creator, epithet for God, 26
Creed, The Thirteen Articles of the, by Maimonides, contain no mention of Israel's election, 57
Criminal procedure, in the Mishnah, 2
Criticism of the wise, prevents repentance, 331
Cursing the many, prevents repentance, 330

Daniel, Rome in the vision of, 100
Daniel, the Book of, cited, in connection with God as a teacher of the Torah, 43, with the extent of the Torah, 122
David, the consequences of the marriage of, with a captive, 212-13, name given to the *Evil Yezer* by, 243, banishes the *Evil Yezer*, 271, slays the *Evil Yezer*, 275, made to sin as an example of repentance, 317-18, and Jeroboam, 319, confident of God's forgiveness, 326, confesses his sin, 336
Dead, the, and the doctrine of imputed sin, 196, and the *Zachuth* of posterity, 198, prayers for, 198
Death, caused by the *Evil Yezer*, 244-7, caused by sin, 245, 247, of children, 254, the contemplation of, conquers the *Evil Yezer*, 276, the punishment of the sinner, 293, 294, 304; an atonement, 304, 307-8, 310
Death, the Angel of *See* Angel of Death, the
Death-bed repentance, 340-1.
Deborah, the generation of, has a single heart, 257
Decalogue, the, the tablets of, suggest an explanation concerning the *Evil Yezer*, 274-5
  See also Law, the; Torah, the
Defilement, term applied to the cardinal sins, 205, 206.
  See also Impurity
Defilement of the land, caused by idolatry, 223, caused by pride, 223, caused by murder, 226
Deification of man, objected to by the Rabbis, 38-9
Deluge, the, and the doctrine of imputed sin, 195; generation of, rebels, 219, 222, causes pain to God, 219-20, robbery the capital sin of, 227, and the Tetragrammaton, 239, give the *Evil Yezer* sway, 271, warned to repent, 315
Depravity in children, left unprotested, prevents repentance, 331.
Desert, the, reason for giving the Torah in, 131
Deuteronomy, the Book of, cited, in connection with Moses' acknowledgement of God, 26, with the might of God, 38, with the justice of God, 38, with the faithfulness of God, 38, with the unity of God, 48, with Israel's exalted place, 48, with the election of Israel, 58 (*bis*), 63-4, with the kingdom of God, 67 (*bis*), with love of God, 67, 68, 69, 79 (*bis*), with man's righteousness and the kingdom of God, 90 (*bis*), 91, with the kingship benediction, 96, with the superiority of the Torah, 118, an *Imitatio Dei*, 119, cited in

connection with the commandment of forgetfulness, 149, with the joy of the Law, 150, with performing the Law with a view to reward, 162, with *Zachuth*, 179, with the *Zachuth* of a pious ancestry, 182, 183, against imputed sin, 185, 186, cited in connection with the duties of a court of justice, 193, with imputed sin through posterity, 196, with walking in the ways of God, 201, with the imitation of God, 203, with cleaving to God, 204 (*bis*), with jealousy, 204, with marriage with a captive, 213, with a rebellious son, 213, with the law of goodness, 214, with pride, 223, 224, with the Shechinah, 224 (*bis*), with heresy, 225, with the *Evil Yezer*, 242, 243, with the good heart, 259, with remedies against the *Evil Yezer*, 277, with God's regret at having created the *Evil Yezer*, 284 (*bis*), with free will and the *Evil Yezer*, 286 (*bis*), 288, with the communal sacrifices, 301; with the justice of God, 305, 306, with the repentance of Manasseh, 318, with God's attribute of mercy in relation to repentance, 322

Devious ways, and the imitation of God, 204.

Devotion, a necessary element in prayer, 156-9

De Wette, definition of mysticism by, 77

Dibbur, as used by the Rabbis, 43 n

Dietary laws See Forbidden food

Dining-table, the, the atoning power of, 312.

Dishonesty, a widespread sin, 250, 260

Disobedience. See Sin

Disrespect, removes the Divine Presence, 232.

Divine Presence, the. See Shechinah, the

Divorce laws, in the Mishnah, 2

"Duties of the Heart," by Bachye Ibn Bakudah, quoted, 68-9, 72-3.

Ecce Homo, quoted, on the ideal of Jesus, 112

Ecclesiastes, the Book of, cited in connection with corrupt government, 107, with the weakening influence of sin, 238, with unintentional sins, 240, with the heart as the seat of the *Yezers*, 256, with the two *Yezers*, 265, with the good uses of the *Evil Yezer*, 267; with man's responsibility for the *Evil Yezer*, 268.

Edom, the prototype of Rome, 99, 108

Egypt, the people of, cause pain to God, 219-20

Eighteen Benedictions, the, prayer for grace to conquer the *Evil Yezer* in, 280

Eleazar ben Jose of Galilee, on allegoric interpretation of Scriptures, 41 n.

Election of Israel, the, treated by the Agadah, 3; indicates the close relation to God, 57, an unformulated dogma, 57; in the liturgy, 57, in the Scriptures, 58, the Rabbis on, 58-64; reasons for, 58-62, predestined, 59; not exclusive, 62-4

Eli, the sons of, deny the kingdom of God, 87.

Eliezer, Rabbi, Chapters of, on God before the creation of the world, 80, on repentance, 128; on free will and the *Evil Yezer*, 288-9.

Eliezer ben Azariah, and the *Zachuth* of his ancestors, 176

Eliezer of Worms, quoted, on love of God, 74-5, on *Chasiduth*, 210.

INDEX

Elijah, held up as a model to Hiram, 39, rebuked for excessive zeal, 52–3, and the inheritors of the future world, 166, rebuked for excessive severity, 204–5, and the law of saints, 216, banishes the *Evil Yezer*, 271; reproaches God for the *Evil Yezer*, 283

Elisha, why made to supersede Elijah, 53, 205, urges Gehazi to repent, 333

Elohim, God as judge, 35.

El Shadai, the God of pardon, 35–6

Enemy, name for the *Evil Yezer*, 243

Enosh, generation of, rebels, 219, cause pain to God, 219–20

Envy, causes death, 245, 246, serviceable for a good purpose, 267

Epithets for God, 21–2, 26–8, 34, 35–6, as used by the Rabbis, 39, in the liturgy, 44

Esau, identified with Amalek and Rome, 99–100, 108, supreme in this world, 100; the Torah offered to, 132

Eve, God at the wedding of, 37, 203

Evil, name for the *Evil Yezer*, 243

Evil, the punishment of the sinner, 293, 294

Evil eye, the, causes death, 245

Evil inclination, the *See Evil Yezer*, the

Evil thoughts, indulgence in, prevents repentance, 330

Evil Yezer, the, and the love of God, 67–8, suppressed by Israel to acknowledge the kingdom of God, 97–8, Scriptural passages on, 242–3; names for, 243–4; activities of, 244–7, 248, corresponds to lust, 246, punishment meted out by, 246–7, and vanity, 248–9, 276; instantaneous resistance to, recommended, 249, connected closely with idolatry and adultery, 250, and scepticism, 251–2; disparages charity, 252, when it takes possession of man, 252–5, the heart the seat of, 255–61; not equivalent with the heart, 258–9, has no dominion over the heart filled with Torah 259, prominent in Jewish literature, 262, the leaven in the dough, 262–3, a creature of God, 264–6, God acknowledges the creation of, 266, 280–3, uses of, 266–7, called a good quality, 267, the servant of man, 267, man responsible for, 268–9, created for man to overcome, 269, can be overcome by man, 269–70, can be turned to good purposes, 271, how to banish, 271–2, the *Good Yezer* to be stirred up against, 272–3, two weapons against, 273, conquered by the study of the Torah, 273–5, conquest of, an honouring of God, 275, conquered by the contemplation of death, 276, various remedies against, 277–8, grace needed to conquer, 278–84, 289–90, God regrets the creation of, 284, and free will, 284–9, to cease with the advent of the Messiah, 290–2, the appearance of, to the righteous and the wicked, 290, Israel's reward for banishing, 292, repentance for, 304, 313, 314, God prays for the destruction of, 316, killed by a confession of sin, 338

Exaltation, and the imitation of God, 204

Exodus, the, due to the *Zachuth* of the Fathers, 174, 180, 185 n, denied by the perverter of justice, 230, fulfilment of the commandment on usury, a condition of, 230–1.

Exodus, the Book of, cited in connection with the might of God, 38, with the mercy of God, 38, with the pride of a mortal, 38; with Jethro's acknowledgement of God, 25, with the name of God, 35, 36, with God's presence at Mount Sinai, 36, with God's speech with man, 41, with God as a man of war, 43, with the affliction of Israel, 44, with God's dwelling on earth, 48, with God's paternal interest in Israel, 50, 51, with Moses as a sacrifice for Israel, 53, with the election of Israel, 58, 63, with the glorification of God through creation, 80, with the kingdom of God as established by Israel, 85-6, with the sanction of the Law, 116, the legal part of the Torah begins in, 120, the book of the covenant mentioned in, 121, cited in connection with Israel's holiness, 168, with the *Zachuth* of the Fathers, 174, with the *Zachuth* of a pious ancestry, 181, with imputed sin, 185, 187, with exaltation, 204; with sexual immorality, 206; with murder, 213, with adultery, 214, with mercy, 215, with humility, 223, with the sight of the glory of God, 236 (*bis*), with the weakening influence of sin, 239 (*bis*), with the Tetragrammaton, 239, with the tablets of stone for the Decalogue, 275, with the disappearance of the *Evil Yezer* in the Messianic time, 291 (*bis*), with the atoning power of the righteous, 310, with Pharaoh's hardened heart, 332

Extermination, penalty for adultery, 224

"External" books *See* Apocalyptic, Apocryphal

Eye, term for the relation between God and Israel, 47

Eye, the evil, causes death, 245

Eye of the world, epithet for God, 26.

Eyes, the, cause sin, 208, 214; agents of sin, 258

Ezekiel, the visions of, and God's heavenly abode, 28-9

Ezekiel, the Book of, cited, in connection with the pride of Hiram, 38-9, with Israel's relation to God, 44, with the kingdom of God, 71, 88, with imputed sin, 187, 196, with robbery, 228, with the *Evil Yezer*, 243-4, with the sinning soul, 261, with the *Evil Yezer* regarded as *stone*, 275; with the grace needed to conquer the *Evil Yezer*, 281, with the punishment of sinners, 293; with repentance human and Divine, 328.

Faith, the Rabbis quoted on, 14, the reason for Israel's election, 59-60

Faithfulness, the, of God, 38

Family, the, and the doctrine of imputed sin, 192

Family of God, Israel, 200

Fasting, a sacrificial atonement, 308, cannot replace repentance, 335, with repentance, 339-40

Fasts, public, the *Zachuth* of pious ancestors invoked at, 172

Father, term for the relation between God and Israel, 46, 49, 50-6, as used in the liturgy, 155.

Father of the world, epithet for God, 26.

Fatherhood of God, the, to be acknowledged by Israel, 50-1; Luther on, 51 n; an unconditional relation, 51-6; in the liturgy, 54-6, changed by apostasy, 55 n

See also Reciprocal relation

Fathers, the, in the sense of the three patriarchs, 171, imperfections and distinctions of, 173-4

See also Patriarchs, the.

INDEX

"Fathers, the, the Chapters of," character of the contents, 2

Fathers, the, the merits of. See *Zachuth*

Fear, an expression for love with the Rabbis, 72, a constituent of the Torah, 146.

Fear of God, the, not in the power of God, 285

Fiend, name for the *Evil Yezer*, 243

First-born son, term for the relation of Israel to God, 46

Flock, term for the relation of Israel to God, 49

Folly, a description of sin, 236-7

Foolish old king, name for the *Evil Yezer*, 244, 254

Forbidden food, causes impurity, 206-7

Forgetfulness, the commandment on, illustrated, 149

Forgiveness, for sins, attained through repentance, 293-4, 335, resides with God alone, 294-5, through suffering, 309, five classes not subject to, 328-30, granted three times for the same sin, 332

See *also* Atonement, Reconciliation

Freedom, attained through the yoke of the kingdom of God, 70

Free will, and the *Evil Yezer*, 284-9

Future world, the See World, the future

Gabriel, angel, not a mediator, 45, 67, may not approach Moses, 238

Galgalim, the, surrounding God, 32

Gamaliel the Second, Rabban, alluded to, 176

Gehazi, ruled by the *Evil Yezer*, 271, urged to repent, 333

Gehenna, children save parents from, 197, repentance in, 341 n

Gemara, the See Talmud, the.

Genesis, the Book of, cited in connection with the dignity of men, 120, value of, 121, cited in connection with the protective power of the *Zachuth*, 190, with the imitation of God, 202, with the *Porek ol*, 221 (*bis*), with bloodshed, 226, 251, with the Tetragrammaton, 240, with the *Evil Yezer*, 242, 243, 264, 265 (*bis*), 266, with overcoming the *Evil Yezer*, 270, 283, with the *Evil Yezer* as *stone*, 274

Gentiles, the, transitory character of opinions on, 9-10, magnify God, 58, God's relation to, 62-4, of the kingdom of God, 106, refuse the Law, 131-2, refuse to share in the Law with Israel, 133, rebellious under suffering, 310

See *also* Kingdom of God, the universal

Geonic Responsa, quoted, on prayers for the dead, 198

Geonim, the, and the visible universal kingdom of God, 95-6, and the national kingdom of God, 97

Gluttony, incompatible with holiness, 211-12, auxiliary to the *Evil Yezer*, 277

God, man's relation to, treated by the Agadah, 3, epithets for, 21-2, 26-8, 34, 35-6, man's nearness to, determined by his conduct, 33; an *imitatio hominis*, 37-8, attendant at the wedding of Adam and Eve, 37, 203, as used by the Hellenists, 43 n, the unity of, emphasised, 43-4, worship due to him alone, 44-5, relation of, to the world, 21-45, relation of, to Israel, 46-56, terms for the relation of, to Israel, 46-7, applies his own attributes to Israel, 47, and the angels, 49, before the creation of the world, 80-1, removed from the world by sin, 83, teaches Israel how to pray, 157, to be imitated by men, 201-5, the denial of, the essence of sin, 233, name given to the *Evil Yezer* by, 243, responsible for the existence of the *Evil Yezer*, 266, 280-3, regrets the creation of the *Evil Yezer*, 284

See also under Forgiveness, Kingdom of God, Transcendentalism

Gods, a term applied to Israel by God, 47, 49

Golden calf, the, indicative of Israel's rebelliousness, 86, the sin of, counteracted by the *Zachuth* of the Fathers, 174 (*bis*), 180, and the doctrine of imputed sin, 189, the sin of, permitted, to teach repentance, 317

Good inclination, the See *Good Yezer*, the

Good Yezer, the, in the Book of Chronicles (I), 243, term of a late date, 243, the heart the seat of, 255, 256, 257, 259, represented by men, 262, a creature of God, 264-5, preferred by the righteous, 271, to be stirred up against the *Evil Yezer*, 272-3, prayers for, 279-80, in the Messianic time, 291

Goodness, the law of, akin to holiness, 214, defined by Nachmanides, 214-5, and insisting upon strict justice, 215

Goodness of God, manifested in the creation, 80

Goodness of the world, epithet for God, 26

Gomorrah, and the doctrine of *Zachuth*, 190, the people of, rebels, 219, 222, the people of, cause pain to God, 219-20

Government, a corrupt, incompatible with the kingdom of God, 106-9

Grace, Rabbi Akiba on justification by, 15-16, the reason for Israel's election, 61-2, the revelation an act of, 133-5, needed in connection with the Torah to conquer the *Evil Yezer*, 278, prayers for, 278-9, prayers for, in the liturgy, 279-80, the need for, implies God's responsibility for the existence of the *Evil Yezer*, 280-2, needed to subdue the *Evil Yezer*, in the world to come, 282-3, granted to Abimelech, 283-4, man must show himself worthy of, 289-90, Akiba on, 306, reserved for this world, 307, repentance an act of, 324

Graciousness of God, the, to be imitated by man, 201-2

Guilt offering, the, ensures forgiveness, 293, accompanied by repentance, 296.

Habakkuk, the Book of, cited, in connection with the *Mizwoth*, 140; with bearing witness, 247

Hagiographa, the, sometimes excluded by the term *Torah*, 118, included in the term *Torah*, 121-6, frequently quoted by the Rabbis, 122, included in the Scriptures, 123, benediction for, 123, how cited in Rabbinic literature, 124-5

See also Wisdom

Halachah, the, not subject to miraculous proof, 7

Halachic discussions, epithet for God in, 34

Hallam, quoted, 39.

Hallevi, Judah See Judah Hallevi

Hamnuna Zuta, on the contemplation of death, 276

Hananiah, justified in rebelling against Nebuchadnezzar, 107.

INDEX

Harnack, on Pauline Epistles, 18

Hatred, a greater sin than the cardinal sins, 227, causes death, 245

Hausrath, disparages the Jewish Sabbath, 153

Heart, the, causes sin, 208, in Jewish literature, 255 n., as the seat of the *Yezers*, 255–61, the agent of sin, 258, not equivalent to the *Evil Yezer*, 258–9, good, 259, accused of inconsistency, 259, equivalent to the soul, 260–1, in the righteous and the wicked, 270

See also Soul, the

Heaven, as the abode of God, 28–9, 30–1, 32, notion as such leaves Rabbinic theology uninfluenced, 30

Heaven, epithet for God, 21, 28, does not imply remoteness, 46

Hegelianism, and the Rabbis, 19

Height of the world, epithet for God, 28

Hell, endowed with pre-mundane existence, 128

Hellenism, and the Rabbis, 39–40, 42–3, and its use of God, 43 n

Heresy, akin to adultery, 225–6

Herod, king, alluded to, 93

Hezekiah, king, alluded to, 177

Hidden-One, name for the *Evil Yezer*, 244

High One, epithet for God, 28

High priest, the, the vestments of, have atoning power, 300

Higher criticism, the, on the literature produced under the predominance of the Law, 116

Hillel, Rabbi, not a miracle-worker, 7, as a modern altruist, 18–19, on the resurrection, 102 n, on the oneness of the material and the spiritual life, 145, on material uses of the Torah, 154, 159, on individual righteousness, 182, worthy of the Divine Presence, 238

Hillel, the school of, on the creation of man, 8, on the atoning power of the burnt offering, 299

Hiram, of Tyre, reproved for pride, 38–9

Holiness, the Law a source of, 168, a motive for the performance of the Law, 168–9, the culmination of the Law, 199, grows out of the kingdom of God, 199, an *Imitatio Dei*, 199–200, 201–5, divisions of, 201, and separateness, 205, destroyed by impurity, 205–9, abstention from things superfluous, 211–12, abstention from things permitted, 212–13, and the law of goodness, 214, and communion with God, 218

See also *Kedushah*, *Chasiduth*

Holiness, a name for God in Rabbinic literature, 199

Holy, applied to the patriarchs after their death, 173, attribute applied to Israel by God, 47

Holy Land, the, talk of the people in, called Torah, 126

Holy One, the, epithet for God, 21, most frequent name for God in Rabbinic literature, 199

Holy Spirit, the, dictates the Torah, 120–1, *Chasiduth* leads to communion with, 217–18

Hope, term for the relation between God and Israel, 46

Hosea, rebuked for excessive zeal, 53

Hosea, the Book of, cited, in connection with God as a man of war, 36, with God's love for Israel, 61, with the manner of performing the Law, 161, with *Zachuth*, 178, with man's worthiness of grace, 289, with repentance for many sins, 325; with confession of sins, 338

INDEX

Hoshayah, Rabbi, on wisdom, 127
Humanising of God, 37–8
Humanity, the essential principle of, in the Book of Leviticus, 120
Humbleness, the reason for Israel's election, 60
Hushai, the Archite, reproves David, 212–13
Hypocrisy, detrimental to belief in the unity of God, 68–9
Hypocrites, excluded from the Divine Presence, 232.

Idolater, the, animosity to, dates from the revelation, 131, a *Porek ol*, 220, names for, 222–3, compared to the unmerciful, 231–2
Idolatry, laws on, not a practical consideration, 141, a cardinal sin, 205, transgression of the dietary laws leads to, 207, consequences of, 223; pride, a form of, 223–4, anger, a form of, 224, a contamination, 233, described as folly, 237, and the *Evil Yezer*, 244, 250, the cause of sin, 291–2
See also Polytheism.
Idols, defined, 67
Imitatio Dei, holiness is an, 199–200, particularised by Abba Saul, 201–2
Immorality, dirties the Torah, 234
See also Adultery, Sexual immorality
Immortality, treated by the Agadah, 3
Impurity, in the sense of sexual immorality, 205–6, of body, 206–7; caused by a disgusting act, 267; caused by a transgression of a Biblical law, 208–9, of thought, 210–11, 232
See also Levitical impurity
Imputed righteousness *See Zachuth*
Imputed sin, the doctrine of, a counterpart of *Zachuth*, 170,

Biblical authority for, and against, 185–7, and the sin of Adam, 188, and the sin of the golden calf, 189; through contemporaries, 191–5, and secret sins, 194, and the revelation, 195, through posterity, 195–7
Incest, laws on, not a practical consideration, 141
Inclination, the evil. See *Evil Yezer*, the
Inclination, the good. See *Good Yezer*, the
Incontinence *See* Sexual immorality
Individualism in religion, 76–9
Informer, the office of, performed by the *Evil Yezer*, 252
Inheritance, regulated by the Mishnah, 2
Initiative, in repentance, 324, 327.
Isaac, God condoles with, 37
See also Fathers, the; Patriarchs, the
Isaac, Rabbi, on the Prophets, 124.
Isaiah, the condition of his prophetical call, 52, the mouthpiece of the Mosaic revelation, 124
Isaiah, the Book of, cited, in connection with separation from God, 33, with the intimate relation of God to Israel, 47, 50, with the rebelliousness of Israel, 52, with Israel's filial relation to God, 54 (*bis*), with Abraham, 59, with God's relation to the Gentiles, 62, with the glorification of God through creation, 80, with universalism, 106 (*bis*), 131; prophetical portion for the Day of Atonement from, 119, cited, in connection with the *Mizwoth*, 140 (*bis*), with humility, 223; with robbery, 228, with nearness to God, 233 (*bis*), with the attribute of mercy, 240, with the *Evil Yezer*, 243; with the heart,

258, with remedies against the *Evil Yezer*, 277, with grace to conquer the *Evil Yezer*, 281, with free will and the *Evil Yezer*, 287, 288, with man's worthiness of grace, 290 (*bis*), with the atoning power of the righteous, 310, with things that prevent repentance, 331

Ishmael, Rabbi, on the pre-mundane existence of repentance, 314

Israel, God teaches Torah to, 37, attributes of God applied to, 47, higher than the angels, 49, prayer by, acceptable, 49, 50–1, high responsibility of, 51–2, prophets and patriarchs, atone for, 53, attributes of, qualifying it for election, 59–60, elected by God as the first-born, 62, establishes the kingdom of God, 85–6, 88–9, rebellious against the kingdom of God, 86–8, connected in the liturgy with the kingdom of God, 97, suppresses the evil inclination to acknowledge the kingdom of God, 97–8, the redemption of, and the kingdom of God, 98–103, the depository of the kingdom of God, 105, what constitutes it a nation, 105–6; mission of, to destroy a corrupt government, 108–9, the kingdom of God dependent on, 114–15, endowed with pre-mundane existence, 128, the Torah pleads for, and against, 129, wedded to the Torah, 130, why made the bearer of the Torah, 131–2, to share the Torah with the Gentiles, 133, its view of the Torah, 137, commended for joy in the Law, 149–50, taught by God how to pray, 157, holy through the commandments, 168–9, lives through the *Zachuth* of the Fathers, 175, the solidarity of, 191–5, the holiness of, 199–200, dietary laws the special privilege of, 207, delivered to the sword by idolatry, 223, the sanctuary of, destroyed by bloodshed, 226, redeemed from Egypt to fulfil the commandment of justice, 230, redeemed from Egypt on condition that it obeys the commandment on usury, 230–1, purified by the Day of Atonement, 234, the sin of, removes the Divine Presence, 236, 238, weakened by sin, 239, apostasy of, due to the *Evil Yezer*, 242, needs grace to extenuate its guilt, 282, and the disappearance of the *Evil Yezer*, 291, rewarded for subduing the *Evil Yezer*, 292, the solidarity of, and the atoning power of sacrifices, 300–1, repentance of, 304, to be punished in the future world, 307, humble under suffering, 310, the righteous and the children atone for, 310–11, given opportunity for repentance, 316, made to sin, as an example of repentance, 317, encouraged to repent for great sins, 326, met halfway by God, 327, must confess sins, 336

See also Election of Israel, the; Kingdom of God, the

Israel, the kingdom of, identified with the kingdom of God, 103, safeguards the conception of the kingdom of God, 104, adds the feature of material happiness to the kingdom of God, 109–14

See also Israel, Election of Israel, the, Kingdom of God, the national, Kingdom of God, the visible universal

Israel, the relation of God to, 46–56, terms for, 46–7, reciprocal, 47–9, 50–1, paternal character of, 51–6, changed by apostasy, 55 n , indicated by election, 57

INDEX

See also Israel, Election of Israel, the

Jacob, and the kingdom of God, 84, chooses the world to come as his portion, 100
See also Fathers, the, Patriarchs, the
Jealousy, and the imitation of God, 204, Elijah rebuked for, 204-5
Jehoiachin, the repentance of, acceptable, 326
Jehoiakim, spites God, 220
Jeremiah, the Book of, cited, in connection with reward for proper zeal, 53, with the election of Israel, 58, with God's relation to the Gentiles, 63 (*bis*), with the kingdom of God, 99, with joy of the Law, 151, with prayer, 156, with the attachment of Israel to God, 200, with the Shechinah, 225, with the inconsistent heart, 259, with the study of the Torah as a weapon against the *Evil Yezer*, 274, with the grace needed to conquer the *Evil Yezer*, 281, 282, with the justice to prevail in the future world, 307, with repentance human and divine, 327
Jeroboam, the division of the kingdom under, rebellion against God, 87, urged by God to repent, 319-20
Jerusalem, identified with the kingdom of God, 99, cause of the destruction of, 215, a resident of, and the continual burnt offering, 300
Jesus, the son of Sirach, on wisdom, 70
Jethro, illustrates the attitude of a proselyte, 25
Job, Satan's good intentions concerning, 268, argues with God regarding the *Evil Yezer*, 273, 280
Job, the Book of, cited, in connection with man's rebelliousness, 83, with the spiritualisation of Scriptures, 103, with adultery, 214, 224-5, with heresy, 226, with the justice of God, 305
Jochanan, Rabbi, on robbery as a capital sin, 227-8
Jochanan ben Sakkai, as a modern altruist, 18-19
Joel, the Book of, cited, in connection with man's direct relation to God, 44-5, with being called by the name of God, 201, with the *Evil Yezer*, 244, with fasting and repentance, 339
Jonah, the Book of, quoted, in connection with efficacious repentance, 335
Jose, Rabbi, quoted on the reward of the righteous, 14
Jose ben Chalafta, Rabbi, on the qualities of God's chosen ones, 61
Joseph, rules over the *Evil Yezer*, 271, the brothers of, defended by the Rabbis, 281
Joseph Askari, on the joy of the Law, 151
Joshua, Israel under, accepts the kingdom of God, 87
Joshua, the Book of, cited, in connection with Rahab's acknowledgement of God, 26
Joshua ben Levi, Rabbi, and the law of saints, 216, enumerates seven names for the *Evil Yezer*, 243-4, on repentance in Gehenna, 341 n
Joy of the Law, an essential element in the understanding of the Law, 146, 148, illustrated in the commandment of forgetfulness, 149, Israel commended for, 149-50, Scriptural and Rabbinical quotations on, 150-1, mediæval writers on, 150-1, a modern illustration of, 151-2, illustrated on the Sabbath, 152-4, illus-

INDEX

trated in the prayers, 154–9, a motive for the performance of the Law, 168–9
See also Law, the, Torah, the

Judah, the princes of, rebellious against God, 87–8

Judah, the Saint (Rabbi), on the time when the *Evil Yezer* takes possession of man, 253–4, prays for grace to conquer the *Evil Yezer*, 279

Judah (Judan), Rabbi, on man's direct relation to God, 44–5

Judah ben Ezekiel, Rabbi, defines *Chasiduth*, 209

Judah ben Ilai, Rabbi, limits the paternal relation between God and Israel, 54, on the imitation of God, 203

Judah Hallevi, on the inclusiveness of the Torah, 146 *See also Kusari*

Judaism, and individualism, 76–9, to convert the world, 77, aims to establish the visible kingdom of God, 79, teaches a universal kingdom of God, 93, views of, on poverty, 110, view of, on suffering, 111, insists upon man's happiness on earth, 111
See also Rabbis, the, etc

Judges, the Book of, cited, in connection with the administration of justice, 229

Justice, in God, 38, the execution of, conditions the Torah, 143, and the imitation of God, 204, bad administration of, a form of bloodshed, 229–30, superior to sacrifices as a means of atonement, 296, God's attribute of, evoked by sin, 239–40, the Rabbis on, 304–6, prevails in the future world, 307, and repentance, 322.

Kaddish, the, and the kingdom of God, 95.

Kedushah, holiness within the limits of the Law, 201, 209, original meaning of, 205, the reward of, 217–18
See also Holiness, *Chasiduth*

Kiara, Simon *See* Simon Kiara.

King, epithet for God, 21

Kingdom of God, the, defined by the Rabbis, 65, conception originates in the Scriptures, 65, divisions of, 66, universal in its aims, 93, conception narrowed and enriched by national aspect, 103–4, bad government incompatible with, 106–9, material features of, 109–14, dependent upon Israel, 114–15, confers authority upon the Law, 116, holiness grows out of, 199, the yoke of, thrown off by the *Porek ol*, 220–1, the yoke of, thrown off by the respecter of persons, 230

Kingdom of God, the invisible, how to receive the yoke of, 66–7, not a burden, 70–2, and the dangers of quietism, 78

Kingdom of God, the national, in the liturgy, 97, 105, connected with the redemption of Israel, 98–101, 114–15, opposed to the kingdom of Rome, 101, the features of, 104, the spiritual features of, 104–6, penitents and proselytes in, 106, and material happiness, 109–14

Kingdom of God, the universal, in the *Shema*, 64
See also Gentiles, the.

Kingdom of God, the visible, the aim of Judaism, 78–9, divisions of, 80

Kingdom of God, the visible universal, dates from the creation of man, 81, 82, impaired by sin, 83, restored by Abraham, 83–4, taught by Jacob, 84, established by Israel, 84–6, 88–9, Israel rebellious against, 86–8, received by Israel under Joshua, 87, in this world, 89, terms for, 89, established by man conscious of God's nearness, 89-90, an ethical concept, 90-1, and the Torah, 91-2, not political, 92, 93, in the liturgy, 93-6, and the unity of God, 96, connected with the kingdom of Israel, 104-6, 114-15.

See also Israel, the kingdom of

Kingdom of heaven, the, defined, 65-6, 89

See also Kingdom of God, the

Kings (I), the Book of, cited, in connection with God's closeness to the earth, 29, with Elijah's excessive zeal, 52-3, with jealousy, 204 (*bis*).

Kings (II), the Book of, cited, in connection with Naaman's acknowledgement of God, 26, with imputed sin, 187, with sin as rebellion, 219, with the repentance of Manasseh, 318, 319

Kingship, the, of God, and his abode in heaven, 31-2, begins with the creation of man, 81, 82

See also Kingdom of God, the

Kneading, forbidden on the Sabbath, 153

Korah, alluded to, 222, given opportunity for repentance, 316

Kusari, the, by Judah Hallevi, quoted, 146

Lamb, term for the relation between God and Israel, 47

Lamentations, the Book of, cited, in connection with Jeremiah's proper zeal, 53, with the kingdom of God, 67, with the weakening influence of sin, 239, with the attribute of justice, 240

Law, the, not connected with hardness, 34, the allegorising method directed against, 40-2, fulfil- ment of, easy to a child of God, 55, derives its authority from the kingdom of God, 116, not a correct rendering of Torah, 117; holiness the highest achievement of, 199, relation of *Kedushah* and *Chasiduth* to, 201, overruled by God, for the sake of repentance, 322.

See also Joy of the Law, Legalism, Leviticalism, Mosaism; Torah, the

Leaven in the dough, the, the *Evil Yezer*, 262-3, identified with the *Evil Yezer* in a prayer, 265-6, God takes the responsibility for, 266, 282, good purpose of, 266-8

See also Evil Yezer, the

Legalism, charged to be the predominant element in Jewish theology, 23-4, misunderstood, 117

See also Law, the, Leviticalism, Mosaism; Torah, the

Legends, on the revelation, 130-5; universalistic tendency of, 131-2.

Levitical impurity, sacrifices intended for, 296, the Day of Atonement concerned with, 301

Leviticalism, not antagonistic to Prophetism, 119

Leviticus, the Book of, cited, in connection with binding laws, 13; with the election of Israel, 58; with the sanction of the Law, 116, Scriptural portion for the Day of Atonement from, 119, contains the essential principle claimed by Christianity and humanity, 119-20 (*bis*), cited, in connection with the intention to underlie sacrifices, 160, with God's covenant with the patriarchs, 172 (*bis*); with the doctrine of imputed sin, 192 (*bis*), with the holiness of Israel, 200, with holiness through separation, 205, 211, with sexual immorality, 206; with relations between man and his fellow, 215, with love of neighbour, 226–7; with justice, 230, with spiritual corruption, 235, with unintentional sins, 241 (*bis*), with the good heart, 259, with the removal of the *Evil Yezer*, 292; with the punishment of sinners, 293, with the limited efficacy of sacrifices, 295, with the size of the sacrifice, 297, with the scapegoat, 301, with encouraging sinners to repent, 321

Liars, excluded from the Divine Presence, 232.

Libertinism, and the observance of the Torah, 211

Life of the world, epithet for God, 26

Light, the, of the first day, concealed by sin, 237

Light of the world, epithet for God, 26

Limitation theory of the Cabalists, 128

Lishmah, defined as single-mindedness in the performance of the Law, 159–61, attained through the performance of the Law, 161, excludes the idea of reward, 162–3
See also Reward

Liturgy, the, a source for Rabbinic theology, 3, 9–11, as a theologic test for the Talmud, 10, early origin of, 11, in the Talmud, 11, free from alien epithets for God, 44, the fatherhood of God in, 54–6, the election of Israel in, 57, the kingship prayers in, universal in tone, 93–6, the kingdom of God in, 97, 105, on the Torah as a source of joy, 147, and the doctrine of *Zachuth*, 184, and prayers for the dead, 198, on holiness, 218, prayers for grace to conquer the *Evil Yezer* in, 279–80, daily prayer for repentance in, 341
See also Prayer, Prayer Book, the, Prayers, the, of the synagogue

Lord of the World, epithet for God, 21, 26

Lost things, keeping, prevents repentance, 330

Love of God, the, the reason for Israel's election, 61, defined, 67–70, unconditional, 68, incompatible with love of self, 68–9, a longing for God, 69–70, 73–6, must be disinterested, 72, 74; and the visible kingdom of God, 78–9, a constituent of the Torah, 146, 147, the only proper motive for the worshipper, 163, the motive for performance of the Law, 167–9

Lovingkindness, works of, a weapon against the *Evil Yezer*, 273, have atoning power, 312
See also Charity

Lust, corresponds to the *Evil Yezer*, 246, in the soul of man, 260, the world based on, 267
See also Sexual immorality

Luther, quoted, on the intimate relationship of God and man, 51 n

Luzzatto, Moses Chayim, on love of God, 69–70, on the joy of the Law, 151, on *Chasiduth*, 209 n.

Lydda, alluded to, 216

Maacah, mother of Absalom, alluded to, 213

Maimonides, and Israel's election, 57, on the *Mizwoth*, 141, on the Sabbath, 152, on the fulfilment of the *Mizwoth*, 165, on repentance, 331, on the nature of repentance, 335, on prayer and repentance, 339

Makom *See* Space

INDEX

Malachi, the mouthpiece of the Mosaic revelation, 124

Malachi, the Book of, cited, in connection with the greatness of God, 58, with purity of motive in performance of the Law, 160–1, with heresy, 226, with God as judge and witness, 247, with the encouraging of repentance in sinners, 321, with repentance human and Divine, 327

Malady, the name for the *Evil Yezer*, 244

Man, the creation of, and God's kingship, 81, 93, a free agent, 81–2, the centre of creation, 82, in rebellion, 83, effect of his consciousness of God, 89–90, the master of his inclinations, 270–3

Manasseh, a *Porek ol*, 221, his repentance acceptable to God, 318–19, 326, his repentance not the highest degree, 320

Manners, good, God a model of, 203

Marcion, Harnack on, 18

Marriage laws, in the Mishnah, 2

Martyrdom, enjoined to prevent the commission of the cardinal sins, 222

Mashal, the See Allegoric interpretation of Scripture

Master of all Creation, epithet for God, 22, 34

Masters, slights put upon, prevent repentance, 330

Material, term not used in Rabbinic literature, 144

Material happiness, a feature of the national kingdom of God, 109–14, and religion, 111

Mechilta, the, censures Israel for deferring the kingdom of God, 86, numerous citations from the Prophets and Hagiographa in, 122

Mediatorship, denounced by the Rabbis, 21, 45

Meekness, the reason for Israel's election, 60

Meir Ibn Gabbai, quoted, on love of God, 69, 75–6

Memra, epithet for God, 35, (Word) as used by the Rabbis, 39, 43 n

Men of the Great Assembly, and the *Evil Yezer*, 246–7, 250

Menelaus, high priest, alluded to, 92.

Merciful One, epithet for God, 34.

Mercy, God's attribute of, turned into justice by sin, 239–40, and repentance, 322–4, represented by the "right hand" of God, 323

Mercy of God, to be imitated by men, 201, 202, in the interpretation of the Law, recommended, 215–16, lack of, equal to a denial of the law, 231–2, the world based on, 267

Merits of the Fathers, the See *Zachuth*

Messiah, the, pre-mundane existence of the name, etc, of, 13 n, 59, 128, and the kingdom of God, 100, 101–3, poverty delays the coming of, 114, exalted beyond the patriarchs, 174, the advent of, to banish the *Evil Yezer*, 290–2

Messianic aspirations, treated by the Agadah, 3

Messianic time, the, and the unity of God, 96

Metatron, read into the Book of Exodus, 41

Micah, the Book of, cited, in connection with the *Mizwoth*, 140, with the grace needed to conquer the *Evil Yezer*, 281, with the atoning power of the burnt offering, 299

Michael, angel, not a mediator, 45, 67, may not approach Moses, 238

Midrash, the, on the narratives of the Bible, 120

Midrashic works, theologic sources, 3

Midrashim, the   *See* Rabbis, the, Rabbinic literature, the

Ministering angels, surrounding God, 28, 32

Miracles, in Rabbinic literature, 5-8

Mishael, justified in rebelling against Nebuchadnezzar, 107

Mishnah, the, character of the contents, 2, drawbacks as a theologic source, 3-4, liturgical passages in, 11, on the *Evil Yezer*, 245, 246

Missionary enterprises, and the Rabbis, 132

Mizwoth, the, complementary to the Torah, 117-18, the number and divisions of, according to R Simlai, 138, 141-2, denounced as a burden, 138-9, the number of, interpreted homiletically, 139-40, which were obsolete in the time of the Rabbis, 141, which were restricted in their application, 141, character of, 142, inclusiveness of, 142-4, how considered by Israel, 148, salvation not dependent on the number fulfilled, 164-6, a source of holiness, 168-9, doctrinal value of, 231

"Modernity," and the Rabbis, 19-20

Moloch, laws on sacrifices to, not a practical consideration, 141

Mommsen, on the cruelty of the Roman government, 108-9 n

Montaigne, quoted, 39

Moral principles of the revelation, unacceptable to the nations, 132

Mosaism, not antagonistic to Prophetism, 119

   See also Law, the, Legalism, Leviticalism, Torah, the

Moses, form of his acknowledgement of God, 26, appearance of God to, a proof of God's omnipresence, 29, buried by God, 37, offers himself as an atoning sacrifice, 53, 310, exalted place of, as a prophet, 118, 124 n , captures the Torah from heaven, 130, instructed in all the deductions from the Torah, 134-5, and the appointment of judges, 143, invokes the *Zachuth* of the tribes, 172-3, invokes the *Zachuth* of the Fathers, 174, the meekness of, 223, the effect of sin on, 237-8, name given to the *Evil Yezer* by, 243, reproaches God for the *Evil Yezer*, 283, prays for the regeneration of the sinner, 316

Moses Loeb, of Sasow, on scepticism, 111.

Mother, term for the relation between God and Israel, 47

Mothers, the, in the sense of the wives of the three patriarchs, 172

Murder, and the doctrine of imputed sin, 196, a cardinal sin, 205, different kinds of, 213, unknown, sacrifice for, 301, not subject to repentance, 333

   See also Bloodshed

Mystic, a, on repentance, 334

Mysticism, and God's abode, 28-9, 32, in Judaism, 76, defined by De Wette, 77, and law, 78

Mystics, the, on the reciprocal relationship of God and Israel, 47-8, on the love of God, 68-70, 72-6, on the creation of the world, 128, and combinations of letters, 129, their view of the Torah, 135, on unintentional sins, 241, on the heart as the seat of the *Yezers*, 256

Naaman, illustrates the attitude of a proselyte, 25-6

Nachmanides, on imputed sin, 186 n ,

on *Chasiduth*, 211–12, on the law of goodness, 214–15
Narratives, the, of the Bible, how regarded, 120
Nationalism, and the Torah, 105–6.
Nazarite, a, cuts off hair to subdue the *Evil Yezer*, 277.
Nazir, the, the holiness of, 211–12
Nebuchadnezzar, justified rebellion against, 107
New Testament, the, the Prophets and Hagiographa called Law in, 125
New Year, the, the kingdom of God, in the liturgy of, 93–4, 105.
Nezikin, Talmudic tractate, attention to, identified with *Chasiduth*, 209.
Nimrod, a rebel, 219
Nineveh, the repentance of the men of, 326
Noah, and the doctrine of imputed sin, 195, saved for the sake of his children, 196, the dietary laws distinguish Israel from the descendants of (*see also* Gentiles, the), 207
Nomism *See* Legalism
Nomos, not a correct rendering of Torah, 117, applied to the Prophets and Hagiographa, 125
Numbers, the Book of, cited, in connection with the faithfulness of Israel, 59, with the superiority of the Torah, 118, with the joy of the Law, 150, with the holiness of fulfilling Biblical commandments, 208, with the *Porek ol*, 221, with humility, 223, with the weakening influence of sin, 239, with the Nazarite, 249, with free will and the *Evil Yezer*, 287, with the intention underlying sacrifice, 298, with the atoning power of the continual burnt offering, 299

Oaths, administration of, in the Mishnah, 2
Obadiah, the Book of, cited, in connection with the kingdom of God, 100
Olah, the *See* Burnt offering, the
Old Testament, the, the economic ideal of, 112.
Only One of the world, epithet for God, 26
Ophanim, the, surrounding God, 28, 32.

Palestine, laws on the conquest of, obsolete, 141
Pantheistic notions in Jewish writers, 27–8, 30
Pappos, on the arbitrariness of God, 305
Paradise, endowed with pre-mundane existence, 128.
Pardon *See* Forgiveness.
Patriarchs, the, atone for Israel, 53, 310, teachers of the kingdom of God, 92; have dominion over the *Evil Yezer*, 271
    See also Fathers, the.
Paul, apostle, antinomian influence of, 4, attitude of commentators on Epistles of, 18
Penitence, qualifies for the kingdom of God, 106
    See also Repentance.
Pentateuch, the, often equivalent to Torah, 118, sometimes considered higher than the prophets, 118, contains more than law, 121, importance of, in the Messianic time, 124 n , the Prophets depend on, 124
    See also Law, the, Torah, the
People, term for the relation of Israel to God, 46
Persecution, the reason for Israel's election, 60
Personification of the Torah, 129–30

INDEX

Perushim, those who abstain from things superfluous, 211.
Petra, an epithet for Abraham, 173
Pharaoh, type of man deified, 39, why God hardened his heart, 332
Phenomena, natural, warn men to repent, 315
Piyutim, fictions, term applied to the narratives of the Bible, 120
Pledge, taking the, of the poor, prevents repentance, 330
Ploughing, forbidden on the Sabbath, 153
Polytheism, disguised, detrimental to belief in the unity of God, 68–9
  See also Idolatry
Poor, plundering the, prevents repentance, 331
Porek ol, defined, 220–1
Poverty, inconsistent with the kingdom of God, 110; the Rabbis on, 112–13, a remedy against the *Evil Yezer*, 278
Power, the, of God, 38
Prayer, heard instantaneously by God, 31, defined by a mediæval Rabbi, 42, by Israel, acceptable to God, 49, 50–1, characterised by the Rabbis, 156–7, devotion indispensable in, 156–9, proper motive for, 162, renders the *Zachuth* of the Fathers efficacious, 180, invalidated by robbery, 228–9, 234, accompanying repentance, 338–9
Prayer, a, by a girl regarding the *Evil Yezer*, 265, by a Rabbi regarding the leaven in the dough, 265–6, by a Rabbi regarding the *Evil Yezer*, 277
Prayer Book, the, and the charge of a transcendental God in Rabbinic theology, 22–3, 29, term for the kingdom of God in, 89
  See also Liturgy, the, Prayer, Prayers, the, of the synagogue

Prayers, by Rabbis, for grace to conquer the *Evil Yezer*, 278–9
Prayers, the, of the synagogue, illustrate the joy of the Law, 154–9, composed by the Rabbis, 155
Pre-mundane existences, 13 and n., 59–60, 80, 127, 128–9, 135, 314.
Presence, the Divine. *See* Shechinah, the
Pride, a form of idolatry, 223–4
Profanation of the name of God, caused by idolatry, 223, a sin not subject to repentance, 328, 329
Prohibitive laws, the number of, 138
Property laws, in the Mishnah, 2
Prophecy, equivalent to holiness, 217; on the punishment of sinners, 293
Prophetism, not antagonised by Mosaism, 119
Prophets, the, atone for Israel, 53, 310, plead with God for Israel, 53–4, demand punishment by death, rather than repentance, 323
Prophets, the, the books of, sometimes excluded by the term *Torah*, 118, sometimes considered less than the Pentateuch, 118, included in the term *Torah*, 121–6, lessons from, accompany the Pentateuch portions, 122, frequently quoted by the Rabbis, 122, benediction for, 123; dependent on the Pentateuch, 124, how cited in Rabbinic literature, 124–5.
Proselytes, transitory character of opinions on, 9–10, inclined to transcendentalism in acknowledging God, 25–6, and epithets for God, 46, in the kingdom of God, 106
Proverbs, the Book of, cited, in connection with the wisdom of God, 38, with the glorification of God through Creation, 80, with

wisdom, 127, 129, with the ways of the Torah, 143, with the *Zachuth* of a pious contemporary, 190, with the doctrine of imputed sin, 193, with the *Zachuth* of a pious posterity, 197, with the strict interpretation of the Law, 216 (*bis*), with pride, 223, with the contamination of sin, 234, with unintentional sins, 240, with the *Evil Yezer*, 243, with sin as the cause of death, 247, with free will and the *Evil Yezer*, 287 (*bis*), with the punishment of sinners, 293, with the limited efficacy of sacrifices, 296, with atonement through suffering, 309, with death-bed repentance, 340

Psalms, the, cited, in connection with Araboth, 28, 31, with the abode of God, 32, 36, with the wealth of God, 38, with Israel forsaken by God, 43, with the title applied by God to Israel, 47, with the election of Israel, 58, with the unity of God, 69, with longing for God, 70, with the kingship of God, 82, 90, 97, 98, 99, and the Law, 116, cited, in connection with the power of God's work, 121, with the extent of the Torah, 122, with the Torah as the bride of Israel, 130, with the *Mizwoth*, 140, with the inclusiveness of the Torah, 144, divested of individualistic tendency, 155, cited in connection with devotion in prayer, 156, 157, with performing the Law without reference to reward, 162–3 (*bis*), with the essential commandments, 164, with negative and positive virtue, 167, with the *Zachuth* of a pious ancestry, 183, with revenge, 204, with exaltation, 204, with pride, 223, with the weakening influence of sin, 239, with the *Evil Yezer*, 242, 243, 244 (*bis*), 245, with sexual intercourse, 253, with the clean heart, 258, with the study of the Torah as a weapon against the *Evil Yezer*, 274, with grace to conquer the *Evil Yezer*, 78 (*bis*), with free will and the *Evil Yezer*, 286, with the punishment of sinners, 293, with pardon granted by God, 294–5 (*bis*), with the intention underlying sacrifice, 298; with humility in suffering, 310, with the act of revelation, 311; with mercy through repentance, 313, with God's instruction in repentance, 314–16, with repentance human and Divine, 327 (*bis*), 328

Pseudo-Jonathan, on the *Evil Yezer*, 242

Punishment, the, of the sinner, 293, 294, 304

See also Reward and punishment

Queen, epithet of the Sabbath, 154

Rab, and the strict interpretation of the Law, 215–16

Rabba, defines *Chasiduth*, 209

Rabba Bar bar Chana, and the strict interpretation of the Law, 215–16

Rabbinic literature, as a theologic source, 2–9, 11–16

See Rabbis, the

Rabbis, the, supposed characteristics of, 2, as miracle-workers, 7, on faith, 14, on sin, 14, on the closeness of God to man, 24–8, 29–30, 31, 33, epithets for God used by, 26–8, 34, and the doctrine of a personal God, 30, their view of the Law, 34, on the names of God, 35–6, on corporeal terms applied to God, 36–7; delight in humanising God, 37-8, object to deifying man, 38-9, and the allegorising method, 39-44, reverence of, for the Scriptures, 42-3, substitute the Tetragrammaton for the epithets for God, 46, terms applied by, to the relation between God and Israel, 47, on the reciprocal relation between God and Israel, 48-9, 50-1, on the fatherhood of God, 51-6, on the election of Israel, 58-64, define the kingdom of God, 65, on love of God, 66-8, 79, on freedom in the kingdom of God, 70-2, on the character of the reward of the righteous, 78, on the creation of man as a free agent, 81, on the kingship of God, 82, on Israel's establishing the kingdom of God, 85-6, 88-9, on man's righteousness and the kingdom of God, 89-91, on the Torah and the kingdom of God, 91-2; on the form of government, 92, on the national kingdom of God, 100, 101-3, 105, 114-15, on what constitutes Israel a nation, 105-6, on the Roman government, 107-9, on material happiness connected with the national kingdom of God, 109-14, on poverty, 110, 112-13, the economic ideal of, 112, object to speculation, 112-13, on the relation of employer to employee, 113, on the connection between Israel and the kingdom of God, 114-15, on the sanction of the Law, 116, on the relative value of Moses and the other prophets, 118, on the books of the Prophets, 119, 124, on the Torah as the word of God, 120-1, on the Book of Genesis, 121, on extra-legal elements in the Torah, 121, frequently quote the Prophets and Hagiographa, 122, include the Hagiographa in the Scriptures, 123, extend the use of Torah beyond the Scriptures, 126, on the Torah as wisdom, 127, attitude toward missionary enterprises, 132, on the pregnant meaning of the Torah, 134, on the Torah as God's will, 136-7, *Mizwoth* obsolete in the time of, 141, on the inclusiveness of the Torah, 142-4, make no division between material and spiritual, 144-6, the Torah a source of joy to, 146-7, 150-1; on the Sabbath, 152-4; accused of mechanical tendencies, 155, the composers of the liturgy, 155, on prayer, 155-7, on purity of motive in the performance of the Law, 160-1, on reward and punishment, 162-3, on negative and positive virtue, 166-7, on love as the motive for the performance of the Law, 167-9, on the ancestors whose *Zachuth* is invoked, 172-3, on the Fathers, 173-5, on the *Zachuth* of a pious ancestry, 176-7, 181-5, limit the *Zachuth* of the Fathers, 177-8, impute unlimited efficacy to it, 178-81, on imputed sin, 186-9, on the *Zachuth* of a pious contemporary, 189-90, on the solidarity of Israel, 191-5, on imputed sin through posterity, 196-7, on the *Zachuth* of posterity, 197-8, on holiness as an *Imitatio Dei*, 199-200, on the imitation of God by man, 201-5, on sexual immorality, 205-6, on the dietary laws, 207, on acts provoking disgust, 207, on *Chasiduth*, 209-10; on the law of goodness, 215-16, on communion with God, 217-18, define sin as rebellion, 219-20, on usury, 230-1; on separation from God, 232-3, on the contamination of sin, 233-6, on sin as folly, 236-7, on the blighting influence of sin, 237-40, on unintentional sins, 240-1, on the two *Yezers*, 243, give various names to the *Evil Yezer*, 243-4, on the activity of the *Evil Yezer*, 244-7, on the period in which the *Evil Yezer* takes possession of man, 252-5, do not consider man corrupt, 262, keep to the golden mean, 264, on the leaven in the dough, 266, on weapons against the *Evil Yezer*, 273, on the uses of the study of the Torah against the *Evil Yezer*, 275, on ascetic remedies against the *Evil Yezer*, 277, on grace to conquer the *Evil Yezer*, 278-84, on the punishment of sinners, 293-4, on the intention underlying sacrifices, 297-8, on the Day of Atonement, 301-4, on the justice of God, 304-6, offer themselves as an atonement for Israel, 311, on God's instruction of men in repentance, 314-15, on relapsing into sin, 339

Rahab, illustrates the attitude of the proselyte, 26

Reaping, forbidden on the Sabbath, 153

Rebellion, against God, the first sin, 83, the sin of Israel, 86-8, definition of sin by the Rabbis, 219-22, 233

Reciprocal relation between God and Israel, 47-9, 50-1

Reconciliation with God, through sacrifices, limited in efficacy, 295-7, through death and suffering, 307-8, through confession of sin, 338

See also Atonement, Repentance.

Regulations of Chasiduth, by Eliezer of Worms, quoted, 210

Religion, place of material happiness in, 111

Remnant, the, of Israel, establishes the kingdom of God, 88-9.

Renan, quoted, 155

Reparation, a condition of acceptable repentance, 333

See also Restitution

Repentance, treated by the Agadah, 3, accepted instantaneously by God, 31, endowed with premundane existence, 128, 314, restores efficacy to the *Zachuth* of the Fathers, 180-1, 185 n , ensures forgiveness for sins, 293-4; ways of achieving, 294, must accompany sacrifices, 294, 296-7, 313, on the Day of Atonement, 302-3, for the *Evil Yezer*, 304, 313, prayer for, 313, the only means of atonement, 313, urged by God himself, 314-16, 319, possible for the greatest sins, 317, 318, 325-6, 333-4, Manasseh an extreme instance of, 318-19, 320, through fear, of a low order, 320, and restitution, 320, encouraged through intercourse between saints and sinners, 321, opposed by the angels, 321-2, and God's attributes of justice and mercy, 322-4, the good portion assigned to this world, 324, an act of grace, 324, depends on the initiative of man, 324, 327, 334, false shame not to stand in the way of, 324-5, need not be public, 326, a mutual relation between God and man, 327-8, inefficacious in five cases, 328-30, 333, prevented by twenty-four things, 330-1, Maimonides on, 331, 335, 339, inefficacious after three warnings, 332, must be accompanied by reparation,

333; a mystic's view of, 334, the nature of, 334, consists of acts, 334–5, must be accompanied by confession of sin, 335–8, and prayer, 338–9, and fasting, 339–40, on the death-bed, 340–1, daily, 342, during the Ten Penitential Days, 342, not limited to special seasons, 342–3
See also Penitence

Restitution, a condition of atonement for moral sins, 296, 303, and repentance, 320
See also Reparation

Resurrection, controversy about the Scriptural authority for the belief in, 124–5

Reuben ben Astrobolis, Rabbi, on the time when the *Evil Yezer* takes possession of man, 252

Revelation, the, indispensable to the existence of the world, 128–9, the day of, in Rabbinic literature, 130–1, universalistic feature of, 131–2, 133, 135, moral features of, unacceptable to the Gentiles, 132, an act of grace, 133–5, due to the *Zachuth* of the Fathers, 174, and the doctrine of imputed sin, 195, the act of, made dependent upon the children of the Israelites, 311
See also Law, the, Pentateuch, the, Torah, the

Revenge, and the imitation of God, 204

Reward, the, of the righteous, R Jose on, 14, not the motive for the performance of the Law, 167, 169
See also *Lishmah*

Reward and punishment, in the Rabbinical system, 162–3

'Right hand," the, of God, represents the attribute of mercy, 323

Righteous, the, reward of, 14, compose the kingdom of God, 106, how they differ from the wicked, 270–1, and the appearance of the *Evil Yezer*, 290, the atoning power of, 310

Righteous One of the world, epithet for God, 26

Righteousness, imputed   See *Zachuth*

Righteousness, treated by the Agadah, 3, establishes the kingdom of God, 89–90, 93, culminates in holiness, 199, and the *Zachuth*, 176, 180, 189–90, of God, to be imitated by man, 202

Ritual observances, attacked by the *Evil Yezer*, 251

Robbery, a form of bloodshed, 227–9, invalidates sacrifices, 228, invalidates charity, 228, invalidates prayer, 228–9, 234, not subject to repentance, 333

Rome, identified with the enemies of the kingdom of God, 99–101, 106–9, obedience to, enjoined upon Israel, 107, objection to the government of, 107–8, considered corrupt by the Rabbis, 108–9

Saadya, Rabbi, on what constitutes Israel a nation, 105, defines the worshipper, 164, on relapsing into sin, 339

Sabbath, the, man the lord of, 152, attacks upon, 152–3, illustrates the joy of the Law, 153–4, celebrated by the observers of it, 153–4, epithets given to, 154, profanation of, due to the *Evil Yezer*, 246

Sacrifices, invalidated by robbery, 228, accompanied by repentance, 294, 296–7, limited in efficacy as a means of atonement, 295–7, charity superior to, 296, efficacy depends upon the intention, 297–8, atoning power assigned to, by the Rabbis, 300–1, suffering compared to, 308–9, death compared to, 310, the Torah and charity compared to, 312, demanded by the Torah, 323

Safety, term for the relation between God and Israel, 46

Saintliness *See Chasiduth*

Saints, associate with sinners to encourage repentance, 321

"Saints, The, Chapters of," miracles reported in, 6

Salvation, not dependent on the number of commandments fulfilled, 164, secured by the fulfilment of one commandment, 165–6, secured by negative virtues, 166–7, depends upon the actions of man, 182, 189

Salvation, term for the relation between God and Israel, 46

Samael, identified with the *Evil Yezer*, 246, 262

Samaritans, the, on what is to be included under Torah, 122

Samuel (I), the Book of, cited, in connection with the foundations of the world, 173, with the *Zachuth* of posterity, 197

Samuel (II), the Book of, cited, in connection with Israel in rebellion, 87, with the righteous as the pillars of the spiritual world, 89

Samuel de Ozedo, quoted, on disinterested love of God, 72 n

Samuel Hakaton, worthy of the Divine Presence, 238

Satan, identified with the *Evil Yezer*, 244–5, 251–2, 268, harbours good intentions concerning Job, 268, cannot enter the Beth-Hammidrash, 274

Scapegoat, the, the atoning power of, 301.

Scepticism, reason for, given by Moses Loeb, of Sasow, 111, due to the *Evil Yezer*, 251–2

Scoffers, excluded from the Divine Presence, 232

Scoffing, prevents repentance, 331

Scriptures, the, the conception of the kingdom of God in, 65–6, included in the term *Torah*, 121–6, knowledge of, required of the Talmid Chacham, 122.

See also Law, the, Pentateuch, the, Prophets, the, Torah, the.

Secret sin *See* Sin, secret.

Sectarianism, how dealt with in Rabbinic literature, 10 and n , opposed by the Rabbis through Scriptural interpretations, 36–7.

Seder Elijah, the, term for sin in, 233

Seducing, the function of the *Evil Yezer*, 248, others, prevents repentance, 329, 330, 333

See also Tempting.

Self, love of, incompatible with love of God, 68

Self-aggrandisement at the expense of others, prevents repentance, 330

Separateness, and holiness, 205; Nachmanides on, 211–12

See Holiness

Separation between God and man, caused how, 232–3

Seraphim the, surrounding God, 28, 32

Serpent, the, identified with the *Evil Yezer*, 246, 262, 282

Sexual immorality, denounced by the Rabbis, 205–6, due to the *Evil Yezer*, 246, affects the minority of men, 250

See also Adultery

Sexual intercourse, subject to restrictions, 211; tainted with sin, 253

Shame, not to stand in the way of repentance, 324–5.

Shammai, not a miracle-worker, 7
Shammai, the school of, on the creation of man, 8, on the atoning power of the burnt offering, 299
Shechinah, epithet for God, 35
Shechinah, the, as used by the Rabbis, 39, removed by idolatry, 223, removed by pride, 223, not respected by a violent man, 224, removed by adultery, 224–5, removed by murder, 226, removed by slander, 227, removed by the bad administration of justice, 229–30, removed by disrespect, 232; removed by sin in general, 232–3, 238, classes of persons excluded from, 232, revealed upon the removal of the *Evil Yezer*, 292
Shedding of blood   *See* Bloodshed, Murder
Shema, the, and the universal kingdom of God, 64, and the kingdom of God, 65, 66–7, 71, Israel's confession of faith, 119
Shepherd, term for the relation between God and Israel, 46, 49
Shirah (Song), the, and the kingdom of God, 85
Shofar, the sound of the, an invitation to repentance, 342
Simlai, Rabbi, on the *Mizwoth*, 138–40
Simon, Rabbi, on Israel's connection with the kingdom of God, 98
Simon ben Jochai, on the responsibility of God for the existence of the *Evil Yezer*, 281
Simon the Just, on the *Evil Yezer*, 248–9
Simon Kiara, on the *Mizwoth*, 141
Simon ben Lakish, Rabbi, on the abode of God, 30–1, sums up the activity of the *Evil Yezer*, 244, 245
Sin, treated by the Agadah, 3, the Rabbis on, 14, separates man from God, 33, has no effect upon the paternal relation between God and Israel, 54, angels incapable of, 81, disfigures man and the world, 83, counteracted by the *Zachuth* of the Fathers, 174; caused by the heart and the eyes, 208, defined by the Rabbis as rebellion, 219–22, causes the separation of man from God, 232–3, 241, various equivalents for, 233–5, a symptom of corruption, 235–6, described as folly, 236–7, has a blighting influence upon the world, 237–40, man persuaded to, by the *Evil Yezer*, 245, 260, death the consequence of, 245, 247, children immune from, 254, the agents of, 258, sways the soul, 260–1; relapsing into, 339–40
    See also Evil Yezer, the, Imputed sin, Sins, Sins, the cardinal, etc
Sin, imputed   *See* Imputed sin
Sin, secret, and the doctrine of imputed sin, 194, classified with blasphemy, 222
Sin, unintentional, held in abhorrence like others, 240–1, a sign of carelessness, 240–1, Nachmanides on, 241, sin offering for, 296
Sin offering, the, accompanied by repentance, 296
Sins, the number of, not to stand in the way of repentance, 325; the character of, not to stand in the way of repentance, 325–6, 333–4, repentance for, inefficacious if repeated, 328–9, 330
Sins, the cardinal, enumerated, 205–6, sins of rebellion, 222–32; have appurtenances, 223, exceeded by hatred, 227, called evil things, 232.

See also Adultery, Bloodshed, Idolatry

Sins, the confession of   *See* Confession of sins, the
  See also Evil Yezer, the, Sin, Sins, the cardinal

Sister, term for the relation between God and Israel, 47

Skinning, forbidden on the Sabbath, 153

Slander, a form of bloodshed, 227, called an evil thing, 232, a common sin, 250–1, habitual, prevents repentance, 330

Slavery, describes the relation of Israel to God, in certain conditions, 55 and n

Social misery, inconsistent with the kingdom of God, 110

Sodom and the doctrine of *Zachuth*, 190, the people of, rebels, 219, 222, cause pain to God, 219–20, warned to repent, 315

Solidarity, of Israel, and the doctrine of imputed sin, 191–5
  See also Community, the

Solomon, throws off the yoke of God, 87, name given to the *Evil Yezer* by, 243

Solomon, The Psalms of, not useful as a source of Rabbinic theology, 4–5

Song of Songs, cited, in connection with the sweetness of the Law, 137, with the contamination of sin, 134

Soul, the, the mystics on, 241, equivalent to the heart, 260–1
  See also Heart, the

Sowing, forbidden on the Sabbath, 153

Space of the world, epithet for God, 26, 34, does not imply remoteness, 34, 46

Spinning, forbidden on the Sabbath, 153

Spiritual, term not used in Rabbinic literature, 144

Spite towards God, 220

Spoiler, the, name for the *Evil Yezer*, 244

Statutes, the, observance of, undermined by the *Evil Yezer*, 251

Stay of the world, epithet for God, 26

Stone, name for the *Evil Yezer*, 243, allegory on, 274

Strange God, name for the *Evil Yezer*, 244

Strength, epithet for God, 34.

"Stretching the hand into the root," blasphemy, 222.

"Strong hand," the, equivalent to the "right hand," 322

Students, and the doctrine of imputed sin, 193

Stumbling-block, name for the *Evil Yezer*, 243

Suffering, treated by the Agadah, 3, inconsistent with the kingdom of God, 110–11, the punishment of the sinner, 293, 294, 304, an atonement, 304, 307–10, to be accepted submissively, 309–10.

Supreme, epithet for God, 21

Suspicion of the upright, prevents repentance, 331

System der Altsynagogalen Palastinensischen Theologie, by Weber, charges Jewish theology with excessive legalism, 23–4.

Taanith, Talmudic tractate, miracles reported in, 6.

Tabernacle, the laws about the, obsolete, 141

Talmid Chacham, the, knowledge of the Scriptures required of, 122

Talmud, the, as a theologic source, 5–6, 9–11, composite character of, 9–11, liturgical elements in, 11.

Talmud, the Babylonian, epithet for God in, 34

Talmudical works, theologic sources, 3
Tanna, the, of the School of Elijah, on Israel's election, 61-2
Tannaitic times, origin of the liturgy in, 11
Tanning, forbidden on the Sabbath, 153
Targum, the, on the *Evil Yezer*, 243
Targumim, the, epithets for God used in, 35, commentators on, not systematic theologians, 15-16
See also Rabbis, the
Tempting, the function of the *Evil Yezer*, 248
See also Seducing
Ten Penitential Days, a call to repentance, 342, ascetic practices connected with, 342
Tetragrammaton, the, applied to the God of mercy, 36, 239, connected with the Scriptural description of the sacrifices, 45, ordered to be pronounced, to guard against heresies, 45, substituted for epithets for God, 46, a pre-mundane existence, 80
Theocracy, a, the only form of government known to the Rabbis, 92, 93
Theology, Rabbinic, sources of, 2-6, 9-11, not a formal system, 12-17, impulsive character of, 12-13, lacks logicality, 13-15, 30, difficulty of systematising, 16-17, Jewish attitude of author to, 17-18, attitude of author to, not apologetic, 18-20, exalted character of, 20, charged with having a transcendental God, 21-2, 23, not influenced by mystical and pantheistic notions of God's abode, 30
See also Rabbis, the
Theosophy, and the Torah, 135.
Thieves, partnership with, prevents repentance, 330.

Throne of glory, the, 28, 32
Tochachoth, the, make the Book of Deuteronomy an *Imitatio Dei*, 119
Torah, the, and the creation of the world, 81, and the kingdom of God, 91-2, makes Israel a nation, 105-6, forced denial of, absolves from obedience to Rome, 107, the term misunderstood, 116-17, not correctly rendered by Law, etc, 117, what it conveys to the Jew, 117, 125, *Mizwoth* complementary to, 117-18; often equivalent to Pentateuch, 118, Scriptural warrant for the superiority of, 118, the Prophets a commentary on, 119, dictated by the Holy Spirit, 120, legal part of, begins in Exodus, 120-1; not always confined to the Pentateuch, 121-6, name applied to the Prophets and Hagiographa, 125, extends beyond the Scriptures, 126, as a revelation and a promise, 127, identified with wisdom, 127-8, 129, 135, endowed with a mystical life, 129-30, wedded to Israel, 130, captured from heaven, 130, refused by the Gentiles, 131-2, intended for the Gentiles as well as Israel, 133, potentialities of, 134-5, the Rabbinical view of, 136-7, character of the laws in, 142, inclusiveness of, 142-4, 146, based on the execution of justice, 143, the *Kusari* on, 146, a source of joy to the Rabbis, 146-7, how considered by Israel, 148, joy an essential element in the understanding of, 148, material uses of, deprecated, 154, 159, disinterested performance of, 159-69, occupation with, a positive virtue, 167, love the motive for the performance of, 167-9, a

source of holiness, 168, 208; observance of, and libertinism, 211, correctives of, 212–16, a merciful interpretation of, recommended, 215–16, with holiness brings communion with God, 217, how regarded by the *Porek ol*, 220–1, denied by the usurer and the unmerciful, 231–2; defiled by immorality, 234, the study of, a weapon against the *Evil Yezer*, 273–5, how it operates, 275, grace needed for efficacy of, 278, on the punishment of sinners, 293; the atoning power of, 312, demands sacrifices rather than repentance, 323; and God's attribute of mercy, 323

See also Joy of the Law; Law, the, Legalism, Leviticalism; *Mizwoth*, the; Pentateuch, the, Rabbis the, Revelation, Scriptures, the

Torah, the, yoke of *See* Kingdom of God, the

Torath ha-Adam, the Torah in its universalistic aspect, 133

Tosephta, the, on the commandment of forgetfulness, 149.

Tower, generation of the, rebels, 219; conceal the light of the first day, 237; warned to repent, 315

Transcendentalism, charged against the God of Rabbinic theology, 21–2; disproved by the Prayer Book, 22–3, 29; disproved by the Rabbinic sources, 24–8, 29–30, 31, 33–4; a failing of proselytes, 25–6.

See also under God.

Treasure, term for the relation of Israel to God, 46.

Tribes, the, the *Zachuth* of, invoked by Moses, 172–3

Tumah, term applied to the cardinal sins, 205, 206

See also Adultery; Sins, the cardinal.

Ula bar Koseheb, and the law of saints, 216

Unchaste thoughts, equivalent to adultery, 214.

Unchastity, included under adultery, 225

See also Adultery; Sexual immorality

Uncircumcised, name for the *Evil Yezer*, 243

Unclean, name for the *Evil Yezer*, 243

Uncovering of faces, the, and the *Porek ol*, 220–1.

Unintentional sin *See* Sin, unintentional

Uniqueness of Israel, 48.

Unity, the Song of, quoted, 27–8; 158–9

Unity of God, the, emphasised, 43–4, declared by Israel, 48, things detrimental to the belief in, 68–9, and love of God, 75; to be realised in the Messianic time, 96.

Universal character of the kingdom of God, 93.

Universalism, repugnant to the Rabbis, without the Torah, 105–6.

Universalistic features of the Sinaitic revelation, 131–2, 133

Usury, fulfilment of the commandment on, a condition of the Exodus, 230–1; a sin equal to murder, 231; a denial of the Law, 231–2.

Vanity, exposes one to the *Evil Yezer*, 248–9; the *Evil Yezer* chiefly representative of, 276.

Vile language, incompatible with holiness, 211–12.

Vine, the, a symbol for Israel, 175.

Vineyard, term for the relation of Israel to God, 49.

Watcher, term for the relation of God to Israel, 49

Wealth, the, of God, 38; desire for, not counted among the great passions, 250, in the soul of man, 260, auxiliary to the *Evil Yezer*, 277

Weaving, forbidden on the Sabbath, 153

Weber, charges Jewish theology with excessive legalism, 23–4

Wicked, the, forfeit the *Zachuth* of the Fathers, 179–80, how they differ from the righteous, 270–1, and the appearance of the *Evil Yezer*, 290, association with, prevents repentance, 330

Widows, plundering, prevents repentance, 331

Will of God, manifested in creation, 80

Wine-drinking, restricted, 211

Winnowing, forbidden on the Sabbath, 153

Wisdom, the, of God, 38, Jesus, the son of Sirach, on, 70, the yoke of, a glory, 70, equivalent to the Torah, 127, 129, 135

Wisdom (Hagiographa), on the punishment of sinners, 293

Wisdom literature, the, and the Law, 116.

Wise, attribute applied to Israel by God, 47

Women, looking at, prevents repentance, 330

Word See Memra

Work, thirty-nine kinds of, forbidden on the Sabbath, 153.

Workmen, treatment of, urged by the Rabbis, 113–14

Works, Rabbi Akiba on the justification by, 15–16, and the love of God, 75.

World, Lord of the, epithet for God, 21, 26

World, the, relation of God to, 21–45, epithets describing God's relation to, 26–8, fate of, may depend on a single action, 189–90, chosen as his portion by Esau, 100, the seat of the kingdom of God, 104, purpose of the creation of, 80–1, plunged into chaos by sin, 83, is the kingdom of God, 89

World, the future, chosen as his portion by Jacob, 100, persons destined for, 165–6, the *Evil Yezer* subdued in, 283, justice to prevail in, 307

Worship, due to God alone, 44–5

Writing, forbidden on the Sabbath, 153

Yezer, the, equivalent to the *Evil Yezer*, 262

Yezer Hara See *Evil Yezer*, the.

Yoke of the kingdom of God, the See Kingdom of God, the, Kingdom of God, the invisible, Kingdom of God, the visible, Kingdom of heaven, the

Yoke of the Torah, the See Kingdom of God, the

Zachuth, acquired through the commandments, 164, place of the doctrine in Judaism, 170, etymology, etc, of the word, 170–1, divisions of the subject, 171–3, and individual righteousness, 176, 189–90

See also *Zachuth*, the, of the Fathers, etc

Zachuth, the, of a pious ancestry, 171, 175–7, 181–5, defined, 175–7, individual righteousness and, 176, extension of, 181–3, does not relieve the individual from responsibility, 183–5, in the liturgy, 184, and trust in God, 184–5

Zachuth, the, of a pious contemporary, defined, 189–90, and Sodom and Gomorrah, 190

Zachuth, the, of a pious posterity, 195, 196-7, limited, 197, and the dead, 198
   See also Children
Zachuth, the, of Israel, and the kingdom of God, 98
Zachuth, the, of the Fathers, in relation to the patriarchs, 171-5, called a rock, 173, historical events attributed to, 174-5, limited, 177-8, unlimited, 178-81
Zachuth, the, of the Mothers, in relation to the wives of the three patriarchs, 172, invoked at public fasts, 172.

Zadok, Rabbi, prayer by, regarding the Sabbath, 153, on material uses of the Torah, 154, 159.
Zebaoth, God in war, 35
Zechariah, the Book of, cited, in connection with God's relation to the Gentiles, 64
Zephaniah, the Book of, cited, in connection with God's relation to the Gentiles, 64
Zerachya ben Shealtiel, on the spiritualisation of the Scriptures, 103
Zohar, the, on the *Evil Yezer*, 246

www.ingramcontent.com/pod-product-compliance
Lightning Source LLC
Chambersburg PA
CBHW050610300426
44112CB00012B/1445